THE COMPLETE GUIDE TO

LIVING WITH MEN

by
E. James Wilder III
Copyright 1993, 1997, 2004

Published by
Shepherd's House Inc
P.O. Box 40096
Pasadena, CA 91114

Selected portions revised from *Life Passages For Men* and *The Stages Of A Man's Life*

The Complete Guide to Living With Men
By E. James Wilder Ph.D.
© 2004

ISBN 0-9674357-5-7

Published by:

Shepherd's House Inc.
P.O. Box 40096
Pasadena, CA 91114

Distributed by:

CARE Packaging
9731 South M-37
Baldwin, MI 49304
CAREpkg@triton.net
www.care1.org
(231) 745-4950

Living With Men is a Life Model Book

Cover Photo by Chris Coursey

To my father

Reverend Earl J. Wilder, Jr.

who explored this trail before I did.

Acknowledgements

I live in a spiritual world that affects the way I think. I'm a Christian. I won't try to hide it and you can enjoy or ignore it if you like. It used to embarrass me to be a Christian, considering the things well known Christians would get caught doing, but I've seen enough immaturity in all kinds of leaders that I don't think there is a better group to join. Which leads me to my last confession. I am a tall, pigmentationally challenged, bald, married heterosexual, middle aged, middle class, male Christian. Can it get any worse? Yes, it does! I think I have some answers.

I have spent a lot of time with men. Many weekends with men at retreats have cleared my mind and brought into focus the goal men live and die to reach. In places like Van Nuys, Costa Mesa, Acton, Long Beach, Goleta, Cottonwood, and Calgary I have seen men setting their sights and souls on their goal—just to be a man.

Dave Came of Servant Publications helped create the first version of this book published in 1994. Ingrid Trobisch helped refine these ideas for the second version published by Quiet Waters Publications in 1999.

When I took a year off to write this book my wife Kitty graciously took over the family finances and worked three part-time jobs. Drs. Laurie and Paul Kayne generously provided encouragement and additional funds for me to write without having to worry about money. Kitty and Ruth Ann Koepcke carefully read each chapter checking for errors and unclear content. Gary Bayer helped me with the story telling sections in several chapters. Kent and Connie Shaffer lent me their cabin for a week to finish editing this manuscript. Sad to say, the California fires of 2003 reduced their cabin to a cinder.

These basic ideas about maturity became part of *The LIFE Model* developed at Shepherd's House[1] in California where I have worked for over twenty-five years. The Shepherd's House staff has helped people with immaturity and malfunctions while looking for better ways to heal and avoid future problems. Anne Bierling has been particularly dedicated to refining the maturity steps using her training in developing *idealized models*. My deepest thanks to all the people who have helped me figure out how maturity worked through their thoughtful questions, careful listening, and personal experiences. David Brown, John Lehman, Ed Johnson and Ruth Ann Koepcke helpfully and creatively developed the theoretical material in this model with me.

---

1 Shepherd's House Inc., P.O Box 40096, Pasadena, CA 91114.

LIVING WITH MEN

Something to be Said For Mature Men
An Introduction

Maturity means we are fully developed for our age. A mature apple blossom is a flower. A mature apple is a fruit and a mature apple pie is nothing like the flower or the fruit. Unfortunately, most of us lag far behind the optimum maturity for our physical age. Life does not stop while we catch up--if we are even trying. At the age when most of us should be ready for apple pies, we are still little green apples.

Maturity can be measured in stages. Each stage can be distinguished by the way people receive and give life. When we look across many cultures we find there are five life stages after birth. These stages and their characteristics are the same for men and women. Here are the five stages:

STAGE	PATTERN OF RECEIVING AND GIVING LIFE
The **INFANT**	-- receives without having to give (is cared for)
The **CHILD**	-- learns to take care of one (self)
The **ADULT**	-- cares for two or more at the same time
The **PARENT**	-- gives life to others without receiving in return
The **ELDER**	-- cares for the community and those without families of their own

To reach the goal of full development, everyone must go through these five life stages and complete the required tasks. Each stage builds on the one before rather than replacing it. We can't skip stages. We can't stick the ingredients in the oven and hope it comes out a pie. It is not a triple if we run straight to third base without tagging first or second. We have to go back and run them in the right order or we are out. We are also not adults if we didn't do infant and child tasks correctly. Full development at each stage means that there is a lot to learn and practice. The goal is worth it!

All maturity is a human responsibility requiring both individual and community effort. The individual must work at his or her tasks while the community must provide the needed materials for her or him to succeed. Like most goals, maturity requires individual effort, team support, and group strategy.

This brings us to another truth about maturity. No one can get mature ahead of schedule. We aren't ripe until harvest time. We can't be a parent at seven years of age, an adult at ten, or an elder at 21. The ideal model presented here constitutes the *fastest possible* route to the goal. On the other hand, we can be far behind and still be infants at 65 with biological grandchildren who are more mature than we are.

MATURITY AND MEN

In my daily life, at work and at church I have experienced more immature moments with both men and women than I need to count. So why have I written a book about maturity and males? First, it is my personal impression that men are, on average, more immature than the women. They need maturity more obviously. Second, the topic of male maturity is of great interest to women. Women are interested in and motivated to help their "boys" grow up. The women I have watched are having no success maturing the men in their lives. This book should really help.

With my first three books for men I observed, and was told by publishers, that men required a book specifically for them. Men will not read something written for women or even for general audiences. They require something specific, to the point, immediately applicable to them. Something, I suppose that the woman in their life can leave on the bed stand with a bookmark or dog-eared corner strategically chosen. So I wrote a book for men, using their terms. Only later did I find that it was not testosterone or Y-chromosomes that limit men but, once again, it is their lack of maturity.

When I asked women to read *The Stages of a Man's Life* as a guide for their own maturity needs (it remained the book I like best for women as well as men until this one got finished) I discovered that women at the INFANT level of maturity could not apply a book written for men to themselves. It became clear that the reason most men required a book written specifically for them was that most men in America are at INFANT maturity. They still need to be told what they need, what they feel and who they are.

The men's movement of the 1990s originally focused on the desire of males of all ages to become men. When leading my first men's retreat I simply conferred manhood on each one present. For many it was a moving experience. Dr. Steve Brigham, who was present that weekend, pointed out later that a number of men were simply not ready for manhood. They were missing something necessary for the task. With his help we identified the needs and the tasks for infants (or unweaned boys as we called them then) and those for boys. These requirements enabled us to discover when men were actually ready and able to become adults. While well-prepared men only required a rite of passage to be on their way, most men were not even sure what it meant to be a man. These were the men who formed most of the men's movement; infants who willingly and persistently sought someone to answer their questions about themselves.

Oh the alarms that go off when I say that most men are infants! Many people become quite sure that this statement will offend men and end their participation in the discussion. This has not been the case. On men's retreats, men have been very willing to identify themselves as boys and infants. They are relieved to know at last why nothing works for them. This reveals the central truth about maturity--we are where we are. We must participate in life however immature we might be and live now if we wish to grow farther. We live each day "right now" ready or not--but it takes about fifty readings of a book like Ecclesiastes for this truth to register. Life is our main gift from God and we must live it fully with whatever maturity we possess while we examine how far we are from the goal of mature identity.

Besides, maturity is not value. Becoming more mature does not give us the slightest bit more value. Being infants does not take away the tiniest bit of our value. In fact, when have we ever been more convinced of someone's value than at the moment they are born! If we can't figure that each tiny baby is a treasure we will never understand value at all. But I am getting way ahead of myself.

Every man and woman goes through a life-cycle of growth that seem both familiar and alien. We are born babies and grow into children, then adults, often becoming parents and finally grandparents or elders. This process was easier to see when the world didn't move so fast and communities were more stable. Today we need to sit down for a few hours and review how growing up works. When you are done, I hope you will say, "I knew that but I never thought of it that way before."

Each phase of life has a main task to master and each following stage builds on the previous one, just as the primer and finish coats are added, one step at a time, to the thing we are painting. Growing up is a five-step process. If we get the steps in the right order and do a reasonably good job at them we will be satisfied with the results, otherwise, like a bad paint job, we will be cracking, blistering and peeling every time things get hot.

DO YOU HAVE A FEAR OF MEN?

We can't fully jump into maturity for men until we address our fear of men. Sometimes people hear every positive statement about men as a denial of the damage men can do, or as a negative statement about women. This is not what I mean to say. It is doubtful any one of us would even recognize *man* as God first intended him. Malfunctioning men are nothing like mature men and can be very hazardous. With that in mind perhaps we should be particularly eager for men to grow up right.

When I say that to be a man is good, I don't mean, "as compared to being a woman or a tree." Instead it is a reminder that when God looked at the world God said his work was good just as it stood. Then God proceeded to improve on that which was already good. A baby, boy, man, father, grandfather or elder is a "good thing" getting better just as a girl, woman, mother or grandmother is.

Whatever we may see of a man outwardly conceals the real person within who can only be seen through the "eyes of Heaven." Through the eyes of Heaven we are known for who we are and who we were meant to be. This deep way of knowing is what the ancients called the "heart." Only in our heart can we find our true self or that of others. When we have lost the heart we have lost the real man. This is a spiritual problem requiring a spiritual solution. This is reflected in the simple, and to some offensive, phrase, "let Jesus into your heart" by which we understand that the heart is in better shape with a little of heaven in there.

Whether you believe in a God or not, no one can observe men for long without coming to the conclusion that something is wrong with a bunch of them. To escape being a hazard to others and to fully mature requires restoration of a man's heart—his identity. Redemption is what Christians call God's contribution toward restoring the connection between this inner man and the visible man. When we have been put back on target our hearts reactivate our growth toward maturity.

Chapter Zero
The Goal

Hot chicken soup saved my life. The wind twisted over a low ridge and both rocks that stood between me and Iceberg Lake. Hidden in my North Face sleeping bag, I was shaking uncontrollably from hypothermia. "What am I doing out here with this idiot?" I kept saying to myself. About a thousand feet above me, flashlights provided security for two climbers roped for the night to a sheer rock face across very thin air from the Keeler Needle. Alfonse handed me the hot soup even as its warmth ebbed away. "Who could believe he was on the Sierra Madre Search and Rescue team," I thought. I was too exhausted to speak.

One full day, and 3,000 feet below, the North Fork of Lone Pine Creek splashed across the last spot I had seen of the Mt. Whitney Trail. There, at 8,800 feet, Alfonse had pointed me up the mountaineer's route along the left side of North Fork Creek. In a few minutes all traces of the trail had disappeared.

"We should be here," Alfonse said, looking at his topographical or "topo" map. He had climbed this face of the mountain before, so I followed him up the stream. We could see from the map that the trail would cross the stream again.

After an hour, the gorge narrowed to the width of the stream. "We should be here," Alfonse said. Left with no way but up, we climbed the cliff, a difficult effort with external-frame backpacks and no ropes. Whitney gleamed gray and white in the distance above us as we dragged ourselves up a tree root to the rock ledge at the top of the gorge.

Making our way from ledge to boulder, we headed toward 10,000 feet where we hoped to find the trail as it met the stream again. Two hours of climbing over rocks brought us to a spot a few hundred feet above the stream. "We should be here," Alfonse said, looking at his "topo" map--but we weren't. It was about noon.

The granite behind our backs went up Pinnacle Ridge to Thor Peak and back down before it met the main Whitney Trail to the south. It would take the rest of the day to get out that way so we pushed ahead. We crossed the tree line and headed toward Iceberg Lake--not that we could see a lake.

About five-thirty that evening we located the mountaineer's trail on the other side of the stream. The genius of having the trail on that side became starkly clear as the cold granite slammed into the sky directly ahead of us on our side. To go anywhere, except back the way we had come, we needed to cross the stream.

There was exactly one way to cross. In front of us was a waterfall. Half way up the falls, a stone ledge jutted through the spray. On our side, this shelf was about 12 inches wide. It looked to be about half that wide where the dripping gray rock emerged from the far side of the stream. "We should be here," Topo Man said, "Iceberg should be right over this ridge."

"So the waterfall we are about to crawl across is the water flowing out of Iceberg Lake," I said to myself and the wind.

"We should be there in a half hour and make camp. We'll heat up some chicken soup." With that he began to inch sideways across the face of the falls holding onto rocks through the rushing water. In the long afternoon shadows, his backpack stuck out at an angle that seemed destined to pull him backwards into the remaining beam of sunlight. I hoped he didn't fall because he was carrying our only stove. We had split up the supplies for the trip so we each carried half of what we needed--I had the tent, he had the stove.

The water made a fantail off my boot as a knife of ice water cut off sensation in my hands. I felt for the ledge with my toes and leaned my face as close to the madly leaping wall of water as breathing would allow. Fortunately, the water was not very deep. The first twenty feet through the spray were uneventful. With about the length of my body to go, the ledge narrowed to three inches wide, moss appeared on a few rocks, and my fingers quit reporting to my brain. I made a clear decision not to go back the same way.

Five minutes later, the wind off Iceberg Lake bit me in the face. Around me, and behind all the big rocks, was a group of ten climbers in their tents and sleeping bags. I couldn't walk any farther--I was shaking too hard. I fumbled to get my sleeping bag off and open. Alfonse opened his pack to make the soup.

"Hmmm. Smells like gas in here," he said. He pulled out the Primus and shook it. "Yup! Out of gas. It's all over my clothes."

I didn't care. "Well, refill it. Let's get some soup."

Alfonse looked uncomfortable, "I thought one tankful would last the trip," he said. "I didn't bring a refill." I was speechless. My internal map said, "You are here," pointing to high danger.

Was it rage, fear, cold or exhaustion that made me shake so hard the rock next to me seemed to move? I was out of options. After a long time, Alfonse wandered back into camp with hot soup. "Here you go!" he said, all smiles. "Some guy let me use his stove."

There is no better soup in the world than that cup of Lipton Cream of Chicken Soup. *Life soup* I call it now and keep a packet in the cupboard, at all times, in case of emergency. After a while I stopped shaking.

2

When I next discovered I was alive, it was morning. Iceberg Lake was covered with ice, clearly indifferent to the demands of August. The wind carried with it a complete explanation. I chipped a spot and got water.

The trail we had wanted went up the right-hand side of North Fork Creek. We missed the trail by 15 feet when we headed up the left-hand bank. From then on, we were never where we should have been. With the help of a map, we eventually got back on the trail but I might have died anyway were it not for those who were there ahead of us. I had trusted an unreliable guide and traveled unprepared. From then on, when in the High Sierra, I carried everything needed for survival in my pack. I was always prepared and knew where I was.

The phone rang and I answered it, as I hate to do. A man introduced himself. "Hi. This is Billy Solomon. My wife says I need to talk to you." We set an appointment for the next day.

Billy walked into the office wearing work boots and sat on the edge of the couch. "I'm goin' to kill the 'son-of-the-perverse-rebellious-woman,[2]" he said. "My wife is sleeping with some snake and she tells *me* to get counseling," Billy was shaking so hard that he couldn't sit still. He half-fell and half-leapt off the couch and rushed to the window. I thought he might go through it. "She is the only woman I ever loved, Doc!" He stood there trembling, then spread the mini-blinds with two fingers and stared out the hole. "Where am I?" he whispered hoarsely. "How did I get here?"

"This is going to take more than chicken soup," I thought.

He was thinking, "What am I doing here with this idiot!" To me he said, "No offense Doc, but how are *you* going to help me get her back?"

Billy's maturity was somewhere in early childhood while his life's trail was somewhere in mid-fatherhood. Like so many men, he had no idea what had just happened to him. He had worked at the same garage for sixteen years. He paid the bills, kept the kids in line, and took the family on vacation each year. He had made a way through the mountains of his life and was stepping from just another ledge to just another boulder when something in his wife gave way. Now, next to my window, Billy's hand raked down the mini-blinds as his arms dropped. Shaking uncontrollably, he registered signs of shock.

Maybe in a gorge or when the trail disappears; high on a ridge or after a near fall; when a bear gets their food or when the sun is setting; men look around and ask the wind, "Where am I?"

Well, here is a map. We will trace the trail for men starting from zero. Since you are old enough to read this, you are also old enough to have been off the trail by now--not just once but many times. Like Alfonse, we

---

[2] King James Version translation. See 1 Samuel 20:30.

often think "we should be here"--but we are not. I've prepared this book as a "topo" map for those who are lost. I've included a supply list for those who are planning trips for themselves--or their sons. But, a few of us are in real danger. We will die tonight unless we find a fellow climber, with a working stove, to give us *LIFE soup*.

Let's begin looking for the little arrow that says "*You* are *here*." Where you are *now* is where you must start. Any rescue or growth starts right here. You cannot be someone else or someplace else. Life is here--or nowhere. We can't memorize a trail to follow because each day the trail changes. Our goal is to live for each step, whether on the trail or off. When we do, we get someplace.

THE MALE LIFE CYCLE FROM BIRTH TO DEATH

Both men and women need to understand these growth stages but for different reasons. There isn't any difference between the life cycle for boys and girls. They must pass through the same stages and transformations, but this book will use mostly male examples. We need to have clear pictures of what male maturity looks like at each stage. Perhaps because so few men mature, they need a clear trail to follow. Men need examples that aren't too bland. Women need to recognize maturity and the lack of it in men, or they will end up depending on men like Alfonse or Billy. Both men and women will need maps and supplies so they can raise their sons to be men, husbands, fathers and elders.

THE FIRST GOAL: BABY

In chapter one we will look extensively at the INFANT STAGE of the baby boy. The infant must experience strong, loving, caring bonds with his parents. These bonds must meet his needs without his having to ask. He must receive life, and learn to express the life that is in him, to everyone's delight. During infancy the baby learns to live joyfully in his mother's world.

The first four years are the baby years. Babies need to receive all good things and learn to express themselves. Each baby learns the value of "just being me" without having to earn anything. During this time his identity will either be built around joy or fear. The child whose "backpack" is filled with joy becomes strong. He will not fear the trails or mountains.

Keeping baby from beginning a life of fear requires breaking life into baby-sized pieces. Each effort leads to letting baby rest in a timely way. The baby years are synchronized to baby's needs. When life comes in his size, baby learns to synchronize and control his mind and emotions. He learns to quiet himself and soon is ready to synchronize himself with others. Relationships that are both joyful and peaceful result from getting his timing right.

These years of infancy prepare him for weaning. In our culture, weaning from the breast or bottle is rarely timed to coincide with when the child can take care of himself. We rush our children into independence as fast as possible. Weaning from infancy is the change from baby to boy. Once a baby has learned to take basic care of his needs, he can transform into a boy who can begin living in his father's world. He moves from life in his home toward life in both his home and community.

The goal for infancy is for babies to organize a strong, joyful, synchronized identity.

THE SECOND GOAL: BOY

The CHILD STAGE begins as the baby becomes a boy at about age four. We will explore the boy's world in chapter three. Once weaned, and able to begin taking care of himself, he will be called a boy and will get quite angry if called a baby.

A boy is more complex than a baby. Boys must learn to ask for the things they need. They must make themselves understandable to others. Boys must discover what satisfies them each day. To do this, each boy must learn to act exactly like himself--like the boy he is in his heart. Boys must develop their talents and resources. Their performance must be self-expression but not as a way to earn approval or love. Boys must learn to receive and give life freely. They must learn to do hard things, things that they don't feel like doing at the time, but which are important and satisfying later. Each boy learns how to pack and carry his own backpack, read a map, keep moving on the trail and enjoy the view.

In preparation for manhood, boys must learn the "big picture" of life. This overall picture of life and maturity becomes his "topo" map. He must also learn the history of his own family because his big picture of life must first apply to people he knows. Family history tells him where *he* is on *his* map.

The goal for childhood is to teach a boy to take care of one person--himself. Taking care of himself must be second nature before he can take care of two or more people at the same time, as men do.

THE THIRD GOAL: MAN

Ideally, the ADULT STAGE begins at age thirteen. The well prepared boy can take excellent care of one person, himself. Given the necessary guidance, the young man is now ready to satisfy the needs of more than one person at a time. Like the other transformations, this one is physical as well as mental and social. His identity will try to reorganize itself and without an older guide, he will end up in a disorganized state. We will look at this in chapter five.

It takes a while to climb the many peaks that separate a self-centered boy from a both-centered man. Adult terrain is where he learns to drive a hard bargain, fair for him and fair for the other. A man looks out for the needs of others as though they were as important as his own. When a man does business, the person he is dealing with gets equal, fair treatment. This stage of development usually takes men into their early twenties. By that time, a man should be able to bargain hard, get a fair deal, not be intimidated by other men, protect others from himself when necessary and take care of a small group to everyone's satisfaction.

A man wants his effects to reflect his personal character and style. Everything he does must meet this heart-based standard. His adult identity finds its highest challenge in marriage. A man is ready for marriage near the end of the adult stage. By that time he is proficient in sharing life for mutual satisfaction. Because he and she are both adults, they can each take care of themselves and others simultaneously. This kind of partnership is characteristically adult. Sharing life in a way that creates a mutually satisfying story--or imprint on history--brings great joy to adults.

The goal for men is to become a satisfying part of history. A man knows that what he does impacts other people. Therefore he carefully insures that his impact on history (his story) is a good one.

THE FOURTH GOAL: FATHER

In the PARENT STAGE a man uses all he has learned in the first three stages to reach his highest peak--giving life. He already knows what he needs and feels. He is looking out for others like he does for himself. He now learns to give without receiving in return, as we will see in chapter eight. This makes him a father.

You know that you are a father when your child keeps you up all night, screaming in your ear, spitting up on your shirt, and then showing no appreciation for your efforts. You could have bargained hard, like a man, and said, "I'll stay up with you tonight but tomorrow night you must carry me around," but you didn't. Instead you gave without demanding in return. This is the mountain peak you have trained for all your life. As you start this ascent, you know you are a dad.

The father knows what he needs. He already reached his infant goals. No one stays up all night and says, "I never need to sleep." He can

6

express his feelings about it as well, "I'm tired but I love my child." He can take care of himself in the morning using the skills he learned as a boy. When his wife takes over, both are satisfied with the baby's care. At work he drives a hard bargain, but at home he climbs above the tree line into unselfish giving. Only the man who has completed the first three stages can enjoy the climb.

Dad passes on the gift of grace by his unselfish giving. His child learns about having value without having to earn it. By staying up all night Dad says, "My child, you have great value to me. Even if you keep me up all night, spit up on my shirt, mess in your diapers and scream in my ear. Even if you do not care that I am here, you have more than enough value to lose sleep over." That is a dad's heart.

Dad represents God to his family. The chance to portray God is the greatest honor that anyone can have. The father becomes an example of God's heart and character through his unselfish giving.[3] This takes a while, and a father is getting the hang of it about the time his children become teens. By that time, unselfishness should be second nature to Dad, he will need it.

To be a giver of life, a father must have received enough life that he can spare some. He must share a home where he can protect, serve and enjoy. He must have a share in finding the resources that allow his children to mature.

The goal of fatherhood is to give life joyfully. As a father gives life, his children grow strong.

THE FIFTH GOAL: ELDER

An elder is a father to his community. He is able to treat children who are not biologically his children with the same unselfish care he learned to give to his own. We will study the ELDER STAGE in chapter twelve.

After his children have become men and women, a truly *grand*-father becomes a guide. He helps those who are climbing for the first time. He rescues those who didn't bring maps, forgot their supplies, or even got lost. Elders give life to the "familyless"--the widows, orphans and strangers. They help their community to mature and reach its identity.

---

[3] I know that some of you have forgotten already that fatherhood is after adult mutuality. Adults understand that representing God to children is a mutual task. Father and mother both represent God. Immaturity makes us think that it must be one or the other. It is both parents as well as either one.

Trust is built by elders because they live transparent lives. They no longer hide what they feel so they can be "cool." They are real in ways they haven't been since they were children. They no longer need to protect themselves because they have learned to suffer well. Elders don't withdraw when things go wrong and people fail to live from their hearts. Through authentic involvement, elders resynchronize their community from its broken relationships, failures and failed trust. Elders may not do the work but they help others get their timing right. "This is not the time for that," they say and then again, "this is the time to do something else."

Many people could use an elder or a *grand*father. In our society we expect older people to buy a Winnebago and drive into the sunset. We, therefore, have few elders, few spare fathers, few guides, and few people helping those in need. There is a great lack of elders in our churches and communities. We need men who have been to the mountain.

Old mountaineers die when they have no one to guide. Each elder must have a community of his own, a place where he is recognized and trusted as an elder. Elders must be given a proper place in the community structure for they would not use force to take it.

"I know just what you need," must echo again in the canyons.

Every elder prepares to face his greatest transformation--a plunge into Iceberg Lake. When elders die, it is a time of great blessing. This is the final decontamination process from all that may have gone wrong on his journey. Everything about him that received and gave life emerges beyond Iceberg Lake. Anything about him that gave death, stays in the lake forever.

The goal for elders is to help their community grow up. Elders raise communities the way parents raise children. Under elders, communities reach their full maturity.

If I had my way about it, I'd forget this book and have each of you sit with an elder and learn to see yourself through the eyes of heaven. They would serve you hot *LIFE soup*. With their help you would find your own level of maturity, get outfitted, reach the trail again, and climb your mountain.

THE FIRST
METAMORPHOSIS

*

BABY

*

THE INFANT STAGE

BABY
The Infant Stage

IDEAL AGE
Birth through Three

NEEDS
•Strong, loving, caring bonds with parents
•Important needs are met without asking
•Others take the lead and synchronize with him first
•Quiet together time
•Help regulating distress and emotions
•Be seen through the "eyes of heaven"
•Receives and gives life
•

TASKS
•Receiving with joy
•Learn to synchronize with others
•Organize himself into a person through imitation
•Learns to regulate and quiet every emotion
•Learn how to return to joy from every emotion
•Learns to be the same person over time
•Learn self-care skills
•Learns to rest
•

Life is to be lived every day. Live it NOW!

10

Chapter One
Becoming a Baby Boy

*A woman giving birth to a child has pain because her time has come; but when her baby is born she forgets the anguish **because of her joy** that a child is born into the world.* **Jesus** (John 16:21 NIV)

THE INFANT BOY AT BIRTH

"It's a Boy!" What a good thing has happened. Almost everyone likes him right now. I started out that way myself. The first words spoken over me were by the nurse.

"What a schnazola!" She said.

Words to live by, I would think. Perhaps this was the beginning of my becoming a well-bonded individual because, as we will soon see, bonding starts with the nose.

"It's a Boy!" Tomorrow we will want to know how many ounces he has lost, and the day after that how many he has gained. The measuring of his progress is well under way. He is completely a boy and yet so much less then a boy must become.

"It's a Boy!" He is a product of the history that went before him. That history will even determine his name. And he is an enigma right now because his very birth has started history in a different direction. No one knows where it will lead. New fathers and mothers can feel overwhelmed at the potential and the needs.

"It's a Boy!" That means blue clothes. He will shop in auto parts stores. On the average, he will receive far fewer offers to hold a baby or sew a dress. He will be left out of discussions about mascara. We have ideas as a culture that will shape his growth.

A boy has been born and that is just what God wanted this time. Purpose and promise make him very valuable. After such a good start will he become the man that God intended him to become?

Becoming a baby - INFANT is the first stage. The baby boy's task is creating a working identity out of what he receives and does over the next four years. The first half of this stage most people will call him a baby and the second half a toddler as he practices becoming a person but we will use baby and infant to describe the first four years of life. The goal of infancy is growing a synchronized self that moves with his body's rhythms and fits well with the people around him. Every baby must work his way along this difficult process, learning as he goes what he needs and who he is. He will become as strong as what he receives.

My friend Chris came to see me one day. He is an unusually sensitive man.

"Jesus wants me to tell you that he created little kids with lots of be-like stuff," he said.

Had it been almost anyone else, I would have suggested medication. But, Chris had a good track record although I could not make any sense out of his statement.

"What is B-like stuff?" I asked him.

"You know, something to help him be like other people--something that lets him take their shape, to be like them. Little kids grow up to be like their parents. That is how they were made."

Two years later I was listening to a lecture by Dr. Schore,[4] a well-known expert on the development of the child brain. He commented that there is part of the brain that begins growing at three months of age that creates a baby's identity by letting his mother control it until he can copy the way she does it. This area, known as the prefrontal cortex, comes to occupy 35% of the adult brain. That is a lot of be-like stuff!

Meanwhile a baby is a sponge or maybe more of a vacuum cleaner, sucking in everything around him. A baby becomes what he receives.[5] Receiving comes before giving. It is part of our dependency on God and others that we never outgrow. Even Jesus started out receiving. It seems to bother some Christmas storytellers that all we have recorded about Jesus as an infant is that he received from others. There are no miracles for little drummer boys, no healings, no dividing his lunch among 5,000 people. In spite of our favorite carol's statement that while in the manger the little Lord Jesus did not cry, there is no scriptural support for the theory. Every indication supports the idea that he expressed his needs and feelings and received from others what he did not earn.

Babies eventually learn to express needs knowingly. By the time infancy is over, every baby should have mastered expressing his needs and feelings and receiving what he needs without shame--but then a cow could do that! To be human requires more. It is the joyful character of the relationship between the one who gives and the one who receives that make us alive. A baby comes to be-like whoever gives him joy.

---

[4] In this chapter I will simplify the works of doctors, Schore, Siegel, Erikson, and van der Kolk in particular. Details of their work can be found in Appendix B. No endorsement by them of this writing is implied.

[5] Erik Erikson, see Appendix B.

12

BECAUSE OF JOY

Babies require us to understand joy. Being human and wanting joy are inseparable. We humans are creatures of joy. We like joy. We seek joy. We never outgrow our desire for joy. Joy is even characteristic of our eternal existence. God makes "everlasting joy" a promise for his people through the prophet Isaiah; and who would not want it? (Isaiah 51:11)

At its essence, joy is relational. Joy is the delight we experience when someone really connects with us. They want to be with us and we with them. Our faces glow. Our eyes grow big and sparkle. We smile and laugh and our hearts and senses open wide to gather them into us. Joy means someone is with me and I like it!

Joy is present even before birth. In the Bible story of the birth of Jesus, Elizabeth tells Mary, "the babe leaped in my womb for joy," (Luke 1:44b KJV) making joy the youngest recorded emotion in scripture. Joy is also the first emotion that infants will seek on their own. Seeking joy is the primary, and perhaps strongest, human motivation. Joy is the centerpiece of human personality and brain structure. In fact, joy and the search for joy form the basis for all healthy bonding between parent and infant.[6]

Joy is what we feel when someone is glad to see us. When their face lights up, we feel joy. We are loved, enjoyed, appreciated, served and protected and it gives us joy. Our eyes want to look to them. Our feet want to run to them, jump, skip and dance. We want to sing. Joy is being with someone who is glad to be with us.

Mothers are usually a baby's biggest joy. If we picture the adventure of raising a child as though it were learning to camp, then a mother's first goal would be setting up a base camp at the foot of Mount Joy. *Joy Camp* would be our place to live and grow strong. It would be the place to build a strong, joyful identity. All our expeditions would begin from Joy Camp and end when we got back to Joy Camp.

JOY CAMP

The first three months of life are devoted to establishing Joy Camp as the base of operations. During those twelve weeks a baby feels joy from being close to his mother. Activities like nursing, rocking, sleeping near the baby or carrying him near her body are very beneficial. This joyful state is the root of all human development. Living in Joy Camp is the basis for understanding mother-love, home, belonging, peace, security and all our

---

[6] Schore, see Appendix B.

treasured experiences. No matter how far we may roam in our lifetime, Joy Camp is where we wish we were each night as we fall asleep.

During the first half of our time in Joy Camp our joy comes from mother's smell,[7] from being fed and staying warm.[8] These three experiences bring joy and create the beginning bond between mother and infant. Particular attention is needed to make sure the baby's needs are met when feeding so that the baby can be joyful and bond. Parent or clock-controlled feeding schedules are very destructive at this age. Eating and regulating his own temperature are new skills for the baby. Any success with those two tasks brings joy for the first six weeks of life. Failure blocks and may even damage nerve endings in the developing brain.

Smell is the first sense to be used for bonding because it is the best developed sense at birth. Babies and mothers both use this sense to identify each other. There is a lot of "baby sniffing" between mothers and their newborns.

It may be wise to keep the baby's life free from artificial smells during the first six weeks when bonding is largely by smell. One wonders what effect smells can have at this age. For instance, what if mother smells of alcohol or tobacco? Bonding with cigarette smoke or alcohol on the parents' breath, the smell of fresh paint in the baby room, or perfumes may include these smells among those which will say comfort, love and belonging for the baby's whole life. Under stress they will seek these for comfort. One mother helped her children by giving them each a small bottle of the perfume she had worn during their infancy as they left home.

Our life-long goal becomes returning to Joy Camp each and every night. Just as salmon go back in search of the smell of the place where they were hatched, we go back seeking the smell of Joy Camp. Smells become a way to repair bad days. That might not be totally bad if we head toward mother, talcum powder, baby oils, or even fresh paint, but seeking alcohol, tobacco, or chasing perfumed women who smoke might be.

Two different women with severe early bonding problems and inability to regulate their emotions have told me that during their first year of therapy with me they went to stores smelling all the deodorants trying to locate the one I used so that they could have my "smell" with them. Although they both were very ashamed of themselves for invading my privacy, their growing confidence of a return to Joy Camp let them tell me. In both cases they had located the correct brand--a generic product not available in most stores.

---

[7] Schore, see Appendix B.

[8] Schore, see Appendix B.

14

The second half of Joy Camp is touch centered. After six weeks, the touch centers of the baby's brain are developed enough for touch to become the strongest sense. From six to twelve weeks, touch becomes the main source of infant joy. This new awareness is possible because the baby's developing brain is now able to sort out and remember skin sensations. Without touch, as with other stressful conditions, his body will generate cortisol--a stress hormone that will literally kill off some of his brain cells.

Through smell, taste, temperature and touch the baby comes to understand himself as a person in relationship to his mother. That is why eating when he is hungry, being touched when he needs to be held, being able to find and smell his mother are so important. This is Joy Camp. Parents make him feel good. His important needs are met without asking. A strong, loving, caring bond is growing with his parents as he begins to organize himself into a human being. By now his emotional thermostat is well on the way to being set. What his body has felt for these months becomes the "normal" state he will seek for the rest of his life. If his thermostat has been set to Joy Camp that is what he will seek. If he has been set on anxiety and adrenalin that will become his normal state. Now he is ready to attempt the seemingly impossible task of teaching his brain to be like his parents' brains.

By three months the baby has developed enough to picture, in his mind, what his mother feels about him. From now on joy becomes very interactive. Until now the baby's capacity to feel joy has been very small and easily filled. After three months the main joy structures in the brain begin their serious growth spurt.[9]

CLIMBING JOY MOUNTAIN

As I mentioned, joy is very relational because the way our minds form our identity is relational. The way our self-concept develops is always based on how we think others see us. Our deepest sense of self is in relationship to a face looking at us. By studying this face and eyes we know what they feel about us. Babies take all these facial expressions personally. A sad face means, "I make people sad," a glad face means, "I bring joy." Fortunately, tired mothers have had two or three months to recover from giving birth before babies need their smiles.

At three months of age, babies already have an image of how their mother sees them. Not surprisingly it is stored, without words, as an image of her face. It is also no surprise that climbing Joy Mountain has to wait

---

[9] For a serious discussion of neurobiological development in the infant you may read two books by Dr. Allan Schore.

until the visual areas of the brain mature at two or three months of age. By then the visual cortex has been "hardwired" into place making vision the dominant sense. What babies begin to look for are eyes that are looking at them with joy. Joy means, "Someone is thrilled to see me."

Joy is the emotion that babies will willingly seek on their own. Because they are motivated to have increasingly high levels of joy, they will keep working toward joy even when things go wrong. As they climb to higher and higher levels of joy, babies literally build brain capacity. The capacity to experience strong joy develops between three and twelve months of age as an infant attempts, repeatedly, to reach higher and higher levels of joy--if he has his parent's help.

Nothing interests a baby more than looking at faces and eyes. Whenever he sees joyful eyes looking at him, the joy in him explodes. In a matter of five or six seconds he can be smiling and giggling--full of excitement and joy. Each time he sees joyful eyes, a face that lights up to see him, he makes another attempt to climb Joy Mountain until, by his first birthday, he can regularly reach the top and feel joy as powerfully as a human can feel anything! Hours of this practice cause him to grow a strong and joyful self.

JOY AND THE HUMAN BRAIN

At two to three months of age a region of the brain, which was not developed at birth, begins its growth. This area, called the right prefrontal cortex, will become the top of the command center in the brain. It has the last word on control of all the body and mind systems and will grow to become about one sixth of the adult brain. It is the first to know everything from inside or outside the body. But this region is not an "it." In fact these circuits are built as an image of three joyful faces looking at each other--mother, baby and father. The strongest bond is usually between the mother and child face with the father looking at them both. This relational image of the self with joyful parents is stored as our identity at the top of the four-level control center of the brain.

Our primary identity, at the apex of the neurological control structure of the brain, is a relational one. For the moment we will call this relational identity "*They*". If "*They*" are oriented by love we can bear all things, endure all things and return to joy. Joy is our strength. If "*They*" are oriented to fear then our identity readily becomes unstable and disorganized. Isn't it like God to design a brain that only knows itself in relationship, and then only when that relationship is one of love? It is love that rejoices in knowing us that makes us know ourselves. This entire region is developed without words because the baby has no vocabulary. Its growth is nearly half over by the time he can say "mama."

The control center of the self is grown in response to his mother's facial expressions and stored in the baby's brain as an image of her face. This visual image will interpret the meaning of his being and life. There is room for more than just his face and hers in the image. It is a three-way image of two people gazing at each other with a third face watching. Sometimes father and child are close while mother watches. Sometimes baby watches mom and dad interact. Other faces can become the third face from time to time and form a stable bond if they are in harmony of expression. Baby's attention will be drawn to the most intense face and eyes. He will match his face to theirs, his mind to theirs and grow his own copy of the strongest connection he finds. Let us hope he finds joy on all the faces. He will learn to be joyful like them. This will charge his inner being with joy. This will provide the strength he will use to fill his "backpack" for life. If not, he will fill up with fear. It will be one or the other--fear or joy.

This prefrontal cortex has its main growth from three to eighteen months. But unlike the rest of the brain that gets "hardwired" and stops growing, this part stays young all our lives. The joyful identity region in the right hemisphere undergoes growth spurts again at four and eight years of age, at the beginning of significant relationships, the birth of one's child or grandchild. At these identity formation times, bonding is at its best. They are also the times when repairs can most easily be made to weak bonds. Often adopted children or those whose mothers were sick or working can form remedial bonds during these times. These are:

AGE	STAGE	FOCUS	OTHER
0-2 years	Early infant	Mother	Father
4 years	Early child	Father	Siblings, friends
8 years	Late child	Friends	Remedial
15 years	Early adult	First love--mate	Remedial
First child	Early parent	First baby	Remedial
Grandchild	Elder	First Grandchild	Remedial

The overwhelming euphoria that accompanies the growth of our "joyful identity control center" (in the right prefrontal cortex) is what we felt with our first love, our first baby, and our first grandchild. Looking in their eyes or seeing their smile threatens our brain with overload. Our brains flood with new nerve endings and the necessary brain chemistry needed for life called serotonin, endorphins, and dopamine. On either end of the joyful look the results are the same. We climb Mt. Joy.

We are creatures of joy so babies that do not see joy on their mothers' faces become full of fear. If they attach to someone who is afraid, angry or distressed they learn to watch for threats. If they do not find eyes that are watching them with joy, they will not attach securely, or if there is no one there at all, they monitor the world for anything that will make them feel bad. Their control center becomes desynchronized. They spend most of their mental energy trying to keep their equilibrium. They develop fear bonds and fear based identities that we will study more in Chapter Two. They live by avoidance because they have no hope of receiving help finding joy if something should go wrong. Infants need someone who is paying attention to them and will help them feel better. They don't explore or even seek trails that lead back to joy. As they grow older, people who never receive this loving bond are always searching for someone or something to make them feel better. In our culture this most often means drugs or sex, power or money.

Joy and Strength

This capacity to feel joy at high levels achieves many purposes, but it is most clearly the source of personal strength. Our goal is to grow strong children. Babies "work out" by climbing Joy Mountain to develop a strong self or as psychologists call it "ego strength." As scripture says, "The joy of the Lord is your strength." (Nehemiah 8:10b KJV) At nine months of age babies will spend up to eight hours a day building their brains by smiling with their mothers. Mothers who get nothing done around the house and only "play" with their baby should know they are building their baby's brain and strength for life.

The strength of a human being is limited by how much joy he can "pack." Joy sustains us through suffering, illness, loss, mistakes, and disappointments. If you look at the people you know who have great joy, they are very resilient, even under great hardship. Like the first century story of Paul and Silas singing their way back to joy in jail after being beaten, the person with joy is strong. Even when facing simple problems, like surviving in school, the child with joy is popular, attractive, and appealing.

Those with little joy are often overwhelmed. Their personalities are weaker and without vigorous workouts on Joy Mountain their brains are underdeveloped. Underdeveloped structures in the joyful identity area of the brain have been found in such diverse conditions as: depression, schizophrenia, attention deficit disorder, eating disorders, borderline personality and autism. All of these suffer from an inability to maintain joy. They also suffer from an inability to recognize facial expressions correctly. For instance, they see tired faces as angry so they are easily hurt and upset.

18

They are also unable to recover from upset feelings in a timely way. Their brain's control center easily becomes desynchronized and consequently their relationships and emotions are unstable.

Climbing Up and Getting Down

Strength is actually a capacity to control our own brains during high levels of emotional arousal. Since babies will only seek joy it is the emotion we must use for training. Baby must learn to get to a high arousal state and then learn to calm back down voluntarily. The rising joy gives him a chance to develop and control his dopamine system. Dopamine is a big part of your "go for it!" system. That sluggish have-to-have-some-coffee feeling is low dopamine. Learning to quiet himself and get arousal back down teaches a baby to develop and control his serotonin system. Serotonin is your "I'm fine" system. That irritable and unhappy, channel surfing, restless feeling is low serotonin. Inability to control these two systems greatly contributes to addictions of all kinds.

The boy who can raise his energy and respond to life has "drive." The boy who can calm himself when emotions heat up had poise and confidence. Climbing Joy Mountain and getting back down is how a baby learns these two opposing and essential tasks needed for a well-trained brain. While the biology of the five different value systems in the brain is very complex and little understood, the training is straightforward: learn to produce and control a natural joy high and a natural calm to bring you back down. The same sort of control a baby learns with joy he will need to learn with his unpleasant feelings after his first birthday. We will look at the negative feelings later in this chapter.

More Benefits of Joy Mountain

Until he has developed his full strength of self, the baby will be overwhelmed by joy every time he gets too high on the mountain. This feels like when we get tickled too much and can't stand it. Joy turns to pain as a baby reaches "overwhelmed." If a mother is using her baby to make herself happy she will keep trying to get him to smile and overwhelm him instead. A good parent will notice that her baby has had too much joy and will look away for a moment to let him rest. When her baby looks back at her, the parent knows it is time to start climbing again.

Studies indicate that too much stimulation is even more harmful than not enough[10]. Alternating joy with resting quietly together allows the

---

[10] Schore page 424.

baby to synchronize his own mind as well as his relationships. So, to develop a well-coordinated brain the mother must synchronize her cycle of joy and rest to match the baby's need and capacity. As a result her baby learns to be energetic, calm himself, develop emotional capacity and synchronize with mother.

This process is repeated thousands of times until baby can reach the top of Mt. Joy. But all these starts and stops on the way up bring hidden bonuses. The baby learns that he can survive being slightly overwhelmed, that he can recover by resting, and that he can return to joy. These steps, repeated many times, teach him how to regulate his own emotions. Experiencing how his mother lets him rest, teaches him how to avoid pushing others too hard. He will be respectful and not overwhelm others with his feelings.

I have noticed that the ability to handle *overwhelmed* is a sort of dividing line between people. There are those who will do anything to avoid getting overwhelmed. When they get overwhelmed, they collapse and don't know what to do. Others view being overwhelmed the same way they would react to feeling very cold or hungry. Certainly the feeling isn't desirable, but it can be endured for important causes. They continue to act like themselves even when overwhelmed. In the end they will not be daunted by any mountain or storm. St. Paul talks about being overwhelmed in this way on his trips and perils--and yet has enough joy packed to continue on his mission.

All of us know people who don't know when to stop. These people also have great trouble regulating their own feelings (acting like themselves when they are upset) and certainly don't get back to joy very easily. They failed to learn how to deal with overwhelmed feelings while climbing Mt. Joy. Their parents did not back off when they reached "overwhelmed." They did not learn to rest and return to joy. They can't quiet themselves very well. Their control center gets desynchronized and they "lose it." This probably happened because the parents needed the child to be happy, make them feel and look good or because the parents were simply not available.

Hearing and Joy

By his first birthday, the baby's hearing has developed enough to process sounds rapidly for meaning. While he doesn't know what most words mean, he can "read" voice-tone. He can tell when the voice is warm and joyful. For the second year of his life, voice-tone becomes as important as the sight of a joyful face for reaching joy. A joyful voice-tone reaches around corners or when they are both watching something and he can't see his parent's delight in him directly.

Singing is one of the leading sources of auditory joy. Fathers and mothers sing to their baby and bring joy. In time, singing becomes a major way for children to reach joy on their own. The second year of life is also devoted almost entirely to joy but with some important differences we will soon examine.

Summary of Bonding Development and the Senses[11]

0 - 1.5 months	Taste, smell and temperature
1.5 - 2.5 months	Touch
2.5 - 12 months	Visual (facial expressions of emotion)
12 - 24 months	Auditory (voice tone)

Each of these supersedes the ones before by becoming dominant. Later modes of bonding add to, but do not eliminate, the earlier ones. Whichever mode is dominant works by receiving input that helps the child's feelings move toward joy and euphoria. Infants bond to whoever provides this effect, and they become like them so that they can do the same thing themselves after that.

Importance of Joy to God

Why dedicate two whole years to building joy into a child? Some people have trouble believing that joy can be this important. Most of us are simply amazed by how early in life the strengths built on joy develop. As a culture, we overlook the importance of growing joy--out of ignorance. But if building strength for a lifetime isn't reason enough, the place of joy in God's kingdom makes joy an eternal-life issue. The Psalmist says, "In thy presence is fullness of joy." (Psalms 16:10b KJV) God lives at the top of Mt. Joy--an excellent reason to help babies get there.

Jesus gave joy as the reason for his teaching. "These things have I spoken unto you, that my joy might remain in you, and that your joy might be full." (John 15:11 KJV) Jesus was training mountaineers.

The source of joy is attributed to God's face in a scripture that occurs in both the Old and New Testaments. This important text is part of the first public announcement of the good news of the Kingdom at Pentecost. Peter quotes from the Psalmist, "Thou hast made known to me the ways of life; thou shalt make me full of joy with thy countenance." (Acts 2:28 KJV) God's face fills us with joy just as the delighted parent's face fills a baby with joy.

---

[11] Schore, see Appendix B.

Another psalm lists both sources of joy (auditory and visual.) "Blessed is the people that know the joyful sound: they shall walk, O LORD, in the light of thy countenance." (Psalms 89:15 KJV) God fills us with joy with joyful sounds and a face (His face) that lights up to see us. This blessing gives us strength. We should do the same for our children.

FINDING THE WAY BACK TO JOY CAMP

About the time of his first birthday our hardy little hiker can reliably reach the top of Joy Mountain. This strength will be put to use during the second year of his life. During this year his mother will teach him how to return to joy from all the unpleasant feelings in life. When a baby has a secure bond with someone who will help him feel better after a painful emotion, he will grow strong and face hardship with hope.

Anyone who has taken young children camping knows how carefully they must be watched to be sure they don't wander off and get lost. When children learn how to get down off the rocks safely, find their way back from the hill on their own, and get back out of the woods without getting lost, parents heave a huge sigh of relief. Their child can now find camp from anywhere around. Camping becomes safer and far more fun.

In the same way, infants must learn the path back to Joy Camp from all their other feelings. They must be guided from shame back to joy, as well as from disgust, fear, sadness, disappointment, anger and humiliation. Once the infant knows the path back, he will not be intimidated or deterred by his feelings. Another way to say this is that the baby can now quiet his own brain and feeling when they are in an uproar. He has learned to control his quieting circuits, not just when he must quiet his joy but when he must quiet his distress. Building joy is how he developed these circuits and learned to control them.

He will only have as much strength to climb back to joy as he developed by climbing up Mt. Joy. If the sad feeling, for instance, is higher than he learned to climb on Mt. Joy, he will run out of strength before he gets back to Joy Camp. From then on he will avoid that feeling instead of overcoming it. What happens for him is that the control center in his brain does not have enough capacity or "bandwidth" and becomes desynchronized when the distressing emotion becomes too strong. His brain switches from goal directed actions to "help me" and then "make it stop."

Infants must be guided into these demanding feelings and back safely by their parents. The emotion on the mother's face or in her voice is what takes the child out into the woods. Let's say baby sticks his hand in his diaper. He is sure that Mommy will be glad to see him and see what he has done. Instead, Mommy suddenly shows disgust on her face. His brain copies the feeling and just as suddenly he is feeling disgusted and ashamed instead of joyful. Mommy then leads him back to joy by cleaning him up and then climbing Mt. Joy again together. "There! You smell better now!" she says with a smile.

For this to succeed it is necessary for two things to happen. The parent must share the "bad" feeling with the child and then return to joy together. The child's brain exactly mimics the parent's path back to joy. This shows the boy how to feel the feeling, quiet the feeling and stay relational and flexible at the same time. Experiences like this create a "return to joy map" and store it in the right hemisphere of the brain. Sadly, if the parent does not share the feeling and return to joy the child learns that too and will conclude that there is no way back from that "bad" spot. If this happens frequently, the baby will not develop hope and will avoid the "bad" feeling. If the parent will not join him in his feeling, he has no one to mimic and learn his way back. By seeing the same feeling he is having expressed on Mommy's face he will duplicate her emotions, and even brain chemistry, each step of the way back to joy and quiet together. This is the map he will use to find his way back to joy for the rest of his life. Every time he is overwhelmed his brain will switch on the images in his right brain--but pity the child who has none. Keep in mind that at this age the baby has a vocabulary of only one or two words so he learns by imitation.

Hope is grown by linking minds with the baby while he is still in his terrible feeling. Before he gives up hope that he will find someone to show him the way back to joy, the mature parent begins to share his feeling. To the older brain it is not so hard to feel upset and still love. Babies cry because they have hope that someone will find them and bring them back to joy. The parent must not exceed their baby's strength but rather comfort and return with him to joy before the baby's hope is gone. When we destroy a baby's capacity to hope it may well be destroyed for life. Proverbs reminds us that, "Hope deferred [or delayed] maketh the heart sick: but when the desire cometh, it is a tree of life." (Proverbs 13:12 KJV)

Of all the unpleasant feelings perhaps shame is the most important one to recover from easily. Shame is a major component of all social interactions because shame is what we feel when others are not happy with us. Naturally, in the course of social learning, we will do many things that make others unhappy with us. The boy who can return to joy and quiet feelings of shame will be a fast social learner. The boy who cannot quiet shame will either be a social pleaser or demand to be pleased. This condition, known as narcissism is a pain to be around. The boy who can quiet shame and stay relational will be miles ahead in social intelligence.

With practice the baby will find paths back to Joy Camp from everywhere--every difficult and draining feeling and every bad thing that happens. The strength to feel feelings when combined with the path back to joy builds hope, resilience, confidence, and a lack of self-centeredness. This last one may surprise you, but self-centeredness comes from avoiding anything that gives "me" a bad feeling. Children that must avoid feelings spend far more time and effort on their self-interests. Conversely, a strong hope that disappointment will eventually reveal a path back to joy lets children take risks and think of others.

Consistently returning to joy after a hard feeling also makes one less self-centered because it teaches that satisfaction is reached when everyone is back in Joy Camp. Satisfaction comes from shared joy--not just finishing a job.

Not only do mothers help children back to joy but good counselors help people return to joy as well. When people have been traumatized or poorly equipped to return to joy, their "remedial parent" will help them find joy and then find the way back from each and every feeling. Traumas cannot be faced or resolved in any helpful way until there is sufficient joy strength present to handle the intensity of every disorganizing feeling caused by the trauma. This means that the mature guide must be able to share every intense feeling that desynchronized the traumatized person's attempts to stay themselves and return to joy. Counselors must know who they are in the presence of intense feeling, act like themselves, regulate their own emotions and help the traumatized person with theirs as well. Joy in this context means that I am not alone. Someone is willing to be with me, share my feeling, show me how to control it by handling it themselves and still acting like a relational, loving person. This learning, like that with mother, is rapid and nonverbal, using facial expressions, voice tone, and body-cues from one right-hemisphere prefrontal cortex to the other.

Once a path back to joy has been established from each of these overwhelming feelings it is possible to make them a part of one's self and history. Now we can feel these feelings and still act like ourselves. Our brain's control center now stays synchronized under intense emotional signals. Without this way back to joy, people live in terror of their feelings and spend much of their energy avoiding anything that will set off the feelings leaving them out of control and miserable again.

Jesus was a clear example of one who could face life unselfishly because he knew the way back to joy. In the quote that began this chapter Jesus indicated that joy brought women out of the distress of childbirth. Joy also brought him through his hardest hour. "Who for the joy that was set before him endured the cross, despising the shame." (Hebrews 12:2 KJV.) He knew there was a path back from pain and shame. Returning to joy was how he approached his death.

We should not even need to say it, but there are those who teach that Jesus endured the cross for a different reason. They teach that Jesus stayed on the cross because God did not come when he cried and therefore, we also should not come when our children cry! Let me say it again, Jesus was motivated by his desire to return to joy. Babies do not even have this capacity! His hope was greater than the pain or the great distress he felt--and it takes a lot of joy to do that. He could stay on course because he knew the path back to Joy Camp. Babies develop this strength each time their parents comfort them as they cry.

"My God, my God, why have you forsaken me?" is the loud cry that Jesus uttered on the cross. It has been cited as proof that God did not comfort Jesus on the cross, but this is not true. As he often does, Jesus is singing--in this case Psalm 22, the song that begins with just these words. The psalm is a song and anyone who knew it would have recognized the opening line just as we would know *Amazing Grace*. Read the whole Psalm but notice the following verses:

1a   My God, my God, why have you forsaken me?

4a   In you our fathers put their trust;

5   They cried to you and were saved; in you they trusted and were not disappointed.

9-11   Yet you brought me out of the womb; you made me trust you even at my mother's breast. From birth I was cast upon you; from my mother's womb you have been my God. **Do not be far from me**, for trouble is near and there is no one to help.

19   But you, O Lord, **be not far off**; O my Strength **come quickly** to help me.

24   For he has not despised or disdained the suffering of the afflicted one; he has not hidden his face from him but listened to his cry for help. (NIV emphasis mine)

This is an anthem to a trust that was built from birth with assurance that comfort and help were never far away. Even in suffering there was face-to-face contact that quickly brought strength. What a song!

Jesus' next recorded words, and the last words before he died, were also a song. "Into thy hands I commit my spirit," comes from Psalm 31. Songs help us stay synchronized. Since our brain's control center is our center for synchronization, it is little wonder that the control center responds to songs and poetry but not to prose. Singing, even singing to ourselves, helps us stay synchronized in our distress.

There are many scriptures that will tell us that we can return to joy from times of distress.

- Weeping may endure for a night, but joy cometh in the morning. (Psalms 30:5 KJV)
- They that sow in tears shall reap in joy. (Psalms 126:5 KJV)
- From] their shame...and confusion...they shall rejoice. (Isaiah 61:7 KJV)
- I will turn their mourning into joy, and will comfort them, and make them rejoice from their sorrow. (Jeremiah 31:13 KJV)
- Make me to hear joy and gladness; that the bones which thou hast broken may rejoice. (Psalms 51:8 KJV)

Many of these scriptures come from the psalms or songs of God. Singing our way to joy is strongly recommended. Many of the Psalms start a long way from joy and then we follow as the psalmist sings us back home to Joy Camp.

Finding the path back from every feeling starts at age one and takes a year to practice. Four months into this practice the limbic system matures and starts working. The limbic system amplifies the intensity of all the baby's emotions. When the system kicks in at 16 months of age, instead of anger we get rage and tantrums. Instead of fear we get terror and night terrors. For the baby whose brain knows the way back to joy, this is just a harder workout. But for those whose feelings have no path back to Joy Camp, there is terrible suffering.

Two months later, at eighteen months of age, the brain attempts to unify our emotional identity. The plan is to connect all the separate emotional areas within a ring of joy. Perhaps this structure in the brain does not look much like a ring but it functions like one.

THE RING OF JOY

Until a year and a half babies handle each emotion separately, as though they were different people for each emotion.[12] Each feeling has its own brain center that works independently. This is part of why a good mother will teach her child how to return to joy from each feeling. These emotional centers are located around the bottom of the brain. At eighteen months the "joyful identity" region attempts to grow a control network that connects all of these emotional centers together. This "ring" around the bottom of the brain establishes, for the first time, that the baby is the same person no matter what he feels. In time this ring of joy will allow him to act like himself regardless of what he feels.

---

[12] Schore, see Appendix B.

Keep in mind that as this is happening a child's expressive vocabulary is only about 15 words. His sense of identity comes from memories of a responsive face that is present with him no matter what he feels. If he has worked out on Mt. Joy and found ways back from each feeling, he will now grow a strong, united self. If not, the distress caused by his failure to return to joy will become stress and release the stress hormone—cortisol. Cortisol will burn out any weak connections and newly formed connections in the brain isolating that emotional center even further. Without training, these feeling centers will stay disconnected acting like separate selves. These separated regions will always produce a desynchronization of the brain's emotional control center when they are triggered. In the future people will say that he is "moody" or changes when he gets angry or frightened--whatever the disconnected feelings might be. An incomplete or weak ring of joy is an invitation for psychological problems like identity splitting, addictions, mood swings, dissociation and behavior problems.

The main effect of childhood trauma and deprivation is the inability to regulate feelings.[13] In other words, people are not able to act like themselves, maintain a consistent identity or return to joy once they have a strong unpleasant feeling. They do not know how to be like themselves when they are upset. We mentioned earlier that brain activity studies had indicated an underdeveloped identity structure in these individuals who can't regulate or recover from upset.[14]

Sometimes, incomplete formation of the ring produces a strange result. When there are paths back to joy from some feelings but not others, the person will learn to move from a "no path back" emotion to one that "has a path." If a man has no path back to joy from anger then whenever he gets angry (no path back) he goes to hurt (path back.) A different man who has a path back to joy from anger will go from shame or helpless despair (with no paths back to joy) to angry (path back) and start a fight because he learned that sometimes after fights people kiss and make up.

A strong joy ring will help people act like themselves whether they are frightened, angry, sad, hurt or happy. Again Jesus gives us an example. When he was sad he healed, the same when he was tired, we are even told that once he got so angry he healed a man (Mark 3:5.) Jesus always acted like himself. That is why he creates in us the ability to grow joy rings. We are creatures of joy.

The six month period from 18 to 24 months are spent growing a strong unified self. Many trips back to joy from all sorts of feelings establish

---

[13] van der Kolk, see Appendix B.
[14] Schore, see Appendix B.

the first large-scale integration of identity. This also allows the baby to realize that his mother is the same person whether she is angry or joyful with him. All paths lead to joy.

It was Christmas day, the year I was two that my first real test arrived. During Christmas dinner I suffered a stroke that paralyzed half my body. Soon after I was in the grip of a raging fever, ultimately discovered to be viral meningitis. Whenever the fever would lift for a moment, I would pull myself up the bars of my crib and sing "Hosanna to the King of Kings" with all my strength. I was singing myself back to joy--a practice I still continue.

Our baby has spent the first half of infancy getting his personality synchronized. Now the relational side of his identity is in place. He has learned to be like his mother, or whoever was closest to him. This has not been easy. If you have ever started a business or office from scratch you can imagine the challenge the baby's brain faces in organizing itself into a personality. He did it by searching to find out who was paying attention to him and then giving control of his emotions over to their faces long enough to see how they will help him feel better. Infancy is a time of organizing and equipping. It is the only time when a human being's MIND can actually be controlled by another person. This is about to change as the infant reaches his second birthday.

THE SECOND HALF OF INFANCY

On his second birthday the infant is now one half the height he will be when full grown. He can walk, talk, and regulate his own feelings when things go wrong. Almost daily he discovers he can do something he couldn't the day before. During this time of left hemisphere growth he learns thoughtful skills for self-care, self-expression, and self-regulation. The next two years will be devoted to discovering what he can do.[15] "I can do it myself!" is his theme.

As far as parents go, during the first half of infancy the mother had an advantage. She could guess what he felt and needed, help him reach joy, lead him out of Joy Camp and back again. A father is not usually as gifted at these things but during the second half of infancy he now has the advantage. Dads seem to have the gift of believing in their baby's capacity to "do it."

Two-year-olds have a widely recognized reputation. From two to four the baby's identity is focused on what he can do. Parents find themselves busy teaching him how to direct what he does through thoughts and words. Because his capacity to imagine has not yet fully developed, he

---

[15] Erikson, see Appendix B.

still does almost everything by imitation. The parents' tasks are to provide him with a safe environment to explore, discover and grow. They will teach him how to talk about and express who he is and what he finds. They will supply what he needs, set limits and encourage-encourage-encourage.

The first half of infancy was the growth spurt for the right hemisphere portion of the identity structure of the prefrontal cortex. The second half is when the left hemisphere prefrontal region grows to become one sixth of the adult brain. This verbal region lets us think in words about who we are. The left half of our be-like stuff makes us people of words and language. Once again we will become like the people around us in our speech. Words are here to stay.

During this time several problems can develop if parents are not aware of exactly how their child understands words. All too frequently parents increase their conflict with two-year-olds with a simple *parent error*. "I told him not to do it and he looked right at me, defied me and did it!" is a common complaint by parents. This is *parent error*! Let's see why.

When they are first learning language children's brains cannot grasp a negative command. For some children this continues until they reach five years of age. This is particularly true for children under pressure or emotion. At first:

"Don't hit your sister!" means the same as "Hit your sister!"
"Don't touch it!" is heard as "Touch it!"
"Don't leave the yard!" equals "Leave the yard!"

Our brains understand negative statements as positive commands with a stop sign at the end, so we stop. The capacity to add stop signs develops as late as age five. Until then, children can hear the words just fine but they can't reliably interpret the meaning. If I told you to "Stop misatuning!" you might have this sort of problem in reverse. You could understand that you were to stop--but stop what? Children under five understand the "what" but not the "stop." They hear:

"(mumble) hit your sister!"
"(something or another) touch it!"
"(unintelligible) leave the yard!"

As a result two-year-olds will look at their parents to see if they are serious! "Hit my sister? Are you kidding? That gets me in trouble! Oh my though, mother looks serious." And so the dirty deed is done.

This problem is made worse for children who become confused at age two and stop listening to words. Before long the infant is so confused that he will go back to using his right hemisphere and decide what to do by voice-tone. Soon his parents will be saying, "He never obeys until I have to yell at him!" *Parent error* again! The child is sorting out commands by voice-tone because if he obeys them all (both the negative and positive which he cannot yet sort out) he will get punished. This leads children to believe their parents are not fair, lie and torment them. It generates lots of anger for the child who gets punished or scolded for doing what he understood he was told to do. Adding anger to a two-year-old gives bad results.

To correct this problem, stay in tune with your child's language development. All the important commands given to children under five should be positive. If you have trouble making positive commands out of negative ones it will help you understand the impossibility this poses for the two-year-old mind. Negative commands must be translated by the parent's brain into useful instructions the child can follow. For instance:

"Don't hit your sister!" becomes "Play nicely with your sister!"
"Don't touch it!" becomes "Keep your hands down and look!"
"Don't leave the yard!" becomes "Stay in the yard!"

Once these parent errors are eliminated, living with two-year-olds is smoother and at times even exciting. Still, when two-year-olds get upset, everything stops until they feel better. Whenever they find themselves having "bad" feelings, thinking and exploring stop. The control center in their right hemisphere takes over. All of their joyful identity and the maps back to joy should be stored there by now. They shut down the left side of the brain with all its words and thoughts while switching on the "return to joy" map on the right side. They suddenly function like one-year-old babies in that words have no effect. This is how the brain is wired. Of course, if there is no map back to joy for this feeling the toddler will stay in his distress. Only when they return to joy will the two-year-old be back. At this age the two halves of the brain might just as well be sitting in different skulls.

Because of their reputation many people give up on two-year-olds too quickly leaving them lost outside of Joy Camp. Don't call your two-year-old a baby when he gets upset. Help him find joy. Much of the stress we call the "terrible twos" comes from trying to control a child **before** returning him to joy. Remember that while he is upset his word processing left hemisphere is shut off and will only be back once joy is reached. First help him with his feeling then you can instruct him once again. Parents who make their control the number one issue at this age will not produce courageous children. Returning to joy is the number one priority, learning to obey is number two. These two tasks can only be combined next year--after his brain connections grow.

When it comes to maturity, sooner is not better. If you were exploring a road that was just being built and came to a river with a sign, "Bridge to be built next year," would you try to drive your family across the chasm? Let us respect the places where our creator has not yet built bridges in children's minds. Two-year-olds will only explore and discover while they feel joy. It keeps them out of some trouble they can't understand.

Joining of the two hemispheres happens at age three. The connections that begin growing will help the verbal and feeling halves of the infant's identity to discover each other. In this last year of infancy he can learn to put words and feelings together. For the first time he can talk about what he is doing, even when he is upset. He begins learning how to act like himself when he is feeling. He learns what he wants to do and say when things go wrong. This last year of infancy, actions and identity come together. Now he can begin to talk about himself, how he feels, and what he wants to do. No longer does he become a one-year-old when he is upset. Now, for the first time he can think about obeying even if he feels upset.

One researcher discovered that children who had been mistreated failed to develop their left hemispheres very well. Their mental energy was getting used trying to keep an emotional balance. There was little energy left for language learning or thinking about the world. He found that for infant boys in particular, neglect greatly damaged the development of the bridge between left and right hemispheres[16]. In fact, for boys neglect produced worse damage than abuse did.

No learning is automatic. We all know many people who become one-year-olds when they get upset. They can think of nothing else but their feeling. Their right hemispheres have taken over and are not consulting with their left. Words don't help. The bridge is closed or out. They stay upset and only notice voice-tone. They can't go on until they feel better. Other times they may be obviously angry, sad or afraid but the talking/thinking half of their brain has not been notified of this at all. I can remember one man with tears running down his face who had no idea he was sad. He could not explain why there were tears when he spoke of his father's death. This is an extreme example of a common problem.

About his third birthday another amazing capacity develops. The baby's brain can now begin to store long-term memories. With this new capacity and a bridge between words and feelings, the rules of his existence change again. Now what he remembers can change what he thinks. What he thinks can change the way he feels. He can remember things when he stops to try and he can talk about all of it—provided someone teaches him how to do it. The equipment is all there but without training that means nothing. The year between his third and fourth birthday will be his training and practice time.

---

[16] Teicher, Martin H., Scars That Won't Heal: The Neurobiology of Child Abuse, Scientific American, March 2002.

The second half of infancy the toddler has learned all the lessons needed to take care of himself. Soon the responsibility will be handed over to him for self-care and self-expression. Having learned the basics about being human, infancy comes to an end. In four short years the baby has copied the older minds around him and created a working identity. In all likelihood, the mind he has copied most has been his mother's. This bond between mother and son is one we must study further before we can leave infancy behind.

Chapter Two
A Baby and His Mother

And Mary kept all these things and pondered them in her heart. (Luke 2:19)

Our second son was born at home on the kitchen table. Before the cord was cut, our son had cried and started nursing at his mother's breast. His mother had wanted him to be born at home surrounded by family. Linda, our neighbor, was waiting downstairs to hear the news and started the phone calls as soon as the shout reached her through the back window, "It's a boy, Linda!" My wife just smiled and reached for the baby.

We had been to many classes and doctor's visits to prepare for childbirth at home. We watched movies and read books. We talked to doctors, nurses, midwives, mothers who had chosen home-births, and people from Third World countries where children are usually born at home. Unlike all the preparation we needed for giving birth, our baby just did his work. He immediately began to breathe. Within two minutes of birth he had cried, expressing his needs, and received the milk and comfort he needed from his mother. Our baby was growing. To understand his work we must look intimately at his needs from his perspective. Meeting these needs will be his first order of business for the next twelve years.

MOTHER AND HER INFANT SON

Strange that the first thing our baby boy needed was to nurse at a breast. Men find it uncomfortable to think and talk about needs that way. A baby boy needs a breast. It will keep him alive, content, comforted, busy and connected to his world. To him it is love, acceptance, food, life, activity and warmth. It gives him something to smell, touch and see. A breast makes him feel better. The breast becomes a baby's first focus in the life-giving bond between him and his mother.

Take a few moments to imagine a baby boy's world. This new world is very unfamiliar, a place of sudden changes. In the midst of daily confusion there are the regular and relaxing workouts on Mother's breast. To him, this is warm life and dining satisfaction. The baby needs his connection to the breast. This connection brings life. From this connection he begins to understand all other connections in his life.

Soon the baby boy will connect with Mommy's eyes as well, for her loving gaze will nurture his soul the way her breast has fed his body. For about the next three years, until he is weaned and ready to care for himself, she will largely be responsible for the quality of his life.

It is the nature of the bond between son and mother that is crucial for his development. Throughout this chapter we will talk about *mother* while keeping in mind that sometimes *mother* is not the one who gave birth to him. Sometimes *mother* is not even female. Who is his mother? A story from the wise king Solomon answers this question. Two women were fighting over one baby. In that story, Solomon ordered a sword be brought to divide the contested baby in two. One woman said that would be fair, the second said it would be better to give the baby to her rival than to kill it. Solomon recognized the second woman's actions as motherly toward the baby and declared her the mother. You see, mothers find their babies' needs more important than their own feelings. So let's look at a baby boy's needs and his mother's responses.

The mother of a dependent, unweaned infant is truly a marvel of creation. This mother knows not only when he is sleepy, hungry or wet, but when he needs attention and exploration. She is available, knows where he hurts (like when that new tooth is coming in), and keeps him the right temperature. Further, she thinks he is marvelous. Her eyes meet his greatest need, for to be fully alive he must be the sparkle in someone's eye. Mommy's gaze alone will bring him to unbearable levels of euphoria. His rapture is so deep, that the baby must look away to catch his breath.

The baby receives without knowing at first that he is asking or receiving. Mother knows his cry is asking. She knows turning his head toward her is asking. She knows that his tugging at her blouse is asking, so she teaches him by saying "Is my little boy hungry?" Sometimes he is not hungry for food but hungry for connection with her instead. He learns that he needs something and he learns to ask. He did not know that before.

It is with Mother's help that her baby will learn he has needs. Mother guesses these needs from his cries and actions. Her mind is specially designed for this moment and effort. Mommy guesses he is too hot or too cold, that he needs a nap or needs to be burped. Perhaps she guesses his cry means his tooth is coming in, and he needs something to chew. Most times he just needs her. Mother recognizes intuitively that his cries ask for something. From within the core of her motherhood come the words for his request. Slowly, and in time, her baby learns to use words to express his needs until one day they are expected from him. When that day comes, Mother will say, "How do you ask?" which means he forgot to say, "Please."

Mother is the first source of connection for a baby. From his connection with Mommy he learns many things: he learns to eat, sleep, to take in what is good and to cry for what he wants. She is his consumer's guide to all that is good and pleasing. With Mother's help and guesses, her baby boy learns how to find all the essential things he will ever need, such as: comfort, shelter, food, closeness, joy, rest and play. He also learns about his own body--where it begins and ends, its powers and limitations.

A good mother notices her son's growth. She does not limit her focus to the things she gives him but notices what he can give. After keeping him safe, full, and warm she stops to enjoy what her baby can do. The good mother watches her son grow and change. By watching what he does and how he contributes to the world, Mommy can appreciate his uniqueness. In time, he will learn to appreciate himself as well. But, for now, the infant does not know that he is unique.

A baby boy's mother shares her joy in him with others. Love is not threatened by such sharing. She knows that he needs more love than just her own. She knows that her own mind and skills are not complete and must be supplemented for his best development. The good mother finds other mothers for her child, so that he may benefit from more care and attention than she can provide. Often these other mothers are female relatives, sometimes they are friends. Mommy fills his life with good people while he still does not know he needs them. Perhaps the main person that mother shares him with is his dad, but older siblings are very important as well. Together they explore and enjoy the uniqueness of her son. He, in turn, learns that love is to be shared, not hoarded.

LOVE-BONDS AND FEAR-BONDS

Not all strong bonds between mother and child are good. In fact, bonds can be generally sorted into two types. Both types of bonds bring closeness between mother and child and serve to meet needs, but there the similarities end. Both fear and love can bond us to others. Fear or love can motivate our behavior. Fear or love can even produce similar behavior but they develop wildly different brain systems and patterns. But, in the case of a mother-and-son bond, fear produces defective connections. Fear and love are antagonists to each other.

Love allows us to see the other person for who he or she is. Contrary to the popular expression, love is not blind. To mother a baby well, a mother must accurately sense her child's feelings and needs and put words and actions to them. Her child will then feel known, understood, and cared for. When the bond between mother and child is based on fear, his mother can no longer see her baby and his needs clearly. She wraps him in a blanket because she is afraid of what other mothers will think of her. She keeps him from exploring because she is afraid he will hurt himself. She feeds him because she is afraid he will get sick or grouchy. She hushes his crying because she fears others will think she is a bad mother. As a result, her baby will not know his needs or recognize his feelings. He learns his mother's fears instead. For such a boy, *life becomes a long-term effort to keep people from becoming upset or afraid.* He is controlled by his mother, even when he rebels, for rebellion is also fear.

THE DIFFERENCE BETWEEN GOOD AND BAD MOTHERS

The characteristics of a good mother are the emotional equivalents of a good musician: timing, intensity (volume) and tone. Did you ever take music lessons? I took piano lessons. You know, it wasn't easy to hit the right note at the right time and volume. Keeping everything synchronized was hard to learn. Babies come with fairly disorganized and undeveloped brains that must eventually be synchronized into happy kids that talk, smile, learn and are a joy to be around. You might say that the main function of a good mother is to teach her infant how to synchronize his brain inside and out. A quick look at how this is done will help us see the difference between good and bad mothers.

In every working human brain, a four-level control center on the right side of the brain dominates all of life. Most of this center's training is completed through interactions with mother by the end of the baby stage of life. One of the four levels, known also at the "mother core," will get special attention in this chapter because its early growth is heavily shaped through relationship with mother.

Like any part of our mind, the control center can develop well and learn a lot or be ignorant and disorganized. When a mother's brain is ignorant and disorganized emotionally, she will train her baby the same way. When her mind has been blessed enough to receive good training then she will pass that on as well. This synchronization capacity is the main difference between good and bad mothers.

THE BRAIN'S CONTROL CENTER

You didn't know your brain had a control center? Our brains do some things we are aware of and other things we can't notice directly. We are more aware of our temperature than our blood pressure for example. The first two layers of the control center are powerful influences that are below the cortex—the level where we experience our awareness and will. The top two levels of the control center give us some sense of choice in what they do because they are made of cortex. So we have a control center that is half buried below our awareness.

The control center is predominantly on the right side of the brain. This means it focuses primarily on how to get back to peace and joy from distressing states of emotions. These recovery skills will let a boy act in relational ways while he is very upset. They allow him to regulate his own feelings, calm down and return to joy—provided he was taught how. The right side of the brain has its own set of characteristics that influence how the control center is trained and run. For instance, right sided memory is unique in that we are not aware we are remembering when it is activated. When we learn a skill, we must remember what we learned in order to use the skill. The only way I can hold a glass of water and drink it is by learning how and then remembering. But when I hold my glass and drink I have no awareness of remembering, I just think, "I'm drinking." In the same way the control center remembers who we learned to be and how we learned to act but we do not think, "I am remembering who I am," we just think, "This is how I am" if we bother to think at all.

You might say the purpose of the brain's control center is *remembering how to act like myself under any condition*s. Said another way, its purpose is to keep me synchronized inside and out no matter what happens. What "happens" are emotions like joy, sadness, terror, rage, shame, disgust, despair and humiliation. Sometimes these emotions arise from inside and sometimes they come from others around us. If our control center is ignorant or disorganized we lose control under these strong emotions. If our control center is strong and well trained we stay exactly the same no matter how intense these feelings get. The preparation for handling all that distress takes place before a baby's second birthday—if he has a good mom.

Let's take a quick tour of the four levels of the control center. Careful synchronization of brain activity is learned, in stages, by the four levels of the brain's control center. From bottom to top this remarkable structure is a learning machine. Level one forms our basic bonds. Our bonds are extremely specific and sensory. When level one wants mommy, daddy won't do. When it wants daddy, mommy gets pushed away. Level one is below the cortex so it has a will of it's own. Level one determines when you are "in love" and who will not ring your chimes. Our deepest pains and joys come from level one. It is our bonding center. When it is *on* we want to attach. When it is *off* we don't. We could call level one our *attachment light* because when it is *on* our faces signal—I want you!

Like level one, level two is also below the cortex. Level two is our basic evaluation center. It has three different opinions about our experiences: good, bad and scary. Once level two has an opinion it can't be persuaded to change. It is the emotional brain for one and it only cares what it thinks. Unless you are in a rather deep coma, level two of your control center is always on.

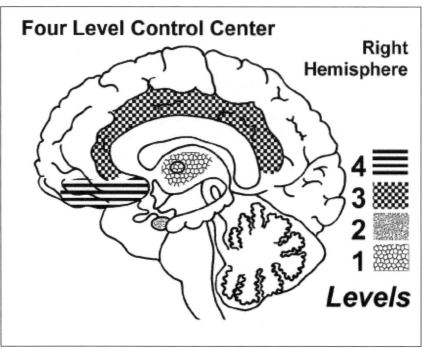

Four Level Control Center

Right Hemisphere

4
3
2
1

Levels

Figure 1 The Brain's Control Center

Figure 1 shows the brain structures most often associated with these four levels of the control center. There is still considerable uncertainty about where some functions start and stop but they seem to be centered in the areas shown on the chart. Level one uses the thalamus and what are known as *deep limbic structures* like the basal ganglia. Level two is centered in the amygdala. The cingulate cortex holds the "mother core" at level three. Best studied is the orbital prefrontal cortex at level four. Together these structures have been called the limbic system.

Level three is the main synchronization area of the control center. It is cortex and open to interaction with other people—particularly those with whom we have bonded. Level three is the emotional brain for two people. It can synchronize with only one other person at a time. Level three does its basic growth and training by synchronizing with mother between 2 and 9 months of age. Level three synchronizes many things. By following a good mom's lead, level three learns to synchronize the lower and higher levels of the brain—those below the cortex with the cortex. Level three synchronizes the different lobes of the brain. It also synchronizes baby and mommy—one brain with another. This is why we call level three the "mother core" because it synchronizes the baby's level three with mother's level three. When mommy and baby are synchronized this way mommy's third level is downloaded into the baby's "mother core." Mother's more developed brain duplicates itself in her baby including what mother knows and how her brain is built.

Level four is our conscious identity center. This is the part of the mind that thinks of itself as *me*. We talked about level four in chapter one and gave it the name *orbital prefrontal cortex*. Here flexible thinking, moral behavior, personal preference and self-awareness reside. The orbitofrontal cortex knows it is *I* who am active and living my life. It is the top level of the control center and, if the four levels are well trained and developed, level four will have the last word about what the brain and body will do. This level four "ability to maintain flexibly organized behavior in the face of high levels of arousal or tension"[17] is what Sroufe calls "a central aspect of a stable individual." Level four is where the capacity for flexible organization resides.

SYNCHRONIZING ATTACHMENT LIGHTS

Synchronization does not just start at level three but much deeper in the brain. There are the 40 cycle per second back-to-front signals from the thalamus, left to right cycles from the cerebellar vermis, heart rates, brain waves, day and night cycles and all sorts of synchronization activities deep in the brain. But the training of a baby boy starts by forming a strong bond with his brain trainer through a process called attachment. Level one of his control center picks out who he will attach to for his training in living. Deep inside the baby feels the impulse to attach as his bonding circuits switch on. Everything hinges on what happens next.

Synchronized: When a baby wants to attach, he looks for eyes, he moves, he makes sounds that to a good mother mean "my baby wants me." His attachment light is *on* so hers comes *on* too. When her baby has had enough for the moment he looks way, gets quiet and lets her know he needs quiet now. Mom follows his lead and needs. His attachment circuits and hers go *on* and *off* together. His basic evaluation at level two of his control center is, "this is good." With that, life is good and he is secure.

Always Off: The baby whose attachment light comes *on* but no one responds is in for an excruciatingly painful time. Nothing in his life will ever hurt as much as having his attachment light ignored. We feel that kind

---

[17] Sroufe (1996, p.159) quoted in Siegel (1999, p. 156)

of pain too when our dog is run over, our child dies or our mate runs away with our best friend. Since the child's need to connect is dismissed or unnoticed his basic evaluation level says "bad." He will try to turn off his attachment light but since it is subcortical with a mind of its own, it won't turn off. Baby's second line of defense is to hide his attachment light. By his second year of life he can begin to fake what is socially acceptable and hide his real feelings. Now he will play quietly by himself and ignore his parents when they come and go. He appears independent and unemotional but inside his little heart is beating hard as he plays it cool. By age thirteen all the outside traces of his pain will be masked so well he won't even know. His attachment level does not come on very often anymore. Only when it comes time to bond with his wife or children will the damage show. They too will get ignored and disregarded. He keeps his attachment light *off* so all his level-one functions are very undeveloped, ignorant, weak and unsynchronized.

Always On: This insecure style of attachment is known for its clingy, dependent and needy style. The funny thing is that unless you pay attention to synchronization, mothers who produce this kind of child are hard to tell from good mothers. The simple difference is this: good mothers synchronize themselves to their baby, bad mothers want baby to synchronize with them. In the case of these bad mothers, they are guided by their own attachment lights and memories of past attachment pains. An insecure and distracted mother looks for her baby when the mother's attachment light comes on and then wants the baby to turn his on also. Whether his light is *off* or *on* is not that important to her, mommy comes when she needs closeness. She overlooks his attachment light signals because she is distracted by her own attachment light. Slowly the baby boy learns to keep his attachment light *on* all the time because he never knows when she might come or leave again. He does not want to miss out on his only opportunity for a while. Unlike "always off" who never seems to be upset, "always on" is always ready to whimper and slow to be soothed.

Chaotic: When the turning *on* of his attachment light produces unpredictable and scary reactions, the baby boy begins to register the approach of his mother as a scary event in his basic evaluation level. He needs her. He wants her, but what happens to him when he gets her attention frightens him sometimes. He does not know how to solve this problem. If the police are likely to shoot you, do you call them when you are in trouble? Three things can make a baby boy frightened of his own attachment light. When his attachment signals produce frightening results like: 1) they make mom angry sometimes, 2) they lead to his becoming overwhelmed by mom's positive emotions toward him at times, 3) when mommy responds but he can pick up how scared she is. Under these three conditions when

40

baby's attachment light comes *on* he fears pain and terror, desires closeness and comfort—but what will happen this time? Since he cannot know and cannot guess he becomes disorganized. This boy is also in for a life-long susceptibility to mental illness and poor relationships.

SYNCHRONIZING ENERGY LEVELS

When I was a boy ukuleles were really big. I spent hours learning to play. In even the simplest song I would have to stop singing and put my fingers on the strings one at a time for the next chord. Sometimes I had to look up chords in a book before I could play them. A good musician could have played along with me easily if she had synchronized to my lack of skill by stopping when I needed to stop. I could never have played along with a good musician—at first that is. After I got better, following the beat and speed of a good player would be just what I needed, but only after I learned the chords. I needed to have certain musical patterns very well learned and practiced before I could play a song smoothly let alone join a band and stay synchronized. A good music teacher would know that and so would a good mother.

As we have seen, the main characteristic of good mothers is that they slow down, quiet down and match their baby's energy and ability. Level three of the control center is particularly suited for synchronizing these energy states in an area known as the cingulate cortex. This area we also call the "mother core" is generally larger in women's brains. When a mother synchronizes her mother core with the same area in her baby's brain, they quickly develop matching brain chemistry, matching brain patterns and finally matching brain structures. In other words, mama can download a working model of her own mother core system into her baby. This can be done between 2 and 9 months of age by face-to-face, nonverbal interactions. All this must be at the mother's initiation because her baby can't match her with his immature and (at first) disorganized brain. If she trains him well, by 9 months of age he can begin to initiate synchronization on his own.

Right-brain-to-right-brain: Synchronization is accomplished by right-brain-to-right-brain communication that is natural and easy if you have a working mother core. The short version of how this works is as follows: whatever your right brain feels is immediately and honestly displayed on the left side of your face. Anyone looking at your face will see the image of your left face and its emotions projected onto the left side of the retinas in both their eyes. The nerves from their left retinas lead immediately to the right side of their brains where their synchronization circuits are given the job of decoding the emotion on your face and responding. Their true response goes on the left side of their face and back to the right side of your brain in the same way. Six complete cycles of these messages pass through both brains each second. Each cycle being slightly amplified so the feelings grow stronger each time around.

Starting and stopping: The most obvious part of synchronizing is starting when your baby's attachment light comes on and stopping when he needs a break. This provides tremendous security to the baby. He does not need to fear being abandoned or overwhelmed. He can focus on learning how to make his brain do what mommy's brain does. If mommy had a good mother core, her brain will read his signals and know just when to start and when to stop.

Climbing together: When mommy first sees her baby is ready to connect with her and link their right brains, she will usually be at a higher energy level than her baby. Her immediate response to linking minds will be to lower her arousal level to match her son's. Her heart rate will drop, her face will relax until their minds are at the same energy level. Together they will increase their joy until the baby's heart rate peaks, his mind can take no more joy and he looks away, disconnecting stimulation to his right brain. This process, which only took a few seconds because the communication is so good, so fast and so mutual, saw mom and baby match smiles, heart rates, brain chemistry and energy levels as high up as baby could make it. That is half the synchronization cycle. The second half is the descent.

This time Mom goes first and baby has to find his own way. Mom knows how to lower her energy levels quickly so she goes to a restful state almost immediately. Baby has to coast to a stop at first. He does not know how to quiet himself. Practice pays off again, however, because the more they practice being quiet together, the faster baby becomes. Being able to quiet himself when he is in an intense emotion will be a very useful skill. We all love to be with people who can become calm quickly when things go wrong. This ability to quiet himself quickly is the strongest predictor of lifelong mental health. A control center that can't quiet itself is the best predictor of mental illness.

Working and resting: A mind that can start when it is supposed to start, stop when it is supposed to stop, get energized when energy is needed, quiet itself when things get too intense, and keep synchronized inside and out will have endurance, resilience and intelligence. We have heard of people who are hyperactive or depressed. These are the people who cannot work when they need to work and rest when they need to rest. They do not synchronize their energy states with others effectively. By alternating working together and resting together *at the baby's pace* a good mother teaches her boy the rhythm of life and relationships. Now he has the beat! Work together—rest together, smile together—rest together, cry together—recover together, first at his pace but as soon as he can keep up he will join the band. A control center with a well-trained third level can begin to initiate synchronizing with others by 9 months of age. An ignorant, disorganized brain may always need others to synchronize with him.

Bad mothers: There is a heavy-sounding term. All of us are bad mothers at moments or with certain feelings. To a great extent, how well we do as mothers depends on what we received—particularly in our first three years of life. When a mother's control center is weak, disorganized or ignorant, she will find her baby's natural disorganization very bothersome. Instead of getting involved with his mind, the deficient mother must struggle to maintain her own stability instead. Sometimes she does this by staying distant, uninvolved and ignoring his cues. She says, "He'll be fine," or "It's no big deal."

A second way a damaged mother keeps herself regulated is to make her baby follow her lead. She tries to "tidy him up" emotionally so he feels what she thinks he should feel. If that worked she would feel more in control. This is the mother who does everything "right" and makes her baby synchronize to her. These bad mothers usually smile more, play more and get more involved with their children than do healthy mothers. They want to be in class with their children. They stay involved, close, affectionate, warm, happy and God knows what other wonderful things so their boy will be happy. Their children do not learn how to synchronize themselves, quiet themselves, or get back to joy from distress.

The third kind of bad mother is the "just make it stop" mother. She is out of control in a very obvious way due to a blown control center, drugs or overwhelming circumstances. Because she wants it to stop she sometimes forces or scares her baby into stopping his emotional demands on her. She explodes at his upsets. "Just shut up!"

What these three types of defective mother cores have in common is that they cannot focus on their child, read their baby's cues or synchronize to their baby. They can't match his energy levels and his rhythm because their own signals are too faint, too strong or too disorganized.

HIERARCHICAL FUNCTION OF THE TOP COMMAND CENTER LEVELS

Timing is deeply important to good brain function. Learning what to synchronize and what to leave out is fundamental for using our heads. A strong and well-trained control center stays synchronized when handling intense feelings. An immature, poorly trained, weakened or chemically disrupted control center falls apart internally. The layers become "delaminated" one layer at a time starting with the top.

When distressing emotions begin to flood the brain the first desynchronization occurs when the right-sided-control-center takes charge and begins to shut down the left hemisphere. During upset feelings the right side is in charge. Gone for now is the left side with its focused thoughts and words. If the control center is working well, the right orbital prefrontal cortex now has "executive control" capacity over the rest of the brain. As the top level of the brain's control center, this identity layer stays on as long as the level just below it (level three) can stay synchronized. For the right orbital prefrontal cortex to stay active, the level three "mother core" must have enough capacity built up to handle this electrical and chemical brainstorm. If the storm gets too strong the control center begins to come apart. The next stage is the loss of level four functions. Level four contains the capacities of the self – our identity – allowing us to act like ourselves rather than become disorganized. When level four is shut off, all the following abilities are temporarily lost.

- **Personal identity**
- **Emotional regulation (individual and mutual)**
- **Joint-focused attention**
- **Switching focus of attention**
- **Three-way bonds**
- **Personal preferences**
- **Creativity**
- **Satisfaction**
- **Goal directed behavior**
- **Moral and social behavior**
- **Correcting our interpretations of others**
- **Time travel / age regression (remembering who we are over time)**
- **Calming/controlling the amygdala (level two)**

Level three, or the synchronization layer, shuts off the top (identity) layer when distress reaches new intensities where there is no previous experience. More nerves are firing or firing faster than this brain has handled before. Now that it has reached a state where the brain has no previous experience to remember, it begins looking for ONE mind greater than itself. He needs one mind with which to synchronize, one mind that has handled this kind of nerve storm before, one mind that can show him the way to handle an upset feeling this big. Mental flexibility is gone, he is focused on finding the ONE. The boy desperately needs someone who will help him get back under control. His mother core looks for someone with capacity and experience to synchronize with him right-brain-to-right-brain and provide an example of being this upset, staying in a relationship and still acting like the same person he or she always was. Synchronization with this "mother" will allow him to synchronize with his higher (prefrontal) brain functions again. A mother with a well-developed capacity could give him an improved control center.

If synchronization of the mother core with a greater ONE fails, the basic evaluation layer (level two) goes to terror and just tries to make it all stop. This subcortical control level always stays on. Desire is gone and the boy switches to fear, withdrawal and avoidance. Gone is moral behavior. Gone is creativity and mental flexibility. This child is now in a high stress state where everything is focused on making it stop. If emotions get intense enough, level two will switch off all possible areas of the brain and declare an energy-conservation-withdrawal-shut-down of all systems. Our boy is now in shock. His control center is desynchronized entirely and he is in trouble. The alternative is to help him grow a strong control center.

During the infancy stage of life a baby boy takes a slowly pulsing mass of cells and transforms them into a synchronized working brain. He learns to synchronize the different parts. He learns to synchronize himself with others. He learns to synchronize words and feelings, effort and rest, relationships and emotions and asking and receiving. If all goes well, by age four he is ready to start taking care of himself. No longer must life be synchronized to him in the ways his nursery provided for him. Now he is ready to begin matching the rhythms of his community. But, suppose his body reaches the age of four while his personality development is still too immature, disorganized, ignorant or incomplete?

DEFECTIVE AND WEAK BONDS

Pity the poor baby whose mother does not sense his needs or respond well to them. She feeds him when she is hungry, or sends him to play when she wants to watch television, and holds him when she needs reassurance. He will not learn his needs or his feelings. Instead, he learns his mother's needs and feelings in a way that makes him feel compelled to meet them. Her mommy-sized needs and feelings will overwhelm a baby because his baby-sized identity disintegrates under such pressure. To survive, he begins a search for someone who will pay attention to *him*.

The baby with weak or fearful bonds senses his desperate need to be connected and lets it be known in various ways. He doesn't understand that his search for attention is a request. Remember that babies must even be taught that their cry is a request. The child who seeks attention has not learned to ask for what he needs. This is usually obvious to adults who say correctly, "He is just looking for attention." Attention is exactly what he

45

craves. If he has not been taught to meet his needs by asking, then he invents other ways to attract attention from his mother or anyone. Maybe he will find what he needs, maybe he will get beat up, or maybe he will get molested. Most likely, he will just get disliked. He is not ready for weaning. He cannot take care of himself.

The poorly bonded baby is in trouble before he reaches the end of infancy. As the time to start taking care of himself approaches, he continues to feel a desperate need to be connected because he hasn't forged a strong bond with his mother. He senses that closeness to others will meet his needs, but his bond with mother is not strong enough to bring satisfaction or security. For him weaning will feel like further abandonment and rejection.

Because it is so upsetting to be abandoned and rejected, an infant with defective bonds will reject his new identity at weaning. Instead of welcoming the goal of taking care of himself, he will try to trick people into taking care of him. He will stay at infant maturity because weak or defective bonds have crippled his identity. This malnutrition-of-the-soul is quite traumatic. Because of it, the baby lacks the necessary good things he requires to grow properly. The development of a boy's brain is more seriously damaged (according to brain scan studies) by neglect than by abuse. We call this absence of good things--type A trauma. The absence of good things will block growth just as as child abuse, illness and catastrophe will do. We call these bad things, type B trauma.

PREPARING FOR WEANING

When an infant has a close bond with his mother, he can depend on her to appear and help him every time something bad happens. From this he learns that bad things precede comfort. He is not alone. He need not fear bad events or feelings. Confidence, hope and faith are built on this simple foundation. Consider the confidence of the man who knows in his gut (prefrontal cortex actually) that something bad is the precursor of something good. Such a man is not easily swayed from his path by adversity or pain. The security of his bond with his mother gives him a strong rope with which to scale the highest peaks of adventure.

The stronger the love-bond between mother and son, the more securely he will climb. The stronger his bond with mother, the greater his capacity to seize life. Knowing he will not be pulled away from his mother's love, he can hold on to wild things and risk what other boys and men would think impossible. He senses his capacity to feel pain, upset and suffering if needed and still stay his course.

NEVER step on a rope. Experienced climbers will tell you that stepping on a rope leaves little bits of sand that grind away the rope as you

46

climb. Then, when you most need it, and tensions are the greatest, the rope will break. Boys must learn to treat their bonds with their mothers carefully. Older children and family members teach boys to honor their bond with their mother and keep it free from fear, contempt or neglect. Mothers must also learn not to step on a rope. Mothers who confess their faults thereby teach their sons to forgive and keep their bonds strong. If you never step on a good rope, your climb will be long and secure.

With a strong love-bond to his mother, a boy can risk involvement without trying to control others, because even if he is hurt he knows that hurt will soon be followed by closeness, comfort and healing. He knows there is always a trail back to Joy Camp. The less he needs to control others, the larger a boy's world can become. More importantly, as a man he will not fear his wife or children. He will not think their needs and feelings are ways to manipulate or control him. The love-bonded baby is the foundation for the life-giving man, but we are getting ahead of ourselves, first our baby must become a child.

A QUICK REVIEW OF THE INFANT STAGE AND WEANING

What a close intimate world surrounds the baby boy. It is a world made for him to the best of his parents' ability. It is a place so intimate that we must take our feelings by the hand just to look inside. It is a world of touching and sensing, of knowing and loving, and once in a while, of holding our noses.

Breathing, sleeping, eating, moving, joy and rest all build a strong bond with his mother during his first year of life. Soon he knows that she is a person with a mind, too. Her mind knows him, helps him, enjoys him, shares good experiences with him. By synchronizing with her mind he learns to synchronize his own. He climbs Mount Joy, resting when needed.

About the time he turns one and begins to walk, his mother, the rock of his security, begins to change. This slow, gradual change allows him to experience tiny doses of frustration and disappointment. No longer does she always come at his call. She will not always guess what is wrong. But Mommy keeps an eye on him and before he can plunge over the cliff to despair she helps him to hope. He learns the paths back to Joy Camp.

But as each day goes past the baby learns to ask and receive. He learns who to ask and how to say it well. "Go ask Daddy to tie your shoes," says Mommy. "Do you want more pureed peas?" or "How's my pumpkin today?" These all herald a passage into a world of words. The baby is preparing to be weaned. We will study weaning more carefully in the chapter about a boy and his father since this process depends greatly on Dad for its ultimate success. With his parents' help the baby boy will leave infancy behind. Soon he will stand on his own. As the end of his third year approaches, he will have developed enough hope to try taking care of himself. These days his mother's words are, "Tell me what you want," or "What is wrong?," or the most dreaded of all, "You'll have to wait until dinner."

Weaning time is dawning although not in the conventional sense. Weaning is the end of infancy. Weaning is a huge transition that can only be made by a well-trained four-year-old brain. A mature toddler with a brain capable of self-regulation, synchronization with others and of guiding his relationships through both words and feelings is ready for the next step. For many, maybe most little boys, this is not the case. He turns four and starts the next stage ill prepared, ignorant and destined to do poorly. His bonds have not prepared him for what is to come.

THE CHILD WITH INFANT MATURITY

Instead of preparing for the goals that come with each new stage of life, the disconnected baby will continue to seek connection. He will want attention and resent it when others get any. He will fail to meet his own needs and demand that others take care of him--if they love him. He will stay an infant as he gets older. Instead of seeking new goals he will always test his connections.

When bonds are based on fears, there is no way that weaning or any other stage of growth can go right. The baby raised on fear will not know his own needs and feelings clearly. If his mother's fears were fairly realistic, then he will cope well with life; if her fears were exotic and irrational he will have little chance of discovering who he really is. Bonds based on fear don't work well. These bonds are always at risk. They can be broken by any fear greater than the fear that bonds.

A true love-bond is characterized by joy, appreciation, encouragement, independence, creativity, flexibility, rest and the ability to risk. The fear-bond is built through control, anger, threats, shame, rigidity, rejection or clinging. As with most of life, nothing is perfect. There are few perfect bonds of love or fear. In these mixed bonds, fear stretches love as though it were a rubber band, if the fear proves too strong, the love snaps and fear takes over. When the fear becomes intense enough the compromised control center comes apart. A weak love-bond will easily be broken by strong fear. Strong love will withstand great fear before giving way. These mixed bonds snap at odd moments and are tremendously confusing to children. They are also discouraging to fearful mothers who want to love their sons.

48

A mother whose own security is not strongly anchored in love will quickly be overcome by fear. She desynchronizes inside and out as her basic evaluation center at level two says, "this is frightening" and seizes control of her poorly developed mind. The frightened or angry mother will not be able to sustain the pressure of the fears inside her and will snap from love to fear as her sense of being threatened grows.

Karin loved her children. She hugged them, fed them, played with them, shared them with her adoring husband. She appeared to be a perfect mommy while Justin was a baby. But Karin had a flaw, a rather deep fear of rejection, which she pushed aside. True, she loved her husband and children and they loved her. When everyone was loving or even sad, she was the mom of moms. But, every once in a while Karin would "lose it" with her son Justin. She was always very sorry for it afterwards, but she just couldn't take it when he refused to do what she told him and ignored her. She would respond by yelling at him and even shook him a couple of times. But that scared her so she stopped. Justin's unresponsiveness awakened in Karin the fear she always carried that her father's unresponsiveness meant he did not love her. This fear led her to try and scare a response out of Justin. This reliance on fear at powerful moments with her son was evidence of the strong fear she always carried toward her father. If Justin ignored her, it reactivated Karin's feelings of being ignored by her father. In those moments, she produced in Justin the same fear that she experienced toward her father. Deep inside, Karin really believes it is fear that connects parents with their children. It is reflected in how she acts.

During the childhood stage, a boy with weak bonds will not be equipped or prepared to reach new goals. Unlike other four-year-old boys who are eager to explore their father's world, take care of themselves, and make friends, he is concerned about being forgotten or left out. During childhood this can best be seen in the way a boy forms friends. Securely attached children are usually invited to play by others and allow other children to join in their play. Poorly bonded children are insecure and beg to join with other children. They are often rejected and play alone. When they do succeed in playing with others, they are frequently displaced or they reject any additional playmates who want to join. Billy was this way. When he had a friend his most common words to others were, "You can't play with us."

MOTHER AND HER BOY

Let us return to our observations of a mature mother with her son as the baby becomes a boy. With Mother's excellent help, a baby comes to find out that he can need, feel, ask, and receive. What a wonderful world this has

49

turned out to be, a world where he can take initiative without having to feel guilt for trying. As he learns to ask more clearly, the infant prepares for weaning when he must make his first solo stand in the world. Successful passage from infant to child requires a solid bond between a baby and his mother. By training him to express his needs and feelings in appropriate words and actions by the time he is four, he is ready.

Weaning marks the time when the child is officially on his own. Weaning, in the sense I am using it, involves feeding, dressing, walking, speaking for himself, and other skills that allow a boy to separate from his mother and achieve a basic level of independence. Mother is no longer in charge of guessing what the child wants. The boy must now ask for himself. Not asking brings with it not receiving, for Mother no longer guesses what is on his mind. Sure, he can solicit help, but even that is now largely up to him. With Mother's help, he has learned to put words to his needs and feelings so that others can know him without having to read his mind. This is the first major achievement of childhood.

The well-bonded mother has her hands full with the weaned boy at first. It is not easy to build his confidence. The newly weaned boy is like a child with new skates or a bicycle. Some just take off while others very carefully test each step. But whether it is through encouraging or trying to keep up, Mother helps the weaned child to become successful at his new stage of independence. She answers a million of his questions a day.

After he has had a successful start, his mother will steadily demand more from the boy. He will learn to ask correctly, at the right time, to the right person. Soon he will be busy learning about his rapidly expanding world. As his perceptions allow more complexity, his requests become more complex. Before long he must begin to calculate time into his requests. This equips him to appreciate his part of history when he becomes a man. To do so he must figure out ahead of time when he will be hungry and how much he will want to eat before he packs his lunch. Mother helps greatly by teaching the boy how to manage his time, such as getting his boots and coat on *before* the school bus arrives.

On the other hand, a boy likes his mother because she keeps the world "soft" when each day it becomes increasingly "hard." His mother continues to be a stable source of warmth and care leaving him free to focus his attention on his world. He is free to try hard things because he trusts his mother's firm support, comfort, and acceptance. His mother helps him stay in the range of manageable mistakes by tracking his development. Since he can count on a soft landing if he falls, the boy can practice climbing enthusiastically. Falls are learning experiences that make him a better climber.

A mother's special gifts of knowing him, which previously helped her know his diapers were wet, now help him know that he is interesting. Mother helps him remember early lessons about his value. She reminds him he has worth just because he is her son, not because of anything he can do. As a result, the boy continues to share the world he is discovering with his mother.

As we have already seen, the unprepared boy is in for trouble. Trying to be a boy when he doesn't know how is very frustrating. He begins to think he is a failure. The child who does not know how to meet his needs by asking will quickly become an angry boy. Unmet needs produce anger, and since no one likes an angry boy, the frustration soon escalates as his anger triggers increasing rejection from others. The mocking phrase, "He just wants attention" is usually close behind, leaving him angrier and more disenfranchised than ever--a casualty of infancy and a badly trained control center.

Sometimes it is Mother who is not ready to let her baby grow up. If she tries to keep him an infant, then they will have endless fights about wearing jackets, boots, or what to eat and when to rest. Sometimes, a mother keeps her son at infant maturity by continuing to be his voice. She tells the world how to understand her son's feelings, reactions, actions and needs. Particularly if the mother relates to her son through her own fears, she will have trouble allowing him to learn from his own mistakes. Not uncommonly this sort of mother makes a career of cleaning up the messes her children make. What a disaster that will be during adolescence when he starts to make a mess of his life!

MOTHER AND THE MAN

My wife Kitty went down to pick up our older son Jamie from college. It was the end of exam week for both of them, since Kitty had started back to college to learn sign language. As they settled in for the two-hour drive home, my son said, "It's good to have you to myself all the way home. There are some things I want to talk to you about." Kitty was delighted. They went on to talk about girls, dating, surpassing one's own parents and many other things.

Young men need to know whether they should fear the new power they have discovered within themselves. They instinctively turn to their mothers to see if they are securely fastened for the arduous climb ahead. Does Mom still find them loveable, or is she afraid of their newfound intellect, body and skills? As each man tries to see himself as he is, he returns to look through his mother's eyes and find out what he can't see for himself. After screening out the things that Mom always says, he finds consolation and hope in her stories about him. She reminds him that, to her eyes he was interesting, lovable, and special even before he could do all the marvelous things he does now. She is a valuable keeper of his history even when it embarrasses him to think that he was once as helpless as Mom describes. They share a little joke when she passes him the sugar.

"Do you want some *oogoo*?"

"Oh, stop it Mom!" he grins. She alone could understand his language when he was a baby.

Now he is the one who strains to understand what others are saying. As a man, who wants to deal fairly with others, he has his first real chance to admire his mother's ability to know what someone else means. This ability to sense what others think and feel helps him bridge the gap to people whose worlds are different than his own. At the same time, it takes him back to his earliest days of life when Mother's attentiveness first broke through the borders of his own existence. His own mother-core is getting a workout synchronizing his newly developed group identity. Like his mother, he now breaks into the borders of other people's worlds--now a blushing girl, then an irritable boss, or then again, a friend who has withdrawn and needs his sympathy. Like his good mother, he enters the lives of the people he meets, seeking to keep their worlds intact and yet make them better because he took the time to know them.

Mother's encouragement means so much at these times. Her faith that he can cross this difficult terrain, even if he is far less skilled than she, brings the hope that he can touch other's worlds and be touched in return. The man who lacks this ability will find himself alone no matter how many parties he attends or how often he gets someone in bed.

The last major challenge of the adult son comes with his marriage. For his mother, marriage brings very important moments of receiving and releasing. Kitty prepared for this experience from almost the moment the boys were born. Each night we prayed for each son and their future wife, wherever that little girl might be in the world right then. We prayed for her safety, her health, and for her soul's welfare. You can imagine Kitty's eagerness to meet them some day. They were beloved strangers she had spiritually covered and waited almost twenty years to meet. Her mother's heart was prepared to receive a daughter-in-law and release her son.

I can hear her excited voice on the phone when Rami said he wanted to bring home a girl for us to meet. After she got off the phone she lay in bed talking excitedly about all the special things she had learned about the girl until well beyond my bedtime. How she liked someone who could love and enjoy her son.

When our boys got married Kitty cut off her apron strings and wrapped them around a book about mother-in-laws as a wedding present.

52

She supported each young bride with a promise that there would be no fight for loyalty or control between them. Mothers have a lot to give their adult sons.

MOTHER FOR HER GROWN SON, THE FATHER /ELDER

Mother-and-son relationships continue to be important throughout the son's lifetime. As a child, one of the things that impressed me the most about my dad was his relationship to his mother. Even as a busy missionary for over twenty-five years, my dad wrote to his mother every week. Every week she would write back. Almost all of her letters ended with, "Well, I see the mailman coming now, so I'd better get this in the mailbox." These words brought a picture to my dad's mind of the little house he had helped build on 422 Bauman Road with lilacs in front and his mother sitting by the window. In the countryside of Colombia, torn by hatred and civil war, amidst constant threats, he was reminded that he was lovable and worth protecting. So it was that his mother reminded him of how God saw him, even though she did not know that was what she was doing.

God's interest in spiritual adoption for fully grown people gives us another hint of the importance of mothers and fathers for men who are old enough to be parents themselves. It is interesting that Jesus spiritually adopted his mother and Saint John the Beloved when they were both adults. (John 19:25-27) Later on we read that the Apostle Paul, who was definitely an adult, had been adopted by Rufus' Mother who was like a mother to him. (Romans 16:13) This he found very precious. Perhaps the man who had learned to be content in any situation liked someone to worry if his soup was still hot and if his tunic needed a little mending. We are never so old that we lose the appreciation for someone with the ability to see us and love what they see.

Mothers are at their best when they can see their son's unique history through God's eyes. Mary kept all the things she heard about Jesus in her heart. This is what a mother does, she keeps the things about her children deep in her heart and treasures them. One young man recently got angry and beat up his fiancée, whereupon she promptly broke off the engagement. When the young man returned to his mother, he said, "I just can't believe I did that!" His mother wisely began at the beginning and reminded him that this was not the first female he had hit. From there she told him who he had been, even back to his childhood. She was indeed a good mother, for she told him not only his history but also who he was beneath the violence--a scared boy who needed help he could not give himself. Their family had passed along poorly running and badly trained control centers for generations. Well past her own children's infancy she began seeking repairs for her own control center. Now she was able to pass some along and let her son know that a problem existed for which repairs were possible. Of course, she said it far better.

WHEN YOUR MOTHER HAS DIED

There are two ways a mother can die. The most obvious death is physical. Once a man's mother has died physically he can only remember her words and actions, and it is important to do exactly that. Proverbs, chapter 31 contains the sayings that King Lemuel learned from his mother. Included among them is training on how to rule and marry wisely. She helps him to see what he really needs among all the options open to a king. "The women who make eyes at kings are not good for you," she tells him in effect, "look for a capable woman." She shares with him her ability, as a mother, to sense what is really needed by telling Lemuel to speak up for those with no voice, the wretched, the embittered, and the poor. The King did well to remember his mother's words about who he was and what he really needed. Scripture still contains his mother's sayings for us to remember. So just as mothers are to remember their children's history, sons are to remember their mothers and treasure them in their hearts. *Never step on a rope!*

There is another form of death which is far worse than physical and much more insidious. Mothers and fathers who die this way still walk around and talk to their sons. These relationships are like marriages that are dead, but the paperwork continues in effect. These mother-and-son relationships are dead, but the facade continues to stand, especially during holidays. Such a relationship is death-giving to the son. If a man comes to realize that his mother cannot see who he is in God's eyes, he is badly in need of adoption by a godly mother. Because she holds our history, a mother reminds us of who we are and how we are connected to others. Spiritual mothers, while they hold less of our history, may well be gifted with more vision about what we are actually like inside. Like the apostle Paul, who treasured his adopted mother, we should not be afraid of spiritual adoption. If saints and apostles need spiritual mothers then all of us could benefit too.

But now let us have an in-depth look at the second goal in life-- becoming a child. If mothers shine during infancy then fathers have their moment when their baby becomes a boy.

THE SECOND
METAMORPHOSIS

*

BOY

*

THE CHILD STAGE

BOY
The Child Stage

IDEAL AGE
Four to Twelve

NEEDS
•Weaning
•Help doing what he doesn't feel like doing
•Authentic help sorting feelings, imaginations and reality
•Feedback on guesses, attempts and failures
•Love he does not have to earn
•Be taught his family history
•Be taught the history of God's family
•Be taught the "big picture" of life
•

TASKS
•Take care of himself
•Learn to ask for what he needs
•Learn self-expression
•Develop his personal resources and talents
•Learn to make himself understandable to others
•Learn to do hard things
•Tame his cravings
•Learn what satisfies
•See himself through the "eyes of heaven"
•

Chapter Three
Becoming a Boy

Our tent was pitched on a slightly level spot between a tree and a rock, one day's hike into the Golden Trout Wilderness. This was our first backpack trip ever. Most of the junior high group from church were scattered around us eating and complaining heartily. Jamie lay in the tent feeling sick.

Macaroni and cheese steamed in a coffee can. Most of the kids ate some. Jamie stayed in the tent. Rami poked at his food but ate almost nothing. When ten and eleven-year-old boys aren't eating, something is wrong. I felt sort of nauseated myself. Were we coming down with something out here in the middle of nowhere?

"Drink a little water and get some rest. You will probably feel better in the morning," I said stuck halfway into the tent like a Pooh Bear.

"I'm not thirsty."

Like childhood, learning to camp in the wilderness requires us to learn many new skills. Each backpacker needed to be able to take care of him or herself. One must stay on trails, find shelter, carry all necessary supplies, not carry too much weight, avoid dangers and animals (like bears), prepare meals, stay healthy, and find safe water to drink. This last task was accomplished on our first trip with iodine tablets that gave the water an unpleasant flavor but killed the parasites and germs.

Getting boys to drink water with iodine proved to be harder than making them clean their rooms at home. Some vacation! The next day it was the same, and the next. By the third day Rami started eating and drinking a little. My appetite returned the fourth day. The main problem was that without food the boys were weak and lacked energy to climb mountains and explore. All the same, we did learn how to backpack.

The High Sierra was beautiful, the trip was so much fun that we decided to go again. This time, I did more reading in preparation. To my surprise, the section on high-altitude health listed nausea, loss of appetite and lack of thirst as symptoms of *dehydration*, a common mountain health hazard. I assumed that if we weren't thirsty, we weren't dehydrated but that was not true. Sometimes we need exactly what we don't feel like having.

Other symptoms of dehydration included swelling of the fingers and extremities. We had each experienced those problems on the first day's climb. But who would think that dehydration could make us swell? I would have guessed it might make us shrivel! Sometimes a problem produces exactly the opposite effects from what we expect. There is a lot a boy doesn't know about taking care of himself.

The iodine in the water kept us from getting sick from parasites but because it made us avoid the water it also led us to getting sick. Sometimes a solution produces a new problem. Taking care of oneself is not that easy. On our first trip we did not know how to make sense of the symptoms of dehydration so we did not drink enough water to correct it. As a result we lost several days of enjoyment, but if the days had been a little hotter the problem could have become life threatening.

By not drinking enough water we lacked a necessary good thing. The lack of something necessary for survival and development is called a type A trauma. The Absence of something needed. Often we cannot recognize what is missing from our symptoms. Sometimes we don't even want what we need, just like we avoided water with a bad taste and got dehydrated. Missing some necessary ingredients for development is the most common problem during childhood. In this chapter we will examine the steps necessary to reach the goal of childhood--taking care of oneself. There is a lot a boy does not know.

WEANING--A NEW IDENTITY

Childhood begins at weaning. The boy leaves infancy behind and with it his identity as a baby. As a baby he believed that others would always take care of him. After weaning the boy-child understands that he can take care of himself. He has a lot to learn. This change radically reshapes the way a boy understands himself. He is a new person now. While we will examine the details of weaning in the next chapter, the importance of weaning can't wait that long.

A boy is not a baby. He is transformed and he knows it. He is a big boy and courageous! This first transformation from one identity to another proves to him that transformation is possible and good for him. The next time he faces transformations he will be free from fear. Each transformation will bring him a new, unknown, and larger self. For the rest of his life, he will not be afraid to leave an old identity for a new one. Instead of repairing old, outgrown identities, he is willing and eager to become someone greater. Weaning lets him know he can make it through change. Transformations are more like a leap than a step.

The four year old is especially ready for his first big change. Trust in his parents is almost total so he will follow their instructions and jump. The strong, joyful baby will make the leap just to see his parents smile. He is almost fearless because he does not understand enough to be daunted. Without a successful weaning at four when they are confident, boys will

58

become afraid to leave their identities behind for new ones later on in life. In the future those stuck in infancy will defend their baby ways instead of transforming into men, fathers and elders. We should note that many, if not most, men in America have gotten stuck at this first identity transformation point.

CHILDHOOD GOALS

Exploration. "Why?" begins with childhood. "Why are you big?" "Why do ducks have feathers?" Children begin exploring their world, trying to understand what they see. Babies can explore their relationships, bodies and homes, but boys are ready to explore the world.

Imagination. From four to six children live in a world of imagination. Even the way a young boy understands himself is built on what he imagines.[18] Young boys can imagine far easier then they can understand the complex reality around them. Their explanations are fantastic and fun. Four to six year old boys will jump off a barn roof with a bed sheet imagining it will work as a parachute and break their legs. They have barely begun to figure out what is impossible.

Their minds are just beginning to detect that contradictory claims can't both be true. For the first time children begin to check and see if parents are telling them the truth. They no longer will believe everything they are told. Now their minds can understand negative instructions so they can decode negative statements like "Don't run," to mean "Stop yourself from running" instead of "STOP RUN."

Doing Hard Things. At five, children develop the capacity to do things that they don't feel like doing. This is the first they know that other people don't always do what they feel like doing. From this, children develop the ability to do hard things. Hard things are things that they don't feel like doing but choose to do anyway. This capacity begins to emerge at five and must be strengthened and developed over the next seven years to be ready for manhood.

There is a ridge below the five Cottonwood lakes that are home to the rare golden trout. Jamie and several others had an introduction to hard things along its endless switchbacks. Their backpack grew heavier with each step. Air was thin at 10,800 feet and all the children were panting and standing far more than they were walking. The more they stood, the stiffer they got and the harder it was to walk. "How much farther is it?" gave way to hot tears and cries of:

"I can't go!"

---

[18] From Erik Erikson's developmental observations. See Appendix B.

"I can't walk any more!"

"I can't move!"

"I want to go home!" Clear proof that we had exceeded their storehouse of joy and a return to Joy Camp was the only goal left. The problem was that our Joy Camp was still uphill from there. Fifty feet below the top of the ridge but before we could see it, we passed two men coming down.

"How much farther to the top?" one boy asked.

"Oh! You're halfway there!" the older man said.

Three boys just sat down and cried. They would not talk or move. Their control centers desynchronized. It was only with great encouragement that they started again. They were delighted to discover five minutes later that the men had been wrong. They made it! They did a hard thing! A flat alpine meadow stretched out the rest of the way to our campsite. I arrived carrying four sleeping bags and Matthew's backpack. Matthew was the youngest boy in the group and not ready for something quite as hard as the others. The boys who weren't dehydrated returned to joy almost as soon as they reached camp. They climbed every rock and fallen tree. They threw every loose stone into the lake.

On later trips we added drinking more water to the list of hard things to do while hiking. It is a hard thing to drink water when you don't feel like it. The goal of childhood is to take care of oneself but there is a lot for a boy to learn.

It is pointless trying to teach children under five to do hard things. Their brains have not developed the capacity. Instead they will become discouraged. Then, when they have matured enough so they could actually succeed, they will feel too hopeless to try. Yet, we all know that infants, who can barely walk, need to do things they don't feel like doing. Until they have developed their wills enough to do hard things we must motivate infants and children by changing the way they feel. Sometimes we help them feel good about things they must do, like, "I'll read you a story when you get in bed." This gives them a positive feeling of anticipation--even when we are only telling them what we would have done anyway. Other times we make children feel more unhappy about avoiding a task than they are about doing it. "You will not get dessert until you finish your asparagus in jalapeno sauce." When they become more unhappy about missing dessert than they are about eating this delicacy they will start to eat--about the same time Iceberg Lake thaws.

Once there is a strong enough identity at age five to override feelings, children can begin choosing to act against the force of their feelings. It is important to start off slowly with this new skill. Five-year-olds can remind themselves to walk when they want to run, and sit still a while when they want to walk. Most of the real practice comes toward the end of childhood during the junior high years. By then children want a challenge. Of course, no boy will want to do hard things, especially at first. He does not like mowing the grass--especially on a hot day, cleaning his room, learning multiplication tables, doing pull-ups, climbing a ridge, completing a merit badge, working until the job is finished or until quitting time, or not acting at the lowest common denominator with every obnoxious child. His character and strength develop as he learns to be more than he was and more than he thought he could be.

There are few naturally occurring hard things for children in suburbia. There are no cows to milk, gardens to hoe, or even newspaper routes before dawn. There are snow blowers and weed whackers only Dad can run, and remote controls for everything else. For decades public schools have had few hard things. One educational theory held that children would naturally learn if they were given good self-esteem and a place to explore the world. This process will never teach children to do hard things they don't feel like doing. While the current political climate favoring high test scores has changed education for the moment, it has not brought joy with it either. Education still misses the joy of doing hard things unless the teacher's own personal maturity can add this essential ingredient.

Much real learning is hard at first. Mathematics, in particular, requires children to think in ways they have never thought before. They must attempt to do something that at first they are unable to do and which must be done a right way. This is hard. The child who has learned to feel satisfied doing hard things will succeed and try even higher goals--perhaps physics or calculus.

Discovering What is Real. Five years of age is also when children learn to judge whether their feelings are realistic. Until now they always believed everything they felt. If a child under five feels scared of ponies, words or explanations cannot change his fears. After five children can change their feelings when their understanding changes. Children who have someone they trust to tell them the truth, can begin to correct the times their feelings are based on misperceptions. If they are told something is an "accident" they can then go back and begin erasing the offended feeling.

Children who do not have parents they trust to tell them the truth will continue believing their feeling instead of what they are told. They will reject explanations and trust their own feelings to tell them the real truth. If they feel it, it is true. If they feel hurt then you hurt them--even if you intended no such thing.

From six to twelve children are what they learn.[19] This is a process of imagining, testing what is imagined against reality and learning from the results. This process produces many failures and many comparisons. Children depend on their parents to tell them the meaning of these comparisons, failures and successes. As a result children learn to separate and correct what they feel from what they imagine and what is real.

Developing His Identity. During this learning time the boy must learn to see himself through the eyes of heaven. It is not enough to be seen that way by others. A boy must begin to recognize his own identity and tend to its growth himself. Taking care of his identity is the most important part of the goal for childhood--learning to take care of oneself.

There are the simpler tasks like asking for what he needs and not waiting for others to guess. And, because his identity is a little different from everyone else, he learns to make himself understandable to others. Instead of withdrawing when he feels misunderstood, the boy learns to make his thoughts, feelings, motives and desires understandable to others. He learns self-expression so that the way he talks and acts reflect his true identity.

Play and a Boy's Identity. Boys practice their identity as they go along. Much of this practice is what we call play. It is play because the outcome is not so serious. In play, boys try out their ideas of how to participate in life. A boy with a poorly built identity can sometimes get by while he is playing only to collapse under real-life strain. But one with a proper identity will build strength and variety during play. Boys need to play.

Play often includes elements of preparation for future tasks. Kittens play in mock fights preparing for territorial disputes later on in life. They practice pouncing and stalking each other in preparation for hunting. Kittens lick each other in preparation for becoming mothers. Little boys also prepare to become men in their play. They may watch super heroes on TV in order to be a hero like Dad when they grow up. In some parts of the world they shoot at melons with their bows and arrows to hone their hunting skills.

The best arena for practicing being a father is in being a brother and a friend to others. Since it is playtime, the roles are not clearly defined. That is to say, a brother can practice being both a man and father with his siblings and a friend with his friends. The boys are merely trying out parts of their identities.

You cannot spend much time around little boys without discovering that "fairness" is a big deal. While some writers think it is a bad thing that boys typically spend just as much time arguing about the rules as playing the

---

[19] Erik Erikson. See Appendix B.

game, I believe that both are essential to play. Arguing is playing at the man's role of making things fair for all sides. Men do this by insuring that everyone is satisfied including themselves. Boys will seek to satisfy themselves if they are mature. If they work things out with each other, they all might even end up back in Joy Camp! People who want to make little boys into little girls dislike this kind of play because it is not harmonious. If we judge by how much fairness boys achieve with their arguments, then we must agree with the critics. In actuality, this type of play usually comes as far from producing fairness as shooting little play arrows into green melons is from hunting wild boar. But play is play. It should not be measured by the same yardstick adults use.

Without the active intervention of adults to help a boy achieve an adult sense of fairness and history, he may turn fairness issues into control fights over rules as he grows older. If he is learning about satisfaction he will soon find control dissatisfying. No one gets to Joy Camp that way. But during play, boys can practice and learn fairness with their friends and siblings.

One way we helped our two sons Jamie and Rami prepare for fairness was to make it a family rule that they must work out conflicts between themselves. Even though Jamie was four at the time and Rami was only two, working things out was their job. We informed them of the simple ground rules. If they brought a dispute to our attention or requested our intervention, they were told to sit at a table, and neither one could get up until the other one gave them permission. Sometimes negotiations were very loud and other times silent. The longest session was close to two hours, as I recall. Did they achieve fairness? I never checked so I don't know, they were just preparing. It did not take long for them, however, to realize the value of mutually satisfying solutions. On one occasion they were simply not able to solve the problem without adult help and both agreed to find that help together. Adult intervention is key at times when real fairness is needed. We will talk more about teaching fairness when we discuss becoming men in chapter five.

Brothers are asked at times to go beyond fairness and care for their brothers and sisters because the need is there, even if it is not fair at the moment. This means doing a hard thing in order to be satisfied. In this way being a brother can also prepare a boy to be a father. Provided that the practice is not too intensive and draining, most boys will find it gratifying. As with piano lessons, too much of a good thing will kill anyone's interest. Lack of encouragement will also destroy a boy's interest in difficult tasks. In addition, there is quite a range of responses between boys. Some respond well, others say they will never play the piano or take care of anyone again. Opportunities do not guarantee success.

Out of all the options open to a boy each one must learn what satisfies. He learns what is just like him, what fits his identity, what expresses who he is in his heart. He learns to apply what heaven sees in him to the life he lives.

A Boy Learns Satisfaction. By the time he reaches twelve years of age, every boy should be very fluent in saying what he feels and knowing what he needs. He should be able to take in everything the world has to offer that is good and reject the bad. The boy should know how to be satisfied.

Finding satisfaction is a very important job. Without it a male person will not be able to meet his needs. It takes a while to learn how to do this well. A long and difficult climb is needed to reach an understanding of a boy's needs and how to satisfy them. Incredible as it seems small children will drink gasoline, drain cleaner, and many others things that older children will spit out instantly, recognizing that gasoline will not quench their thirst.

While finding out what he should drink is part of what a young child must learn, each year the problems become more complex. One sunny afternoon my sons discovered some facts about satisfaction. The lesson came from a ladder they found in the garage. With this new toy, they could climb on the garage roof and see all around. Once, when Rami was on the roof he instructed Jamie, who was still on the ground, to help him get down. Jamie simply pushed the ladder away from the roof, giving his brother a quick ride to the ground. Rami's feelings told him instantly that was not the way to meet his need in the future. Fast results were not the most satisfying.

As a twelve-year-old, one of my sons faced a teacher that was very unfair and controlling. This made the boy quite angry on a regular basis. Expressing his anger directly to the teacher was not allowed, so he decided to escape the teacher's control by not doing any of his homework. This also provided a kind of revenge, because not doing homework drove the teacher wild. She would explode each time the assignments were missing. This solution helped my son express his anger indirectly but did not meet his need to learn. Unlike declining gasoline in favor of water, this conflict of needs and feelings proved harder to untangle.

By the time a boy reaches twelve, he should have learned to be satisfied, and that dissatisfaction is not so bad because it is temporary. The satisfied boy knows how to meet his needs and can choose between competing solutions.

Tragically, the majority of men do not appear to have finished the job of being a boy. Most of us do not know what we feel or how to meet our needs. This leaves us very vulnerable. When we are dissatisfied and do not know what satisfies us we are sitting ducks for anyone who claims to have an answer.

Advertising, for example, is the fine art of creating dissatisfaction. Advertising is designed to create a feeling of dissatisfaction and then tell us what will meet that need. If men and boys knew what they felt and what met their needs, advertising would have no impact. There would be no use for advertising except to tell us the price. The popularity of advertising, and the way most men succumb to it, tells me that men have not finished being boys and do not know what they feel or need. Many men have not taken care of that childhood job.

Being boys is simply our time to learn what really satisfies. We will need this skill in every later stage of our lives.

A BOY'S NEEDS

Boys must have many resources provided for them that they don't even know they need. Without this provision their identities become dehydrated and they don't even know it. Sure they may be angry, withdrawn, lethargic, unmotivated, bored or agitated but they have no idea what is missing from their lives. They can hurt themselves or their grades and not know why.

I often use scuba diving to get myself in shape during the winter so that I can go backpacking in the summer. After feeling so sick from dehydration the first backpacking trip I was even more determined to stay strong and healthy. That winter I took myself on a three-day dive trip to the Channel Islands on a live-aboard dive boat. I had been having trouble "clearing" or equalizing the pressure in my ears along with having a stuffy nose on my last few dives so I took along nasal spray and decongestants. During the trip the congestion got worse each day. On the last day I wondered if I should dive at all. We were going to swim into a beach that was a rookery for sea lions so I overcame my misgivings and dove anyway. My right ear wouldn't clear and I damaged an eardrum. It took a year for my ear to heal before I could dive again. Hundreds of dollars in medical expenses later, my doctor prescribed heavy dosages of decongestants before and during all my dives.

The next summer I was determined to avoid dehydration in the High Sierra by watching when my fingers started swelling and drinking water right away. I wanted to catch the problem well before the nausea started. The first day on the trail I noticed that just before my fingers started to swell my ears would block. Swelling in the nasal tissues around the Eustachian tube that connects the ear and the throat blocked the airflow to my middle ear. As soon as I drank water my ears cleared up. If I waited a little longer before drinking water, my nose got stuffy. It too would clear up when my body had enough water.

In moderately cold water, scuba divers keep themselves warm with wetsuits. It's a bit crude I suppose, but have you ever noticed that when you get cold you need to go to the bathroom more often? A hiker can find a tree but there are no such facilities under water so you can guess what scuba divers do when in need. That is why no one wants to rent a used wetsuit. My first Christmas after I started diving I bought a beautiful blue Harvey's wetsuit of my own. In order to keep it clean I cut down on how much coffee I drank before diving. It was after that the problems clearing my ears and sinuses began. On my three-day boat trip I drank as little as possible. Here was my old nemesis *dehydration* again, and under water no less!

Who would think they would get dehydrated under water? Who would guess dehydration would cause stuffy nose, plugged ears leading to damaged eardrums? Who would think dehydration could cause a lack of thirst, loss of appetite leading to lack of energy. Likewise, children who do not know how to act like themselves will show a wide variety of seemingly unrelated symptoms. The same is true for unfinished childhood tasks and needs that remain unmet. The most common of these unrecognized needs for boys are: unearned love, a sense of family history, the history of God's family, and a big picture of life.

A Boy Needs Love He Does Not Earn. Babies often receive lots of freely given love. Boys also need love that has no performance requirements. A boy needs love that is given because someone knows he is worth it. We call this freely given love--grace. Grace is how we learn about our intrinsic value. The first twelve years of life are the time to learn how to receive. These years establish our value.

All of us have value because we were created with God's life in us. We have value because God values us. It is not because of anything we have done. As babies we should all have the opportunity to learn our intrinsic value otherwise we will think our value comes from what we do. By the time we are two we need to know we have great value without having to do anything at all. From two until four years-of-age our identities become "I am what I do" so it is hard to know if "doing" is what gives us value or not. Children must continue receiving love that isn't earned throughout the child years so they can be clear that *doing* is good but our value comes from *being*.

A moment of self-examination will cause most men to discover that they believe their value comes from what they can do. If a man can't earn a living, talk and think straight, if he can't contribute to his family or society, he thinks he has lost his value. Boys who don't receive grace become men who turn to achievements, fame, and fortune in order to find value. This is how a four year old thinks. If they must *do* something to feel worth, then men do not know who they really are.

Our culture is not going to tell us correctly who we really are. God tells us we have great value for just being made in his image, so it is only if we look at ourselves from his point of view that we realize we have great value even if we can't do anything at all. Boys need to receive love because the need to receive is with us all of our lives.

Family History. As he nears twelve a boy needs to be taught his family history. Preparation for manhood teaches a boy how to take care of himself. Self-care takes many years to learn. In order for the boy to become a man he must learn to take care of two or more people at once. He must satisfy himself and others in a responsible way. He must learn how history is affected by his responsible and irresponsible actions. The only history he will readily understand is that of his own family. Family story telling is a big part of developing a well-balanced brain.

Training a boy between nine and twelve in family history is easy— just tell him stories. These last years of childhood his interest in parents is at its height. He is beginning to study what he will be like as an adult and really wants to know how his parents think and live. Just before junior high is perhaps the best time to teach them how the world of relationships works. Before the crude social power-plays of junior high begin is a great time to fill him in on how people can affect each other. It is also a good time to help him understand the big picture of maturity. He will stay your ally more easily since you have prepared him to grow up. I have written an entire book on this subject entitled *Rite of Passage*.[20]

Tales of the Guardians of Life. The History of God's Family sounds like religion to most people and it turns them off. Suppose with me that God is life. God is what it means to be fully alive and God is passionate that life be full and good. Would the guardian of life not give guidelines for living? Would Life not want people to study and know the ways of life and avoid the ways that lead to death? Boys need to know more than their family history if they are to grow up as men who are alive and life-giving. For their growth and understanding, boys must hear the stories of the people of God—the people who lived and brought life. They need to know life so they will not join gangs that kill, beat their wives and children, pour contempt on those they love and fail to learn about the source of life and goodness. History and movies are full of these themes and yet until a boy realizes that life has a history and heritage in real men and women who made sometimes difficult choices so life could go on, they will not be ready to become men.

The Big Picture. Childhood is also the time to learn the "big picture" of life. This means knowing the stages and goals for each of the five stages of life, much as they were described in chapter zero. People really

---

[20] E. James Wilder, *Rite of Passage* (Ann Arbor: Servant Publications, 1994.)

need a map. It is amazing how much struggle this removes from teen years and the later stages of life. Children who know where they are going will fight their parents far less than those who are just being pushed along without knowing the goal. During late childhood boys can understand goals and are happy pursuing the same goals as their dads. By ten or twelve they can understand how each stage of life builds on the previous stage. Boys appreciate complexity and they are already becoming complex themselves.

When I taught my younger son Rami to drive we took the complex process in stages. First, he worked on the accelerator then the clutch and the brake. My head shook back and forth like a maraca in a Tijuana band while he learned how to use the brakes. When Rami began combining the controls, he would forget what he had learned about the accelerator when he used the clutch. When we added steering, he almost forgot about the clutch. In time, we added driving in traffic to the tasks and thankfully he remembered the previous steps. So it is with growing up, each stage builds on the previous ones. Knowing the big picture helps us fit it all together and look forward to what is next.

In the next chapter we will look at how the father guides and participates in his son's childhood. Dads really come into their own during the boyhood years. These years can be very satisfying when you remember to drink enough water.

Chapter Four
A Boy and His Father

The boy grew and was weaned, and on the day of his weaning Abraham gave a feast. Genesis 21:8.

WHAT IS A DAD FOR?

With a full stack of blueberry pancakes in front of me, I felt particularly useless. A humorless nurse had just sent me away while my wife got "prepped" for an induced labor. Nurses had no use for a Dad.

Very few fathers were allowed into the labor room in the early seventies. Even fewer fathers entered the delivery room. When they were admitted, Dads were "kept in a corner." Doctors had no use for fathers when it came to babies and births.

Our doctor took the radical step of allowing me to stay by my wife for the whole birth, but only after a very careful screening. When our due date passed, the doctor scheduled us for a Monday morning birth-by-appointment. Well, it might not be quite right to say he scheduled *us* exactly, I was, more-or-less, the transportation. Our doctor himself was still in bed when we arrived at the hospital that Monday morning so the nurses locked me out of the labor room. I protested that I had a special Doctor's clearance to be present. That got me a steel-cold glare, a closed door and instructions to go get breakfast--or just do something.

I found the nearby Beaver Grill and got the North-country special. Across the counter, the cafeteria cook stayed busy with his work. He was oblivious to my becoming a father. He had sausage to fry. People ate, pulled on their Paul Bunyan jackets, Co-op caps and left. For them it was just an ordinary day. As for me, I have ordered blueberry pancakes every March seventeenth since then.

When the last fat blueberry was gone, I headed back toward the labor room. I felt my apprehension rising as I got closer. My first child would be here any minute, and I didn't want to miss it. I wanted to know everything about him or her. Anticipation was intense. I wanted to meet the life I had helped form. What if I passed out like they said fathers do? My vague uneasiness about being in a hospital got stronger when I saw Kitty connected to tubes.

"Stay out of the way," the nurse ordered as she left.

Once labor started, we stayed busy breathing. Rubbing sore muscles made me feel useful. Being the official timekeeper for contractions and intervals also gave me a reason to exist. My wife was clearly appreciative of my presence, which is more then some men can say. I sensed in her instructions to keep rubbing that there was room and need for me to be a husband, but what would I do as a father?

The doctor checked me over one last time before we went into the delivery room. "You can always leave if this gets to be too much," he said. Kitty didn't have that option. I wanted to say something like, "If she can take it the least I can do is watch," but I kept my mouth shut and nodded.

Our son Jamie arrived by late afternoon. I was elated to be a witness to something so marvelous. The doctor ushered in this new life then held him up by his neck and the feet. We tried to catch glimpses of him between the green outfits of the medical team on the far side of the room. They wheeled him out one door and my wife out another. I followed her like a puppy on a leash--staying out of the way. Kitty asked about our baby and was told we would see Jamie at feeding time.

My first job as a father was asking the nursing staff if it was feeding time yet. I was like the kid in the back seat asking, "Are we there yet?" By the third time I asked, we were there or perhaps the nurses had grown tired of me. Then, for a moment after he was fed, I held my son. Almost immediately the curtain was pulled back, a nurse pounced and carried him away. I kissed Kitty, took off my funny robe, and went home.

As I called all the relatives to tell them the news, the same question was asked by everyone, "How are the mother and baby?" There was lots to tell, but by eleven o'clock that night not one person had noticed I was now a Dad. I began to wonder whether it mattered. What did it mean to be the father anyway?

It got worse from there. I awoke one night from a dead sleep to find myself being rolled over the edge of the bed and onto the floor. My wife had awakened and, after failing to find the baby, concluded that I must be lying on him. That got me a quick trip to the floor. Only then did Kitty remember that she had put Jamie back in his crib. She ran to find him while I tried to retrieve my breath and wits enough to say, "What on earth!?"

Breast-feeding also did nothing to help me find out what a father was for, except that Kitty took all my handkerchiefs and used them to catch drips! I can see why some men go out and buy the baby a baseball glove or a football, it gives a guy something to hold on to.

My favorite moments were when the little guy was sleeping. After I was sure he was still breathing, I'd stay and watch him until those little eyes finally opened and he would just gaze at me. There was nothing else in the world right then--just the two of us.

It seems Mommy was wired to know when he woke up, because before long she would call out, "Check and see if Jamie is awake yet."

"He is."

"Oh! Bring him here." And the mystery moment was over. I could feel something receding from my face into a lost inner pool the way water drains from the bathtub.

At first, I thought that picking up a baby was like handling high explosives. A quick motion might set something off, or maybe I might drop him and bring disaster. Streams of advice from the ladies did not build my confidence. They gathered like mosquitoes when I got near him. Kitty gave the play-by-play and Aunt Karen added the color commentary.

"Look at the way he holds the head. Not like that! Here, let me show you," my wife said.

"Men!" said her sister, "Don't they know a baby won't break?"

"Well, if they don't break, then what was wrong with how I held his head?" I wondered.

I felt cheated. There didn't seem to be much a father could do, or at least do right. Do babies even need fathers? Maybe fathers are for the time when children grow up, speak, walk, and go fishing. If I didn't find some purpose as a father it was clear that I'd soon be out of the flow of life in this house--relegated to running errands and paying bills. Something inside me burned with desire to know why I was here. It was time I discovered what dads were for before life became a series of quick trips to the floor and lonely stacks of blueberry pancakes. Necessity may be the mother of invention, but desire is the father of discovery.

Dads Are For Discovery. Whereas mothers seem to focus on taking care of babies, Dads want the baby to do something. A baby represents so much potential. A dad wants to see his baby in action. I certainly wanted to discover what my baby could do. After all, it wasn't that many years since I took my dad's Chevy Impala out to see what it could do. A scary thought to some, I suppose.[21]

Now when it comes to *action* babies can seem a little unimpressive at first. Fathers and babies discover mouths, noses, hair, movement, and noises. Once his son can hold up his head, Dad throws the baby boy up in the air to discover flying. Together they bounce, run, race and see what fun feels like. They discover what can be lifted, pushed, and jumped on, even when they must strain to do it. Together they find expression for the life that the child has received from his parents. Why, even the baby himself wants to discover things! Together the father and son will discover the world. They

---

[21] It could do about 135 mph. (The guys reading this wanted to know. The ladies are back to the paragraph about babies by now thinking, "Why can't men…something or another.")

will learn how to protect, serve and enjoy the earth. They will learn to live off the land.

Without Dad's help, Mother might well become the boy's whole world. Dad soon becomes proof that Mom can't understand everyone all the time, and Mom becomes proof that Dad, for all his power, can't move everything. Through Dad he can see that there is no need to be afraid of being connected to Mother. Dad's eagerness to be with her and playful competition with his son for her attention gives proof of this.

Furthermore, the boy need not fear that his mother (and after her all women) will control him or overpower his weak efforts at becoming an individual. His connection with Dad lets him be different than Mom and yet appreciated and admired. The boy can treasure closeness without fear and seek independence with enthusiasm. Dad is a bridge to the wider world and his guide to living off the land.

UNIQUENESS OF THE FATHER BOND

Dad forms a special connection with his child. When you think about it, this alone is a remarkable event. Unlike Mother, who risked her life just to give birth to him, who carried him inside her for nine months, who fed him from her body, slept with him, and sensed his needs and feelings, Dad must bond because someone said to him, "Behold your child." Mother's bond was conditioned by a release of oxytocin[22] when her baby was born. Mama gets more doses of this bonding chemical each time her baby nurses, but dad must bond almost entirely by visual and external means. Fortunately men bond more easily than women. This is good news and bad news. If men do not learn to guard their visual bonding tendencies, they will stray.

The boy's first connections to his mother surround him, and engulf him. He connects to her by taking her breast in his mouth. Dad is an outside force that moves him up and down and throws him in the air. Dad connects and disconnects. Dad puts demands on his body. Dad is the destination Mom chooses for his first steps. With Dad he must be his own person. Dad in turn richly appreciates each thing that makes the boy his own person.

Appreciation, anticipation, holding, comfort, and play are some of the first gifts a son receives from his father. These activities produce a bond between the father and his son that will grow and enrich both of their lives. Early appreciation of his child helps prepare the father in a unique way. He will be a far better guide for his son because he learned to appreciate the boy's characteristics from the very start.

---

[22] This powerful little peptide is the same chemical that lets women have multiple orgasms.

72

Bonding with his baby is not free from turbulence. In cultures where men do not depend so exclusively on their wives to meet all their emotional needs there is less of a crisis for men when Mama has a baby, but the average American father must overcome a bit of resentment. This baby has taken his wife's attention and affection away from him. The baby now has her breasts. Mommy is too tired for hubby. Sex is something you check for with ultrasound scans. Not too surprisingly, many men have their first affair while their wives are having their first baby. They get attached to a babe instead of a baby. No one gave them a "heads-up" about their attachment needs so as the result of having an ignorant and badly trained brain, these men never knew they were about to crave connection and it could get them in trouble.

Because a father with an untrained mind feels these nameless, vague but extremely intense and powerful urges to give life, a power beyond his own will pushes him to bond. He must participate in receiving and giving life. He must join the dance of joy. Someone must light up to see him, be glad to be with him and want all he has to give. A man who has been trained to be a father knows he is getting ready to bond with his son or daughter. The untrained brain is an easy fish to catch and filet.

A BABY AND HIS FATHER

The "mother core" brain training a dad received from his mother many years ago when he was a baby is crucial for a dad to bond with his baby. A well-trained control center will let dad synchronize with his baby, bond with his baby, build joy with his baby and let dad calm himself enough to match what his baby needs. To be a good dad you must be able to do both excitement and calm. The dad who can calm himself and calm others is way ahead of the game. He can use his brain.

Unfortunately for me, when my babies were born I had an ignorant brain. My wife's brain also had little idea what fathers were for so much of the bonding between me and my babies was left to chance. This meant that when mommy was not available and daddy had to take care of the babies the boys were hard to comfort. They were not securely attached to me, my face, my smell or my voice. It was hard for me to calm my sons when they got upset.

The baby boy who discovers his dad early in life discovers a wonderful thing. This creature is the one his mother, the visible source of his life, waits and looks for. He is harder, hairier, usually bigger than Mom. He appears and disappears in an almost random way. Dad represents the unpredictable, the exciting, the one who brings change. Being up on Daddy's shoulders is like riding an elephant or driving a fast car. It is awesome how much power the boy can control and direct. It is here the boy begins to learn of meekness.

The story is told of a Greek general with Alexander the Great who wrote home about his new warhorse. It was, he said, the strongest horse he had ever had. The beast would run almost tirelessly and yet it was guided by the lightest touch, a truly meek horse. Wrestling with Dad, or riding on his back, wrapping little arms around his head and nearly poking out his eyes, the boy begins to learn of meekness. To him, Dad is great power under sensitive control. This teaches him to use his will wisely by imitating his father's self-control. It teaches baby how to stay calm and still have fun.

Boy babies also look to father for examples of how to handle their feelings. Dads have a place in teaching a baby how to climb Joy Mountain and calm back down. Dads also help boys climb the more rugged emotional mountains and calm down safely. Emotions are the most powerful forces a baby knows and dad sets a clear example of how to survive and use these powerful forces. When the baby boy is afraid, in a rage, or even in pain, his father's assuring closeness lets the boy know that it will be okay. Together, a family must explore the whole mountain range of different feelings. The family must also rest in all the calm valleys if they want to develop good survival skills.

To a boy, his father's eyes reveal the meaning of what the world does to him. This right-brain-to-right-brain-communication-link helps make sense of emotional experiences. Seeing dad's reaction to a fall lets him know if it was serious. Seeing dad's reaction to mommy leaving lets him know that dad "has his lights on" and knows what is happening. Dad's look will tell him if Dad knows what is happening to him, too. If there is a bond to dad, baby will use dad's brain to help him calm down when things go wrong.

Baby and His Body. Daddy has the body most like his. Boys learn to use their bodies, walk their bodies, sit their bodies, dress their bodies, feed their bodies like Daddy does. Boys learn the limits of their bodies and how to take care of their needs from watching how Daddy does it. I remember one little boy picking up the communion wafer at church and saying in a loud voice, "What the hell kind of bread is this?" One dad wanted to crawl out of there. The opposite can also happen. Another dad "busted his buttons" when Junior pushed his plastic lawn mower around the yard.

Just as a baby boy needs a breast to receive life, so the baby needs a body of his own to experience that life. Dad, the chap with a body most like his own, is there to help the boy learn to live in his body. And whether or not the aunts think highly of how these two start out, it is Dad who is best equipped to show the boy what he can do. To discover the boy's body and

74

mind, they will play and work together. They will explore his endurance, strength, creativity and abilities. They are preparing to protect, serve and live off the land.

Self Expression. The boy's bond with father teaches him self-expression, how to play, work, make things change, and influence his environment. He needs two influences. Not only is he the sort of person Mom taught him to be with needs and feelings who can take things in but he can also make a change in the world around him. With Dad's help he can do things and make things happen. Even before weaning this fatherly influence begins to pull a rich variety of expression out of the boy.

Dad is very interested in what abilities the boy has inside of himself and wants to try them out. Together they see if he can catch a ball, ride a bike, drive the car while sitting on Dad's lap, or shoot a slingshot. It is said that when Bach would sit down at a new organ he would take it to the limits and see what sort of "lungs" it had. Dads do that. Together he and his boy will explore and expand the limits of his world. With Dad the boy will come into full possession of his body and mind. Together they will play. They don't have to test the limits, they just want to.

Making Mistakes. Around Dad things are always going wrong. The boy learns that Dad smiles when he tries and misses. Together they laugh at mistakes. Together they test the limits to see what is possible today. Together the boy learns to stretch his limits but also how to set limits as well. He can clearly see the difference in power between himself and his dad. He can't do everything Dad can--not yet.

Because his father cares, a boy can see that his efforts mean something, even when they fail. It will come as no surprise to the reader that men are failure prone in most of their efforts. For a baby boy to grow up into a man, he must also get good at failure. One of the essential ingredients of a good childhood is the opportunity to fail without being penalized. Freedom to fail is a big part of preventing sexual addictions. When a boy grows up with freedom to fail he will allow real relationships to nurture his soul instead of living in fantasy or self-generated sexuality. We will get back to this later in the book.

MOTHERS AND FATHERS TOGETHER

Each member of a family exerts his or her influence. Individual uniqueness prevents us from making accurate generalizations about each family member's role, but some generalizations about mothers and fathers will help us divide the work of parenting according to who might be better at a given task. This difference between a mother and a father is mostly a difference in emphasis and speed. Mothers and fathers tend to divide tasks according to who does it faster or better.

Babies don't leave much time. We still laugh at my wife's idea when our first child was born that when she stayed home to be with him, she would have time for projects she had always wanted to do around the house. Time is the critical factor when there are babies at home. This means that whoever is faster will usually get the job.

Differences Between Mothers and Fathers. INTUITION or knowing what others need and feel, is required to guess what babies need. Men usually lose their intuition and sensitivity if they are doing two things at once. The most intuitive of men will usually become oblivious of others if he is trying to sort the mail, cook a meal, or plan his day. Women, on the other hand, can usually do these tasks and still maintain their sensitivity. Consequently, a mother can usually wash the dishes and watch the kids, while Dad can only manage one or the other.

A father may not always be less intuitive than a mother. It is not that fathers totally lack a capacity to sense what a child is feeling or what they need. Fathers can provide these functions quite well, but they must focus and take the time. The average man will just be much slower than the average woman. He will also need to stop whatever else he is doing at the time.

This also gives some hope to single parents who must do everything themselves. The good news is you can do it. The bad news is some things will take you longer and single parents are already trying to do the work of two. This is another place where it is particularly important to recruit other people as supplemental parents.

EXERTION or finding the limits of what we can do, is required for babies' growth. Fathers' abilities to focus on tasks help them take children out of their comfort zone. This capacity to focus also helps them guide children back to joy after a failure or minor injury. Fathers help children build faith in their ability to recover after something goes wrong. Mothers, who can see that something like this would happen, are often more reluctant to try. Mothers are usually more comforting while fathers are planning the next failure.

These are generalizations and in some families parents are quite the opposite of what I have just described. Although men and women can each do almost all the same things the other can, no man will be a mother and no woman a father. Children are simply so complex that they will receive everything both parents can invest.

Both Parents Are Needed Sometimes. Between two parents babies learn to come and go without separation anxiety. They are always aware of going *to* a joyful face more than they are aware of going *away* from the other parent. Two parents reduce the baby's fears in many other ways as well. He learns to receive from his mother and to create from his father. Mother clears the way for the baby boy to know what he needs and feels because she is not afraid of his feelings or demands. Father helps the boy to grow past his fear of failure by enjoying failing together. The boy learns what he can do as well as his limitations.

From his parent's attention and stories a baby learns that he has great value. What he takes in does not give him value and what he makes happen does not give him value. He doesn't do these things to get value or love, they are just part of who he is. His connections with Mom and Dad let him know the value of "just being me." This is the goal of infancy.

As soon as a baby can toddle about, stories become the most important way to keep the family synchronized. Stories are the vehicle that makes our minds understandable to others.[23] The stories I mean are the "stories-of-us" that created and maintain our identity as individuals and families. Parents tell these stories to each other. Together, parents help a baby to tell these stories. The stories-of-us help our minds learn to remember who we are and how we act. Stories-of-us help us make sense of the world. *"Daddy loves to play golf! When you get a little bigger you can play too."* Stories-of-us let us feel close to each other, learn to trust and understand, and even fix things that went wrong. *"I'm sorry I scared you with my yelling. A lizard ran down my neck!"* Stories help us share joy with those who were not there. *"You'll never believe where we went after school…"* Stories help us bring home "owies" to be comforted. *"I lost my favorite jacket."* Stories help learn from others. *When I was your age… (Yeah! Like that is going to work!)* Every day in every life needs to become a story. If you own a mind, you need stories to synchronize all the parts of your mind and make sense of life. *"When something goes wrong in our family we talk it out until we can all be glad to be together again. That is what families are for—helping each other. Mommy is mad because I promised to call and I forgot, so I need to talk to her now and make it better."*

Daddy's stories help baby understand mommy. *"Mommy is going to be right back. She just went to take your sister to school. She didn't forget you wanted to have breakfast so she made your favorite non-sweetened whole-grain granola, tofu and spinach salad puree."* Mommy's stories help baby understand daddy. *"Daddy would like to give you rides, honey but he hurt his back roughhousing with Uncle Mike and now he has to stay in bed all day until his back gets better."* Mommy and daddy's stories help grandma and grandpa understand baby. *"See that! His molars are starting to*

---

[23] Dr. Siegel makes this point over and over.

come in! He is just fussy, but last night he seemed to like sucking on a cold chew ring." Grandma and grandpa's stories help everyone understand the family—and sometimes drive everyone nuts.

One of the best tests of whether someone had a good family is how well they tell the stories of their childhood. The better the family, the more complete and truthful the stories they tell. Of course, they also do better at making themselves understood and understanding others.[24] Mommy and Daddy must work together to help their baby see the other parent through their eyes—by means of stories. Reading stories to your children helps them to learn even more perspectives.

THE FATHER-AND-SON WEANING BOND

As weaning approaches, Dad becomes a larger player in his boy's life. Dad is a good place to practice what baby has learned from Mother. Mother has been teaching him how to ask for what he needs. When he practices on Dad the results are remarkable. Dad responds to his baby's requests. What a wonderful world!

Dad is also the model for the little boy. As they begin exploring the world together, his baby boy notices that Dad also asks people for what he needs and they give it to him. Asking and receiving are keys to living off the land he is entering. The baby boy knows that this enormous person is what he will be like when he is big. Just following the future around is fascinating.

Dad is very important in helping a boy meet his needs. He will teach his son how to live off the land. This becomes the focus of his father's training once the day of weaning arrives.

In more traditional cultures, weaning is a specific time when breast-feeding stops, but for us it means the boy is ready to feed and care for himself. In our culture, little trail markers signal its approach; like the day he holds his own spoon, ties his own shoes, puts on his own clothes and gets into bed on his own. These are all parts of weaning in the sense that I am using the word.

Benjamin had a special baby bottle burying ceremony. He and his dad dug a hole in the back yard. His older sister held the bottles until it was time to throw them in. Mommy brought his favorite cake and ice cream and the whole family partied. Other families have done the same with diapers.

Weaning is the second great transformation in a child's identity. The first metamorphosis occurred at birth and was almost entirely based on his mother's efforts. Weaning is the first major achievement that mother, father

---

[24] Dr. Siegel again.

78

and child reach as a family team, and what an achievement it is. As the boy enters his new identity his joyful identity brain center undergoes a new growth spurt. Dad's joy in his son will result in a euphoric new bond. This is like father--like son time. As the African proverb says, "He who walks with his father will soon be like him."

Early Weaning. Unfortunately, we tend to rush self-care. If we start too soon our baby will not make an identity change. Instead he will come to believe that independence gives him his value. He will continue to think of himself as being what he does.

We can enjoy each step of weaning even if they get rushed a little. They are all a part of our son's history. If all went well during infancy, the baby has learned to "take in" energy from his mother and to "put out" energy from his father. When he turns four we can celebrate his new identity together as a family or community.

Traditional Weaning. When Isaac was weaned Abraham held a feast. The day of his son's weaning was community news and everyone was invited. It was the boy's introduction to his community and their introduction to the boy. The feast made it clear that this boy was important, under his father's care and protection, and in need of the community's involvement. The feast let everyone know that while the boy had depended on his mother until then, his father was now in charge of his nutrition. Even as his mother brought him into the world through her labor, the father now brought him into the world surrounded by the fruit of his labor--the delightful flavors of living off the land.

Isaac began to learn how to ask for what he needed from others. At the feast there was plenty of food to help him learn. For the boy it meant that he was now able to feed himself and everyone was happy about this achievement. He was one of a people now and past his first major hurdle, thanks to his mother's excellent training. A boy who could feed himself was ready for bigger adventures, and everyone rejoiced. This introduced him to the goal for boys--learning to care for himself. For this he needed a family and community. He did not feed himself in isolation. A feast meant that all the community celebrated and rejoiced that they too could feed themselves.

Fathers and Weaning. Weaning is Dad's day in much the same way that the birth day is Mother's day. Neither day would come to be without the other's efforts but special changes take place in a child's identity weaning day that involve Dad in unique ways.

Comforted by his father's voice and surrounded by his father's ample supply, the boy who can feed himself is now ready to learn many new ways to meet his needs. Buying, growing, building, finding, stalking, thinking, gathering, chasing, and waiting are all ways that his father meets his needs, and soon they will be learned by the boy as well.

At weaning the father's role begins in earnest as he takes the boy into the wider world. Each trip goes farther from the familiar base camp of his mother, but with Dad's help the boy child discovers new supply sources. Together they are living off the land.

A BOY AND HIS FATHER

I was four the first time my dad took me blueberry picking. Grandpa Jacobson and Uncle August climbed in our pastel-green 1955 Plymouth station wagon next to our family of four and we headed for a burnt out section of land near Baudette. Grandpa and his brother both sported gray beards and spoke very little. They kept track of forest fires because burnt out areas would have great blueberry crops the next few years. Baudette was a three hundred and twenty mile round trip for my dad who kept track of mileage very carefully. His one-year-old Plymouth was the economy version with no oil filter and Dad was serious about regular oil changes.

It was a blueberry extravaganza. The old men picked quarts of berries. I picked about what I ate. It was amazing to walk, pick and eat. I was living off the land!

Each adventure with Dad starts with leaving home and ends with a return to rest. The boy learns that both leaving and returning are good. Connecting and disconnecting in endless succession, yet with no more fear than he felt releasing his hold on his mother's breast, the boy sets out to learn who he now is. As soon as he learns how it is done, he will launch his own adventures in the care of his watchful community, for his community has been prepared by his father to receive him.

This process is a stress on father, just as teaching the boy to ask for his needs was a stress to his mother. The father's desire to see his son grow provides the motivation to overcome this strain. Fathers who train their sons out of fear push them to perform and achieve rather than teaching them to explore, express themselves, and find satisfaction in life.

Through this maze of confusion, it is the father who guides his son to satisfaction. Back at Camp Joy, Mother's milk was always satisfying--unless she ate certain things. When you are living off the land, the choices are not all good. Does a boy choose chocolate chip cookies or broccoli, potatoes or zucchini, eggs or liver, wine or cola? What should he eat first? When should he not eat?

Learning about food is just the beginning of choosing between options. What clothes should he wear, what friends should he choose, what activities should he spend his play time doing? What goals are worth effort, suffering or pain to obtain? What should be turned down even if it is immediately pleasurable because it is not satisfying? Father is the one who, through finding out what really satisfies in life, can guide his steps and choices. In time his father will show him the difference between pleasure and satisfaction, and in so doing the boy will learn wisdom.

HOW FATHERS SYNCRONIZE WITH BOYS

We have said a lot about synchronizing with babies. First the parent must synchronize to the baby but after nine months the baby can begin to synchronize to the parent—within limits. As a boy gets older those limits need to keep stretching. Dad needs to keep close track of all progress. A positive father will measure progress by the boy while a negative father will measure progress by the goal. A negative father says, *"You are still leaving your room a mess. I told you I wanted everything picked up"* A positive father will say, *"I see you are picking up your clothes now. What are you going to pick up next?"*

The biggest part of growing up is not about the work you do but about how you handle your feelings and impulses. The baby had to learn how to feel joy and all the unpleasant emotions as well, but the boy must take on the urgent drives linked to survival. A baby cannot overcome anything that seems to threaten his survival but the boy needs to master even these feelings so they will not become tyrants. Most often this training falls to dad.

It Isn't Going to Kill You. If mother's favorite phrase was, "Be careful," Dad's is, "It won't kill him." Dads seem to intuitively know that we need to learn to distinguish what will really kill us from what only feels that way. Can you hear dad say, "It isn't going to kill him to: Stay up late, jump in the pool, wait to eat, do something he doesn't want to do, have ice cream before salad or fall off his bike?" This conflict between two necessary forces—safe limits and new growth—often has parents split. While sometimes the battle is between dad and mom, other times it is between parents and child. Boys need to learn to delay gratification and do hard things they don't feel like doing. Not only will it not kill them to suffer these discomforts, but failing at either challenge can prove to be life threatening under the wrong circumstances. We looked at doing hard things in chapter three so let's look at cravings.

The beast each boy must tame is the feeling that roars, "You are killing me" when he can't get what he wants. When he was a baby, both parents would help him calm down when he couldn't get what he wanted. As an infant his parents stopped him from getting things he craved but should not have. Now that he is a boy, his Dad must teach him how to tame a brain that screams, "I'll die if I don't get it!" Dad says, "It isn't going to kill you, son" but then must show him how to live with unfulfilled desire.

The boy is not too sure he won't die because the intense signal he is listening to is coming from his brain's survival center in the limbic system. If he can't control his cravings now he will really have trouble when his adolescent hormones kick in to amplify his urges and desires.

Deep in each brain the *nucleus accumbens* creates overpowering urges for bonding, food, safety and eventually sex. Because these are our strongest survival drives our brain makes their voices intense and urgent. We feel as though we will not live if we don't have these desires. Learning to tame these intense signals is a job that falls largely on Dad. Now, you will no doubt have noticed that a great number of men have had no success themselves dealing with their appetites, urges, impulses and drives. They will, of course be useless in training their sons if they do not learn this first for themselves. Perhaps a bit of religion would do them good.

The nucleus accumbens is such a strong factor in life that most great religions contain teaching about how to train and restrain these drives. Among the Jewish and Christian stories, we read about Esau who lost his birthright to Jacob because Esau thought he would die if he didn't get some lentil stew. Denying all cravings and attachments is central to Buddhist training. The brain that has not mastered its desires is like a wild monkey for Buddhists. Jesus spent 40 days fasting before he began to teach in order to ensure that he would not make his own survival his priority. He had to tame his survival circuits. Muslims practice fasting one month a year. Sexual abstinence is central to the Catholic Church priesthood and those priests who have not tamed their nucleus accumbens have brought the church into crisis. Learning higher values than our own survival and learning to attach our cravings to God are all part of the spiritual disciplines in the Christian tradition.

The nucleus accumbens not only responds to our survival drives like bonds, food, safety and sex but it is also the part of our brains that reacts to cocaine, heroin, alcohol, nicotine, caffeine, ecstasy, "speed," and other drugs. It is closely tied to the cravings that make those drugs addictive. Training the mind to handle this powerful center in the brain that screams, "I'll just die if I don't get it," is a crucial part of avoiding addictions. When teen years come, sexual hormones (testosterone and estrogen) will make the nucleus even more sensitive and reactive. Its training begins when baby screams as though he would die because he wants mommy and he has daddy instead. Dad's presence, closeness and reassurance while he screams as though he would die is the first reassurance that the nucleus is not always right. Of course the dad who has not tamed his own nucleus will be chasing Bathsheba, downloading porn, having a toke, watching TV, playing video games, obsessed with work or eating and drinking.

Controlling these urges involves learning to survive their siren song as well as learning how to control the brain circuits that set off the alarm. To keep the nucleus from getting in a spasm we must be good at producing joy and bringing ourselves to calm—surprise! You can see which one of these two (joy or calm) people have trouble with by looking at the addictions they chose. Addictions typically involve a stimulant for those who do not know how to produce joy on their own or a depressant (like alcohol) for those who do not know how to produce peace on their own. We can crave being alive (stimulants like cocaine) just as we crave becoming calm (narcotics and food.)

Let me tell you a story. Dads have a special part of this means of synchronization. As we have already begun to see, stories help greatly to synchronize the left and right sides of the boy's brain during the childhood stage of development. Children over four have the two sides of their brains connected so they can really benefit from mutual story telling about the emotional events of the day. *"Tell me what happened at school today,"* is an important part of family interactions. Even that simple skill is built learning to, *"Tell Mommy what we did today,"* as well as listening to Daddy tell the stories of his day. Dads who develop the skill can become very good at telling stories of family adventures and misadventures. In fact, telling truthful, authentic, accurate, and complete stories about misadventures and negative feelings helps calm the mind and build peace. A well-trained mind can produce joy when needed and calm itself when needed as well.

I discovered the power of family stories when I worked at a counseling center that saw over 1,000 appointments a month—primarily with women who had been sexually abused. Many of these women hated men. Many of the men they hated were their husbands. I developed a reputation as a miracle worker with their husbands by changing most of them into wonderful guys in only three visits. The men were never to divulge to their wives what I told them to do, but here it is:

1. When you get home each day tell your wife three stories about your day. These stories must involve people you saw or interacted with during that day.
2. Before you can brush your teeth for bed you must tell three *stories of us*. Go through old picture albums to find them if you can't remember any.
3. Get a good storybook and read your wife a story or chapter each night when you get in bed. This helps end the day in joy and since so many sexually abused women didn't have good childhoods or bedtimes it builds good memories to replace bad.

In under two weeks the men went from the bottom of the barrel to the top. Some women's groups would even sponsor three visits with me for particularly "hopeless" men. The results were the same. Of course every woman guessed the storybook at bedtime was my idea, they just couldn't guess how I got the "bum" to do it. They did not guess the nature of the real change in his story telling. The reason I made my instructions secret is that abused women have trouble understanding that men can love intentionally as well as spontaneously so they would have discounted intentional love even though it was real. The only other thing I did in those three visits was to explain the nature of treatment and recovery to the men. No one had ever told them what to expect. Men do much better when they know what is going on.

Singing a song does much the same as story telling. Dads who sing and tell stories, help their children to harmonize the way they think and feel. Singing over your children when they are falling asleep or making up silly songs about them brings joy. It is no wonder that the favorite episode of the enormously popular *Cosby Show* was the one where the family lip-synced a song for their grandparents' anniversary. The world knows Bill Cosby as a man from Joy Mountain who, though not a musician, still sings.

MORE USES FOR FATHERS

Before we get to the bottom of this stack of pancakes I found a few more uses for fathers. It just goes to show what one man's desire can do when his chance to give life is on the line. Feeling useless as a dad can become a self-fulfilling prophesy, but with desire there is hope. We have not nearly tapped the power of the father-child bond. [25]

Cooperation Skills Three-way bonds allow for flexible and helpful interactions between three or more people. Children learn how to cooperate from joining the teamwork between their parents. The obvious joy and peace parents achieve through helping each other, motivates children to work and play cooperatively as well. Dad is a crucial part of children's brain development when it comes to three way interactions. Even in families with lots of siblings, the modeling flows from the top down. Few children will be as smooth and joyful about working together as adult parents can be. If dad and mom possess well-trained, mature brains it will be second nature for them to work together. If one or both parents have an ignorant or untrained brain life is going to be tense.

Group Participation T-ball, soccer, little league, Scouts, camping, band, church and all aspects of becoming a boy will eventually require participation in a group. The skills a boy learns interacting with his parents

---

[25] Dr. Ken Canfield at the *National Center for Fathering.* www.fathers.com 1(800) 593-DADS

and siblings are a big part of his social intelligence. What determines his place in the social pecking order, however, is the motivation he learns to use. Motives will always be either fears or desires. A well-trained control center builds a boy who runs on desire. A father whose pride and joy rolls out the red carpet for his son's entrance to his community removes a boy's fears and strengthens his healthy desires. The boy arrives on the other side of his metamorphosis ready to learn and grow. Abraham, as you recall, held a feast to introduce his son when Isaac was weaned. His father became his advocate, defender, encourager and interpreter in their community.

Tag Team Fathering Boys need more than one father. No child with only one father has enough fathers. Because each father has his own limitations, a father's duty is to secure additional fathers for his son. In so doing, the good father helps his son many ways. By this point, you must have noticed that the men around you have got some things missing. Maybe you do too. Incomplete development leaves men with identities like Swiss cheese. This and several other reasons suggest a need for supplements.

First, just like stacking many slices of Swiss cheese will cover the holes, having many models of mature men will raise a boy with fewer holes in his identity. By adding additional fathers a dad raises his son to become someone greater than himself. By taking in the diversity of different men's fathering abilities, a boy will grow past his father's limitations and blind spots much more readily.

Second, the boy with many fathers learns early in life about the presence and power of the spiritual family. His world is larger, his vision and opportunities are multiplied, and he has much more life to see, explore and receive. He can find an experienced guide for every mountain he wants to climb, every skill he wants to learn.

Third, the boy with many fathers is much safer in times of trouble. Should his father be gone, injured, or die he will have other men in his life. When his parents are overwhelmed there will be places to turn. Should a phase of life be particularly rough at home, like adolescence, he will have mature support to see him through the difficult terrain.

Fourth, the boy with many fathers will be better prepared for future growth and maturity. He will move more easily into his community after weaning and enter the community of men smoothly when he becomes a man. He will even find it more natural to find and receive help from other fathers when he becomes a dad. This support from other fathers is the single most important human factor in becoming a better father.[26]

Evaluating Boys' Efforts Boys learn much from their mothers and fathers, but they practice what they learn with their siblings and peers. As you would expect, they compare lessons with each other as well as practicing on each other. The influence of these practice sessions is considerable in every child's development. Parents who supervise these practice sessions well will find that helping their son evaluate the results strengthens the lessons they want to teach. Unexamined or unregulated play can often teach very different lessons to the boy about who he is or what he can do. The good father is attentive to this possibility and reviews his lessons frequently with his son to be sure the boy's conclusions are satisfying.

DEFECTIVE BONDS WITH FATHER

We can better understand the importance of a boy's bonds with his father when we look at what happens if they are missing or defective. Having no bond to his father leaves the boy adrift within himself and adrift in the world of men. The man who is unconnected with his father does not trust other men. He does not trust his wife or daughter with other men either.

Weak Bonds. The man who is not connected with his father is at great risk of becoming a conformist. He does not know how to be separate and make things happen. He is more prone to be changed than to cause changes. He is not in full possession of his own capacity. This makes it hard to do what needs doing. Dad is the one who teaches us to go after what we want and make things happen.

A weak bond with Dad produces a frantic search for control, power and freedom. Such men need to get away from what they fear will control them. This kind of man fears commitment, challenge, work and struggle. It doesn't matter who gets hurt as he tries to escape. Rather than the connection to his father that tells him he can stay relational and make things happen, there is fear which leads to running away. Escape is necessary when strength is missing--strength to get involved and stay involved. Men run away to work, sports, and study. Some have made minor careers out of trying to be free of any responsibilities in life.

God when portrayed as our Father says, "When you have done everything, stand." Men who know this kind of God don't need to run. God promises the strength needed to stay even when we might suffer.

---

[26] Dr. Ken Canfield again.

We can go, we can do, we can be what is needed but we don't need to run. There is no frantic search for freedom. Jesus did not run around saying, "Let me out of here, these people are trying to run my life."

I get afraid to stay involved sometimes so I run away. I remember one time a family fight broke out on an old subject. I quickly decided to go to the back bedroom to pray. It was the perfect cover. I would gladly have prayed until everything was better, and I could go back out safely. God didn't like my using Him to escape my responsibility so instead of peace my pious escape brought me growing agitation. Before long I had to rejoin the family and take a stand. I don't know that we resolved anything that day, but God knew I could take the heat.

Not only is the missing father a problem, but at times an involved father will fail to be a good model and so create problems by his presence. Each boy is the closest replica on earth of what his father is like. How he feels about his father will have a huge impact on how he sees himself. Even in trying to be very different from his father, the boy is not free from the powerful influence of these feelings.

If a large oak tree drops an acorn that grows into an oak tree, it will be the closest replica of the original oak tree that we can find. Still, the effects of climate, lightening, wind and disease may cause the two trees to grow very differently. In that sense the boy can be the closest replica of who his father was created to be, although through the effects of climate he may grow in very different ways.

God didn't create any trash. We trash ourselves and get trashed because there is evil in the world. But even if your father was the worst father in the world, that is not how his life was supposed to grow. We can say he malfunctioned. Stripped of all the sentimental guilt, evil is nothing other than a malfunction of identity. To see dad through the eyes of heaven, we see an oak tree that never grew up right. The lightning strike of '37 and the winter of '52 took their toll. The seed of the oak tree need not grow that way.

Broken Bonds. If boys or men totally reject their fathers, they reject the model on which they were based. Such a rejection is a rejection of their very selves. Total rejection of parents will trip up our identities. Until each of us can see our fathers through the eyes of heaven and see which parts of Dad are the distortions of evil and what is the created design, we cannot see ourselves correctly either. For men, this acceptance is crucial.

If someone were in a car accident and went through the windshield, we would not assume that what we found was what their face should look like. We can figure that out because we know what faces should look like, but we don't really know what evil does to people's souls, especially when we grow up with them. That face we saw on our father we took to be normal. We could not tell what the scars were unless our father was honest about his history. The truth comes from looking at this history through the eyes of heaven.

To look at injured people with understanding we must know what they were before the injury. People with faces full of glass from the windshield will rightfully see themselves as ugly, but are they ugly? First we must take the glass out and stitch up their faces.

To stretch this analogy a bit, all of us have had our faces jammed through the windshield of sin in the world. (Sin is whatever gives us the ability to not act like ourselves.) We need our faces reconstructed by someone who knows what they should look like to begin with. A plastic surgeon would want a "before" picture. But since our world is thousands of years into the wreck, we have to go back to the Creator for a "before" picture. We can no longer determine whether our faces should look as they do, or if what we see is the result of going through the windshield of malfunction. We ask our Creator to pick the glass out and build our face so that it looks like our father, the way our father was meant to look. In doing this we must come to terms with the fact that our father has also gone through the windshield. His face has also been crushed, and cleaning up his face is God's business, not ours. Often a father has disfigured his son's face to match his own using the same shards of glass. Many a son has undertaken to put glass right back in his father's face to show him what it feels like.

Fear Bonds. At one point in my training when I was being instructed in behavior modification, my services were requested to help a boy who was not doing well in school. We set up a program of goals he could reach. In return he received certain rewards. The reward the boy requested was to spend some time with his dad doing something fun. The father agreed and the standards for success were set. As a result the boy began to apply himself diligently to his studies and earned all his points.

Two weeks later the family came in again. The boy was worse then ever, so I asked what went wrong. The boy said, "I did everything, but my dad would not spend time with me."

I asked his father if this were true and said, "Hey! That is how the world is! You don't always get what you expect. The kid just has to learn to live with that." The dad was happy, he had just taught his son a valuable lesson--what it is like to have your face put through the windshield of life. Now his face would look like his father's. This is how he saw being a good father. He needed to teach certain lessons and get the glass arranged in his son's face the way it was in his own. This is what happens when you don't have the eyes of heaven to see what someone ought to look like.

This father was, as far as I could determine, well intentioned. There is a lot of training that occurs this way by those who don't know how a face ought to look. Deep inside men sense something wrong with the ways they treat their children. And yet, without the courage to face their own pain and their own losses, the trickle-down of cruelty is inevitable. Men, particularly those of this generation, must face the fact that the mentors, fathers, elders, and role models that they seek are not usually available. For this generation the first and last step of grief will be giving what they never received. It is the first step because unless we give, we will not grieve deeply. It is the last because when we have grieved our losses, we will have life to give.

A MAN AND HIS FATHER

It makes me a little uncomfortable to say so, but there have been times when my marriage got a little bumpy. Perhaps you know what I mean. Some bumps have lasted more than a few hours or even a few days. It was on a particularly long bump that I called my dad. He, in his great wisdom, reminded me of my original intentions in marrying my wife. Over the phone he took me back to Bemidji Park and our conversation fifteen years before.

I remembered the day that my dad asked me about my desire to get married. In his opinion and that of the state of Minnesota, I was too young. Did I know, he inquired, of the difficulties inherent in my decision? As we walked through the park at the edge of Lake Bemidji and glanced at the paintings by local artists, we reviewed my life--past, present and future.

"You knew there would be tough times when you got married," Dad reminded me. "I seem to recall that you wanted the challenge." He was right. A man sometimes needs his father to help him do hard things.

My mind flashed to a childhood cartoon. Dad's challenge reminded me of Superchicken's words to Fred, "You knew the job was dangerous when you took it!"

But my father's compassion was deeper than it appeared at first, and we talked at some length about what it means to do things that strain and even hurt. Though he did not particularly agree with me or support all that I was doing, my dad reminded me of my history, my commitments and, most importantly, that there wasn't anything unmanly about feeling pain. The stories-of-us helped me remember how to act like myself.

In my waiting room there is a picture that my son took the first time I brought him blueberry picking. It doesn't show the blueberries we found in the woods near lake Plantagenet, just a funny yellow mushroom. But I remember. We were living off the land.

In later chapters we will learn more about a man and his father and even what to do if your father is dead either physically or in other ways. A man's connection to his father goes on forever. A wise father will try to bring the best out of us, for he can see with the eyes of heaven what there is inside of us waiting to come out. We do well to return often to his words and remember them.

But now our look at what happens to males during childhood is over and we must turn our attention to the next stage in his metamorphosis. If all went well the twelve-year-old boy does a first-rate job of taking care of himself within his family and community. He has seen the world and learned to feed himself well from the best of the land. He is already ahead of the average male in the USA. A huge transformation now awaits him—his passage into manhood.

THE THIRD
METAPMORPHOSIS

MAN

THE ADULT STAGE

MAN
The Adult Stage

IDEAL AGE
Thirteen to First Child

NEEDS
•A Rite of Passage
•Time to bond with peers and form a group identity
•Inclusion by the community of men
•Observe men using their power fairly
•Being given important tasks by his community
•Guidance for the personal imprint he makes on history
•Opportunities to share life in partnership
•

TASKS
•Discover the main characteristics of his heart
•Proclaim and defend his personal and group identity
•Bring himself and others back to joy simultaneously
•Develop a personal style that reflects his heart
•Learn to protect others from himself
•Learn to diversify and blend roles
•Life-giving male sexuality
•Mutual satisfaction
•Partnership

•

Plus
Everything from the Infant and Child stages
Life is to be lived every day. Live it NOW!

Chapter Five
Becoming a Man

Dan Struble threw another log on the fire. It was a "dad" kind of evening, one with plenty of interruptions. He and I had finished a discussion on weaning and gotten something to drink from the kitchen. His baby daughter Amanda had just started crawling around. She was too young to benefit from our subject. She eyed me carefully as Dan turned and warmed up to his topic for the remainder of the evening.

"We just called-out our third boy at church," he said, after reminding me of the ritual described in great detail by Gordon Dalbey in his book *Healing the Masculine Soul*. "Pastor Steve's younger son Adam just turned thirteen. Steve asked him to choose seven men in the church whom he respected to teach him how to be a man. I was one of the men he chose.

"On the appointed day the six other men showed up at Adam's house and called him out. They took him to dinner together to celebrate his becoming a man. I was part of the calling out and dinner for the first two boys, but this time I was on Navy duty and returned just in time to prepare my house for the ceremony.

"After dinner, they brought him over to my home where we took turns telling him what he needed to know to be a man. We divided up seven topics and prepared well in advance what we wanted to say. We talked about peer pressure, drugs and alcohol, sexual purity before marriage, pursuing God's will, the importance of God's will, how to date and treat a woman, and man as warrior. I'm really excited about this."

Dan recounted how after the group had prayed for Adam, he had used his naval officer's sword to illustrate the parallels between forming a sword and making a man of character, discipline, and integrity. Everyone was delighted, particularly Adam, who then held the sword through each of the other presentations. The presentations were fast-moving when the men were well prepared and rambled when they weren't. All the men, however, had taken their roles seriously. A tape of the presentations was given to Adam and the evening ended, but not the impact on the men or the boy. Each one knew he was a part of the community of men and a part of history.

Of course, just as it took them twelve years to become boys, it will take these young men many years to fully become men. When, after more than 4000 hours of practice, I was granted my license as a psychologist, I still felt very shaky about being on my own. I was a psychologist, but I knew there was much yet to learn. In the same way, a thirteen-year-old boy becomes a man but knows that most of what it means to be a man is yet to be learned.

WHAT IS A RITE OF PASSAGE?

Anthropologists gave us the term "rite of passage" to describe the ceremony admitting boys to adult life. Yet, if we let the term reduce our thinking to the level of a ceremony we miss the point. Becoming a man is a metamorphosis of identity. MAN is the third identity a male will experience. At birth he becomes a breathing, eating, moving BABY. At weaning he becomes a BOY who takes responsibility for self-care. Now he leaves the security of his known sense of self as a boy for a new, unknown identity as a man. Unlike his weaning, he goes into this crucible of change with his eyes open. It is a frightening moment.

The confidence of his mother, father and the community of men help this boy take the scariest of all journeys. He has some idea of who he will become, but at a profound level he still doesn't know. If it goes well he will not fear any future transformations. Once he makes the journey from one identity to a greater one, he realizes that he can survive the passage into the unknown. Fear will not overwhelm him when God calls him to other moments of transformation. He will be ready.

God transforms us "from glory to glory" in a series of identity changes throughout our lifetime unless fear stops us from changing. Each stage starts out with a time of growth that slowly turns into maintenance and repair as the end of the stage approaches. Just as an old car becomes too unreliable, so, too, our identities stop working for us and we want to be more than we are now. At the end of each stage we leave behind the comfort and restriction of knowing who we are for the greater glory of becoming someone we do not yet understand. Those who have experienced a rite of passage from boyhood to manhood will understand God's excitement at taking us on a journey, even though we never know the outcome in advance.

It might not be apparent at first, but the passage into young manhood is also preparation for death. In his rite of passage a boy makes the transition to a new identity among the company of men and his family. He learns that a man can face and survive the unknown, a challenge he must confront again at death. Life as he knows it ceases to exist and a transformation takes place. He plunges into Iceberg Lake knowing almost nothing of the new identity and existence beyond.

Even in death he is not alone, for he is surrounded by a "great crowd of witnesses." In animist societies, the spirits of the ancestors fill the role that the witnessing spirits do for Christians. No mere mortal can understand who we become when our bodies are motionless and cold, but we do know that we can survive radical changes in our "selves" and live. The rite of passage reduces our fear of death. Faithful guides have led us through one passage and we can survive others. Followers of Jesus take him as a guide from glory to glory--even at death.

Both Parents' Role In a Rite of Passage. Gordon Dalbey suggests in *Father and Son* that a great struggle to separate a boy from his mother and unite him with the community of men is what ushers a boy into manhood. In his early writings Dalbey sees the rite of passage as separating the boy from the woman in the form of his mother. Other writers in the men's movement, such as Robert Bly and Sam Keen, concur.

I see this rite as simply a passage from boyhood into manhood. While many authors believe a boy must struggle to separate from his mother and women, I believe that a boy who bonded with his father as an infant, whose father showed him what he could do while he was two, will already have a strong independent identity. If his father took him out to see the world at weaning, he will not have an identity dominated by his mother. Therefore, a rite of passage doesn't need to separate a son from his mother. He will need the support of both his parents to transform his identity from boy to man. Both have prepared him and both must affirm and enjoy every sprouting sign of manhood. After all, the adult stage is one of mutuality and parents are the best examples.

Supported, instructed, encouraged and enjoyed by his parents, the properly prepared boy will succeed. Because he was raised to express his true self and find satisfaction, he can leave behind a child's identity and become someone new. After carefully raising their son through childhood his transformation should now receive the same care as his birth.

HOW A BOY BECOMES A MAN

His Family Helps Him Expect a Transformation. The preparations for manhood begin long before the boy turns thirteen. Each boy has already been through two complete cycles of growth-maintenance-transformation. The first cycle lasted nine months and was done for him by his mother. His transformation is marked by his birthday and each year his family celebrates it.

His second growth cycle began as he learned to breath, eat and receive everything he needed for a joyful identity. Toward the end people began to get tired of maintaining his baby ways and prepared for his transformation into a child. You are not a baby anymore they told him as he learned to feed himself, get in bed and put on his clothes. This transformation in his identity required his help as he joined his father in the feast of his weaning and put food into his own mouth.

The third growth cycle has taken him through learning to care for and satisfy himself. As he nears the end of this phase he maintains and repairs his self-centered identity. People around him begin to hope for more and sense it is time to prepare him for a new identity. By reviewing his past growth and transformations and showing him examples of who he will be, the boy gets motivated and inspired for another transformation. Some boys watch their fathers at home or go to work with them. Other boys see men on television, visit Grandpa, or watch men at church, parks, and family gatherings.

Dad Makes Final Preparations. A trip with dad to learn how to be a man is the first concrete step in a boy's developing manhood. By going on a weekend together before the boy enters junior high school, the father is able to prepare his son for the changes ahead. Each boy needs to know that he will be growing in power--personal, sexual, intellectual, emotional, financial, social, and spiritual power. How he uses this power will determine what part he will play in history. The boy and his view of the world are getting bigger. Parents who don't prepare their children will later appear to be stupid in the eyes of their youngsters. This is an impressionable time for boys, a time when they really want closeness with their fathers and will readily listen to what they have to say.

One important childhood task is learning the big picture of life. This trip with father is an excellent time to insure that the picture is clearly visible. Chapter zero of this book explains the stages and tasks each boy should learn. Dad can review or teach the five stages that will guide a boy through his life. To make the lesson stick Dad must tell his son both of their stories. First he can tell how he reached each stage of maturity and completed his tasks. Next he can remind his son how the boy progressed and what is still ahead.

"You know, son, it took me until I was 37 to learn how to return to Joy Camp from disappointment. Until then I thought I was worthless whenever I disappointed anyone. One time when I . . . "

"You were already seven by the time I learned these five stages so we never had a weaning for you. In fact, I wasn't home much at all before then because I didn't know what dads were for. What I did do was teach you how to fish. That is where you learned how to take care of yourself outdoors. Your Uncle Chip would come by . . . "

"Mama and I forgot to teach you how to do difficult things. I had to do everything for myself when I was a boy because my parents could barely keep food on the table. They were always gone working or too tired when they got home. I had to work to buy my own shoes when I was 12. Your mama's dad drank too much and he sometimes made things hard for her when they didn't need to be so we both wanted things to be better for you and you sister. Sometimes we make things too easy for you. Do you remember the time you didn't want to . . . "

I have devoted an entire book to this trip entitled *Just Between Father and Son: A weekend adventure prepares a boy for adolescence.*[27] On this trip

---

[27] E. James Wilder, *Just Between Father & Son*, InterVarsity Press 1990. Available from C.A.R.E. Packaging (231) 745-4950. CAREpkg@triton.net or www.care1.org

the father has a chance to pass on the very best of himself to his son. It is surprisingly simple but profoundly moving. One friend of mine described the trip with his son as a sacred moment. "The only thing I can compare it to was my honeymoon," he said.

The boy who knows that he will become a man at the appointed time is free to take full advantage of his childhood. He does not have to interrupt childhood by trying to prove he is a man when he isn't. He can grow and repair the flaws in his self-care until the time of metamorphosis arrives.

The Rite of Passage. The initiation or rite of passage means a change of identity for a boy. Although it is frightening to leave behind one identity in search of another, two things can make it easier, the company of those who have already made the journey and the support of other boys who are making the same leap. Jewish boys usually go the first way and Masai boys the second.

Passage for One. It was this solo initiation that Dan Struble performed, according to the model developed by Gordon Dalbey. Jim Martini created his own variation for his son Mario. Structured as a back yard barbecue on Mario's thirteenth birthday, Jim invited a group of carefully chosen men to welcome and train his son. He had already taken Mario on the father-and-son trip so the teaching was done.

Mario's little sister made a collection of pictures with captions that gave a sense of his history. She and his mother helped prepare the food and home and then went shopping for the evening. Each man who arrived that night was chosen for his demonstrated achievement in some area of life and his commitment to help Mario mature.

After the meal as the sun set, Jim lit a candle and prayed. Jeff, the scout leader, spoke of citizenship. Bob, the horticulturist, encouraged work. George, who almost never misses a weekend adventure, welcomed Mario on any trip his family took fishing, boating, skiing, or dirt-biking from that night until he turned 18. Others spoke on education, girls, spirituality and family. Most gave symbolic gifts--like the fishing pole from George. Mario liked that part best.

Group Passage. A Lutheran church in Long Beach includes a rite of passage as part of their confirmation class. The Saturday before they are confirmed all the men from the church gather for a barbecue. There are grandfathers drinking lemonade, fathers talking business, teenagers playing volleyball, little boys chasing the dogs, and toddlers getting knocked over.

When the food is gone, this year's crop of boys sits inside a circle made up of all the other males in church. Little boys appear on shoulders or between legs, a few old men find chairs, and everyone listens. Fathers or mentors go into the center of the circle and lift up their boy by the hand when his name is called. The boy gives his statement of faith. This young man is beginning to proclaim his personal and community identity. He is becoming a Christian man not just any kind of man.

Next the men encourage and bless him by telling him what they have appreciated about his life in their church community. This is the time to publicly affirm the main characteristic of each boy's heart. He will learn to express his unique kind of Christian manhood.

When it was Sergio's turn, Brian's dad said, "Whenever you come over to our house to play with Brian you are always considerate to his two little sisters. I really admire that about you."

Peter's uncle put a hand on his shoulder, "You weren't the best player when you joined my Little League team," (there were general snickers just then) "but you kept coming back and doing the drills until you became our best infielder." Sergio gets slaps on the back.

Brian spoke up, "You are my best friend and I hope I always know you." There is a general "Hummmm" of approval from the men and a sniffle from Brian who is suddenly taken by his Nikes.

When the circle is empty, most of the boys are standing with their father's arms around them while the pastor blesses them in prayer and dedicates them as men. Thirteen is a great year. Now they will join their father and his friends and practice manhood.

A TIME OF FORMATION

Dad and his men must deliberately include each young man in ways that show him how men work together for mutual satisfaction. Very quickly, the men must also give each new man important jobs to do before the young man becomes disillusioned and bored.

Mother's pride, encouragement, and natural concerns help this newly initiated youth experience that being a man is a good thing for women. Mother helps him remember what he learned as a baby and a boy as the young man grows. Without this balance, new growth might crowd out the old, leaving the young man to wither. Just because you are a man doesn't mean you don't need your oatmeal and sleep!

Mother, father, peers and community work together for a time of shared life. Together they can observe and encourage the young man to see his impact on history. This is a time to take him seriously. During this time young men learn their adult tasks.

- Develop a strong group identity bond with his friends
- Bring two or more people back to joy simultaneously
- Protect others from himself when necessary
- Achieve mutual satisfaction - fairness
- Develop life-giving sexuality
- Contribute to his church, home, and friends
- Proclaim his community's history and identity

- Learn to live in a way that expresses his heart

Solid Growth and Solo Flight. As with all stages this one begins with a growth spurt. We will examine all the elements of this growth in the next chapter. Once a young man is established he will need several years of solid work before he can achieve mutual satisfaction with personal style. He will need places to share life with adults and hear their evaluation of his impact on their lives. The young man expresses and explores his needs in discussions about what satisfied him and what didn't. Thus, he begins to understand the impact of his achievements for himself and others.

Some boys never become men and others must overcome large obstacles when they finally do. Some boys have only their mothers and women helping them. Most often these mothers are quite concerned about their boy's development but feel inadequate and worried. Unfortunately, many of these worried mothers are married to or divorced from a father whose contributions are of doubtful or poor quality.

WHEN A BOY HAS NO MAN TO HELP HIM

Single Parent Mothers. When mothers take their sons through their rite of passage without a father's help, they take the mountaineer's route. This is definitely the hard way to climb a mountain. Mothers will have a very good chance of success if they know a mature man or a community of men who will adopt her boy as a member. Mothers can provide all the training and encouragement a boy needs but cannot welcome him into the fellowship of men. It takes men to tell him, "You are a man like us."

Mom can easily teach a young man about his heart, how to protect others from himself, to see the effects he leaves on others, and how to satisfy himself and others at the same time. She can teach him all the other adult tasks as well. Mom would be a big part of her son's training even if a father were doing his part. Without a dad's help however, her son will almost always have trouble accepting her training as genuinely *manly*. Because boys often fear being dominated by their mothers, they are more likely to resist mom's instruction and try to find out for themselves. Just a little encouragement by mature men, or even a book like this one, will help these young men verify they are on the right trail.

No Community of Men. Without a community of men, young men cannot practice or become sure of themselves. Clumsy, limited and insecure, they either isolate or go the opposite direction and dominate others. A lack of male community can happen in two different ways. Most often the missing ingredient is a lack of mature men who can include and train young men. But a lack of community can also be caused by a lack of peer companions. Learning together with other beginners is necessary for mutuality and partnership to grow the best.

The lack of a male community for their sons afflicts some married mothers just as it does single mothers. Fathers who are loners often produce the same results in their sons as single mothers because they have no group of men where they can take their sons. Mature men will generally have a community of men around them.

No Mature Men. The boy and his mother are left to find their own way when there are no mature men in the community. Much of the boy's growth will be delayed until he can find mature men later in life. If his mother will point out this problem to him, he will at least know what is wrong and what he needs to find. When there is no community of men the strategy is the same, tell the young man what he is missing. In time he will locate a community of men and be included if he knows he should look for one. It will be a lonely pilgrimage until then.

Boys who receive no instruction don't know what they are missing. When they have no training from their mothers, no community of men to include them, no mature men to train them, they simply don't make it.

BOYS THAT DID NOT MAKE IT

Perhaps it will not surprise you to hear that many men have no idea when or how they came to be men. The three boys that Dan has helped to become men will probably have no such problem. The boy who passes thirteen without recognition begins to feel the internal tension of being a man without a rite of passage and an idea of how to proceed. He is left on his own and to the mercy of his peers to invent a way to be recognized as a man. In fact, men often take very circuitous routes to prove they are really men.

Most often these boys grow up trying to impress, intimidate, achieve, humiliate or lie their way through life. They often fear and manipulate women because they feel controlled and cheated by the women who withhold the good things from them. Most are, of course, obsessed with sex, money, drugs or power. For them, manliness comes from destructive activities, as we will see later in this book.

For now we will turn our attention back to normal development during the adult stage. Marriage and fatherhood are on the horizon. But before we reach those goals, we will examine closely the actual building of a man.

Chapter Six
The Power Years

The glory of young men is their strength. (Proverbs 20:29a KJV)

Gomez was the first to lose his breakfast over the truck's railing as the roads of Antioqia snaked their way into the mists below us. The bass guitarist staggered through the exhaust fumes and the rocking instruments to join him for a duet. Frank[28] and Gomez had started the band named *JOY* and worked well together by now. Tim, my brother and lead guitar, had his nose stuck through a flap in the truck's canvas cover searching for fresh mountain air. We were proclaiming the Gospel in ways only teenagers could appreciate.

My parents sat in the cab with the driver making sure that we arrived in Manizales for the concert that night. Like the youth convention we had just played, my Mom's contacts opened this door. Her friends and reputation got us into almost every place we played. She hated rock music but used her relational network and reputation to open doors so that we could let the world know who we served. My dad raised the money for us to take this short-term missionary tour through the Andes. He made sure we got from place to place but the rest was up to the "boys in the band."

Manizales apparently did not ground its electricity because when I picked up my guitar for the concert that night I felt the power moving through my fingers. I found the driest spot to stand and play but the buzz kept going--turning my fingers to numb ice. Halfway through the outdoor concert the light bulb inside the drum went dim. We put it there to keep the drums warm and dry enough for Gomez to play. When the voltage dropped below 70 volts, our vocal amp cut out. Working together we improvised solution after solution with the same teamwork and tempers we had used to build gear and write songs.

The next day we left on the train. As always there was lots of banter and discussions about how to divide the work fairly. "El Director," as I was unflatteringly called by the band, was chosen to ride in the baggage car with our gear. At one of the little mountain towns where we stopped, the police dragged in a dead man on a two-by-twelve plank and dumped him at my feet. He had been shot at the *cantina* the night before and was being returned to his hometown. Two cops in green uniforms sat in the boxcar door and

---

[28] Francisco Rodriguez and Wilfren Gomez founded *Voces Alegres* whose meaning roughly translates *Joy Singers*.

swapped stories that matched the number of bullet holes I could count. When they heard about it, the rest of the band stopped complaining about the seats in third class. Suddenly sober, we thought about life and why we were living it the way we were.

YOUNG MEN AND POWER

I loved to jump out of the truck and talk our way through military roadblocks. It gave me a sense of power and influence when I persuaded them to let us pass. Frank loved to turn his amp up loud and play. It was like controlling raw power. Gomez liked working the snare drum and talking to girls--well, we all liked talking to girls. We liked the social and personal power their attention and recognition brought. Tim liked writing a song with deep lyrics and having the biggest amp. We all liked the crowd's response when we played. We were alive and strong--the glory of young men.

Thirty years later I was sitting in a mountain retreat with Dr. Charles Kraft, the famous missionary anthropologist.[29] We lit a fire and looked down the valley a quarter mile to the San Andreas Fault. San Andreas represents a sort of power that Californians respect.

"This is beach front property," the manager assured me. Chuck hardly needed that inspiration to start a round of his favorite jokes.

We shared the retreat center for the weekend with Kim, a young woman from Indiana, who was changing the inner city of Fresno for World Impact and Jesus. She and her team were about to move into a neighborhood of Hmong people. Dr. Kraft taught her how to pronounce the "H" in Hmong by blowing out his nose. Like the young men and women mentioned over 100 times in scripture, Kim was busy making things happen. Conversation quickly moved to spiritual conflicts and power. Kim asked Dr. Kraft many insightful questions about spiritual power and how to use it. Power and young adults go together.

Later that day, Chuck commented to me about three methods of deliverance (exorcism) he had observed, called: power encounters, authority encounters and truth encounters. These, he said, were drawn from the three main components of Christianity: power, relationship and truth. Authentic Christianity is built on all three.

Power, relationship, and truth, are also the three preoccupations of young adults. Particular attention must be given to their development during the POWER YEARS of young adult life. The *JOY* band and Kim illustrate how power, relationships and truth blend the many tasks and needs of young adults. The band, for instance, gave us time to bond with peers and work out

---

[29] Dr. Kraft is the author of *Christianity With Power* along with many other books.

fair ways to divide responsibilities. Frank and Gomez developed a partnership that became the band. We learned to bring ourselves back to joy together when we got mad at each other or things went wrong. The many jobs involved in touring helped us develop our personal styles, diversify and blend roles, and make an impact on history. My parents included us into the adult community of churches and conventions where we were given a significant task. We proclaimed our spiritual identity as Christians as well as our personal identities as players, and group identity as a band. All of which amounts to learning to use power in relationships based on truth.

Kim also experienced many of these factors in her missionary experience in Fresno. Characteristic of young adults who are doing well, she had found a significant role, a place in the community structure, a group of peers, and was proclaiming the many aspects of her identity against heavy odds. Like many Christians Kim was at home with truth, like most young women she was rather skilled in relationships, but like all young adults she needed guidance with power.

Power. Most of the action and physical service recorded in scripture is attributed to young adults. Young men were the messengers for David, warriors, explorers, lovers, guards, and even the ones to bury Ananias and Sapphira. If teenagers are going to have conflicts with their parents it will usually be over how quickly they should receive power. Proper development requires that a young man:

- Observe men and adults using power wisely
- Do important tasks for his community
- Make an impact on history
- Learn significant roles
- Use sexual power wisely
- Protect others from himself

Relationship. Mutuality, the key skill of adult life is central to the relationships that develop during adulthood. Group affiliations and partnerships are the matrix for growth. Young adults need opportunity to be co-partners with peers and junior partners with older adults. Young adults must be drawn into the community structure and given important jobs. This is how they become part of the church and its mission. For this to develop correctly a young man must:

- Bond with peers
- Be included in the community of men
- Develop partnership relationships
- Achieve mutual satisfaction
- Bring himself and others back to joy simultaneously

Truth. About thirteen years of age the brain develops the capacity for abstract thought. Young adults can now make decisions and live according to principles and truth. The first application of this search for truth is to find his true group identity. A young man needs both an individual and group identity. Brain changes taking place at just this age help him grow a new sense of identity. The identity area in his prefrontal cortex, the principle level of his brain's control center, has just undergone a major disorganization in anticipation of a new identity. To help establish this new identity a young teenage man seeks his true friends. He develops his power as they practice and proclaim their group identity. For this to succeed a young man must:

- Discover the main characteristics of his heart
- Develop a personal style that reflects his heart
- Proclaim his true identity
- Personal identity
- Community identity
- Spiritual identity

Gangs proclaim their identities by "tagging" or what we call graffiti. Cults, armies, revolutionaries, and movements from hippies to punk rock have grown on the power of young people seeking their true selves. Uniting together, supporting a cause, proclaiming their group identity and making an impact draws both Vegans and Marines. They think they are right, they want to be strong, and they band together to win.

True identity is found in the heart. For this reason each young man needs to know the main characteristic of his heart. In chapter five we discussed how the community of men uses the rite of passage to help each boy find at least one characteristic of his heart. Without this true identity all power and relationships become twisted.

YOUNG MEN AND THEIR HEARTS

*Young man, make the most of the days of your youth; let your **heart** and your eyes show you the way; but remember that for all these things God will call you to account.* (Ecclesiastes 11:9b NEB. Emphasis mine.)

The heart is the place where we know truth. In the ancient wisdom literature the heart is the seat of knowing. We might be tempted to think these ancients a bit stupid about anatomy because we know the heart circulates blood. The ancients knew this too and chose the heart for just that reason. For them, the blood symbolized LIFE and at the center of life was the heart. The quality of the heart determined the quality of life. A healthy heart could discern truth, a sickly or hardened heart could not. The ancients

104

were very big on the quality of life so the heart symbolized the quality of life in circulation. The deepest truths about life were found at the center of its distribution--the heart.

Young men are advised to guide themselves with their heart and their eyes. Both are ways of seeing. Eyes see the outside, the heart sees the inside. The eyes see physical things, the heart sees spiritual things. Maintaining a healthy heart is a major goal of the wisdom literature. This begins by using the heart to see (discern) God and then see oneself. All paths, truth and wisdom are found by the heart that sees both God and self.

Finding His Heart. No two hearts are alike. Young men must identify the main characteristics of their hearts. Some will be kind, some courageous, some bold, some speak truth, some seek righteousness or justice, some have dead or hard hearts already. Receiving a good look at themselves through the hearts of men in their community is a part of the rite of passage as we have seen in chapter five.

Knowing what their individual heart is made of also helps young men understand their characteristic pain. Kind hearts are hurt by meanness, truthful hearts by deceit, accepting hearts by rejection, and loyal hearts by betrayal or abandonment. They will need support in the years to come as they learn to live with a heart like theirs and everything that brings pain. Without this help many will abandon their hearts, stop caring, and find ways to stop "knowing."

The community must prepare for the purification brought by these young hearts. They will be bothered by the deceit, injustice, rejection and other pains they feel and bring older community members to account. A wise community will be corrected, while the foolish will silence these young men and their hearts.

As the community instructs a young man about his heart they must teach him to use his heart to find his true identity, find God, and act like himself. All spiritual communities know to do this and we need say no more about this ancient practice.

Caring For His Heart. After finding their hearts, every group of young men should be taught the proper care and maintenance of the heart. Without a working heart, life is pointless. Every spiritual community has disciplines that must be practiced:[30] prayer, meditation, fasting, giving gifts, study of scripture, singing, feasts of remembrance, rites and ceremonies. Traditions vary, but central to all Christian practice are prayer, confession,

---

[30] Fortuitously, these spiritual disciplines are also the means of mastering the strident voice of the self-preservation center in the brain. The Nucleus Accumbens, if untrained, will dominate life with its urgent cravings—craving that lead to addictions of all kinds. Contrary to its screaming urges, we will not surely die.

baptism, communion and proclamation. For those who have not first found their hearts this is deadly, boring and lifeless, for it becomes maintenance of tradition not care of the heart. First a young man must find his heart so that he can know both God and himself, only then can he maintain his means of knowing--his heart.

GROWTH IN POWER, RELATIONSHIPS AND TRUTH

Power, relationship and truth are so blended that it is impossible to address one without touching on the others. Power is learned in relationships, given in relationships, used in relationships. Power must always be guided and directed by truth if it is genuine power. Power and relationships must reflect the truth about our individual and group identities. We must know the truth about our use of power, realize our impact, develop our style and examine our intentions. In this way our power leaves a fitting impact on history.

Young men must be taught and corrected as they learn about their power. This requires that they learn in a group context where they can experiment and practice doing things that matter. It is up to their family and community to provide this monitored freedom.

Bonding With Peers Produces a Group Identity. Scouts, Christian Service Brigade, youth groups, bands, gangs, sports and teams, school activities, sharing drugs, hanging-out, clothing styles, and entertainment are some ways that young adults form groups. You may immediately notice your preference for the methods that require a community sponsor. When communities provide a time, place and bonding activities, young adults find important roles where their power makes a positive difference. Left on their own, young adults gravitate toward destructive power. They damage the community that has not received them. Just as often, they destroy themselves.

Significant Roles in the Family and Community. Immediately after the rite of passage men enter a growth phase in which they are given increasing power and responsibility. The roles available for young men often spring from the normal activities of life. Something as basic as helping parents with hospitality, making sure everyone is fed, and guests are participating in activities is a simple start. Sometimes these jobs will fit their heart and personality and bring out their individuality. More often young men find jobs anyone could do. With common jobs they learn to put their hearts into the common things of life, lifting the ordinary up to life-giving through their participation.

Almost any job or role will teach the basic skills of responsible participation in community life. Finding odd jobs teaches fairness through negotiating the payment for mowing a lawn. Painting a garage may take repeated efforts to achieve mutual satisfaction. Taking pictures or playing the piano for the neighbors' fiftieth anniversary develops many skills and roles and make a difference in the lives of others. Some of these opportunities are provided but most are earned. Young men need both--some jobs they can find on their own, other opportunities must be provided. This is true whether they participate as junior partners with adults or co-partners with peers. Most of the time they work to build strength, not to earn money.

Co-partners With Peers. In spite of all that practice arguing over baseball rules in grade school, a young man's first roles with his peers are not glamorous opportunities. Car washes for class trips, pooling money for a video game cartridge, cleaning the garage so the band has a place to practice, and planning a camping trip together are usual starting places. Power, relationship and truth develop in these small interactions with friends.

Frank and I decided to share a hammock on our first camping expedition, about the time I was fourteen. We were headed to Chinche, some 10,000 feet up the Andes mountains. The hammock was easy to carry and the webbing looked wide enough for the two of us to sleep. Of course, we never tried it out before the trip. We arrived cold and very tired but mutual sleeping satisfaction was never reached that foggy night. In fact, it was some considerable time before Frank returned to joy since I slept quite soundly at his expense. Frank sat by the fire most of the night suffering the pain of injustice more than the loss of sleep. This injury was more grievous because it was actually Frank's hammock.

Moments like these, and the recovery time afterwards teach young men to become friends and buddies. Trying to cook beans, clean up, move gear and get places together provide hundreds of small opportunities to return to joy together. Later they learn to be friends with young women and finally, as we will see in chapter seven, life partners.

Junior Partners With Older Adults. Young men need their community to provide junior partnerships. Whether they are interns at the White House or singers in a Jesus band, they must be provided with important jobs and places in the community structure.

My friend David Brown tells of a mission group in the Church of Our Savior in Washington D.C. that grew so large they believed God wanted them to get an office. They drew up a plan for what they needed along with a budget. They entrusted two teenagers who were active members of their group with the time consuming task of finding office space. The real estate agent didn't believe the teenagers' claim that older adults had appointed them to find an office. After the leaders confirmed their story, the surprised agent took them around to weed out sites. The two teens found a suitable office at a price that wasn't believed possible in D.C.

Very often the men of a church will plan to help someone who is invalid, sick, abandoned, or impoverished. Younger men can be actively involved in taking inventory of needs, planning what needs to be done, or even taking charge of parts of the project that fit their skills, like making sure that all the watering and weeding is done in an invalid's yard. Young men glory in their strength, but they are not cheap labor. They need to be a part of decisions such as who the men will choose to help this week and why. Listening to the young man's heart on these occasions can also keep men from becoming so busy working that they forget to care about the one they are helping.

Families also need to involve their sons so that they learn how power is used for everyone's benefit. Asking the young man to help plan his portion of the family budget, or who to include on family trips, vacations, holidays, and activities teaches him to keep his family joyful. Planning activities that reach out to neighborhood children who lack stable homes or the lonely and elderly can help the young man balance his own needs with those of people who do not have the resources he has.

Sometimes a young man can be selected for a special task in order to help train him. Greg was picked by his father to choose the right site and boat rental for the men's fishing trip his dad was scheduled to lead. He helped Greg list the different features and advantages he needed so he could compare boats. Then he let his son call, negotiate, and finally select the best boat and site for the trip. It took quite a bit of time, more time than it would have taken his dad, but the training and sense of accomplishment that Greg experienced when he headed out with the men made it worthwhile. Greg was given a real role and real power. As he traveled with the men and saw how his choices made a difference to their trip he began to care about how the older men enjoyed their trip. His care brought real relationships and taught Greg the truth about the difference he could make.

Proclaiming His Group Identity. A child makes himself understandable to others. Adults make their group understandable to people from other groups. Cults are plentiful among young adults because they give them important tasks proclaiming the group's identity. Gangs wear colors and "tag" walls and signs with their marks for the same reason.

Recently two young men wearing white shirts and ties approached me on the street. Their pockets had signs identifying them as Elders of the Latter Day Saints Church. I asked the older one how many of his friends from his home Ward in St. George, Utah had gone on missions. "All of them," he said. They were proclaiming their group identity to anyone who would listen.

Telling others took Kim to Fresno and the *JOY* band to Cali and Medellin--future homes of the Colombian drug cartel. This is an important job in any group that wants to grow or make a difference. Proclaiming, preaching, announcing good news, whatever you want to call it, has a major place in Christianity. As my friend Chris says, evangelism is people letting others know their real identity. Young people have enormous energy for proclamation. Young hearts are strong and pump a lot of life. Each community must make room—for this is power, relationship and truth.

RETURN TO JOY FOR TWO OR MORE

In chapter one we found joy as the central feature of a strong identity. The capacity to return to joy creates resilience. Life holds no terrors for those who know the path back to joy and quiet from every kind of distress. Joy means someone is glad to be with us. Mothers bring infants back to joy and teach them that there is a way to quiet themselves. Children bring themselves back to joy or ask for help when it is too hard. Adults work together to be sure everyone in their group makes it back to joy.

It should not be too surprising that as young men develop a community identity it would feature returning to joy for everyone. The wonderful discovery of adult life is that *we can do this together*. The thousands of hours of phone calls, eating together, going shopping, hanging out, talking, and even doing drugs together, represent ways young adults try getting back to joy as a group.

Joy means "someone is glad to be with me" so those with shadows in their lives must be met in the shadows. It also means being glad to be with "me," not with "who you think I am" or "who you think I should be." So shadow people gather together in the shadows feeling sure that others will not want to be with them. To return anyone to joy means joining them where they are first.

When the band called *JOY* played Cali, we were confronted by an old lady who told us we were playing the Devil's music. It was a rare Sunday morning church appearance and her condemnation left us all very angry just as church was starting. We were a long way from joy by the time communion was served so the whole band declined participation for fear our anger might be sin. The pastor who had invited us observed what we did and talked to the band after the service.

We were quite nervous about getting in trouble as Pastor Salazar began questioning us. To our surprise, he explained that our anger was normal and not a sin. He let us know that being condemned would make him feel angry also. He invited us to participate in celebration with the rest of the community. By joining us in our troubles the pastor returned the whole band to joy in a matter of minutes.

On another occasion, we tried working out problems ourselves. CC sang with us and played the tambourine in a way that seemed below our standards. Our attempts to correct the problem resulted in CC quitting the group. There were quite a few hurt feelings as a result and we didn't make it back to joy together. In later years I tried playing a tambourine for several hours at a time and found the beast harder to tame than I thought, but that humility came too late to help CC back to joy.

Achieving Fairness. Let us suppose for a moment that life is normal. We have a normal thirteen-year-old boy who knows what he feels and is able to express his feelings clearly. The boy knows what he needs and what will satisfy him. Although he is not perfect in these regards, he knows how to ask for the help he needs when he needs it. The boy knows that he has great value because God said so and therefore he is entitled to receive all the things he needs. In other words, this is a normal thirteen-year-old. Yet, the boy has observed that there is more to life than what he experiences. Men, it seems, have a power with each other that is out of range for him. He senses the pressure when men collide, and yet like the mountain rams, walk away unharmed. He is ready to discover a new meaning for a word he has known since preschool--fairness.

For the first time in his life, the developing male becomes responsible for tending his neighbor's needs in the same way he has cared for his own. "It's not fair" for the child means that his own needs and feelings were being ignored. "It's not fair" for the man could just as easily mean, "Your needs and feelings are not to be ignored."

The boy, who until this point has had his own needs to meet and his own satisfaction to seek, is about to meet his first major challenge. To be a man is to realize that his actions have an impact on others for whom he has responsibility. The man must work to see that others' needs are given the same consideration as his own. As the man's power increases, it is possible to take unfair advantage of weaker or less knowledgeable men, women, and children. A man will see to it that this inequity does not happen--first, because it will not be satisfying and, second, because it will mar his contribution to history. A man must love his neighbor as himself. Fair is fair.

Protecting Others From Himself. As he learns to use power, each young man realizes that he makes mistakes. He realizes that not all uses of power are a good expression of his heart. He learns that his best intentions sometimes don't bring the results he seeks. Sometimes he uses his relationship skills to get his own way with those who are weaker or less mature than he is. As his heart and community point out these failures, he learns to protect others from himself. The way older men and women around him protect him from themselves is a great example for him. Men and women who dress modestly protect each other from the full power of their sexuality. They avoid verbal bulldozing[31] in discussions and take care not to overwhelm others with their feelings or needs. Most importantly, they take notice when others say "ouch!" A safe person is one who will protect others from him or her self.

A YOUNG MAN IS A PART OF HISTORY

The step into manhood for the normal boy is found in this awesome discovery. He is a part of history. He is now ready to know that because he has lived, life will not be the same for other people. He will have his effect whether it be for good or ill. Understanding how he is to participate in history will be his challenge for the next decade or so. To start him out right, his father and the men of his village, those who know their history, will instruct him on how history works. Since the normal boy understands satisfaction, he immediately wants to know what sort of participation in history will be the most satisfying. By learning these secrets he will become a wise, good man.

Perhaps it is not right to call the means of participating in history "secrets" because they are so plainly seen, but to the untrained eye they appear as secrets, and the boy's eye is new at all this. By examining the history already passed, the boy can learn of the history yet to come. Still the 13-year-old is not skilled at seeing large patterns, so the history he must hear first is that of his own family and people, his own town and life. If he first understands what is near by, he will soon grasp that which is far away. These are the stories that make a man. They are the true stories of how he came to be, who he is, and how through him others will come to be who they are. These stories synchronize the right and left halves of his brain and let his thinking make sense when they are true.

Boys learn to be men through stories, his-stories. A man knows that he is not the only part of history. He wants his interests and those of others to be fairly represented. When he is 13 the new man starts thinking, "What is a fair bargain? How do I deal with others so that it meets their needs and my needs?" He thinks to himself, "What I do will have an effect on other people." That is how he does it.

Stories will lead all young men to several important crisis points. Are these stories primarily about him? Are they primarily about his people?

---

[31] Dr. Dallas Willard's term for Jesus' teaching in the sermon on the mount. Matthew 5:33-37.

Are they primarily about his God? When each young man wrestles with his survival center and its cravings and urges, he must answer the question of who his stories have for a focus. The result may be a suicide bomber, a patriot or a president Clinton. For the young men who are Christian, this is the time when they must decide if Jesus is LORD. If indeed life is God's story and our self-preservation is not the highest value, then we must concern ourselves with living from our hearts, for the benefit of all the life which God created and cares for on earth as members of the family of God. Young men will live, die and even blow themselves up based on the stories they believe—stories that answer their questions about power, truth and relationships. The course of world history is shaped by young men's stories.

Life-giving Sexuality. With the current infestation of predatory and opportunistic sexuality, young men need real help learning to live with teenage sexual feelings. The sex hormones testosterone and estrogen make our brains much harder to calm. As a result, our capacity to find peace and rest is reduced in the early teen years. The brain must find new ways to settle down and have quiet together. Interestingly, sexual arousal is produced by the quieting (parasympathetic) half of our nervous system. While these new, irritable and hard to quiet nervous systems are installed in teenagers to motivate them enough to form new group identities, the possibility of malfunctions early on are quite high. Sexual activities are the single largest area of regret in men's lives as they look back at their effects on history. Pregnant girlfriends, abortions, affairs, pornography, incest, and sexual obsessions leave men, from clergy to grandfathers, chagrined and ashamed of their histories. Instead of giving life they find they have ruined lives for women and children and the men who will pick up the pieces. Sexuality gives men a major opportunity to protect others from themselves.

The commitment to always serve, protect and enjoy all life we conceive is part of life-giving sexuality. Another commitment is that once shared, life-giving sexuality will never be withheld. This celebration of life touches our deepest joys and calls us to return again and again. To find the gate barred makes us suffer just as being replaced would do. This is part of returning to joy for lovers.

Life-giving sexuality is not just for lovers. It also protects the life-giving sexuality of others. By recognizing a treasure in the sexuality of others we cover and protect it. This affirms their value as well as ours. Like our national parks, we protect beauty when we find it.

SOLO FLIGHT

Independence arrives within five years of becoming a man. The independence and confidence developed among the community of men and from one's own family soon require decisions and consequences to rest on the young man's shoulders. The next step may be finding a job. It may mean moving into an apartment or going away to college. Solo flight usually involves making decisions like buying a car and other financial considerations such as deciding when to spend, save, or borrow money. Solo flight is never accomplished completely alone. In fact, deciding where you will work or who you will rent with are parts of the risks in taking responsibility for your own life. The soloist must decide when to ask for help and advice and what mistakes or losses are tolerable.

Simon was a junior in advanced placement classes when he decided to exercise the option of skipping his senior year and entering college early. He had many ideas of what to do with his life, which in one way means that he had no idea what to do. Simon had started taking evening classes in junior college in order to learn Japanese. Instead of a graduation present, he asked his parents to send him on a trip to Japan. After careful consideration as a family, it was decided that he and two friends would take a seven-week trip through Japan. It was somewhat of a sacrifice on the part of his parents to send him there, but more importantly they wanted him to see what it was like in other cultures.

To make the trip work out, Simon had to plan it with the help of many people. Friends of the family and other parents helped Simon figure out transportation, lodging, food, and other needs for each day of the trip. When he actually arrived, he discovered that traveling in Japan, living in Japanese homes, and experiencing minority status left him constantly in need of negotiating what was good for him, his traveling companions, his hosts, and the friends he made.

When he returned home and started college, Simon was a changed man. His appreciation for his family, friends, and the help of others was greatly increased. Simon sought counsel from older men about career choices, changes in majors, and schools. He looked out for the needs of his friends and roommates as well as his own. Unlike many other college students, he loved to call home and tell his parents what he was doing and received both their advice and admiration. In addition, he continued to discover what was satisfying for him and what was not. From calculus to aquariums, bicycles to sushi, sleeping with the window open to helping people escape cults, Simon examined it all. He was flying.

But whether the soloist succeeds completely or not, his results are part of the family history to be applauded, analyzed, and in time refined for future flights.

LIFE PARTNERSHIP

By now our young men are well versed in fairness, mutual satisfaction, returning two people to joy at the same time, protecting others from themselves, life-giving sexuality, leaving a history to be proud of, expressing a group identity, while living all this from their hearts. To reach the next level of maturity will require many of them to find a life partner who shares their desire to give life. It is time to look among their many woman friends for someone to court.

When two people light up as they see each other, admire each other, seek chances to encourage each other's heart, experience joy easily, and return to joy quickly together, they will begin looking in their hearts to see if they have found the gift that only God brings. As bonding euphoria gives way to deeper appreciation each young man finds his power, relationship skills and knowledge of his true identity stretched beyond its limit. We will study this testing of a man in our next chapter.

Chapter Seven
Testing a Man--Men and Marriage

Fifteen feet ahead of me, Molly kept trying to stick her head between her legs. "Is that nitrogen narcosis?" I wondered as her bubbles disappeared in the bluish haze above. Her dive partner swam off down the canyon looking at sea fans, without noticing.

Our dive master's warning went through my mind. "We can only stay four minutes on this deep dive without risking the bends," he said pointing to his slate with the calculations. "Everyone to the bow in five minutes. We'll descend together."

I swam quickly toward Molly who by now was bent over with her feet and face down and her rear up. She kept thrashing and pointing between her legs. Close inspection revealed a fishing lure imbedded in the seat of her wet suit and a monofilament line heading up the way of our bubbles. I recalled that as we had headed to the bow of the boat we had passed a deck hand with a fishing pole. A few moments with a sharp dive knife and Molly swam away free to find her dive buddy. There were two and one half minutes left.

Deep dives test every bit of equipment, skill and ability a diver has. Following the anchor rope we needed to descend at 60 feet per minute in order to make it back safely. This meant reading depth gauges, watches, clearing masks and ears, maintaining buoyancy, tightening gear as the pressure made our wetsuits shrink, and other parts of diving, all needed to be done without slowing the descent. With each kick of the fins the water became darker and colder. My mask began leaking water at about forty feet down after a kick in the face by a careless classmate. I needed to clear my mask with one hand, hold the anchor chain with the other, and maintain the rate of descent. This is harder to do while upside down because of the way our noses are designed. Except for a little water in my nose it worked.

Now, more than 100 feet under the Pacific, I watched my dive buddy swim off down a different canyon from the rest of the class. With barely a minute left I wondered whether to let him disappear from view into the dim, deep, darkness or swim off after him. He was swimming away from the class, the anchor line and the way back up. I turned back and just reached the instructor as time ran out. He held up his slate with our depth and time. We quickly checked our dive tables and calculated the length of our decompression stop at ten feet. The instructor checked me off his list and signaled me to ascend. When we finally reached the surface I re-located my dive buddy about thirty feet away swimming through a school of jellyfish. He was doing his own thing. I was rather glad I hadn't needed him.

Dive partners can be the worst part of diving. Back on board the boat, I watched the coast of San Miguel Island while remembering an incident from my first dive class. We were practicing buddy breathing in the swimming pool. For this to work, two divers must share the same air tank and pass the air hose back and forth between them. This prepares divers for out-of-air emergencies under water. As we were passing the air, I noticed the panic in my buddy's eyes as he clutched the regulator to his mouth. It was clear he wasn't going to give it back any time soon. That was O.K. in four feet of swimming pool water--I just stood up.

Since then I have had many bad, and a few dangerous, dive buddies. Even a tankful of air spent with them is too much. It makes me pity their wives. I won't dive with them twice. This time I asked the dive master for a new partner.

Marriage is a mutual effort like buddy breathing. It means sharing your air supply with someone under every condition life can throw at you. Marriage is arduous but well worth the effort. Being prepared, trained and skilled for marriage can really save your heart and maybe your life. Why isn't there a certification card for participants? Before they let us loose in the ocean, our instructors made sure that we were proficient at a list of skills, had the necessary equipment and knowledge, and had time to practice.

Whether he pursues marriage, schooling, or work, the contented, satisfied man can experience an increasing complexity in the goodness of being male. Single men as well as married men need to give life to many people or they will become shriveled and unhappy. Marriage, however, is both-centered and requires a man to increase his complexity so that neither he nor his wife becomes shriveled and unhappy.

Marriage requires that a man have something to offer from many different aspects of himself. It is like working out on many different kinds of equipment at the gym to develop a wide variety of muscles. Women tend to put demands on many different facets of a man simultaneously. A man needs to enter marriage knowing he has many things to offer. A young man who has developed a rewardingly complex sense of himself will view all his actions and relationships as opportunities.

STOCKING YOUR CONTROL CENTER WITH STORIES

One way of looking at the different aspects of a man's identity is to picture them as a stock of "acting like myself" stories stored in the

116

prefrontal cortex. The words for these stories and their autobiographical memories stored neatly in the left-brain. The pictures and behaviors for each story are stored in the right brain for rapid deployment.

Before marriage, a groom should have experience living many different relational story lines. A "pre-dive" checklist for grooms might look like this:

Pre-Marriage Check List

Do you have well-developed adult maturity?   ☐ yes

Can you give life with style?   ☐ yes

Do you have experience giving life as a:

    ☐ brother

    ☐ friend

    ☐ priest

    ☐ lover

    ☐ warrior

    ☐ king

    ☐ servant.

    ☐ all these together

What do we mean by *well-developed adult maturity*? As we pass through the six stages of life we go from a rapid growth period at the beginning of a stage to a period of maintenance and repair near the end of a stage—just prior to our next metamorphosis. During the tail end of a stage, learning gives way to productivity. It is this kind of mature adult who is ready for marriage. By now the different aspects of his adult identity have been learned and practiced enough to have some proficiency.

A man must practice until his adult abilities are expressed with a style that is uniquely personal. He must know the basic story lines for men and have some experience expressing and blending them because to marry is to blend two families and their histories. Each must be done to a level of mutual satisfaction. Naturally, a young man will want to improve his style or diversify and blend his stories but some experience is required!

Learning to express one's masculine power in these different stories is learned while a man is single. The stories are learned as a means of self-expression for adult men married or not. A word of caution to single men, however, is that once you are good at these stories it will be hard to stay single.

MAN AS BROTHER

The identity of a man as a brother is one that carries over from childhood. Boys learn to be brothers. As men they learn to expand brotherhood beyond the biological family. This is to say that men have brother-to-brother or brother-and-sister relationships with an expanding number of people. This component of a man's identity contributes greatly to his sense of fairness. A brother learns, long before he becomes a man, that the needs and feelings of his siblings matter. His entire family will have taken pains to point this out. Yet with siblings there is often a note of competition, or perhaps even the feeling that there isn't enough to go around. This must be corrected in the man. Each man must know in his heart that there is enough goodness for everyone so that he will always pursue the common good. Enough for us and some to share is a brother's standard.

Brothers also learn that kinship is not based on behavior or emotion. A brother bond is beyond human power to break. Even when one brother can't stand another they are still brothers. When a sister acts like she doesn't know him, she is still his sister. He learns to *live into* kinship relationships because they exist and are real. He does not create the relationship, he just grows into it--even with people he has never met. Often we hear stories of people who discover they have a brother they hadn't known of before. Their reactions are usually intense and hopeful. They hope to grow into what existed without their even knowing about it.

Dating is one extension of the brother bond beyond childhood. Marriage is also a special brother-and-sister bond. That shocks us but was known in the ancient wisdom. In his great love poem, *The Song of Solomon*, the king sings, "You have stolen my heart, my sister, my bride" (4:9). He refers to his beloved as his sister because romantic love is sister love--plus. This is hard for the average red-blooded American boy to grasp. Our view of romance has no bonding component at all, unless you consider "chemistry" a form of human relationship. I can't say I'm too impressed with the average romance and marriage in our day. We would do far better to approach our dates as sisters than as entertainment or pleasure.

It is clear that trying to bond with a wife as though she were one's mother is a disaster. A parent-to-child bond is very one directional. The appropriate marriage bond is the mutual bond that we find in the brother-and-sister relationship. Marriage is a specialized, life-giving, brother-and-sister bond that only lasts as long as they are both alive. The power of the sibling bond is that it does not depend on emotions or behavior. The bond withstands even the years the brothers and sisters hate each other. This is essential for marriage, although two adults who return to joy quickly will never need to live through hating each other.

Dating should also build toward permanent relationships. Why waste our life-energy? Why mess with our attachment circuit that is at level one of our brain's control center? When I was dating, I noticed that most of the girls I dated were mad at the boy they had dated before me. Not uncommonly he had taken some liberties with her feelings or body that left her hurting. Knowing that someday I would be marrying one of these girls caused me to wonder what shape I would like my bride to be in when I received her. The maxim, "Do unto others as you would have them do unto you," took on some practical meaning. My dating goal, which I also taught to my sons, became dating in such a way that were I ever to meet the husband of a girl I dated, he would want to shake my hand and thank me. I wanted to be the source of life and good things.

Even the word dating gives the impression of making an impact on history on a given date in time. A further spiritual truth was suggested to me by the view that we are the bride of Christ and consequently my treatment of all believers will fall in this category when I meet the "Groom."

MAN AS FRIEND

Like being a brother, friend is another bond that boys carry over into manhood. Like brotherhood, friendship develops with age. The man has more depth to bring to a friendship. It is a relationship for all seasons. Friendship for children provides a crucial source of comparison with others that is necessary for identity to form correctly. Children spend considerable effort comparing everything about themselves with others. While such comparisons can be used destructively, their healthy use is necessary for proper development. Friends are the yardsticks against which we measure ourselves. People tend to find yardsticks about their own size to make their measurements.

Friendships also help children learn to appreciate people who are different from themselves. Men need friends for both stretching and measuring. Men need friends for fun. Friends are the greatest help in developing a personal style, for they help us to know how to express the things that make us uniquely ourselves and point out when that uniqueness is offensive. A man will often develop a style that complements his friends' styles. That can be good or bad, but the man without friends is usually an offense to eyes, ears and nose.

It is worth noting that men typically have a problem developing deep and lasting friendships, particularly with fellow men. The lack of these close friendships among men has been attributed to many factors. Perhaps the most frequently mentioned reason is homophobia. This theory has gained some recognition among intellectuals but continues to receive the disregard it deserves from men at large. I believe that for most men their avoidance of close relationships with other males really stems from an unspoken fear of rejection by the male subculture, which is characterized by insulting and slightly hostile repartee. Men call it "just kidding around." The insults usually come in the form of "put-downs" under the cover of harmless banter about sports, sex, cars, and the news.

"Just kidding around" can be deadly, especially in its cumulative effect on men who get "put down." These put-down "attacks" are common compared to the minor number of homosexual seductions or assaults a man will experience. Put downs create an emotionally charged climate of shame and humiliation that is experienced by nearly all men. Even men who fear their homosexual feelings have an even greater fear of rejection by other men. No one wants a life bereft of joy.

As interesting and even plausible as the homophobia hypothesis sounds, a much simpler and compelling explanation is available. Men simply expect and fear that other men will be disinterested and reject them, based on what they have experienced with their fathers and among their peers. What truth there is in the homophobia hypothesis may lie in the perception of some men that the only man who would take a real interest in them must be sexually motivated. When Tom backs down from picking up the phone to call Dave, even if he is homophobic, he is probably less afraid that Dave will make a pass at him and more afraid that Dave won't even care that he called.

In contrast to the shame threat our male subculture poses to deep and lasting relationships among men, we can find male friendship where joy and loyalty are practiced. King David said, "I will have none but the most loyal as my friends" (Psalms 101:6). A friend is loyal at all times, not just when it's convenient, or when you happen to be having a good time together. Convenience is the great enemy of friendship. Inconvenience is

120

seen as a bad thing in our culture. We have convenience stores, remote controls, and automatic *everything*. In the parable of the friend who knocked at midnight, Jesus points out that even if it is rather inconvenient to get up, unlock your house, and find the food required, yet because the one who knocks is a friend he will receive what he requested.

Nowhere is the lack of loyalty more easily recognized as when marriage partners fail to become or stay friends. Men who have never been friends with women should not expect that marriage will somehow make a friendship appear. Like all survival skills, friendships with women need to be practiced and learned from childhood or studied intensively before they can be used under stress. We had to practice clearing our masks of water, retrieving our fins and regulators in swimming pools before our scuba instructors would take us in the ocean. Practice, practice, practice! Even if one is certified, if he or she hasn't been diving for awhile it is good to practice before taking a dive trip--maybe even take a refresher course. Marriage supplies even tougher conditions than diving. A dive boat won't go out in a storm but your marriage will.

MAN AS PRIEST

The priest keeps things covered. No, not covered up but covered. Men find both joy and quiet in covering. The consumer-boy believes that there is satisfaction in uncovering. "Take it off." "Tell us your deepest and darkest secrets," the talk show hosts say. More than one police show has made in on the air by sneaking a peek at the misfortunes of others. But the priest keeps things covered. He has no room for gossip, tales, and the rumors that keep *People* magazine, the talk shows, and crime shows in business. He knows the difference between discovery and exploitation.

The priest keeps things covered but not through denial. He practices intercession both before God and with those who need to learn mercy and forgiveness. The priest keeps the channels clear and good faith between people flowing. The priest never diminishes the size of a sin, but seeks to increase the size of the repentance and mercy. By making sure that each infraction is forgiven and cleansed, the priest covers. The priest wants history to be spotless and clean so that God's decontamination and repair of all our malfunctions will be complete. To this end, each priest adds his own style and flair. Men find covering very satisfying.

In a Christian marriage both of the partners are priests. It is beautiful when both can cover and both can keep the home clean and redeemed. This is part of the reason why marriage only works between two *adults*. This is a mutually shared simultaneous responsibility. Like diving with a responsible partner, any trouble is easier to face and our hearts can rest happily when we are covered.

MAN AS LOVER

"Love covers a multitude of sins," Scripture tells us. Man as lover is in harmony with man as priest because both cover. In a limited sense, "lover" refers to a man's sexual passion, but the lover is much more than sexual in his love for his beloved. Perhaps because of the strength of love, it highlights each man's style more than any other side of his personality. The greatest attribute of the lover is his fearlessness. "Perfect love casts out fear," Scripture says, so the lover is more fearless than the warrior.

The lover is known by what and who he loves. The good lover loves God more than life, the giver more than the gift, the woman more than sex, the child more than results. The lover celebrates life without fear, freely giving life and strength to others. The lover pursues, embraces, laughs, releases, and then pursues again. In all these movements, he includes the elements of his own style that will please him and his loves. The man is lover to boy and girl, grandmother and grandfather, dog and cat, and, in time his bride and wife.

The boy cannot be a lover because he thinks too much of his own needs, feelings, and satisfaction. Having learned that his own need and satisfaction is on the same level with that of another frees the man to be a lover by appreciating both his own feelings and those of his love.

A marvelous thing happens when the lover is around because of the high levels of joy, excitement, and enjoyment that he brings. Young, new love will even bring a sudden flurry of growth in the special part of the brain's control center devoted to joyful relationships.[32] Like the many blossoms on a pear tree, both his and her brains will produce more happy nerve connections than they can ever use. Just remembering the lover's eyes, face, voice and excitement to greet them sends off shivers. In time the brain will trim off the excess ones and they will think straight again. Still the lover will always bring joy unless one dreadful thing happens.

Should there be bad feelings between the lover and his beloved that are left there overnight, the body's stress hormone cortisol begins to burn out the joyful places in the brain. Short upsets are no problem, they even build strength and hope when the lovers return to love, joy and rest. The love song of Solomon even includes a lovers quarrel which does not last through the night. The lover returns to joy before the flame goes out.

---

[32] Level four of the control center is in the right orbital prefrontal cortex

MAN AS WARRIOR

The men's movement has brought with it the return of the warrior, this time not as a destroyer but as a defender. Their warrior is the heroic one in the epic stories and poems, Gilgamesh and Hercules, not G.I. Joe and Rambo. But clever as Ulysses was with the Cyclops and as inspiring as myths can be, Gordon Dalbey probably got closer to the truth when he said that the warrior carries the sword of truth.

Ultimately the warrior knows that there are things more important than his own life, some value greater than himself. The warrior ultimately seeks a king or prophet to outlive him should his own life be lost in the struggle for what is greater than himself. The boy will always seek his own survival as the greatest good because that is the boy's task. Men must consider others as well as themselves, or they will end up fighting out of greed, revenge, or the desire to gain advantage. That is not the warrior, but an assassin at work. It is the killer-boy who lives by fear, never knowing the greater power of love. Whether he is an intercity gang member, Ku Klux Klansman, terrorist or the driver who swerves into another's lane to show his anger, it is the killer-boy at work.

King Saul's son Jonathan was as delightful an example of the warrior as we will ever see. He protected his friends and served his God more than family loyalty or ambition. He never fought to prove his power yet he would take on an army with just his armor bearer for support when he had God to guide him.

The apostle[33] Paul tells us that we who serve the Mighty Warrior must ourselves fight, not against mere flesh and blood, but against the evil of the age we live in, the dark imposter who would destroy lives and mock our King.

Perhaps the most endearing trait of the warrior is that he protects others from himself. This is the essence of a safe person, for he recognizes the ways he can injure others and protects them from his own weapons. A warrior husband will protect his wife by warning her where he is still immature or hurtful and take responsibility for finding a solution. He can be counted on to hear his wife's request for protection from any unhealed or unredeemed bits of himself. The warrior never says, "You made me hurt you—or hit, yell at, go someplace else for sex, get mad at, swear or even be rude." A warrior is responsible for his weapons.

---

[33] An "apostle" is someone on a mission from God. No, I don't think the Blue's Brothers made the cut.

The warrior's greatest weapon may also be a surprise. He fights with the words that come from God (Ephesians 6:17). He avoids the killer words the enemy uses and knows that there is no life-giving power in his own words. The warrior seeks the words of life, words of the Spirit, the words that speak miracles into existence. Like all warriors, he studies, practices, guards, polishes these weapons and keeps them with him at all times. These words make his heart light up. Speaking words of life seems more like him than anything else he could say because he knows he is a life-giving man.

MAN AS KING

Every man, slave or free, poor or rich, has his area of dominion. Wisdom literature is full of instructions for kings. The prospect of a fool becoming king is too horrible to describe, according to the ancients. Much of our dominion is shared with others. The more exclusive our dominion and the higher we rise in power, the more our kingdom reflects our style, values, and investment. If earlier generations erred in asserting their dominion too rigidly, this generation has forgotten what it means to be king and see to it that justice and truth prevail in their domain.

David, who was a king in many ways said, "I will sing of your love and justice.... I will walk in my house with blameless heart... No one who practices deceit will dwell in my household; no one who speaks falsely will stand in my presence" (Psalms 101:1,2,7). Even if one's kingdom is no bigger than one's own home, the king rules. What I mean by that is that the king insures that the values worth dying for can live in his kingdom.

This is quite different than what a boy-king would seek. The boy-king would want ruling to give him his own way. That is terrible and oppressive domination. Only a man is ready to be king. A man's rule seeks values greater than his own life and provision for others as well as himself. He protects and cares for the widow, orphan and the poor. But these efforts belong better at the elder stage of maturity, for a man can only be king with elders to advise him.

In his own home, a man may have dominion alone until he marries. After that he shares it with his wife and later his children. Sharing dominion is clearly a man-sized task. No boy could consider all the needs involved in such a position of authority. The man who has never been a boy is even more lost for he does not even know himself.

Being king demands a certain style from the man, for to rule well is to express beautifully the deeper values inside you. The passion of a poet and the wisdom of the sage are fitting in a king; and well satisfying.

124

MAN AS SERVANT

The servant is the expression of a deep and satisfying understanding of the needs of others. Like the wise virgins of the Apocalypse, servants have covered their own needs and are ready to attend to others. In Christian hierarchies, the more people you rule over, the more people you must serve. The husband, as head of the home, is therefore the servant of the home. It is a sign of his greatness to see and provide for each one's needs. No one will beat him to the job. The boy cannot serve in this way for he will mistakenly conclude that serving makes him the lesser, not as important as the one being served.

Whether it is P. G. Woodhouse's masterful butler Jeves or the late Mother Theresa of Calcutta, the distinguished servant is known by his or her understanding of the master's needs and wishes. The style of service has been perfected by long hours of practice so that the complex now appears effortless. The servant's pride is in his intimate knowledge of the master's needs ensuring that preparations have been made before the request comes.

Jesus had such style in serving that even under the duress of knowing he would be tortured to death in hours, he could say, "In my Father's house are many mansions. I go to prepare a place for you." Now that is room service with style!

PUTTING IT TOGETHER

In all these sides of his personality a man is still himself. Each story in his control center allows a man to express another aspect of who he is and what he can be. Some parts of manhood may be more comfortable than others. A man may express himself well as a servant and feel out of place as a king, yet, all these dimensions should be explored by every man as he grows older. These are not roles he must fit into but parts of a man that he must bring out of himself. A man cannot become a role and be satisfied. Each different story represents one dance he can learn, one tune he can sing, one job he can do and one further expression of the life within him. When he hears the story told with integrity by an older man he will feel something within him synchronize with the story and begin to feel, "That could be me!"

It isn't enough for each man to blend these dimensions of himself in isolation, he must first blend them with his community and then with his wife. We need a community and family close around us if we expect to succeed at anything as challenging as marriage. Like deep diving, we want a good boat, knowledgeable deck hands, and a dive crew with experience. We need parents ready to be in-laws, family to support us and friends who encourage us through the rough times. Otherwise, like Molly, we will find ourselves being dragged away by some unseen hook in our rear end put there by the very same people who were supposed to be helping us.

MAN AS HUSBAND

Marriage is the adventure that tests every bit of equipment, skill, and strength a man has. It is not recommended for all men because marriage is not an accomplishment but a relationship. Marriage is certainly not recommended for boys and infants! Marriage is a commitment to share life with one particular woman. The call to be a husband is the most intense human expression of the task of being a man. In order to survive and enjoy the experience, the man must have his personal style working smoothly so he can plunge himself into this joy experience. To be a husband means being all he can be to his wife, a satisfying: brother, friend, priest, lover, warrior, servant, and king. He must be a son to her parents, brother to her siblings, a friend to her friends. All the while he cannot forget who he is or his effects on history.

If you recall, a man is to consider the needs of others as equal to his own. Nowhere is that task more passionately practiced than in marriage, where two become one. Not only must the man consider the needs, satisfaction, and feelings of another person, but he faces a woman who is not like him in many ways and hard to figure out. On top of that, he must meet her needs as he would his own[34] at a very intimate level and in almost every aspect of life. That is no small challenge. One shutters to think of the disaster that would follow if a boy attempted to do such a thing. Worse yet, suppose an infant boy who did not even understand what satisfied his needs tried to get married. *Kyrie Eleison*! Lord, have mercy!

As you read these stories about men, doesn't some part of you wish you knew more men like these—or maybe even one man like this? When these are the stories and pictures in the control centers of men's brains then men can share life with style. Even the most cynical reader will find a twinge of longing for such men.

---

[34] Mutual meeting of needs between men and women is only possible when both have reached adult maturity.

TAKING A DEEP DIVE

It is really quite exciting when men begin to develop a variety of these manly aspects of themselves. Many young men will not be polished before marriage. In fact, a man's personal style develops over most of his first forty years of life. Let's consider one example of a man who found out there was more to him than he knew.

Don always dreaded visits by his in-laws. By the end of two days the house was a mess and tension reigned supreme. It soon degenerated into feigned politeness between adults, while his in-laws criticized their daughter and her children--her decisions, tastes and vocabulary. They were quick to point out how lucky she was to have married Don. He really did not appreciate their support.

Don wanted to be a warrior and throw Dad and Mom out of the house, but that did not seem right with the family. So he turned into a servant instead. He waited on his wife and her parents to try and make them more comfortable and agreeable. However, they used this opportunity to reinforce to their daughter how *extraordinarily* lucky she was to have found such a husband. In return for his service, his wife served him up a stare that would freeze a dinosaur.

Don then turned to the role of a priest. He wanted to cover his wife by helping her deal with the problems that came to the surface whenever her parents visited. Yet she was not very open to this approach when her parents were there and although several problems were covered, overall, she felt that Don was siding with her parents against her.

It was only after talking with a friend that Don began to realize that he was king in his home. The rules in his kingdom were set by him and his queen—including, how visitors were to treat the queen. "Your parents may be visiting royalty," he told his wife, "but we are the responsible rulers here. Whatever happens in our house we have to answer for and not your parents."

The very next visit the situation changed. There were no confrontations, no laying down the law, just simple statements like, "That is not how we handle criticism here. We encourage the person to do better." Once the king and queen knew *their* home was *their* dominion, and all visitors enjoyed *their* hospitality, it changed patterns profoundly. The values worth dying for began to live in *their* kingdom. The lover in him found room to pursue his beloved before tension burned them out at night. King, warrior, priest, lover, brother, and servant led the way back to husband and wife as friends.

The different life-giving dimensions in a man can blend together at times. They harmonize well with the life in women and children. Picking the right blend for the occasion really satisfies a man and gives him a sense of style. By now we know how important that satisfaction is to a man. Now we can see how his many sides provide him with almost unlimited options to satisfy his need to be life-giving.

Marriage signals the most common culmination of adult life. It is the most complex of all life-sharing activities. Marriage is the height of what two adults can do together. It means satisfying two people--at the same time--for the remainder of a life span. More than any other human activity, this prepares the couple to have a unique and profound effect on history--together they can start another human life.

THE FOURTH METAPMORPHOSIS

*

FATHER

*

THE PARENT STAGE

FATHER
The Parent Stage

IDEAL AGE
From his first child until his youngest child becomes an adult

NEEDS
•To give life
•An encouraging partner
•Guidance from elders
•Peer review with other fathers
•A secure and orderly community for raising children

•

TASKS
•Giving without needing to receive in return
•Building a home
•Protecting his family
•Serving his family
•Enjoying his family
•Maturing his children
•Synchronizing the needs of children, wife, family, work & church

•

Plus everything from the Infant, Child and Adult stages

Chapter Eight
Becoming a Father

"Yes," he said, peering into my mouth, "If all is going well I'm becoming a father right now!" Somehow he didn't seem as excited as he should be.

"Open wide," he said, and I did. Phil had always been a strange dentist but this definitely topped it. When I came in, he would hand me a teddy bear, stuff suction tubes in my mouth, and then talk non-stop.

"Yeah, my wife is in England getting pregnant right now. We tried for years and finally had to go the in-vitro way. It turns out," he said looking for something behind my molar, "that it is cheaper to fly to London and get it done there than to pay the doctors here. I would have gone along but someone had to pay for the trip." With that he took out his handy-dandy air-and-water sprayer and aimed it at my face instead of in my mouth. Water splattered everywhere.

"Oh! Did I miss again? I must be out of practice!"

"Hhaaurr eeyyuuu wwea! Quii aaaa!"[35] I answered as his little suction tube grabbed hold of my tongue. I'd never been with a man when he was becoming a father before.

Phil was clearly pleased. "You know, if you were burned up in a plane crash I wouldn't need X-rays to identify these teeth," he said. Then he drifted back to his main theme and filled in some details. "She just stays in a hotel room until they have succeeded. She should be back in a couple of weeks. Who knows, maybe I'm a dad right now!"

"Chhoongaauuaaheunn!"[36] I told him, and meant every bit of it.

The average man comes to the moment of becoming a father a bit differently than Phil did. There is a mystical passage for a man the moment he discovers he is now a source of new life. Not every man will recognize and seize the moment, but for those who do the universe momentarily disappears and then returns with a penetrating brilliance. History is inexorably changed for him and the whole world, for who knows what this new life will bring? This is his run for the roses. Becoming a father is the starting gun of the great race he has trained for all his life.

He started out as a baby himself, it seems all males do. As an infant he learned to express his feelings and regulate his body's joy and peace systems. In time his father introduced him to the wide world of satisfaction and exertion and he went from baby to boy. A few short years later he

---

[35] "Sure you are! Quit that!"
[36] "Congratulations"

became a master of knowing and satisfying himself. The boy then faced the challenge of leaving behind his boy identity for a new one through a self-observed metamorphosis. While becoming a young man he used everything he had learned as a boy as the community of men taught him how to participate in building their future. Shakily at first, but with rising strength, this young man learned to meet others' needs along with his own. Fairness and hard bargains became his rules. He learned to protect and serve. The most enjoyable part of this stage was finding a woman who could be his equal in the task of life-giving.

Once again, no sooner had he mastered this adult identity when something deep, unfulfilled, overwhelming, and yet good began to tear apart the man he knew himself to be. No boy or infant could feel these urges without fear. The desire to give life began to challenge him to be more than he had known. He wished to become a father. This was his mountain to climb. This was his goal to reach. This was his life to give. Fatherhood, more than anything else expressed the life-giving man in him.

All his life the mystery of the father has pulled at him, calling for something beyond bargaining and fairness, something that gave without being repaid. Fatherhood was a strange path for it led toward paying another's bills, even suffering for things one didn't do and for things one didn't deserve. To do all this with satisfaction is the secret joy of being a father. This he now wanted for himself. Here it was--the goal of a lifetime. Does it sound familiar to you?

No doubt you have heard women say they wanted a baby. You may even have seen some women cry for the lack of one. Recently one generation of women woke up late and only felt the urge to have babies in their forties—but no one was completely surprised. Many men who partially raised one family discovered that their second (and younger) wife wanted a brood of her own. But do men want children?

The answer is that only men who have a reasonably working control center have access to their attachment drive in level one. Mess up a control center and you have a man who does not grow up, does not use his feelings well and is captive to his cravings. An undeveloped man bonds to God-knows-what if he bonds at all. Three quarter or more of the men in the US will revert to infant level maturity under any stress. Not even their mothers told them stories about how they would love to be fathers one day.

The last quarter century, becoming a father has become less about children and more about marriage or the lack of it as unwed parents and divorces have proliferated. We have lumped marriage and children together, forgetting that they represent the culmination of two *different* stages of life. Marriage is for *adults* and children are for *parents*.

Furthermore, childbirth increasingly ties fathers to Lamaze classes and the community of women with fewer ties to the fellowship of men. Men hear and tell few stories about becoming fathers. Yet becoming a father is a male event, participated in only by men, never ever in the absence of women, of course. From a child level of maturity and ignorance, becoming a dad is often viewed as what ties a man-and-woman together rather than what ties a father-and-child together. (I make the point only to contrast the immature view of childbirth as a "couple thing" with the adult view of parenthood as a "family thing." The adult understands that man-as-father does not diminish man-as-husband, because having a baby is the highest expression of the life-giving properties in both men and women).

There is a general undercurrent of belief in society that men are not drawn to being fathers as strongly as women feel the call to motherhood. Some people feel that women want to get married and have children, but men like to roam and have sex. Yet it is my contention that any man who does not become a father in some meaningful way is doomed to a life of unfulfilled misery. He becomes an airplane that never flew, a ship that never sailed, a racehorse that stayed in the stable, an aborted birth. Imagine building a house for twenty years and then not moving into it, preparing twenty-five years for the Olympics and then not competing in your event. Such a tragedy would probably warrant its own made-for-TV movie. Such is the fate of the man who fails to become a father.

To be a father is to give without receiving in return. It is a chance to be rich. All men are destined to be fathers and will remain frustrated, unhappy and unfulfilled if they do not reach this calling. Unlike the gangster mentality, I do not mean the men must get a girl pregnant; that never yet made a man a father. All men have within them the need to be the source of life to others and to give without seeking to receive--this is what it means to be a father. It is the giving of life that every man must experience. Otherwise, he condemns himself to a miserable, unfulfilled existence. It is not enough to give life randomly, like some tomcat pursuing a queen in heat and then disappearing. Men need personal commitment and personal cost. The effort must be long, long enough to see a life grow--the preferred minimum length of time being just a lifetime. Anything less and a man feels diminished. So what if his climb took him to the top of the compost heap—a man needs a mountain.

Without giving life to a child, a father becomes a eunuch on a honeymoon. It is in the strain and effort, and even failures in fathering, that the really best parts of a man are revealed, tested and strengthened. For this reason the father welcomes the suffering and cost to himself. If the goal had been easy it would not take much of a man or show his mettle.

Why does the athlete compete? Why does the actor anxiously wait for the curtain to go up? Why is the Indy 500 driver eager for the green flag? Why does the salesman gear up for a big presentation? Why does the mountain climber seek Everest? The answer to all these challenges is the same--because it will bring out the best in him. Yes, deep within each person is the burning desire to see what is best in him or her on display-- tested, tried, demonstrated and tangible. It is the desire to be known mixed with the call of glory. Only being a father can bring out the very best in a man.

What torments contestants endure to demonstrate the best they have. Race drivers crash, burn, break bones and come back. Football players play with broken hands. Mountain climbers lose their fingers and toes to frostbite. Gymnasts and skaters give up their entire social lives for years of grueling practice on the mat or the ice. Actors live in their vans and borrow money until their friends and relatives can hardly stand to see their tired faces, and yet they persevere. All these contestants endure hardship for the chance to discover and display what is best about themselves.

Suppose a great Russian weight lifter stood backstage after a lifetime of training, sniffed the acrid jolting shot of ammonia and walked out to the weight room confident that he could set a new world's record. As he stood before the judges and audience the judges told him, "Weight lifting is no longer of any value and will not be allowed. You are a Russian. Dance like Nureyev." If compelled to dance, he would be humiliated and laughed to scorn, for dancing is not the best of him. Yet Nureyev would have felt, in an instant, that dancing would bring out his best while lifting weights would not.

Find a man who has no opportunity to express that which is best about him and you will find a despondent, irritable, restless, unfulfilled, and miserable man. It is worth noting that this desire is not about competition but about the goal. What really satisfies is the chance to show what is best about us in a way that can be seen. When our best is eclipsed by another who is greater than ourselves we become invisible and unhappy. When our skill is far better than the competition but we do not achieve our best, we find no joy. Take the man who plays tennis against a far inferior player and wins with no effort; he will have less satisfaction in winning than he would in losing by a narrow margin to anyone seeded at Wimbledon. Satisfaction comes from expressing that which is best in us.

The boy trains to meet his needs, the man trains to meet his needs and those of others. This prepares him to have a self--a big strong self. He is a person in history, full of life. He is now ready to run the good race, fight the good fight, dance the great dance, he is ready to give life. Only in giving life will he find the deepest, most satisfying expression of what is best about himself. This is the main event. This is the real man at his best. To do so earns him the title of *Father*, a title that would mean nothing if it did not express the very best of him.

Life is a mystery. What makes one frog alive and another dead? What makes a tree alive and a board not? What makes a flower burst out of a seed? We do not know; it is a mystery. To think that life might spring up where there was none before compels us to look at spring leaves or follow Jesus to Lazarus' tomb. And when a man has found that he can bring life into being, it is the most godlike feeling he can experience without sinning. It is the very best part of him.

STORIES OF FATHERS

My friend Rick helped me see how this worked. He had a ten-year-old daughter when he and his wife conceived again. Together we all shared the excitement for about three months, then the baby died. Rick's wife miscarried as far as the doctors were concerned, but to Rick, his baby died. He mourned for over a year. To this day he will get tears when I ask him about it. One morning over breakfast he said to me, "You know, my feelings about my baby are a little bit selfish. Part of what hurt so much is that being a father brings out the best in me. These are the deepest strongest feelings I know. And then, to have it all torn away . . ."

Rick's father had not known the deep satisfaction and joy Rick knew. As he grew up, Rick's dad had told him, "Don't be like me." In fact, he seemed to think that the best thing he could do for Rick was to leave his son alone and let as little as possible of himself rub off on the boy. To this man being a father only showed up the worst things about himself. Leaving his son alone struck him as the right thing to do. It was his best shot.

Travis, my cousin, was looking for a safe and normal life when he had an experience similar to Rick's. One terrible morning he and his wife woke up to find their only child had died of crib death. As we sat by the window looking out at the San Gabriel mountains, he told me, "When that happened it changed my life forever." Travis changed careers, lifestyle and even who he was. Later, as I watched him hug a young bereaved mother, I could see the best in him still looking for a way to be expressed. It was just like his father-heart to hurt for lost children.

Mark had a similar story. His son Jonathan had Down's Syndrome and after a short life died from medical complications. Mark was inconsolable with pain. Some of the best of him was cut down in its prime. Mark was a teacher. He knew that Jonathan would need the best of his teaching abilities to make it in the world. Mark knew, from his own painful path, how to fit into a world that thought he was different. He knew people would never fully accept him no matter what he did. In spite of the battle, Mark remained authentic. This quality was in the very best part of Mark for he had a steadfast father-heart as well. He took all that he treasured and poured it into his son and planned to give him even more. When Jonathan died some of the very best part of Mark died too.

Mark found the best part of himself as a father, Travis found his deepest understanding, and Rick felt his potential to love. Inside each man was a father's heart with its own unique touch. Mark longed to teach, Travis to comfort, Rick to connect. Each man learned the strength of his own heart from the strength of his pain.

The tragic contrast between Rick and his father points out the difference between men who have learned that they have something to give and those who haven't. Rick had something to give and knew that fatherhood would bring it into full view. He was ready to run the race he had trained for his whole life. Even those bleak days with his own father had helped him see the importance of what a father needed to give and so Rick set his goals high.

The significance of a successful transformation from man to father goes beyond one lifetime, however, because fatherhood is an eternal business, at least for sons of the God who created life. Giving life is the family business. Unlike the marriage bond which is temporal and endures on a good run until "death do us part" and then reverts to a brother-sister bond, paternity is an eternal arrangement. Parent-and-child relationship is still operating in heaven; otherwise, the promises to Abraham that he will be the father of many nations is a meaningless gesture. In fact, we see this bond in action when Jesus tells us that after Lazarus died, he was comforted by his Father Abraham. Fatherhood is therefore a spiritual bond as well as an emotional one.

Spiritually speaking, our entrance into eternal life (not Heaven) is predicated on receiving and giving life. We receive this life and pass it on to others. The way of life in God's kingdom is one of life-giving not of killing. The life-giving family line endures eternally, not so with the biological family. I hope that each biological family will also become a spiritual family so that they will participate in a family that is alive forever. Biological "fathers" can wander off, spiritual fathers cannot.

THE COST OF FATHERHOOD

Eternal bonds between father and child are neither easy nor cheap. For just those reasons they are all the more meaningful to the man who possesses them with understanding. In some ways, they cost the father his life, whether you measure that in time, energy or resources. The cost of giving without receiving in return is a kind of dying. With each sacrifice, the father must die a bit and rejoice that he was worthy of the glory.

Becoming a father is paradoxically a dying process, as are all passages. The new father must leave behind his old understanding of who he is if he is to participate in something new. Most dads do this joyfully with just a bit of apprehension and fear. Each man must feel his own pain for himself. At times he must hurt like a father would hurt. It is part of the climb toward the goal.

The first cost of fatherhood is the man's possessive enjoyment of his wife. If he has been blessed, his wife has been his garden of delights and he, her lover--the object of her devoted love. Yet, when she becomes pregnant, her body, mind and feelings turn to another, a beloved stranger. This stranger can keep his wife awake nights without her objection. If he woke her up like that she would be mad! But now she smiles and says, "I felt the baby move."

The man-husband becomes an escort and support, almost an understudy in his wife's heart. There is little that is his alone anymore. He must learn again that intimacy is for a time and place and not diminished by being shared. The mature man knows how to satisfy two or more people at the same time so he can now stretch to become a father.

The newborn emerges from the very privacy that he once called his own exclusive domain. He would have felt like killing anyone else who dared enter there. Now his child emerges and immediately lays claim to his wife's breasts. These were also his alone, but now the baby takes over without a care in the world about Dad's feelings. The mature man (who was first a boy) is transformed in these moments into a father. His baby's devoted lack of concern about his father's feelings will bring joy, for he knows how much better it is to give than to receive. So it is that the husband becomes a father. He now has a family to serve, protect and enjoy.

It is the cost that lets us know that someone loves us. When someone has a good time for us, it doesn't count for much. If someone is willing to suffer for us, then we pay attention. The gift of being a father is to give without return, to suffer what you would not have had to suffer on behalf of someone else. In doing so, the father makes an example of God the Father's love in ways that will become understandable to his own children. It is not in contrast to the mother that he does so, but in concert with her. Together they will provide the home they both will need for this stage.

While being a father is a man's greatest expression of himself, he is still pushed beyond his limits. When men are stretched to new lengths, they *really need encouragement*. There was a time when all a man needed to say was, "We are expecting a child," and friends and colleagues would pump his hand and fill his ears with congratulations. That isn't the typical reaction anymore. Passing out cigars to cheering friends is becoming rare. When a man announces that his wife is pregnant, people say, "Did you want it?" or, "Can you afford it?" or, "Are you going to keep it?" Is this good news or not? The politically correct response is to ask if the child is wanted before congratulating. From there the discussion usually turns to the enormous cost. What is lacking in this discussion is the encouragement and joy needed to help a man be all that he can be.

Having babies costs a lot. Raising children is expensive. Dad is supposed to pay the bill according to the neo-traditional formula, although that is less and less often the case. "Deadbeat Dads" as these infant males are called, do not even give money to their children. The man at the adult stage of maturity at least knows how to take care of children together with his wife. Only a child or infant in a man's body would withhold life and money from his children.

The father longs for the opportunity to demonstrate his love. He is eager to fight the good fight because it shows the best of who he is. As his child grows, the opportunities increase. As his child grows older, he continually provides something more. Each level of his child's development brings out more of the best of him. The opportunities afforded by his children trigger his father's heart to become more than he ever thought he could be. His children will find more in him than he ever knew he contained. Sons and daughters will each bring out different aspects of his heart, as will their differing personalities.

Yet realistically, not everything that comes out of fathers under the strain of growing is wonderful and life-giving. Growing and stretching also means exposing hidden inadequacies. When a man comes to the time to produce his best only to discover he is crippled or disfigured he will be upset. The usual response is one of rage, shame, and distance; sometimes he withdraws sometimes he intimidates. The rage of feeling disqualified for the race he trained for all his life can make a man into truly bad company.

Equally destructive is the fear of being disqualified. Fear keeps men, like Rick's dad, from even entering the race. This fear is a two-fanged monster. One tooth drips with the fear of pain. Its twin fills with fear of his own rage and what he might do. Fleeing this monster, children in men's bodies push away their children or leave them to their mothers. Yet if there is a dark side to the father who stumbles across his crippling rage, there is also hope. He can find healing for the boy inside himself if he will persevere and face the pain. Perhaps it will not be in time for his children's childhood but perhaps in their lifetime.

SYNCHRONIZING COMPLEX NEEDS

As we have seen in each previous stage, maturity means increasing complexity in the rhythms we must synchronize. Starting with synchronizing his own body and emotional rhythms as an infant, he added words, social rhythms and eventually a group identity with its patterns and cycles. These rhythms were practiced with his natural and spiritual families until he became familiar with his own "instrument" and contribution enough to have some style. Somewhere along the way he began to juggle a job and career as part of his daily rhythms. When synchronizing all of that seemed too little for him, our man added synchronizing with a woman and her rhythms on a full time, life-long basis to give him a little challenge. It was quite a stretch but it did him good. Now he had a full time place to practice all the storylines in his identity—well, actually not. There was another storyline missing, that of father. He now wanted to synchronize the needs, feelings, expressions, joy, quieting and returning to joy of children: in a family, with a wife, and a job, and a community, and schools, and church and with his and her relatives. This man wanted to synchronize all those activities with the goal that everyone would be satisfied together. This guy loves his complexity doesn't he? So! He invited his wife out to a candle light meal to demonstrate his sense of style and said, "Honey, let's have kids." At least that is the way it is usually done.

Synchronizing all these diverse needs in a way that brings daily satisfaction and develops trust in him from all these people and groups is the work of the fatherhood stage. You can see why a man would need: a well-trained control center, to get back to joy easily, to bring others back to joy quickly, to have tamed his nucleus accumbens and to have a synchronized group identity so there would be a rhythm to his community life. Both he and his wife would need well-developed adult abilities to satisfy two or more people at once before this plan could be anything but a disaster. Yet, it is the dependable way in which a father synchronizes all these complex needs that will lead to trusting him as a father.

It will take every bit of joy a man has built plus the joy he builds each day to carry him through this twenty-plus-year effort. This is the main event! Let's explore what is needed to reach maturity as a father.

Chapter Nine
Fathers and Their Children

... the essential attribute of the macho - power - almost always reveals itself as a capacity for wounding, humiliating, annihilating. Nothing is more natural, therefore, than his indifference toward the offspring he engenders. He is not the founder of a people; he is not a patriarch who exercises patria potestas; *he is not a king or a judge or a chieftain of a clan. He is power isolated in its own potency, without relationship or compromise with the outside world. He is pure incommunication, a solitude that devours itself and everything it touches. He does not pertain to our world; he is not from our city; he does not live in our neighborhood. He comes from far away: he is always far away. He is the Stranger.*[37]

Octavio Paz
The Labyrinth of Solitude

In his classical statement of the male worldview, Octavio Paz has provided a definition of masculinity from a large segment of his Latin culture. Men exist in a labyrinth of solitude. "We are alone," he says, "solitude, the source of anxiety, begins on the day we are deprived of maternal protection and fall into a strange and hostile world."[38] So men resort instead to "the pistol, a phallic symbol that discharges death rather than life..."[39]

Man is seen as death-giving, father is death-giving, even humor is death-giving bringing unexpected annihilation, dust, and nothingness. Power is measured in units of death, by the ability to destroy and consume. Little wonder that the child deprived of maternal protection is plunged into anxiety, if this is the nature of the father. Millions of people hold some variation on this view of fathers. Many of those millions are fathers.

Contrasting with this indifferent, hostile view of fathers is the father figure described by the ancient prophet Zephaniah (Zephaniah 3:17). He is a father who is among his children, like a warrior keeping them safe, rejoicing over them, singing songs for them, quieting each one with his love, and exulting over them with shouts of joy. This father is not a stranger. His city is our city. He is pure communication. He gives life not death.

We can take note how closely the Zephaniah father matches a well-trained control center in the male brain. He is attached to his children and wants to be close to them (level one.) He recognizes danger and keeps them

---

[37] Octavio Paz, *The Labyrinth of Solitude* (New York: Grove Press, 1961), 82.
[38] Paz, The Labyrinth, 82.
[39] Paz, The Labyrinth, 82.

safe (level two.) Zeph's father alternates between joy and quiet while guiding his children into both (level three-mother core.) The next verse in Zephaniah says that he "comforts those who mourn" indicating the ability to return to joy and peace from distress. He sings over his children, clear evidence that his right hemispheric communication is working because music and rhythm belong to the synchronization circuits in the right brain. This is a well-synchronized father who is able to synchronize his children in joy, quiet and distress. Such creativity and flexibility is a clear sign that this father has his (level four) prefrontal cortex on. His internal story tells him that he is a comforting, protecting, singing, joyful and quieting kind of father.

Paz tells the story of a man of fear. He knows no bonds or connections (level one is unsynchronized). He gives the same destructive responses even when there is no threat (level two is stuck.) This father quiets no one except to kill them. He brings no joy. His power is always out of proportion to the moment (level three—mother core is untrained.) So we know that the only desires he will have are the untamed cravings linked to his survival nucleus: sex, food, alcohol, drugs or thrill seeking. He is driven by his fear and not by the desires of a well-developed identity in his prefrontal cortex (level four is off.)

Do you have a preference for either the Paz or Zeph kind of father?

Which story is the truth about fathers? Which is more realistic? What behavior can we expect from a father? Psychologists and therapists often side with Paz. They argue that fathers are not deeply bonded to their children, particularly compared with mothers. Therapists might not go as far as Paz goes with his definition of the masculine soul, but they often seem to believe that men have to "get in touch with their feminine side" in order to be nurturing. There is a wide-spread view that men who do not embrace their feminine side and, in addition, reject their masculine proclivities should never be allowed around children. In this view, held unconsciously by many professionals, men are pure isolation--an isolation driven toward sex and power. Being exposed to this sort of "masculine" influence is precisely the fear that torments the children "deprived of maternal protection" in the macho world Paz describes.

Yet, if this destructive nature is not actually masculinity in action but the rage of men with broken bonds, insecure attachments and the inevitable brain malfunctions that follow, then men who bond in masculine ways will resemble Zephaniah's description of a father's love. If disrupting a man's attachment center (level one) causes severe pain and can lead to rage then we may have a clue to the macho man Paz describes. While no one doubts that taking her baby away would cause severe pain and rage to a mother, the cold indifference of the macho father who shows no sign of pain

142

when leaving his children leaves a different impression about his soul. Could violence be a sign of bonding pain? Could a man have such deep pain and not know it?

Let us start with the bonding pain question. Pain can lead to rage. If you stick your finger in a man's eye he will usually get mad. If you cut off the favorite part of his body you can expect him to get unpleasant, maybe even violent when he is in a position to retaliate. In fact, if you cause a man pain for a long time, he may become very hostile toward everyone. Thus, a man separated from his deepest source of satisfaction, meaning, and love may become destructive to himself and others in his life. Nothing hurts worse than a jab in the (level one) attachment circuit, so if men have a working attachment center it is going to hurt if it gets injured. Our worst suffering comes from bonds that are torn apart. Since it is precisely an injury to our attachment center during infancy and childhood that produces emotional instability, incapacity to regulate intense emotions and loss of relational ability, we have an agonizing wound directly linked to the loss of capacity to handle that agony. If this is true, then deeply bonded men should be less hostile, destructive and angry because they can remember who they are even when in pain. Bonded fathers should remember to protect, serve and enjoy their homes and families. Men with early attachment wounds could act like Paz describes.

It may be that men bond more readily than women, although that view will surprise many readers. Many who quote experiences with men like Paz described will vigorously contest this view. However, the existence of so many men in the macho category may be evidence that men are more prone to bonding than they appear to be. Their very bravado suggests to me that men are hiding a point of great vulnerability and pain. What greater pain is there than a damaged attachment?

Much more common even than machismo, is the man who will not bond because he fears attachment pain. He can best avoid the pain he fears by keeping his bond center cluttered with what I call junk bonds. He can love his car, his sports on TV, his fishing or golf, his booze, work, religion, computer or his neighbor's wife. If men bond easily then even objects and activities will work to form bonds. It has been shown that damage to level four of the control center (prefrontal cortex) makes people bond to objects and animals instead of other people. We also know that a poorly functioning control center will have level four turned off—another reason they might choose candy bars over people.

In any conflict the combatants seek to cover up their areas of vulnerability. If men are most vulnerable in the area of their bonds, and primarily their bonds to their children, then men who wish to avoid the risk of pain must find ways to stay disconnected from their children. To do so they must clutter up or destroy their bonding capacity so nothing will stick. Only someone with a tendency to bond would have to work so hard to prevent it. If so much effort must be exerted to prevent bonding, and men insulate themselves from the pain so strongly, then they must bond rather easily.

DAD'S CONTROL CENTER

It should be obvious from the comparison between the macho and synchronized fathers that the brain's control center has a powerful influence on parenting at all four levels. As you may remember from Chapter Two, the first two levels of the control center are sub-cortical. Operating in the deeper areas of the brain, their activity is not under the control of our wills or open to direct conscious observation. These areas are very similar to the portions of our brains that control our blood pressure. Whatever knowledge of them or effect on them we can have is indirect and yet they are vital to our survival.

Here is a quick review of the four levels.

Sub-cortical

Level one – attachment circuits (attachment light)

Level two – basic values and safety functions (good, bad and scary)

Cortical

Level three – synchronization (mother core)

Level four – personal identity which can be flexibly applied to all circumstances

If we were to describe how each of these four levels contributes to good or bad fathering, we would have another whole book. Instead, we will just take a quick look at level one. Here we can begin to understand the bond between father and child and how it can go bad.

In Chapter Two we explained the four different patterns that our attachment circuits can develop—only one of which is desirable. All other patterns are unhelpful and produce weak or insecure attachment bonds. The one good pattern produces secure attachments. In this healthy pattern, a man's attachment light goes on and off in synchronization with those of his child and loved ones. He hurts when his loved ones are not there to respond but he has enough joy strength to wait for them to come back. He continues responding when they are available once again.

The three insecure attachment styles are all ways of dealing with attachment pain produced by having one's attachment light ignored. While the pain of having one's attachment light on with no response is intense and severe, it is also sub-cortical so unless men are taught to name it, they can live their whole lives and not know what this severe craving actually is. This is our first hint that men could have a pain they could not name. Not having a name would not stop men from attaching, but it would sure render any stories useless. Without a name, men cannot know that a story about loving his children applies to him and could guide his life. But let's go farther, could men mistake their attachment pain for something else the way they mistake heart attacks for pain in their left arm?

The answer to this question lies in the general-purpose pleasure center dominated by the nucleus accumbens. Because the attachment circuit uses the nucleus accumbens to express "I'm going to die if I don't get my attachment," anything that brings pleasure will turn off the nucleus and temporarily mask the attachment pain. Anything that produces a rush in the dopamine and serotonin circuits of the nucleus accumbens will appear to be the answer to the attachment cry. The brain then makes the mistaken conclusion that what he wanted was whatever brought the rush. High sugar foods, alcohol, escaping danger, cocaine but most importantly sexual arousal and orgasms can give just that rush. Even murder has been known to blow the pleasure center's lid and trigger orgasms for both men and women. Boys and men can learn to stimulate the nucleus accumbens pleasure center to mask the signals of the unhappy attachment circuit effectively blocking their attachment pain. Once a man learns to masturbate to shut off his unidentified and unnamed attachment pain we have a sex/pornography addict on our hands.

Here we have a man who has no idea he craves attachment but who knows he has a severe addictive compulsion to something that gives him a rush. He cannot understand stories about attachment bonds in any personal way. He has an irritable and unstable control center that is set off any time his desire to attach is triggered—however, he would be the last person on earth to know that was what he really wanted. Is it any surprise that domestic violence and rapes are usually set off by a woman's attractiveness? Doesn't it follow that batterers respond to vulnerability with violence? Is it any wonder that drinking and drugs are usually involved as men try to make the cursed nucleus shut up! They haven't a clue and it makes them quite dangerous. Paz told us it could happen.

One further step is to use sex to shut off the attachment response to specific individuals. If a man uses sex to turn off real attachment messages to specific people in his life then he will sexually approach those he feels the urge to bond with—his children, wife's friends, children's friends, attractive people he meets, altar boys, congregants, interns, counselees and secretaries. Since the man's sub-cortical goal is to shut off his attachment light he loses all sense of synchronization and his sexual activity, once triggered, becomes a ritual. His ritual runs until the attachment light is out or masked and he stops. Quiet together does not follow his orgasm, only stone-cold death, a *"pure incommunication, a solitude that devours itself and everything it touches,"* as Paz would say.

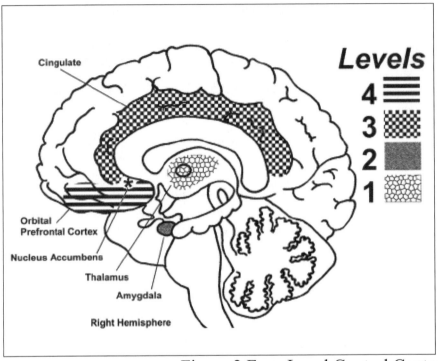

Figure 2 Four-Level Control Center

Once a man uses sex to turn off his attachment light with an unsuitable sexual partner (like his child,) the road to a healthy attachment is forever closed guaranteeing that his attachment light will be on again with no good solution available so the abuse and molestation will continue. On top of that, the man must now revert to fear bonding to cover his tracks and make sure his attachment victim does not expose him. The tragedy is compounded by the fact that it may well have been a real attachment response that started the disaster. Now the man must become a closet terrorist to avoid detection. This produces the disorganized attachment pattern we discussed in Chapter Two. The same person you want to attach to has become the source of your fear.

IDENTIFYING AND MANAGING ATTACHMENT PAIN

When the continued and persistent response to his attachment light is a plunge into shame and hopeless despair, level two of his control center begins to regard the attachment light as bad. If the child is later able to block his awareness of his attachment light and reduce his conscious level of pain, level two will find this good. Anything that blocks the attachment light will be seen as good in this arrangement. In this way, shame and hopeless despair become neurologically linked to the desire for attachment, resulting in an avoidance of anything that might trigger desire for attachment. This man will keep his attachment light off for people and dismiss feelings as unimportant if he notices them at all. Since it is quite possible for us to learn to avoid noticing what our brain is doing when we are motivated to stop pain, we have the final clue to our question about whether a man can have a severe attachment pain and not know it. The answer is a resounding YES. We have also seen that the potential for violence, assault, abuse and addiction become very high with this condition. Indeed, the man with a tormented attachment level in his control center is a man to avoid.[40] Warning: Do not attempt repair at home. You or your children may get injured, killed or acquire sexually transmitted diseases—besides, it won't work. We will look at possible solutions in Chapters Seventeen and Eighteen. For now let's get back to other ways infants manage attachment pain.

If attachment happens randomly during infancy then the control center's level two will encourage keeping the attachment light on all the time to see if the baby "wins the lottery." By always looking for attachment, he will be ready when opportunity strikes. His whole life becomes about winning the "feel better" lottery. When he grows up he finds a woman who makes him feel better. In time they have a child and his child becomes another way to feel better. Children easily respond with joy to their father's interest so they become a good source for a fix and the pattern is passed on to the next generation. These men are sitting ducks for sexual addictions. They may even become sexual predators or child molesters if they suffer certain kinds of head trauma, particularly damage to the back left side of the head.[41]

Some fathers bond when their children are young only to break the attachment later. This is also a function of pain. A dad, like any parent, will likely stay bonded with his children up until the age when the children are

---

[40] That will help him a lot, eh?

[41] Dr. Amen in *Healing The Hardware of the Soul* has reported what other researchers have also found, that many sexual predators have marked brain problems and histories of head trauma.

recapitulating the highest level of dad's maturity. That is the point where his bonds broke and his pain started. So, let us say that dad got through weaning and then got stuck at five-year-old maturity. This Dad will still bond but in an impaired way. He will enjoy closeness with his child until the youngster reaches age five. When the child begins to navigate the same problems that stopped the father's growth, problems will arise. The father then has three options: 1) face his own pain, 2) disconnect or 3) keep the child crippled at age-five maturity with him.

We all admire the father who chooses to face his own pain. In a very real sense, a dad must review and retrace all the developmental stages with each of his children in order to maintain his bond with them. Once a child reaches the place of the father's defeat, Dad must confront the problem that once defeated him, but this time successfully, in order to keep the bond with the child intact and healthy. Gordon Dalbey tells in his story *One Ice Cream At A Time*[42], how he faced such a crisis. When his son John Miguel asked him for ice cream one hot afternoon, Gordon refused until he became aware of what he was doing. Gordon realized that he was refusing to buy John Miguel an ice cream because Gordon's father would not buy him ice cream. A small pain perhaps--not being allowed to ask Dad for the things you want--but enough to cripple father-and-son moments in the hot summer sun.

If Dad won't face his pain, his pain will force him to withdraw from the child and break his bond, or else he will cripple the child in the same way he was damaged. My guess is that most men disconnect. Either way, the bond is broken and his child won't keep growing properly. You see, the point at which the father stopped maturing marks the place where he lost track of how to act like himself. As a result, he lost his flexibility and stopped adding to his own complexity.[43]

So for all us wounded and immature men this means that, for our children to mature, we must face our pain and seek healing. We need a moment of God's restoration that will give us the life our children need from us. We may need the help of our communities as well. It is the strength of the love in a father's heart that has brought many fathers through the pain of recovery. Often, the bond with their children is the only bond strong enough to keep wounded fathers from running away.

Take, for instance, Joe. He was the perfect father until Joey was old enough to sleep in his own bed. Joe played and laughed, while Joey played with his bottle, learned to crawl, stood on his own, and learned to walk and talk. Joe was patient and enjoyed helping his son even when Joey couldn't succeed. When Joey was scared at nights and wanted comfort, Joe got him

---

[42] Gordon Dalbey, *One Ice Cream At A Time*. www.abbafather.com Tape A12 "Honor the Child."

[43] Siegel. See Appendix B.

148

out of his crib and brought him to bed. But one day Joey turned three. By that time he slept in his own bed and wandered into his parents' room whenever he felt the need at night. Joe found himself telling Joey sharply that now that he was three he needed to stay in his own bed at night. He would have added, "and don't cry," but he didn't believe that story anymore, so he stopped before he said it.

The first bad night that brought Joey wandering into his parents' bedroom after that drew surprising anger and frustration out of Joe. His wife said, "What's gotten into you? You never used to be so harsh. Now you scared him." Joe was surprised at himself, but he said inflexibly, "He has to learn to stay in his own bed." Joe could suddenly neither calm himself nor his son.

A peek at history would reveal that Joe's father had become sick at the same time that Joe's younger brother was born, just after Joe turned three. What had been a pleasant childhood became a rather unforgiving climate, as his irritable parents tried to cope with tough times. In order to continue being the kind of father he was in his heart, Joe had to be healed and correct his own distortions about being three. Without his son's tears, Joe would have run from his pain and played "hardball" with his son. Joe decided instead to face the truth about his parents' limitations and his own pain. Then he was able to discover, along with Joey, what a three-year-old boy really wants and needs in the middle of the night.

Joe was the kind of father described by the Personal Fathering Profile®[44] as an overcoming father. He was motivated by love for his children so he faced the pain of his own developmental deficiencies and stayed bonded while his children grew.

OVERCOMING FATHERS

I saw one example of this overcoming kind of father bond each Tuesday morning at six when Wayne showed up at prayer breakfast with his adoptive daughter Melissa. (It used to be a men's prayer breakfast but with changing times it became a prayer breakfast.) Melissa was only two and Wayne was too old to really care about his next birthday party. Wayne was a farmer's son from Iowa, fixed his own cars and taught math. He was not a man known for being deeply in touch with his feelings. His development suggests that he was raised with a dismissive form of attachment and

---

[44] Personal Fathering Profiles are available from the National Center for Fathering. 1-800-593-DADS or www.fathers.com or 10200 W 75TH Street, Suite 267, Shawnee Mission, KS 66204-2223.

learned to keep his attachment light off or at least unnoticed. Melissa was not biologically related to him, this side of Noah, that is.

At breakfast each week Melissa crawled up on Daddy's lap, put her arms around his neck, and curled up for ten to fifty minutes. Occasionally, she would poke or swat at Dean who could be a pest. Dean sat next to Wayne and asked her dumb questions. Melissa fussed about her orange juice and made Daddy cut up her food. On Mondays, Wayne would take Melissa to parent-and-child play times at the university, where he was usually the only father present. Wayne was a pacifist, hardly ever lost his temper, and opposed the death penalty. He is a little unusual, and yet most of us know someone like Wayne.

Rick was home with Ryan. Like Wayne he took to fathering like a duck to water. When he dropped Ryan off at the play area in the fitness center, Ryan often clung to him awhile. This behavior mystified the women that ran the center. Why would this little boy cling to his father? Rick said that it was worth having his business go bad to have the time with his son. Rick did not own a gun. He was never violent or abusive. He could be moody and his early attachment history included having his mother hospitalized for large periods of his infancy. Rick got some good brain training from a loving aunt who cared for him at times when his mother was too sick. Rick's attachment level stayed on and wanted to win the lottery just as Ryan's tended to do. Rick and his wife learned the stories of the family of God, and began to work with his erratically functioning control center so that they might live differently than he did growing up. Rick found that medication helped him a lot.

Bob, whose father was also his grandfather, came home to find his wife in bed with her boss. He did not try to kill the other man. Bob did not have a good bond with either of his parents. In fact his parents were of the scared and scary variety that produce disorganized attachments. Bob had been working for years to be able to attach securely with his own children. He sang stories to himself about the family of God and chose to live out a different set of stories than he learned growing up. Bob was not affluent and his health was not great, but his loyalty to his children made it hard for him to move out when his wife refused to change. Bob main focus was finding a way to care for his children and keep them safe.

In a similar but even sadder situation, Dr. Sam slept for months on the couch after his wife threw him out of the bedroom to make room for her boyfriends. Dr. Sam was raised in orphanages and foster homes and found it almost impossible to think of leaving his own children no matter what his wife did. Sam had his doctorate in psychology, but that did little to help. Psychology fills your left brain with explanations but does not retrain your control center. In addition, the last half-century of psychology has done little

150

to help fathers. Sam eventually found a safe home for himself and his children. He continued to be a quiet, even-tempered man in spite of the terrible training his brain received when he was a child. By keeping his life in a workable range he could now live out the new stories he learned from Zephaniah and others.

Incidentally, men who care about their bonds are not just interested in their children, the sexual and marital bond is also very important to men. Like a broken parent-child bond, broken or damaged marital bonds can also be a source of great pain. Once level two in their brain's control center decides that it is bad or scary to have their "attachment light" on, men may try to avoid sexual/marital bonds as well as parent/child bonds. It appears that both Dr. Sam and Bob's wives were busy preventing any sexual bonding with their husbands. They did this, as many men also do, by copulating indiscriminately. There is nothing like lots of matings to prevent bonding. No bond--no pain is the level two knee-jerk reaction. When we notice that level two is not cortex and can't reason, we also see why this strategy is doomed to fail. A synchronized control center is needed for healthy marital bonds as well as parental bonds.

THE MAIN EVENT

If it were only an academic issue it would not matter how fathers bond with children. But it is my contention that this bond is the main event for all males. Without it men are doomed to unhappiness. At the risk of being run out of town as a heretic, I might even say that parenthood is more the point of our life than religion. The preacher in Ecclesiastes warns against being too religious and recommends daily enjoyment of one's wife. God Himself did not tell the pair in the garden to meditate on his words, sing worshipfully, or play the harp, but rather to multiply and fill the earth: dad-and-mom stuff.

Good father bonds come in many different flavors. Bonds change with each stage of a child's life and are different with each child. Father bonds are slightly different with sons and daughters, or first and last children, but they are more alike than they are different. Bonds are the places where who I am touches who you are so that we are united, sustained and changed. Bonds are the ways in which we give life. They are usually charged with either love or fear. Father bonds, in particular, are filled with expressions of whatever is in the father's heart, whatever it is like him to give.

Men who believe they are not the bonding type will not try to be close to their children or wife. These are the men who Paz so aptly describes. They are clogged with junk bonds. Perhaps the best known of these bonds are those to gangs, organized crime, military and para-military groups, hate groups, entertainment and even law enforcement. The non-bonded man is often viewed as a type of man rather than the aberration he represents.

Musicians have given us many songs about the non-bonding man. "Papa was a rolling stone," "I keep my sleeping bag rolled up and stashed behind her couch," "I used her and she used me and neither one cared--we were getting our share," "what's love got to do with it," and "I'm free falling," to mention a few.

Doug loved motorcycles and dirt bikes. He had loved power, control and thrills ever since he was twelve years old. Doug's dad was a self-made millionaire and their relationship was distant. When Doug's son was born, and took all his wife's attention away from him, Doug went back to dirt bikes. When he was home he demanded more sex. He did everything he could to keep from bonding with his son and feeling the pain of how distant he was from his father. He even hung pictures of dirt bikes in the bedroom where most fathers would put pictures of their sons. He kept his bonding surface covered with junk and his nucleus stimulated.

Conversely, men who believe that they must become feminized in order to bond with their children will be greatly frustrated in their attempts to be more like a woman. Women compound this problem by supporting the idea that a good father should bond with a child in the same way the mother does, and so become a "back up" mother when she is too tired, overwhelmed, busy or exhausted. Further, when neither of the parents has seen a functional father in action, anyone's guess is as good as another about what a father should be like.

Yet, the climb to fatherhood is not achieved through following well-meaning advice. Fatherhood cannot be done "the right way" but through a heart-felt identity that brings satisfaction. This is why it is so important that each father has first been a boy who learned how to act like himself in satisfying ways. In the parent or father stage, satisfaction comes from giving his life so that his children can mature. The father gives because it is like him to give. This expression of his deepest identity is the goal for each day's living. The context for his life is found at home. A father needs a home and family to protect, serve and enjoy. Yet, because he was first a man, he does not work alone but as a part of a marriage, community and tradition. This allows the father to receive input from his own heart, his wife, children, friends, relatives and even his children's friends.

Men who believe that bonding should be painless will seek to change and control everyone they bond with to insure that they do not experience pain, anxiety or loss in their relationships. They refuse to love anyone who does not love them well enough. These bonds can be strong but

152

they are fear bonds and serve to insure that no one outgrows Dad emotionally. Perhaps this is the most common sort of father. He bonds sufficiently to maintain control but avoids the painful parts of his life where change is needed. Sometimes he wakes up when his wife leaves him or his children provoke him to it. Mostly, he tries to keep everyone in order without ever asking himself if keeping it that way satisfies him or anyone.

Glen was this way. He was always careful to be right, disciplined his children, told them what they should do without really asking for their input, and pointed out their mistakes. His children loved him, feared him, were loyal to him, and kept him at a respectful distance all their lives. None of them could tell you what their father's heart was like although they knew exactly what he believed was right.

As each father's development will affect his fathering differently at each stage of his children's growth we should take time to examine what it is like to be a father as one's children grow up.

THE MATURE FATHER AND THE INFANT STAGE

New fathers enter what Ken Canfield of the National Center for Fathering calls the age of idealism when their children are first born. Due in part to widespread success in achieving the first stage of development, most parents are able to freely join in with their children at this point. Such a bond produces joy and delight between father and child. Naturally, the father who did not bond with his parents even at this point in his own development will have real problems immediately. He will lack an internal understanding of how things work at the infant stage and suffer severe levels of emotional pain.

Some, like myself, will find a capacity to bond but lack stories and understanding about how to live this out. I dismissed myself and allowed myself to be dismissed too easily given my tendency to be "safe" through keeping my attachment light off. Others will find themselves distracted by their own feelings and issues and form weak bonds for that reason. But for the father who is available and synchronized, this is his moment!

During the first four years of a child's life, the baby's growth rate is enormous. The good dad delights in this growth by observing it carefully and encouraging each new step. This is the kind of attention described by John Fischer in his song, "Christopher's Toes."

> *Christopher knows Christopher's toes*
> *He just found them today*
> *Stuck in the air at the end of his chair*
> *Ten little toes just waitin' to play.*[45]

---

[45] Copyright 1982 by Word Music, ASCAP

Not only do children discover their toes but their tongues and voices, and inevitably they find Dad's nostrils are just the right size for a little fingers with fingernails that should have been trimmed. It is a time of discovering their senses and muscles. For the father this is also a time of getting to know his child. It is a time for play and mutual discovery. Dad wants to know what baby can do. Being together is the key to success. The more time spent together the greater the discoveries. Since this stage usually exhausts mother with late night feedings, time spent with Dad is welcome respite for her. It also allows both parents to revel in the life they have created together. This is a new form of intimacy for parents who are not used to being close when a third person is involved. Mom, Dad and baby are learning what it means to be a family.

For Dad, knowing his child becomes a form of rediscovering the world himself. It is a chance to enrich his own discoveries that may have languished since infancy. In this awakening, the father will experience a feeling much like falling in love with his son or daughter. This rush of fresh life occurs as everything becomes new and alive again. Joy is tempered by the exhaustion that most parents experience in the early years of childrearing in a culture that isolates parents from other support.

The father who was raised in relative isolation and never participated in raising other children must overcome his early years spent alone and his limited sense of self. Repulsion with diapers, fear of holding babies, and reluctance to coo and snuggle must be overcome to form a close relationship to his baby. This is all part of the discovery of himself and the world that the first-time father experiences.

A father learns more about being a dad from his first child than from his other children. The first father-child-bond a man forms is a unique bond that requires more time to produce. What a father learns with his first child prepares him to appreciate his later children more precisely and quickly. Because he practiced on the first child, he can meet needs more accurately for his other children even with less time available per child. In its own way this provides a needed balance, for with each new baby, the father is able to focus more acutely on the uniqueness of that child.

THE WOUNDED FATHER AND THE INFANT STAGE

The father whose own development crashed at the baby stage is faced with a monumental task in raising children. He will either prove to be neglectful and distant, overprotective (in a controlling way) or frightening with his children. Amazingly, this overprotectiveness is the source for much emotional and physical child abuse. These fathers badly misjudge the force they are using to control their children and instead of protection they produce destruction. When their brain's control center becomes desynchronized internally they thrash about. They pressure their children and family in order to settle themselves and their own feelings.

The father who was sexually abused at this stage will typically experience his desire to bond with his child, whether male or female, as a sexual impulse. He does very poorly at managing his craving for closeness. Closeness for him equates to sexual activity and may result in repeating the abuse. Some men control their impulses by rigidly removing themselves from their children in angry isolation.

There are two types of trauma that can stop maturity. The first is obvious and includes all the bad things that happen to children. The second type is easier to overlook and involves missing the necessary good things. An obvious example would be missing vitamins in babies' diets. If important nutrients are missing children can even die.

Wilber was one father who did not make it through his own infancy intact. In fact, while his parents neither abused nor neglected him in any criminal way, they treated him in the same way one might treat a prize-winning cow. He received his food regularly, his stall was clean, his pasture fenced, and he got his shots on time. The only cloud in the sky seemed so natural that he never saw it. His father and mother worked hard but never stopped to find him interesting. Wilber was not the twinkle in anyone's eye. As a result, it never occurred to him that he or, later, his six children were the least bit interesting. This might seem odd for a man with a doctorate in counseling, but these things happen.

Each of Wilber's children received his or her food regularly, each was always clean, their back yard was nicely fenced and each one got his or her shots on time. Wilber never thought to notice the gifts his children brought him or what they made in school. He didn't think to play with their toes or fingers, or blow on their tummies. When they grew up and met partners, he never thought to ask their boyfriends or girlfriends what they liked, believed, or even where they wanted to live.

At his retirement party, many students from his school claimed he had been a guiding influence on them--after all it was his job and he worked hard--but his own children did not all attend. Some declared they had no tribute to give. Wilber didn't seem to notice. He didn't see how his children would be interested in him, anyway. He expressed no need or feeling and sought no satisfaction. He simply cared for his children with a dispassionate interest that seemed right, familiar and painless. Wilber was disconnected from infancy. He had no stories-of-us. He now dismissed his feelings and those of his children leaving a very weak bond he never seemed to notice.

Due to the interest shown by some family friends, some of Wilber's children began to express their needs and feelings. Soon the family began to disintegrate. Wilber never thought to look at himself to see if he were part of the problem because he found himself totally uninteresting. Wilber got lost as a baby, long before he was weaned. He had no sense of being loved for who he was, no sense of being someone special. No one told him in time.

While it is unlikely that any severe abuse at an infant age will be corrected without a great amount of difficulty, most fathers were happy babies. They discover only mild deficits requiring them to overcome discomfort, anxiety and embarrassment about their own infants. Entering their baby's world means enjoying baby things and baby activities. The father who knows what satisfies him will excitedly plunge through this barrier into baby world, splashing water, taking baths, crawling around, making noises, gumming toes and trying all sorts of new things again. With a reasonably healthy mother core (level three) he will synchronize his joy and quiet to his baby's needs and capacities. Ah! The fun of it! And, to think that this is serious maturity building!

THE MATURE FATHER AND THE CHILD STAGE

As the self-care of childhood approaches, a father finds himself increasingly teaching his child about life. It is the time to answer incessant "why" questions and explain everything in the world. The father who has explored the world with his infant for the last several years will find these questions excite his own curiosity and add zest to life. Teaching and learning go together.

This is also a time where fears can grow. As weaning approaches the child discovers that everyone else in the house is better at taking care of themselves than he or she is. Others--usually siblings--increasingly compete for his or her coveted spot. Jealous rage, possessiveness, and a desire for exclusive relationships with parents characterize this age.

The mature father takes time to teach his children about inclusive love that does not fear others by teaching his children how to take care of themselves, pets, toys and younger children. This is at the level of caring play and not adult level responsibilities. He teaches sharing toys or Daddy's knee and helping little sister or brother stay on Daddy's back for a ride.

The mature father approaches weaning his child with anticipation. Once weaned, children are able to explore the world with Dad much more freely. Weaning can cause some anxiety to children and it helps to have Dad close. Dad is the one who keeps the secret knowledge of the good things inside each of his children. With patience born of faith, he searches diligently until the good part of his child is discovered, or a lesson is

156

learned. At these times the child learns to be more than he or she was before because not everything we discover is there before we begin the search. Becoming what one has not yet become is much harder to hope for, especially when the new thing cannot yet be understood.

Early childhood is a time of imagination as much as a time for facts, because children find it easier to imagine the impossible than to understand the actual. Fantasies of being big and living in Daddy's world have special meaning. Little boys want to be like Dad and marry Mom, while little girls want to marry Dad and take better care of him than Mommy does.

Very soon school will begin and with it the need to understand the outside world of strangers. School is like a giant bicycle for the child to ride and master. Parents prepare each child to master these demands even when the start isn't smooth.

Around age six children pass freely from imagination to learning. One key area of learning at this age involves the conscience of each child. Within a warm relationship with parents, rules and examples are carefully matched to see if the rule maker follows the rule. Without judging by satisfaction, however, rules become a method of moral control over others, rather than a way to bring out the best in us. For instance, instead of making everyone line up by height and serving in that order like they taught in school, sometimes it is more satisfying to bring Grandma her food first, so she can sit down and rest while others are being served.

Dad and Mom are the main solution to their children's need to know the meaning of what they learn, particularly through comparisons. It is easy for people to see what they are not, until too much attention to the fact causes them to develop defenses that blind them. During the child stage, fathers help their children learn to use comparisons, rules and competition to measure their own growth, not their own value. Expressing and demonstrating what the child has learned is subject to constant comparison; otherwise, the results are meaningless.

Jimmy always answered questions more slowly than his classmates. Some of them suggested that Jimmy wasn't all that smart. In fact, Jimmy was unusually bright and reflective. He pondered questions before answering. His answers were often unusual as a result. When the teacher asked, "If Tommy has ten apples and he takes seven from Billy and gives three to George, how many apples does he have?" Jimmy thought about why Tommy would take Billy's apples when he could have given three to George and still had seven, which was more than he could eat anyway. The kids laughed at his answer. They said it was dumb. It was obvious he was slow.

Jimmy needed his parents' help to understand the comparisons he made with other children. Was he really dumb? Unfortunately he did not ask his mom, he thought she was already too worried. He did not ask his dad.

Dad had left with another lady and Jimmy didn't see him very often. Maybe he wouldn't come back at all if he knew that his son was stupid. Jimmy needed to know that it wasn't bad to be thoughtful and slow. It was twenty years before he found out. By then he was at the top of his philosophy class where a teacher told him the truth. A rare event in philosophy class, I suppose.

THE WOUNDED FATHER AND THE CHILD STAGE

The father who has not navigated this time in his own childhood without mishap will not know how to guide his children through their sense of jealousy and fear. He will already have struggled with jealousy over his wife's attention to their children. He may have pressured her to wean babies too early. Consequently, the children may be clingy, jealous and resistant. Often such a father has isolated his wife from her friends, and so she is more vulnerable to exhaustion and discouragement and more dependent on him. Yet he cannot support her without anger.

In response to this crisis, the immature father will often angrily or coldly reject his sons and foster his daughter's immature jealous attachment to himself. In doing so he seeks to keep what his children give for himself rather than teaching them what they have for others. He is giving *so he can receive in return*--this is backwards. For his daughter this often means she must stay Daddy's girlfriend forever. For his son it means performing and bringing glory to his father. The son becomes a slave who cannot compete for Mother's attention with his father, except when Dad is away. This is an open training ground for mistresses the son may have later on.

Tom was a father who had his life fall apart during his child stage. His parents took to fighting and his dad left. As time went on, he began to call his dad by his first name just like he did with his step-dad. In reality Tom had no dad. Since, like all children at this age, you are what you learn he learned to be his own dad. He went on to one school after another, he got degrees in religion and business and education.

Tom married young and had three children who did well until they reached school age. From there on Tom's anger grew, he angrily compared his children with each other, he compared them with others outside the family, he compared them with the rules he had set, and they failed miserably. Tom compared his wife with other women who were smarter, thinner, more pleasing, less passive, better dressed, had bigger breasts and smaller butts and were better with money. His family began to like it when he was away on business because they were tired of being yelled at and feeling angry or afraid.

Tom could not see why they simply didn't learn to be what he told them to be, what the Bible told them to be, what good psychological theory told them to be, what any intelligent person could see they should be. Had Tom ever stopped to ask, he might have noticed that he was not satisfied with life, but rather than seek satisfaction he made rules and berated his family. They, in turn, learned to feel bad, sneak around his rules, counter with rules of their own and likewise be dissatisfied. If it wouldn't have made them "bad," they might have wished him dead.

Meanwhile, Tom regularly became dissatisfied with his church, his friends, his job, his house or the part of the country where he lived. No one and no place *gave him* enough. He would move to a new location dragging his unhappy family with him. In this, he had improved on his own father, for he did take his children out to see the world without abandoning them. He only made them wish at times that he would.

Tom simply could not see why his family did not learn to become the people he wanted them to be. He didn't know that while it is important to produce products for your efforts, that principle works for things not for people. In a perverse twist on a father's hope, Tom became a source of despair, seeing in his family only what they were not giving him.

THE MATURE FATHER OF YOUNG MEN AND WOMEN

Contrary to popular belief, I do not believe that there is much difference between a father's relationship to his daughters and sons. The primary difference involves the way in which a father affirms his children's sexual identity. For the son the message is, "Your sexuality is like mine and that is very fine." For the daughter the message is, "Your sexuality is different from mine and that is very fine." For both sexes of children the major factor is the father's respect for his own sexuality and lack of fear of theirs.

A father's capacity to be calm about his children's sexuality flows from his capacity to calm his own feelings, his victory over his own cravings, the successful mastery of his nucleus accumbens with its "I'm going to die!" Since this father has at least two decades of experience protecting others from himself, he is quite able to teach the same respectful sexuality to his children. This is the father that earns his trust.

The father of young men and women enjoys the onset and development of true friendship with his children. Having reached the crucial goals of development together, the father must first allow the independence of his children, followed by their return. Each of these times back together allows for review and celebration of progress. Life becomes a dance with the endless rhythm of goings and comings. The first of these movements away from Dad is likely to be painful because the new adult must find his or her own identity separate from Mom and Dad.

Separation from parents is encouraged by a mature father through a rite of passage. His children and their peers become members of their same-gender community and begin to form a group identity. Fathers, uncles and grandfathers provide opportunities for young adults to be together, enjoy each other and contribute to their community.

The first step in separation from parents is for young adults to declare themselves different from their parents on some important point. Suddenly having very short (or very long) hair is essential. If parents like long the young adult likes short--you get the picture. To some parents, this appears to be rejection but it is only the first step of the dance. Daughters want to be women and have their own boyfriends. Sons want to be different in ways that often means ignoring Dad for a few years in favor of their own friends and interests. If Dad is prone to fear rejection, he will withdraw from his children rather than encouraging their individual development.

As adult children approach different milestones, they turn first to their father for encouragement, then run off and forget him only to return later for his praise, interest and appreciation of their success. Should, per adventure, their efforts result in failure, their return is likely to be quicker. When faced with his children's failures, Dad gets a chance to relive a little of the "kiss the boo-boo" days before the cycle repeats. Major milestones are first dates, driving the car, getting a job, going to college, getting engaged and then married, buying a car or a house or even new tires.

I recall trying to decide whether I should buy steel-belted or radial ply tires and asking my dad--Mr. Steelbelt--to help me choose. I asked dad which car battery was best. Should I get a seventy-two month battery if I was only keeping the car three years? Life insurance policies and that sort of thing brought me back to Dad long after I was married.

The character of father-and-child relationship in adulthood becomes increasingly like that of adult peers. One day they discover they are as old as their parents used to be. As children approach the age of their early memories of their parents, sharing the stories-of-us takes on a special sweetness. Children eagerly compare their experiences with what their parents felt back then. For parents this fulfills the old prophesy that, "You'll understand when you're older," and provided that they let their children make the point, it cements their bond.

A father is gratified with each burst of his children's interest in his heart and life. Each return trip allows him to express how much of his children he has treasured inside. His children trust him.

160

THE WOUNDED FATHER OF YOUNG MEN AND WOMEN

The father who fell as he attempted passage into manhood is in for a bumpy time when his children make the leap. He will find strong impulses to react the way his parents did or react precisely the opposite. Since the most common symptom of this problem is a continuation of the reactive identity of early teenage years, this father is usually marked by being reactive and negative toward his children. He may criticize the way his children dress, their choice of friends, their personal styles, their choice of work or school and their personal habits. If they choose it he won't like it.

A reactive identity is one where the person defines himself in terms of what he is not. It can range from the response, "I'm not stupid, you are," to the complex, "I'm not like my parents and family." It is seen in tastes and choices. "I hate onions," when Dad likes them, or, "I will never drink coffee," when Mom is a seven-pots-a-day Java fiend. Reactive identities know what they don't like, don't want, and don't value. They don't yet know what they do like, want and value.

The second sign that a father experienced trouble during his early adult stage is a tendency toward extremes--that is to say, his style is reactive. He is either too involved or too withdrawn, too controlling or too permissive. He provokes stand-offs and draws "lines in the sand," making every move by his child a challenge to Dad's authority. Even steps toward normal growth become major risks for the child because Dad says, "If you move out, don't expect any help from me!"

Billy had such a father. Billy's dad was an assistant pastor in a large church. Whenever anything went wrong in Billy's life, his dad was quick to point out which transgression caused the trouble. Billy felt he could not do anything without provoking his father's anger. One day at school Billy's best friend was shot to death right in front of him by another kid. The police said it was probably a random gang killing. Billy did not dare to tell his father what had happened, because the boy was already upset enough without having his father yell at him for "hanging around" with the wrong friends again.

Immediately, Billy's grades dropped. He could not concentrate in class and was afraid to go to school. His father was outraged that Billy was not getting good grades and grounded him from everything but church. He yelled at the boy almost every day and even took him to the youth pastor at church to have him correct the boy's "rebellious attitude." Perhaps it will not surprise you that before six months were up, Billy was thinking seriously that his dead friend had it better and was making plans to join him. Nothing would induce the father to spend time with Billy or even take a day away for his son. "When he gets his grades up, we'll talk about it. He is lazy and I won't reward bad behavior." The more his dad reacted, the less Billy wanted to tell him of his pain and loss. Billy's life hangs in the balance. Billy does not trust his father.

Lesser versions of this scenario are the most common counseling problems for teenagers and young adults. Most fathers who are caught in this trap can't believe the family's problem is more about them than about their children. These fathers are trying so hard and doing the right thing that it can't be their fault! Never do they stop to ask if they are satisfied, or if they are expressing what is in their heart. Instead, they concern themselves with being justified. Typically, they react against their wife's observations of the hurt they create. They reject the feelings of their children with more self-justification. Since they have not become men, they do not seek the correction of other men either, although if they did they might turn their hearts back toward their children.

There is always hope for a dad who will face his pain. It is the strength of the father's heart-bond with his children that inspires him to provide for his children the very things he did not receive. His heart moves him to feel with them the emotions he was not allowed to experience. By giving his life to his children, the father finds the very best part of himself. We explore that in the next chapter.

Chapter Ten
The Father's World

The father is a source of life to children. Every man who does not give of his life to children will remain unfulfilled and miserable. The man who lives to be a consumer will die with the most toys to be fought over by his heirs. In the end he still gives his life, but only when he can no longer enjoy doing so. Who can say if anyone but the IRS loves him for it. Many men die without ever finding the inside of the father's world.

The father world is a very special world produced by the very nature of the father's own heart. By nature he should protect, serve and enjoy the earth. (Genesis 2:15-16) His world is the best expression of himself, colored and textured by the quality of life he gives. It is here, in his home, that he can become fully human, created in God's own image. It should not surprise us then that the father image we studied in the last chapter is a portrait of God's heart. Through the voice of the prophet Zephaniah we get this glimpse: (Zephaniah 3:17)

1. The Lord your God is **with you** - *present*
2. The Mighty one **will save you** - *protective*
3. He will **rejoice over you with delight** - *attentive and special*
4. He will **rest you in his love** - *quieting*
5. He will be **joyful over you with singing** - *enjoying*
6. He will **gather those who mourn the appointed feasts** - *comforting*

This character was put into humans before they were male and female so it is in all of us. It is equally true of mothers and fathers. But, perhaps we need to hear again that it is true of fathers. The father is present, protecting, attending to, calming, serving, enjoying and comforting his family. Everyone knows that they are special when father is there.

Perhaps you have heard of a father's world that is not like the one I just described. Ever since we have been able to decide for ourselves what is good and evil, some fathers have done whatever pleased them. Fathers of all sorts justify their actions. It is my contention that we have stopped acting like ourselves. Men are malfunctioning in such large numbers that malfunction has become the standard. We are in a sorry mess. Even those who don't agree about the source of the problem agree with that.

God has made it possible to be ourselves again through Emmanuel, whose name means God with us. (Matthew 1:23) Through his redemption we can again mature into fathers and mothers who act like ourselves. We can receive and give authentic life. Let me compare a restored and an unrestored father and see what sort of worlds they build. For those of you who are about to gag right now, let me say that showing up in church does not equal restoration. Unrestored fathers are wounded, desynchronized and immature children, creating life in their own image.

1. Father is Present *The Lord your God is in your midst*

The wounded father withdraws. He can be emotionally absent, physically absent, hide in the garage or through TV viewing, he can duck out when there is trouble and he can abandon his family.

A natural human father would seek his children, engage their attention, notice their lives and reactions, stay involved when there is conflict or difficulty, and be accessible. This father lives with his family and shares life with them.

2. Father is Protective *Like a warrior to keep you safe*

The wounded father is a defeated father. He feels weak, threatened and ineffective. Worse yet he may not protect his family from himself or from each other.

The mature father will protect his family from himself and each other. This is the first line of protection and separates safe people from hurtful ones. He will keep children safe from being exposed to shame, ridicule, humiliation, excesses of power, exposure to harmful people and materials, not leave their lives uncovered around danger. He will particularly protect them from threats or blame. (1 Pet 2:22,23)

3. Father is Attentive *He will rejoice over you and be glad*

The wounded father is bitter, he hates himself and his life. Sometimes he is depressed plodding along with too much to do, grieving a divorce or other loss of children, or he feels guilty. There are many ways to be absorbed, depleted, or distracted. Over-work and distractions are two of the most common ways to lose a father. The average father spends most of his life servicing debt--paying off loans. Debt and payments absorb most of his available mental and emotional energy.

The mature father delights in his children. He carefully sees them through God's eyes and pays attention to their interests, progress, discoveries, thoughts, feelings and needs. He knows his children well, so well that each one can see that they are a very special individual to their father.

4. Father Calms *He will rest you in his love*

The wounded father is a restless man. He is often reactive, reacting with anger, arousing and agitating rather than quieting his home. His control center delaminates with regularity. He does not engage with upset family members to share their pain and bring peace. He creates fear rather than tranquility, he scares his kids and exasperates them. He may be a driven man or one who drives his children. Like him they must be hard, strong, fast, productive, independent and winners. He has become the bad shepherd of Ezekiel 34:4 who drives even the strong sheep severely and does not let them play. Often he is impatient, restless, tense and sometimes cold. His family does not expect care when dad is home.

The restored father holds his children with non-sexual affection that quiets them. They rest because he doesn't arouse or unsettle. He creates an atmosphere where his family can put down their guard and express their needs. They look for dad when things go wrong so that they can get back to joy. Everything is better if father is home, and his presence is always home even when he is away.

5. Fathers Enjoy *He will be joyful over you with singing*

The wounded father has been shouted at but not joyfully. Oh, how it stings to be berated. Was he wrong, stupid, too strict or too soft, too slow or too careless, a perfectionist or a slob, insensitive, too rigid, not spiritual enough, just like his father, or brother--the bum. The wounded father has rarely been admired by an older man or even a friend. The wounded father often passes on the treatment he received for his family's edification. Other times he retreats to silence. The wounded father knows that he is inadequate to the task of being a father even if no one has said so. He feels a failure at one of the most important things in his life. He promised himself as a boy that he would do better but he failed. There will be no songs written in his honor and he will write none for his children. Silent, self-conscious, and ashamed, he does not enjoy the life he gives or his greatest gifts--his own children.

The normal man will feel wonder at the beauty of his children. His heart will sing over each one. He will rejoice with shouts of joy if he doesn't sing. He will bless his children with his voice so that it becomes their favorite sound each day. Sometimes Dad's exuberance will make them think he is a little nuts. But in the privacy of their home, his joy brings giggles. Publicly his evident pleasure in his children brings pride.

6. Fathers Comfort *I will gather those who grieve about the appointed feasts*

The wounded father scatters, parties, makes himself feel good but does not notice the hurts of his family. If he does notice he may ridicule or blame them for their pain. It hurts to be around him and one must stay on his good side. His children are afraid to remonstrate with him when he forgets his promises or overlooks their needs because he might get mad.

The redeemed father knows that each absence hurts. He knows that the celebrations that were missed because he was too wounded, busy, driven, detained or depressed need to be mourned. He will gather those who mourn what they have missed whether he was responsible or not. He will notice that they missed their weaning feast, rite of passage, that he was not there for graduation or their play. His children's loss will be grieved together so they can heal and celebrate the feasts together. They will find comfort and laughter again in their father's world.

Central to each appointed feast is an appointment with God. This appointment is where redemption is done. Those who have missed the appointed feasts have not been restored. They have missed their scheduled maintenance. They need servicing to stop evil from attacking, to restore them from their damage, and to reconnect them with the flow of life. The un-maintained father does not miss these times and will not comfort his children when they have not been healed. The restored father knows the importance of appointments with the God who can restore his children also. He is a spiritual father.

I'M SORRY

It shouldn't take long to realize that when we speak here of a restored father we are talking about more than the religious belief often passed off as faith. For the restored father, a passionate desire to be fully alive and functioning leads to a dedicated focus on repairing all malfunctions. He not only wants his malfunctions corrected but he wants the desyncronizations of others corrected too—even when they malfunctioned against him. The old word for that is forgiveness. Men in denial won't admit there is a problem so they won't seek to change. Unless we admit we have malfunctioned we cannot be retrained either. Jesus said the sign that we really believe we have malfunctioned is that we see other's failings as malfunctions as well. When we know God as Zephaniah did we will show the same eagerness for other's restoration as we show for our own. The good father can say, "I'm sorry. I failed," as well as, "I forgive you. You malfunctioned."

166

THE FATHER AND HIS WORK

No chapter on a dad's world would be complete without mentioning Dad's work. Most dads find their work to be both the most demanding part of fatherhood and the thing that most prevents them from being the dad they want to be. One friend of mine said that a book on being a dad need contain only one page--a picture of a man taking out his billfold. "Green blood," I call it because a father's time on the job converts his life into cash. One woman said that the difference between a father's relationship with his daughter and his son is that the son wants the keys to the car and the daughter wants the credit card. Credit card, car keys and billfold all depend on a man's work, and yet it is work that keeps Dad from the track meet after school, the violin recital (thankfully) and the class play. Work puts dad in a bad mood by the time he gets home and drains the best of his energy before he can make good on his promise to play ball in the park.

Unlike Matthew, in the John Denver song by the same title, who "rode on his daddy's shoulders, behind a mule, beneath the sun," most American boys and girls do not work with their dads. Some, like the children in *Mary Poppins*, venture into their father's workplace almost in wonder or fear.

To a man, his work is his life poured out minute-by-minute and returned to him in an envelope every two weeks. When the government, unions, insurance companies and other parasites have taken their share, all but the most wretched men will take what is left of their "green blood" home to keep their family alive. It might not seem like much, and in spite of all the quips about "bringing home the paycheck" this too is life giving.

THE FATHER AS A HUSBAND

To the mature man, one who worked out a good relationship with his wife where both of them can be satisfied, fatherhood will present some new challenges. Because he and his wife are raising children together his efforts as a father will touch deep chords in his wife. Every woman has deficits in her bonds with her father, for there are no fathers who can entirely avoid putting some glass into their daughter's face. Her mothering will produce the same problems for him, exposing deficits in his bond with his mother. It is painful when these holes come to the surface and mature couples will momentarily extend a parental hand to each other. That is to say, when one partner slips into their childhood feelings their spouse will respond like a good parent should.

Within a mature couple bond there is room for both partners to be adults at the same time in order to run a household. Both can then be children at the same time in order to play. Occasionally they can even be parent and child to each other in order to heal and mature. It is even possible for the arrangement to be lopsided with one spouse doing more parenting and the other more recovery, provided the arrangement is temporary.

Not all such situations are short-lived. The clearest case I remember was one I observed as a young counselor in a camp for senior citizens. One woman in the camp was an offense to the other campers. She would knock down women with their walkers to get to the front of the food line. She refused to take a shower and was easily recognizable from downwind. She was intensely reactive and hostile if confronted. In all, she was most unpleasant.

Her husband was one of the most educated and interesting men I ever met. Fluent in seventeen languages, he added a wealth of knowledge to any conversation. He was kind, interested in the people around him, and put up with his wife's outrages with saintly patience, all the while redirecting her to better behavior--like a good father would do with a two-year-old.

Disgruntled, I asked him why he put up with a wife who acted so childishly. He told me that she had not always been that way; but only for the last twenty-five years since Auschwitz. A victim of Nazi torture and non-anesthetized surgery on her brain, his wife, who had once been a concert pianist, had been reduced to this state. His stay in the concentration/death camps had gone better than hers and even increased his understanding of other languages, which is proof that some people can find something good anywhere. For years now he had been in a parental position toward his wife, yet with patience born from maturity and deep character he treated her very well.

Many older people find themselves with variations of this problem. My father, like many others, cared for my mother for five years before she died of Alzheimer's-like symptoms. It is one thing for a couple to face the consequences of illness, accidents, calamity and vile evil together but entirely something else to enter marriage in order to find a parent. Most women who try to marry a father-figure are still at the four-year-old level of emotional development. Four-year-old girls want to marry Daddy and are sure they can take better care of him than Mommy can. They don't distinguish fantasy from reality. However, girls who have still not outgrown this stage by the time they marry carry within themselves the jealous rage of childhood. A four-year-old girl wants to be special, the only girl in Daddy's life. She will be an attachment vigilante who will do almost anything to protect her place. Such behavior is tolerable, even a bit cute, in a four-year-old. But when lodged in an adult body with its knowledge and abilities, jealousy becomes a terror.

Four-year-old children in full-grown bodies give care hoping that by giving they will receive care in return. They give in order to consume the results. When they are disappointed (the greatest offense possible) life becomes an endless succession of upsets as hurt rage follows hurt rage. It makes me think of the time I slipped at the top of a sleet-covered stairway and felt my tender parts hit one step after another all the way to the ground floor.

The man who joins himself to a woman after mistaking her devoted love for Daddy with an adult love for a husband will rue the day he said "I do." Not only so, but should the woman outgrow this four-year-old stage at some point, she will lose her interest in taking care of her man, leaving her ex-husband to feel that she took him in with promises of love and then took him for everything she could. Father-and-daughter relationships are an inadequate model for a marriage relationship.

The man trapped in such an arrangement often buys security by using his life-giving capacity to keep his wife from getting mad. He takes care of his wife in return for having her please him. But, such arrangements always backfire because they are contrary to nature. Life-giving carries with it a prohibition--we may not consume the life we give for our own pleasure. Couples are meant to enjoy each other and together give life to their children.

On the mature and healthy side, it is often the woman who encourages her husband to become a better father for their children and in so doing receives some vicarious fathering. By watching her children's father in action, she can fill in her own picture of a father. Since her father is the prototypical male in every daughter's life, she will understand her femininity in relationship to Dad's masculinity. Anything a husband does to change his wife's view of men or her femininity makes him, for that moment, a supplemental father. This will bring some bitter-sweet moments for his wife.

A man told me how his wife had hidden one of his shirts that she did not like. When he asked her to return it, she said, "You can beat me if you want, but I won't get it." Raised by an abusive father, she could not see her husband's smile.

"I knew I was speaking for good fathers everywhere," he told me, "when I said, `I'm not going to hurt you. I just want my shirt.'" Then he gave her a hug. For that moment, he was a supplemental father for his wife. He was a life-giver.

MAN AS FATHER TO HIS CHILDREN'S FRIENDS

Enough for us and some to share. This motto should be found in every home. It is a good measure for the amount of love needed to produce satisfaction. *Enough for us with some to share* is the dosage of attention children need. On open house nights at school, the parents who pay attention to their child's efforts and those of the child's friends or table-mates become the popular parents and spread a blanket of good will for their child to enjoy in school. Even in such places as scouts, baseball leagues, or camps the parents who pay attention to their children's friends really stand out. Not only so, but the parents who send along an extra cookie for the child to share, or make room for one more on the way to the amusement park or church, allow their child to share the best treasure--his parents. Comments like, "Your dad is cool!" or "Your mom is really nice!" please parent and child alike.

If you look around, you will find parents that almost always have an extra participant in family activities. Having *enough for us and some to share* produces this effect. Children in such families are provided the means to give good experiences to friends and prove that their dad and mom are the greatest.

Although they are schoolteachers and not wealthy, Wayne and Judi always found room for some of their children's friends to travel with them to Mexico or Europe. Dean and Diane always made room for Paul's friends on camping and ski trips. Spence and Bonnie fit in kids for high school football games and youth activities. Dick and Nancy always had extra soft drinks when the kids rented a movie.

Willard and Virginia always had cookies on Sunday afternoon for all the kids and their parents who wanted to come over and swim. Hundreds of children learned to swim in their back yard pool. Kids from Africa to Australia look to Willard and Virginia as supplementary parents. While Virginia was the one who seemed to have a way with kids, Willard kept everything safe and operational and provided constant supervision of backyard activities.

I read a true story[46] of a father who allowed his daughter and her little friend to "fix" his hair and then took them both to a restaurant with his outrageous styling job. This allowed his daughter to share her wonderful dad. *Enough for us with some to share.* What a contrast with the woman who told me that she turns to her childhood friend for support these days because she was the other one her dad liked to make out with.

MEN AS GODFATHERS

In various sacramental traditions, the role of the godfather is a very special one. In Spanish, the word for godfather is "conpadre," or literally

---

[46] Of course I can't remember where I read it by now.

"co-father." Besides the spiritual responsibility to bring up children in the ways of God should the father be absent, co-fathers provided real-life security in a world where illness or war could claim the father's life and leave his child unprotected. Thus fathers saw it as a duty before God to obtain a back-up father who would make a commitment to care for each of his children.

Sadly, we know that many times this simply becomes an honorary tradition with little content. But the idea of a father and co-father agreeing to the mutual care of a child has many spiritual, social, and personal advantages. Not only does this provide a way for single men to participate in fathering, it also births children with the sense of a spiritual family that extends beyond their biological ties.

MEN AS FATHERS AFTER DIVORCE

Single-parent Dads. The first and most obvious result of divorce is the presence of two single parents. In addition to the effort caused by single parenting, there is lots of emotional pain in everyone's life that brings out some hidden problems and drives other problems into hiding.

Under this load, the single-parent father must do his best to impersonate both Mom and Dad as we described them in chapters two and three. While this job is impossible, it must be attempted all the same. Not only does this help avoid further polarization of the parents, but the children need more care during a divorce. Each day children need a mother's attention to what goes into them and a father's care about what comes out of them. This leaves single parents to be both father and mother when they have custody. Since the wise father always finds other fathers for his children, he will need to lean more heavily on their help in order to avoid collapse.

Dad and His Ex-wife. Some have said that the mother is the main interpreter of the father to her children. Through her eyes, they come to view his time at work as an act of love or a way to stay away from his family. Never is the father more vulnerable to this process than after a divorce while separated from his children. Wise mothers interpret the father's actions truthfully, not according to their own moods and fears. Immature parents use their feeling to "adjust" the facts.

The dad who knows himself to be a life-giver will continue caring for his children. He will avoid, as best he can, wasting life and resources in fighting his ex-wife. The major trap for divorcing couples is when they react to each other rather than express who they really are. Hurt and trapped feelings lead men to rejection and avoidance, rather than acting like the father they know themselves to be. Vindictiveness has made more than one father become what his ex-wife said he was, amid shouts of, "Well, if she wants it that way!"

The determination to live according to one's own character should rule in relationship to one's ex-wife. The father must do his best to become the faithful interpreter of his own actions--actions that, while loving, may not always be understandable to children. Infants and young children do everything because it is what they want and like to do. Thus, they will interpret all the parents' actions to mean the same. If Dad or Mom are not with them, it is because the parent does not like to be with them. Parents are always viewed as doing what they like.

To avoid making these childish misunderstandings a permanent part of the child's identity the wise father will give an interpretation of his and his ex-wife's actions that is realistic. These interpretations will need to be made repeatedly until the child is able to understand a world in which people do not always do what they like to do.

In all, the goal is to give life to children so if they cannot have one home in which they grow up loved and wanted, they have two homes in which to grow up loved and wanted.

Dad as Stepfather. Divorces tend to happen because people's ability to love is exceeded by the force of their feelings. In other words, people divorce because their feelings change. The most common explanation given to children about divorce is, "Your parents don't love each other any more." This creates a terrifying world for children, who can then never be sure when love will run out for them as well. In addition, they learn that who one loves is not a matter of the heart but of what one feels. This lesson is clearly applied to the relationship to stepfathers. Since mom did not love Dad, just because he was Dad, neither will child love Step-dad just because he is Step-dad. Stepparents, therefore, often inherit the storm of feelings from the divorce that children now believe must rule life. Their understanding of this rule goes something like this: If I love you fine, but if I don't, then anything goes--all rejection is justified. Most children of divorce are left with an internal rule similar to this. It is the bane of blended families.

There are two ways to bond. The first is through building joy together and the second is by returning to joy from upset. While the joy path to bonding may be barred for some step-dads, the stepfather who knows how to calm and settle distressing feelings by synchronizing his right brain with a child's right brain has a wide open door to bond with upset stepchildren. A mature man with a good "mother core" in his control center can share children's distress and still be glad to be with them. He has found the back door to bonding.

Return to joy bonding is relatively easy when the cause of the distress is outside the family. When the distress was caused by someone the child is bonded to it will be harder to address because the child attachment center (level one) will want to exclude a stranger--like the stepfather. When the stepfather caused the upset it will be harder still to know the path back to joy. Hardest of all when the stepfather is being blamed for the upset but really did nothing. Unfortunately, many upset children will mix an unfair accusation with an upset feeling—a combination that can desynchronize all but the best-trained control centers. A man can only climb what he has trained to climb. While training to climb that mountain is beyond the limits of this book, a good father, his coaches and trainers can usually break the problem down.[47] The good father will soon have his (level-four) creativity back on and find a way back to joy now that he knows what mountain he is climbing.

Stepfathers may experience a slow progression toward becoming full fathers. In other cases, which usually involve younger children, men find themselves as fathers so quickly and completely their heads spin. Men find it quite painful when their father-love is rejected by their new children. The man who has not learned the value of love that suffers will withdraw or become controlling and angry. He ceases to love as a dad and becomes the boss.

The man who knows his feelings, his needs, and what will bring satisfaction will find step-parenting to be a satisfying expression of his ability to give his life when he realizes that he has nothing to prove. He is a dad and his job is finding ways to express the best of himself. If his audience appreciates him, that's fine; if they do not, then his character will shine even brighter for he is still a dad whether anyone appreciates it or not. Children do not make one a dad, they only provide the opportunity to express it.

BAD DADS

At the other extreme is the stepfather who, rather than giving life as a father would, consumes it for his pleasure. His attraction to the children is more likely to become sexual as he has not gone through the process of cleaning dirty diapers, getting spit-up on, staying up nights, cleaning snot

---

[47] Ok, ok! The solution requires both truth and emotional capacity. This situation assaults both the left and right hemisphere functions at the same time. Take the accusation first. Asking God, "Is it true?" as is done by prayer healing methods like TheoPhostic® will clear up the lie and pain in the father's mind. Once the stepfather is healed of the stinging effect of the lie he will be able to synchronize minds with the child. He may need to help the child through the same process, as the child's accusation may well represent an old wound in the child's memory as well. More information on TheoPhostic® can be found at www.theophostic.com.

from a filthy face, or getting a finger up his nose. All these irritating moments of closeness help most fathers develop a non-sexual touch and love for their children.

Because it so upsets us, we may be tempted to ignore perverted forms of life-giving. The man who gives life only to insure his own supply of pleasure is shocking to us, and rightly so. This is the kind of person who inspires children's stories of witches that fatten you up so they can eat you. The most common version of this horror is the man who acts fatherly and then sexually abuses the children he lures into his grasp. When this is done by fathers to their children or step-children, we call it incest. When men fatten up other people's children to eat we call it pedophilia. Whatever name we use, the horror remains because life-giving is not intended as a way to insure the life-giver's supply of pleasure.

Three times in Scripture God tells us, "You shall not boil a kid in its mother's milk." The milk that gives a little animal its life is not to be used to enhance the pleasure of eating it. There is an important life principle at work here that applies to other situations as well. How much more, for instance, are we to keep the natural beauty and sexuality of our children protected from the chance we will use it to enhance our own pleasure! We would be more innocent if we cooked our children and ate them. (Deuteronomy 28:53-54)

But some will say, what about the case where the child is not the biological relative of the man? The story of the good Samaritan is well known because it teaches that a neighbor is anyone we meet. Likewise, any man entrusted with the care of children is a father to them whether he likes to think so or not. He will be judged accordingly, with no reduction of standards. The privilege of giving life brings with it the prohibition of consuming the life we give for our own pleasure. Further, we must take steps to protect all children from predators and pedophiles.

VARIETIES OF FATHERS

Supplementary Fathers. Every child is in need of supplementary fathers. These are fathers who assist the child's main father with training, introduction and protection in the community. Because of their personal uniqueness supplementary fathers can appreciate parts of the child and the world that the father does not know, or lacks opportunity to enjoy.

My sons have benefited from supplementary fathers. Wayne Bishop helped my son Jamie rebuild a carburetor, while Chuck Rose showed Rami through the Gospel of John. There is always a need for supplementary fathers, even in the best homes. We should not be misled into believing that additional fathers are only needed in childhood. It is a life-long need.

174

Stand-in Fathers. Sometimes, due to illness, death, distance, moral breakdown, or abandonment a primary father does not provide even minimum requirements for his children. These children require a partial replacement of their father. One young woman may want a favorite uncle to give her away at her wedding after the death of her father, or a young man might want someone to watch him compete since his father left town with another woman. This stand-in father will take the father's place at significant moments in the child's life, perhaps even send a birthday card or Christmas gift. He is like a foster father or godfather.

Replacement Fathers. Faced with a catastrophic loss of a father through violence, crime, moral delinquency or disaster, some people need a new father. Legal adoption is needed for young children and its spiritual equivalent for adults. It has been my privilege to observe many replacement fathers since almost all my close friends have adopted children--some from India, others from Mexico, even one from Indiana.

There are many different levels at which it is possible to be a father. Consequently, since there is a large demand for good fathers, men are never at a loss for opportunities. Since people need fathers at all ages, and no one with only one father has enough fathers, let us consider a few possibilities for men.

MEN AS FATHERS TO OTHER MEN

Fathers encourage and comfort each other. Derrick, a young father, recently approached another young father and asked him if he felt neglected, too. Derrick's own father had been very controlling and on at least one occasion had an affair in front of his son. Now that Derrick's wife was absorbed with their baby and had been short and cross with him for about a year, he was finding the interest shown by other women alarmingly attractive.

Derrick's friend talked to him about the occasional struggles he felt himself when his wife would say, "The baby comes first." By sharing his feelings and encouraging Derrick to hang in there until he earned the special love of his little daughter, the friend became a supplemental dad. He filled in where Derrick's father's failures had left a gap. He illustrated what a good dad would do. Much more extensive relationships are possible between men but a further discussion of stand-in and replacement fathers must wait for the chapters on man as an elder or grandfather.

Although man's basic nature is fatherly, actual examples of fatherliness are sometimes rare. Fathers in such places find high demands placed on them. A source of life is never ignored for long, whether it is a spring in the desert or a herd of zebras on the Serengeti Plain, someone is bound to notice. Life springs up around such life-giving places, and demand often brings with it competition.

There is rarely a fair distribution of resources. Frequently a few fathers do yeomen's share, while other potential fathers do nothing and suffer the pangs of emptiness. Perhaps the easiest case to see is the man and wife who have no biological children of their own. Men in this state often feel the calling of fatherhood most acutely. Some, who for emotional or economic reasons, decide not to have children feel that the best way to protect their children is not to bring any into this cruel world. As fathers to phantom children, they feel the empty yearning of protecting without the joy of giving life.

Many couples are childless for other reasons. Rather than list possible reasons we will focus on the need for everyone to experience giving life. Like the single fathers, who we will study in the next chapter, these fathers must give life to those who need supplementary, stand-in or replacement fathers. In this way, they help balance the load for other fathers and find fulfillment for themselves.

A father who knows he has life to give will have many opportunities to do so. He must be strong or his life will be stolen before he can give it away. He must know who he is or he will be shaped into whatever pleases the consumers around him. Life-giving is the main event in men's lives. It is good to be a father, not in contrast with being a mother, but just because being what God made one to be is splendidly good. In the next chapter we will see how men who have not become fathers biologically can give life.

Chapter Eleven
Single and Childless Men as Spiritual Fathers

He threw the top into the air and caught it effortlessly on its own string then transferred it to his hand and just as quickly to Rami's head where it spun to everyone's delight. Jim Schreiber had been spinning tops for years. Mr. Schreiber collected tops. He had large tops, small tops, singing tops, upside-down tops and every conceivable shape, weight and style of tops. He would do tricks with them spinning them in the most imaginative ways and unexpected places. He was good at it, too, because I never saw him miss.

Mr. Schreiber smiled, laughed, and talked to strangers as if he had always known them. There was always a little crowd around him. Boys and girls of all ages, their parents and grandparents watched and listened as he told stories, taught values, shared his faith and always gave top lessons. Rami was giggling because the top on his head tickled as the top spun.

Mr. Schreiber loved people. He was probably the sort of person anyone would think of as a father but the Schreibers had no children. Mr. Schreiber kept bees and produced his own honey. I think his wife Jemimah baked the bread she served. Mr. Schreiber taught hundreds of children to put honey on the bread first and butter second. "It keeps the honey in!" he would say. Hundreds of satisfied little boys and girls agreed.

Mr. Schreiber loved to fish and take others fishing. Almost every day he had someone who had never fished before in his boatload of people. His way to catch fish was simple. Mr. Schreiber trolled up and down the lake with long bamboo poles for each guest until some northern pike would hit the lure. "Let's bamboozle them," he would always joke as he handed out the poles. All the while he talked, guided, taught about the lake, the fish, the birds, the weather, and how to enjoy the experience.

Back on shore, Mr. Schreiber taught his guests to filet the fish, that is to say, they watched and he talked. In about thirty seconds per fish, supper was on its way. There was always bread, butter, and honey on the table.

I met Mr. Schreiber because he and my dad worked at the same school. We had just moved to Northern Minnesota that summer and I knew no one. After growing up in the Andes Mountains of South America, Minnesota was a strange land where only the drone of mosquitoes seemed familiar. Culture shock, my gangly teenage body and thriving acne did nothing for my social confidence. That summer Mr. Schreiber taught me to fish, but he did more than that. He taught me how to care for the poles, maintain an outboard motor, balance a load of passengers in a boat, watch the weather, give people a safe ride, keep the lines from getting tangled, take fish off the hook, and help women and children feel comfortable fishing.

One beautiful summer day he said to me, "Jim, I'm mighty busy today and there is a group here that would like to go fishing. Would you mind to show them around the lake for me? You know where the lifejackets are."

After that, he met people, invited them fishing, bought gas for the boat and I took them out on the lake. Because Mr. Schreiber liked people and people liked him there was always a group waiting for me to take them out any day the weather permitted. Mr. Schreiber's fatherly interest in me gave me one of the best summers of my life.

Sometimes I filleted the fish when we got back. That took about me two minutes per fish with no talking. Usually Mr. Schreiber made the fish fly into the pan in seconds amid stories and cheers. There was always fresh bread and honey from his bees. He seemed to take endless pleasure in life and knew so many stories that I rarely heard the same one twice all summer.

Mr. Schreiber helped me find a place in a world of people and the world of nature. With each new boatload, he assured us all that I had something of value to give and that we were all worth getting to know. Mr. Schreiber made me popular. He gave me a place and a skill, made me feel indispensable, all because he saw something in me.

It is no surprise that I took my boys to see him when we visited the North Country. Mr. Schreiber was too old to take kids fishing anymore but he could still toss a top fifteen feet in the air and catch it on a string. It was a rainy day and fifteen or so children were listening to his stories and watching top tricks in his cabin. My restless four-year-old Rami was captivated.

The Screibers had no kids I am told but Rami took an interest in tops when he was about 10 years old. He found them hard to manage so he added yo-yos. Rami collected many different kinds and liked to do tricks with them during the camping trips we took each summer. The whir something on a string would meet the hum of the mosquito again and again. To this day, I always have a little honey in the cupboard and put the butter over honey on fresh bread. Some would say the Schreibers had no kids but I'm not so sure.

CHILDLESS COUPLES

The goal for all men is fatherhood. Unlike many women, most men who want to raise a family manage to get married. Their need for children goes unmet only when they are unable to have children of their own for some reason. All of us know a couple in that condition. While people often assume that only the women would like children, it is not hard to find couples where the men are just as sad as their wives. In time they may solve the problem

178

through medical means like my dentist did, through a civil adoption or by becoming fatherly to many children as Mr. Schreiber did.

Men are meant to be dads. Some of my best examples for this chapter eventually married or had children of their own. For a period of time, when they did not know if they would have their own children, they gave themselves to other people's children.

Gary and Susan had no children when we met them. Our boys were pre-school age at the time. Anytime we needed childcare or went out of town, Gary and Susan asked to keep the boys. Gary loved our children and was soon like an uncle to them. We listed Gary and Susan in our will as the ones we wanted to have raise our boys if we died. Eventually, Gary and Susan moved to Texas and had children of their own. More than a quarter of a century later we are still in touch every week.

Dan Struble, who we met in Chapter Five, was a father to many young sailors wherever he was stationed. Long before he had kids of his own his quarters became a refuge for young men away from their families. While on duty in Afghanistan after the September 11th attacks demolished the area of the Pentagon where he was periodically assigned, Dan again took young sailors and soldiers under his wing. Dan liked children, too. He has never been able to pass by children without taking an interest in them. Dan now has two of his own. While on that tour he corresponded with grade school classes by e-mail from the war zone. It is obvious now that Dan has a father's heart but it appeared long before he had children of his own.

SINGLE MEN AS FATHERS

We will look at the many single men who are already biological fathers later in this chapter but first let us look at mature single men. Mature men find something pulling them toward children and something pushing them to be the source of life. Single men have something of great value to give to children. Some will recognize it for what it is, the call to be a father. Because all bonds are real for children and adults as well there is no room for "playing dad." Since young men are not attempting to steal babies but to express the father within themselves, these relationships become part of the extended family or spiritual community and supplement or stand-in for other fathers. Under the guidance of elders this arrangement can be very beneficial.

When these opportunities to be a father come from the spiritual community they often include opportunities to help with the spiritual as well as physical and emotional development of a child. We will examine these opportunities to become a spiritual father in the next few chapters. While young men are often thinking of starting a natural family, it is not too soon for them to begin building a spiritual family either. For some men, spiritual children will be all they have.

Raising Infants There are many places for single men to experience fatherhood. The hardest opportunities for single men to find are in relationship to infants. Few opportunities are afforded, except within the extended family context, unless a single man is dating a woman with children. Giving life to infants must come from one's heart because babies only form real bonds. Consequently a man who bonds only builds toward permanence. When bonding with an infant he never bonds in ways he knows he may not fulfill, like swooping in to be boyfriend/father just to leave in three months when she doesn't work out.

Single men find opportunities to become spiritual fathers to babies in their extended family. This is the most natural place to experience the long-term commitment of fatherhood. Nieces, nephews, and younger cousins all provide opportunities for single men to hold babies. With parents and grandparents around the young man will also learn a great deal to improve his range of fatherly expression. It is a good time to put more father stories in his control center. Good close friends also will share their babies--particularly with godfathers. These relationships can be maintained and grow over the years and serve to supplement the baby's father needs.

Parents should be warned not to share their children with fathers or mothers who live and act alone, trouble will always come of it. By living alone I do not mean people who live by themselves in their own house or apartment, but those who practice solitary parenting, whether they live with others or not. Spiritual fathers and elders will help parents protect their children by teaching these principles. As with biological fathers, spiritual fathers also seek more fathers for their children. *An isolated father is always in trouble* and single fathers should not think that they have been granted an exemption to this rule. Be part of a family group.

Steve came from a family with strong family values. He began dating a young lady with an infant son. Although dating a divorced woman with a child had not been his life's plan, Steve slowly built a relationship with her and the baby. He took pains not to get in the way of her family relationships or obligations and actually helped her live her daily life more successfully by sharing her difficulties with her. They took a full year slowly getting acquainted before they began to consider marriage. Because Steve did not live or date in isolation he had built a wide variety of mutual relationships with her family, his family and even the ex-husband's family by the end of the first year. Steve's life was rich and full when they passed the point of no return and he proposed. He had been a good single father and gained the respect of three families, one fine lady and a happy baby.

Raising Children All fathers are life-givers. A single father should express the life that lies within himself whether it is expressed through cooking, hiking, art, music, sports, working, exploring, or talking. This is the life he has to offer to children. The weaned child is beginning to explore the world and seek satisfaction. He needs the life that the single man wants to give. It is a simple matter to share what one loves with children by including them in activities that fit their age.

All of this fits well with the father's task with children. Father introduces his child to the community and teaches satisfaction. Dad must rely on his own knowledge of satisfaction but the final test is always the child's own experience.

Becoming a father to weaned children is far easier for most single men. In addition to the possibilities provided by his extended family, the spiritual father may seek children within organizations in his community. Not only are there children's clubs, Sunday Schools, and group sports, but many single men find a spot to be fathers in junior high ministries. Junior high is the time that many children experience their first conscious rejection by their fathers. Fathers with badly trained control centers and who lack the help of elders in their parenting often react to their junior high children by rejecting their independence at a time when children are still very concerned about their parent's attention. In many churches, camps and activity centers this parent gap is filled by fatherly single men.

Sports are another place where single fathers congregate. Older brothers, single uncles, and occasional sports enthusiasts become supplemental fathers to the young players. Most single fathers stay at the supplemental father stage. Occasionally an uncle will become a stand-in father for his nephews and nieces, particularly following a divorce or the father's death.

Raising Young Adults Single men have a great opportunity to be spiritual fathers when boys go through their rite of passage into manhood like the men in Dan's church did by surrounding each boy, teaching him about life and making a commitment to follow up their teaching with opportunities to practice. Single fathers have as much to teach boys about history and manhood as married fathers do. Single fathers often have more time available and so their contribution can be greater. If a group of spiritual fathers took on the rites of passage for the boys of their community they would have enough sons to last the rest of their lives.

Fathers are still needed when children become adults. Young men and women often need someone to help them when conflicts escalate excessively at home. Occasionally, a single man will become a replacement father through spiritual adoption or foster parenting. One pastor I know, although he never married, took in a boy and a girl who were abandoned on the street as teenagers. They lived with him until they were adults. He paid for the girl's wedding, and helped the boy buy a car. He became their spiritual father for life.

George is a divorced contractor in his late fifties. George works hard and plays hard and tries to live a life of integrity. That is not what one expects in a contractor. Ten years ago George took in two men in their twenties whose lives were a mess. They had neither the skills nor the energy to manage their lives successfully. Living with George and working in his company has helped one get off drugs. Both have learned trades, skills, and money and time management. They have learned to live with other people and how to work as well as play. George has become the father that neither man ever had.

SINGLE MALE ATTACHMENT PROBLEMS

Most single fathers are the kind with bonding problems who have children but never marry. I don't mean to put the whole load on men either because if women had developed their maturity as well there would not be so many women who get pregnant. But this book is all about men so let's have a go at the single men who leave babies behind. Groups like the National Center for Fathering are working with young unmarried fathers teaching them to care for their children. Their program is excellent. I think it is nearly impossible to overestimate the benefit we obtain as a society when men learn to have peace with their attachment centers and relationships with their children.

Solving this male attachment problem through education is impossible. Education strongly favors the left hemisphere and information transfer. Information does not train our brain's right hemispheric control center. Securely bonded relationships with those who love us and face-to-face emotional relationships are needed to train the brain to bond. Even then, we can only learn something if the other person has a better trained "mother core" in their brain's control center (level three). Schools are not designed for that kind of training—only parents are. Education can only get us far enough to realize we need training, and that is worth a lot!

Solving this male attachment problem through therapy is impossible and impractical. First, where would we get enough therapists? Probably three quarters of the men in the world need some kind of help. How would you get the gangsters, addicts, underemployed, uneducated and disconnected from their feelings to go for therapy? Who would pay for it?

In spite of its many liabilities, the only vehicle that could possibly correct this problem is the family and regrettably it is the cause of the trouble. There are, however, three forms of family: natural, social and spiritual. Of these three forms, only the natural and spiritual have had any success at achieving any large-scale healthy attachments. Social families are often built around economics or ideologies and rarely make it even one generation unless they include the two other forms of family. We will dismiss the social family from our discussion.

I am completely in favor of improving natural family bonds in every way possible and believe that for repair and prevention there is no better place to start. By using the resources of the extended family like grandparents, aunts and uncles to develop joy we can improve future generations. By using extended family financial resources to be sure no mother goes back to work until her baby is at least one and preferably four, we can greatly improve the quality of babies' control centers.

The problem with natural family is that it leaves those lives whose natural families have been lost, left behind, decimated or damaged still untouched. When mother core damage has been passed from generation to generation of unhappy women through slavery, oppression, drugs, alcohol abuse, war and cultural perversity how are we to expect these families to recover? The only available answer large enough to stand a chance is the spiritual family.

SPIRITUAL FAMILY

Not all religions have a concept of spiritual family. Some religions have as their objective the opposite concept—the removal of all attachments. Of those religions that do have a spiritual family, many do not separate the natural and spiritual family. For them, the spiritual family is comprised of dead biological ancestors or they believe the natural family passes on the divine family line and its characteristics. For some religions, the spiritual family is a relationship between the gods. Many Western cults have both a natural and spiritual family but promote the total replacement of all natural family ties with spiritual family relationships, an arrangement that with remarkable frequency means the cult leader has sexual access to all the members. Another version of cult activity uses spiritual family as a justification for polygamy. So you see, spiritual family is not without its dangers.

When spiritual family is linked to ideology it is one of the worst of all conceivable woes. This hybrid sponsors religious wars to eliminate all who are not one of the chosen people or religion. Liberal devils are fair game to kill. When spiritual family is linked to global values like "one world one family" it just as often oppresses those who would have more stringent limits on their spiritual family. Conservatives can be herded into camps to "retrain." A therapeutic spiritual family with the intent of making better bonds would fare no better. This is a perversion of bonds. Bonds are neurologically meant for joy and the return to joy, not ideology. Joy is being glad to be with you because we belong and not because I want to get some result from you. Bonds need joy just as much when there are results as when there are not. Ideology demands results.

One of the bits of genius in the teachings of Jesus is his unusual definition of spiritual family.[48] In Jesus' view, the immediate presence of God in all aspects of human life synchronizes all of existence in a joyful unity for those who will hear and see it. The immediate and long-term results of this synchronization are the formation of loving family bonds with God and among those who participated in the harmony. I see it this way, surpassing our normal view of families is a spiritual reality in which we are all connected. Moving into this realm creates possibilities we would not have otherwise.

If spiritual family is to offer any hope for our practical problem of helping men bond, then it must be a family of joy created by spiritual adoption. Adoption can be defined as, "joyfully receiving as one's own that which is not one's by nature." Such a spiritual family not only provides a means of building bonds with those who have none, but for repairing insecure attachments outside normal kinship limits—including family bonds for single men. In that context, what does it mean to be a spiritual father? It means seeing the human family as God's family and allowing God's Spirit to connect us with those who need a heart like ours. These spiritual connections can be fleeting chances to practice our fatherliness or become life-changing father-and-child bonds.

A father is one who helps his children find their true identity, in spite of cultural distortions and injuries. As spiritual beings, men have something of great value to give because God creates in them the ability to see other people as they were meant to be. There is nothing about getting married or starting a pregnancy that automatically makes a man better able to see others with the eyes of God, so single men can practice spiritual fathering as easily as married men can.

SPIRITUAL VISION

It was the prayer of my teenage years that God would let me see Jesus in others. When I looked at a girl and said, "Now, where do I see Jesus in her?" it had an influence on how I treated her. To this day, seeing Jesus in a boy changes my attitude toward him. My teenage prayer was the beginning of this gift. God began giving me the eyes of Heaven through which people appeared

---

[48] For more details and references to Jesus' teachings on spiritual family see *Bringing the Life Model to Life* by Koepcke, Keopcke, Poole and Wilder, available through C.A.R.E. Packaging at CAREpkg@triton.net or www.care1.org.

quite uncommon. The driver who gave me the finger and honked his horn became blind and small rather than large and threatening. Girls without bras became lonely and needy instead of being the keepers of the great treasure I couldn't have. Seeing people as God would see them helped me act according to a greater reality. I now had a gift to give anyone who would receive it, for really seeing into someone's heart is perhaps the greatest gift a man can give. Fathers give this gift when they help children to see themselves correctly.

The same thing is true for every man. Every man was created as a blessing. It is the only reason why God would have created him. He was not interested in creating his people as curses, but as blessings. That is what he put in your father before you and now in you. Your father may not have followed God's design, but the father within every man is meant as a blessing to his children.

When we see the image of God in others, we begin giving life to them. The desire to do so comes from the father's heart in each man and the mother's heart in each woman. Single men and married men without children are capable of this type of life-giving and will be unfulfilled without it.

SPIRITUAL ADOPTION

All fathers are fatherly because it is their nature. When fatherhood comes from the heart, it is impossible to stop "acting like" a father, but when fatherhood is a role, "fatherly" actions and attitudes will come and go. Fatherhood is a stage of life, a complete identity, and not a role to play. Role-play is for boys.

Spiritual adoption is not a role and it is not just acting fatherly. Spiritual adoption is a permanent, real relationship--a spiritual connection. As a spiritual bond, created by God, it is much more than becoming a father figure. Spiritual fathers report that spiritual adoption felt like something that happened to them not something they did. These fathers knew the connection in their hearts long before they put it into words. A stranger had become their child.

The apostle Paul is an example of a single man who became a spiritual father. His sons included Timothy, Titus, and Onesimus. We still read some of the letters he wrote to them. Obviously, he was an involved and loving father.

One word of caution about spiritual adoptions--they are divine connections. People who promise to be fathers because they feel compassion for needy souls usually crumble under the immense need. They break many hearts. I cannot tell you how many people have been crushed because someone, in a moment of emotion, said, "I'll be your Dad (or Mom,)" thinking of it as a way to help. Helping is a product of child maturity not father maturity. Life giving without receiving in return is for fathers--whether it helps or not. Breaking a spiritual bond is abandonment, betrayal and desertion just like breaking a natural father bond, so don't do it!

FATHERS NEED TO PROTECT, SERVE AND ENJOY

God established men as protectors and nurturers of his garden. That is what it means to be human not just male. Men protect and make things grow. That is why it is good news to have men around. This is the basis of fatherhood. Yet if the man's own history has not been redeemed by God, he will have nothing redeemable to offer to others. Without knowing our own redemption, we cannot see others through the eyes of heaven and so bring them life. When we only see garbage in others, we will not know who they were created to be. For this reason the journey to synchronization with God and participation in a spiritual family begins with the acknowledgement that we have malfunctioned and not always acted like ourselves. We have lost sight of our true identities. We no longer bond, return to joy or participate fully in our spiritual family as we should. We see and admit that our malfunctions have hurt others as well as ourselves and we want them restored as well. None who pass this way will fail to meet God.

Mature men, with the eyes of heaven and redeemed histories, are ready to be fathers. This life-giving strength is to be given away, whether it is to our extended families or our spiritual families. The man who offers such gifts to others is a father whether he is married, has children, or is single.

A spiritual father sees the world as his home to protect, serve and enjoy. He follows his heart to the places that mean the most to him. Because he was first a man, he can contribute to other men's homes in ways that satisfy everyone. He is a father-at-large looking for ways to leave his blessings and they are not hard to find.

UNIQUE GIFTS FROM SINGLE FATHERS

A case can certainly be made that, if one wishes to be a father, it is better to remain single and celibate. Marriages are demanding of time, energy, and resources. First Corinthians chapter seven contains a classic and controversial discussion on this topic that has led many to conclude that Paul was against marriage. In this passage, Paul says that it is better not to marry unless sexual passions get too strong. Many have concluded that Paul thought Christians should stay single, if they can.

This understanding of the passage is based on reading verse 26, which speaks of "a time of stress like the present," and verse 29, which says, "the time we live in will not last long," as referring to the ongoing life of the

186

church. I believe the passage refers to times of extreme stress. Paul was writing to a church under violent, horrifying persecution.

The political context in Colombia when I grew up was exceedingly violent. I lived through times of persecution. Christians were driven from their homes in the middle of the night and forced to escape with their wives and children. In that context, I find Paul's description to be true. When fleeing for his life, a married man is not thinking of the Lord's children, he is thinking about his wife and kids and how to find food and shelter for them. It is, as Paul describes, a bad time to marry and raise a family. Staying single does save grief and pain, if one can handle it, until the brief time of trouble is over. Those who have seen their children tortured or starved to death will witness the truth of this statement.

The single person, on the other hand, can and does devote time to the care of others during times of deep distress. In that sense, the single person can be a supplemental, stand-in, or replacement father, a brother or a friend to more people than a married man can. Pastors and missionaries who plan to go into high-stress locations should listen to Paul's excellent instruction and stay out if they are married with children. In any case, Paul is clear that the single person can care for more children than the married person if he or she is devoted to Christ.

During the 1992 Los Angeles riots I concerned myself with my house and wife and kids. Eileen, my unmarried spiritual daughter, taught in South Central Los Angeles where the rioting was the worst. She concerned herself with the thirty children in her class, plus many children from previous classes. She did what she could to insure their safety and comfort. When her student Ezekiel was shot a few years later, she visited him in the hospital every day and became a spiritual mother to him. This is what Paul was talking about in First Corinthians chapter seven.

Under normal conditions, marriages form the most desirable way of having children because they are the most bonded, uniform and disciplined way to protect, serve and enjoy a home. The non-stop effort required by a lifetime commitment to one's child produces character that cannot be duplicated by any other method. The parent who sustains a child throughout life develops a breadth of love that covers all things. The single person who, in times of severe stress, loves many children and endures the deaths of many children, builds a depth of love that cannot be duplicated either. Both of these loves are strong because they flow from the parent's life itself—life that in turn flows from God.

We should not go on, however, to assume that single men are only meant to parent children in times of stress. True, they are most needed at such times, but the need for single men as fathers goes far beyond stressful periods in history to stressful times in everyday life. Every child needs more dads.

Naturally, if the child has no father, his or her need will be greater, but it is not necessary to find an extremely needy child in order to experience fatherhood.

BECOMING A GOOD FATHER

To fully experience fatherhood, the father (natural or spiritual) must take time to consider what he is doing. Fathers take time to think about being fathers. In each situation, fathers ask their hearts, "What would a father do?" The spiritual father may be misled into thinking that his lack of ideas on how to be a father comes from his lack of biological children, but such is not the case. Even with biological children, fathers learn to activate their father's heart by asking themselves, their friends, family and elders, "What would a father do now?"

After some planning, the father must test each idea to see if it works. The efforts generated by careful planning are then judged to see if they are satisfying, and so each new attempt is refined. This discipline brings out more of the father's best.

Many men find that their first answer to the question, "what would a father do?" involves giving punishment. After all, many people's conscious thoughts about fathers have never been stretched beyond spanking, grounding, growling or shouting. By this point in the book, we do not need to combat those notions, but rather encourage each fledgling father, or spiritual father, to seek the things that make him feel he is giving life to children in his care.

One of my first spiritual fathering experiences was as a camp counselor. Teamed with another young single man, we took on the little "rowdies" in a daily challenge of who would tire the other out first. Believing ourselves to be strong and firm counselors, we were proud of our cabin. We thought of ourselves more as camp counselors than as spiritual fathers at the time. Pleased with our management of the boys, we would brag about our cabin to the other counselors.

Several of the women counselors insisted that the boys were afraid of us. We did not believe it. "Ask them," said the women, so we did. The boys reported that they were afraid which made us rethink our whole approach. This kind of learning was possible only by living in a spiritual community. All growing fathers will combine what they learn from their community with the internal test of satisfaction to insure that they are giving life.

I do not believe that in practice there should be a separation of married fathers and spiritual fathers. What is needed by both types of fathers is the strength and experience of their elders, the truly *grand fathers* of the community. It is grandfathers who help men become fathers, just as fathers help boys become men. So let us now move on to the final metamorphosis.

THE FIFTH
METAMORPHOSIS

*

GRANDFATHER

*

THE ELDER STAGE

GRANDFATHER
The Elder Stage

IDEAL AGE
Youngest child is now an adult

NEEDS
•A community to call his own
•Recognition by his community
•A proper place in the community structure
•To be valued and defended by his community

•

TASKS
•Hospitality
•Giving life to the "familyless"
•Raising and maturing his community
•Building and maintaining the community identity
•Acting like himself in the midst of difficulty
•Enjoying what God put in each and every one
•Living transparently and spontaneously
•Building and rebuilding trust

•

Chapter Twelve
Becoming an Elder

We are heirs to social tapestries woven and sustained by elders--their stories quietly lived out around us. These elders not only look after their own affairs but they keep watch over the results achieved by others. Elders take responsibility for the impact left by their business associates, families and communities. Elders guard strangers from being harmed by the businesses, churches and associations they manage.

I am convinced that the lack of people with earned elder maturity has given us politicians instead of statesmen in government, child molesters instead of priests in the church, agenda pushers instead of judges in the courts, massive waste and folly instead of education in the school system and dishonest accounting instead of value in business. I dare say that a lack of elders (with earned maturity) in business has done more to torpedo the US economy than bin Laden did with his terrorism. Monica, Enron, Arthur Andersen, Jim Bakker and Worldcom would not have been brought to us by elders.

"I don't feel too well," Gary said staring out the windshield of his new SUV.

"Like you want to heave?" I asked. He nodded.

"I haven't gotten enough sleep for three nights. I get home from rehearsals about midnight and as soon as I'm asleep the phone rings. Holly is having contractions and Brian is about to take her back to the hospital again. It has happened the last three nights. If she can hold the baby another three weeks his lungs will be formed enough that he can be born safely. I'm sorry I was late," he was searching for his thermos now.

Each Saturday at 6 AM Gary and I meet to pray. Gary brings the coffee. Thinking Gary was suffering from stress rather than illness or dehydration, I suggested we walk up the hill for some exercise.

Mother Theresa had found Holly as a baby in India. When she was almost three Gary became her dad. Now he was considering being her birth coach when Holly had her first child. This would be Gary's first grandchild. He was excited, but becoming a grandfather was bringing up issues ranging from his ex-wife to his job.

I was no stranger to grandfather complications in my life, either. My son and his wife separated just after our first grandson was born. I went from bliss to anguish in under two weeks. Now, almost six grandchildren later, life's complications have not disappeared. By the time Gary poured the coffee, we had prayed over all our children and situations they faced. We wanted so badly to be in the middle of life but kept ending up on the sidelines.

"Shelley finished her newsletter," he said. Seeing my quizzical look he added, "Didn't I tell you about Shelley?"

"You hit a blank file there."

"She is sort of my spiritual daughter. I met her in Israel when she had just finished serving her time in the IDF. She was good friends with the daughter of my friends, the Kendalls. Her father left the family about the time Shelley was 11 years old. Her mother took her and her two sisters to Israel and they made a*lyah*. Just before I met her, Shelley's mother, her pregnant sister and her nephew were killed in an accident. That left Shelley with only distant family so the Kendalls told her she would always have a place with them. I met her in the midst of that trauma. She is the one who helped me get my cell-phone."

"Oh, yes!" I interrupted. "She was the one with you at the bus stop where the suicide bomber struck." Gary nodded and went on to tell how Shelley had gotten into his heart, the remarkable things she did and how she was growing.

While he talked, I thought about a recent conversation with David Miranda at a fourth of July party. After introducing his teenage sons he pointed to a young couple and said, "She is sort of my God-daughter. When her father was dying I went to visit him in the hospital. I told him, 'Your daughter will never be alone or lack for a father. I'll take care of her.' I wasn't planning to say it but the words jumped out of my mouth. After he died I checked on her and looked over her boyfriends." Officer Miranda smiled broadly at the thought and told me stories. "One day she surprised me by asking if I would walk her down the aisle. It was on the way down the aisle that I realized I had kept my promise."

Gary checked the signal on his cell phone. "You never know when... More coffee?"

When I got home there was a call from Dr. Peters. Dr. Peters was an older and experienced pastor who I had met briefly several years before. Recently he had begun calling about once a week to talk about being a spiritual father. Dr. Peters had biological daughters, a legally adopted daughter and spiritually adopted daughters. He, like I, understood spiritual adoption as God bringing someone into our lives who needed additional, remedial or replacement father bonds.

The essential part of *spiritual adoption* is that God brings people together. Spiritual adoption is not and cannot be something we arrange nor something we do alone. Spiritual family is central to the message Jesus proclaimed. Spiritual parents-child relationships are a salient theme in the lives of His followers like St. Paul.

Among our spiritual daughters, Dr. Peters and I each had one or more who were sexually abused by their fathers or family. These women were adults by the time we met them. Some were married, divorced and others single. Dr. Peters started calling me after he had taken some heat about bonding with a hurt girl in an adult body. I sent him copies of the early versions of this manuscript to study so we could discuss his situation. Some of his colleagues said spiritual adoption wasn't possible, some said it wasn't wise, some said it wasn't Christian, some said it wasn't moral and most thought it wasn't real. In short, his community did not trust him or that his adoptive bond was from God. I've been through the same scene myself and know several older men who can tell similar stories.

Dr. Peters and I talked awhile about how to quiet girls with our love. We reviewed the intense intimacy of a spiritually bonded relationship and discussed the hostility that spiritual adoption draws from the community— even from some in the church. People, particularly those with child maturity, cannot accept that elders could have a non-sexual bond with a hurt child in an adult body.[49] I reminded him that an elder needs to take criticism without fear and build trust in his community. He needed to be an elder to his community as much as to his daughter. Elders need their community in order to survive.

As Dr. Peters and I talked, I looked around at my house. I bought the place from Walter Gilbert, a schoolteacher. The house itself was designed in part by his daughter. Walter was a teacher in everything he did so he involved his children in planning the building. I was sitting at the back of the house in what Walter called his "mother-in-law apartment." Here many people, beginning with his mother-in-law, found shelter. When he retired, Walter took his elder status seriously and helped his pastor with most of those who came to the church for help, drove for those without cars and fed those without food. Walter also helped those who were not from his church. The neighbor in back bought his plot of land from Walter when he arrived in the United States fleeing the Holocaust and war in his homeland. Until his death, this neighbor told us stories about the kindness and fairness of "Mr. Valter."

I had hardly hung up when Eileen, my spiritual daughter, called. She had just heard some good news. For several years we had been following Lumpery's work with the boy warriors of Sierra Leone and refugees in the Gambia. A few months ago Lumpery died suddenly, leaving

---

[49] Children, as you may recall, can take care of only one person at a time. Someone with child maturity simply can't grasp how you can love and bond without it being an exclusive romantic love. If they have not mastered quieting their own feelings, they can't imagine closeness that does not "turn you on."

a wife who was quite weak from sickle cell anemia and their children (his own and some they had rescued) without financial support. Eileen had sent money to help Berta but more than a month passed with no word that the funds had made it there safely.

"Berta's sister just called to say the money got there! I didn't think they would call but I was getting worried that it got lost." This answer to prayer made us both feel much better.

"Bye, Princess!" I blew her a kiss over the phone and got to work writing. It was almost 10 AM. Where does the time go?

WHAT IS AN ELDER?

The elder stage is the first metamorphosis that requires an explanation. We readily understand infants, children, adults and parents because we see them so often. Elder is a word with particular meanings for some groups; and yet, because it describes the outcome of the fifth transformation more closely than any other word available, we will use the term "elder" rather than grandfather, mentor, or "old goat."[50] An elder, as we will define the term, is a parent who has raised children to be adult men and women and is ready to be a father to others outside his immediate family. Age does not make an elder, biological grandchildren do not make an elder, having children outside your own home does not make an elder. It is the readiness to treat others in your community as you have treated your own family that makes you an elder.

There is no shortcut to maturity. Becoming an elder requires a high degree of mastery of each one of the preceding stages. The elder can meet his own baby, boy, man, and father needs with a wealth of goodness to spare. In order to reach the elder stage, all of the elder's children will need to be men or women—that is to say, his youngest is now over twelve years old. Only then can a man consider becoming an elder. The qualification process is arduous and is not for everyone. The damage done to one's own children and to the church and community by becoming an elder too soon is far too extensive for us to overlook as we will see in Chapter Twenty.

---

[50] In many Christian and pseudo-Christian traditions *Elder* refers to a particular church office. Most protestant denominations use elder to refer to a church board member. These individuals are usually elected to run the church or oversee operations. The Nazarene Church uses elder to refer to its ordained clergy. The Latter Day Saints (Mormons) employ the term for their missionaries and leaders, many still in their teenage years. This theological use of the term elder comes from scriptures like 1Timothy and Titus that contain descriptions of elders. Timothy, it appears was not himself an elder although he was a church leader. In one passage he is instructed to correct elders as he would a father.

Fathers become elders by repeatedly going through the first four stages of life in synchronization with each child they raise. This equips an elder with refined and mature knowledge of his needs, feelings, and sources of satisfaction. An elder has followed the path to maturity many times, each time adding skills, facing new challenges and incorporating elements missing in his own childhood. As each of his children grew up, an elder practiced the maturity tasks over and over. For example, he will have introduced each child into the community and helped each child explore and understand his or her world. He will have found elders to serve as supplemental fathers for his own children and learned from other fathers how to teach each child his or her place in the family history. He will have trained his adult children to treat others fairly and drive a hard yet fair bargain that satisfies both people. This kind of experience allows the man approaching the status of elder to understand the needs and feelings of many people within his community. He will have studied how to satisfy them all at once—though usually without success. He will also be aware of the dangers his community contains since he has worked for years to protect his children and their efforts.

The apostle Paul uses many of these characteristics in his description of elders to his spiritual sons Timothy and Titus (I Timothy 3:1-7; Titus 1:6-9). An elder, Paul tells them, should have his home, his beliefs, and himself in good order. At home, an elder should have been married only once and to only one wife if he wanted to develop elder maturity. He must be content to stay with his one wife[51] for no one will trust a man with women if he is shopping for another wife. His children must be orderly or he will be too distracted to help a community. His home should overflow with hospitality, such that his ties to his community are strong and intact and his reputation is a good one. The elder's own life should be orderly. He cannot be violent, greedy, an alcoholic, envious, self-centered, or easily angered—which are all signs of a badly trained control center. Instead he must be a good teacher, just, holy, levelheaded, faithful, and a friend of good. In his doctrine, the elder must know God and God's view of people. He faithfully sees others through the eyes of heaven. Thus, he is able to exercise a spiritual fatherhood for those in his care.

It is apparent from even a cursory examination of Paul's list of characteristics, that an elder is: at home with his needs and feelings, able to satisfy himself and others, well practiced in fairness, an experienced father, one who gives love and one who suffers without growing angry or resentful. Yet, because few have trained to become elders, most applicants reach this

---

[51] Polygamy was a potential form of marriage in that culture but inappropriate for elders.

stage feeling woefully inadequate and quite aware of their own shortcomings. As with all stages, there are no perfect elders. Everyone has remedial work to do.

The rewards for elders are great. Elders are rewarded with many children. The better an elder he is, the more children he will receive. Elders often receive a double blessing for their endurance since they father both biological and spiritual children.

ELDERS AND CULTURES

It is understood in many societies that ruling is left to elders. These elders maintain the history and culture of their people. In India men are expected to reach a point in their life where their concerns expand beyond their own house to include their village. The home is the training ground for the elder who, having practiced on those born to him, can now be trusted with the lives of those he did not engender. In a traditional society elders rule, guard, teach, and oversee. In this way they are fathers to their people, their city, strangers, and orphans.

Octavio Paz said of the macho man, "He is not of our city." The macho ruler is the antithesis of the elder because he measures his masculinity by death and consumption, not by preserving and giving life. When this macho view of life is used by rulers to protect their position and tradition, the results are violent and oppressive as described by Hugh Steven in his book, *They Dared to be Different*. Steven describes the social and spiritual changes that followed the translation of the Bible for the Chamula people of Chiapas Mexico. The Chamula elders had a masculine worldview very similar to that described by Paz. While they saw their community identity as Christian, the Chamulas had a saying, "To deviate is to die." Chamula rulers were the keepers of a tradition that was at times abusive, alcoholic and oppressive. Those who would not drink the sacred alcohol with them and follow their mandates would be killed. These elders had a status and title of elder but their fear-based way of life had not produced elder maturity. Fears do not improve with age.

While cultures can become powerful forces either for or against maturity, we should not assume that Latin culture is the problem. Paz has brilliantly exposed the ways of "machismo" as a cultural insider. His analysis gives us a hint of the diversity within Latin viewpoints. It is not any particular culture that is the issue so much as it is the dominant fears afflicting our group identities. Fears do not improve with culture.

Religious values play a very important part in the development of elders. No culture without religious values will develop elder maturity. Values direct our desires and battle our fears. Even religious values can

196

become interpreted through fears however, taking the vitality from religion. Fears do not improve with religion.

Floriano Ramos Esponda grew up in Chiapas Mexico. His father has earned his elder maturity and Floriano is becoming an elder himself. Floriano's daughters are delightful young women and his wife Lilia is a happy community leader. Surrounded by volcanic social forces, Floriano has warm relationships with his parents, wife, children and neighbors. People from many different churches and countries trust his leadership. He is a resource and source of life.

At any given time, Floriano has 20 to 50 young men he is training to be leaders. Floriano looks after his "Timothys" as he calls the young pastors he is training to become church and community leaders. Taking this name from the loving father-and-son relationship between Saint Paul and his "true son in the faith" Timothy, Floriano carefully equips his "Timothys." For Floriano, part of bringing resources to his community included attracting an international team from "Desarollo Cristiano" to train his young pastors. The team was led by a former test pilot named Randy Whittig from Costa Rica who brought one of his "Timothys" from Argentina.

Chris Shaw started his mornings by ironing his clothes and everyone else's while bemoaning the fact that he had not brought any *yerba maté tea* from Argentina to share with us. It was obvious that he and Randy were delighted to be together. Chris poured life, love and kindness into everyone he met. During his teaching times, Chris vigorously and practically expounded the proper care and training of, you guessed it, Timothys, to the great appreciation and approval of the many leadership couples that Floriano had gathered for the week.

I was in Floriano's parents' home toward the end of that week when word arrived that my mother had died. Warmth, comforting, kindness and sweetness surrounded me in those hours of grief as Floriano, his family and friends shared the loss with me. Chris kindly watched out for my needs. Randy gave me his flight coupons in case I missed any flights. An older man said, "Since your father can't be here I shall be your father," and he held me, cried and kissed my forehead. I have never felt anything like it.

Do a lot of names and places start flying around when we talk about elders? An elder's relational network easily reaches around the world these days and probably always has. The Sunday before I left for Chiapas, I ran into Bob Remington at church in Pasadena. To my casual comment that I would not see him next Sunday because I would be in Chiapas, Bob reached into his case and produced a picture of the Governor of Chiapas along with his phone and e-mail. "Here," he said, "we have been praying for the governor each week. He has a hard job bringing peace to that region." I had just dropped into another elder's sphere of concern. Bob and I had never spoken of Chiapas before but now his network of trust-building relationships was extended to me. Bob was part of a spiritual family.

Let's look at one example of the impact of spiritual family. The Waodani had the most violent culture on the earth in the 1950s. Few Waodani died natural deaths. They came to international infamy when they killed the first five missionaries to reach them in 1956.[52] The Waodani soon began to learn the ways of life from the family members of the very men they had speared to death. As they began to follow God's trail, their culture changed.

Mincaye was a member of the original raiding party that killed the five but he has grown to be an elder. Recently, Mincaye became a spiritual grandfather to the grandchildren of one of the men he helped to kill. In 1995 Steve Saint, son of the murdered Nate Saint, was called back to the tribe by the Waodani elders. The Waodani needed Steve for mutual protection from an outside world Steve understood far better than they did. Together with his wife and three children, Steve moved into the Amazon jungle. The *People Maker* had seen it well that he should come. Mincaye and the children fell in love. They are a giggle to watch. Their relationship is open, joyful, warm, respectful, loving and very full of God. They are a spiritual family.

Tementa, one of the younger Waodani elders, is a pilot. In spite of growing up in the stone-age, Tementa can fly a plane, maintain his own aircraft and even fill cavities in teeth.

"I met Steve in Miami and went flying with Tementa," Gary told me one Saturday morning.

Gary has always wanted to fly and he seemed slightly envious of Tementa. Over some of his special blend of coffee, Gary told me of the concerns Mincaye, Tementa and Steve had for the continued health of the Waodani community. Although they had not been able to put it in words, the Waodani felt increasingly threatened by dependency on outside benevolence. Steve pointed out that if someone brought them meat long enough they would forget how to hunt and their children would never learn to spear. The elders recognized that unless they could balance what they were receiving with what they gave, they would soon lose vitality. We saw it well to pray for them.

In Africa, Celestin Musekura is bringing reconciliation to survivors of violence in Rwanda and Sudan. About a million people were brutally killed in Rwanda including the majority of the men in leadership. The recovery effort has focused upon women. After watching their husbands and families being killed, these women must deal with their own wounds while raising the children from their community who lost their parents. The

---

[52] Previously this tribe was known by the highly derogatory name of *Auca.*

198

average adult woman is raising five or more psychologically traumatized orphans in addition to any of their own children who survived. Some children have not spoken since the day they watched the violent deaths of their parents. Celestin brings a message of forgiveness even though he too lost family.

Elders must look after those with no voice like widows and orphans and find words for the things that no one can say. Celestin, Mincaye, Lumpery, the Kendalls, Bob and Floriano all agree. They are fathers to their communities, bringing resources from long distances if necessary so their people will grow and mature. They build trust between people, teach the ways of life and consider themselves friends of Jesus. Whoever is a friend of Jesus is a friend of theirs. Whoever is an enemy of Jesus needs their blessing even more. Whoever does not know Jesus is much too far from peace and joy for them to ignore. They are part of a spiritual family—a community that transcends time and place.

Mature old men are like prairie grass that lives over one hundred years and has roots twenty-five feet deep. Prairie grass sustains an ecosystem as deep as its roots, grows back after fire and frost and holds its land together. I can, within a mouse click or two from where I'm writing this book, be in touch with Dr. Schore, the Waodani, Israel, Rwanda or Pastor Floriano. This is not remarkable or a sign of my social network (because I'm a reclusive sort of guy.) Instead, these connections flow from knowing elders and fathers like Gary, Mincaye, Bob, Celestin, Walter, Pastor Floriano, Dr. Schore, Dr. Amen and many others. They build trust between people and bring resources to their communities.

I am concerned that we may not be renewing our elder resource. True, a lot of baby-boomers are getting old, but are they becoming elders? Meanwhile elders are quietly passing away leaving a generation obsessed with finding new data. New data soon becomes obsolete. The pages of statistical analysis from my dissertation hardly interest the paper recyclers these days. Yet, we madly pursue the new data, assuming that all old information is now trivial. Our computer mice jump through windows faster and our hard drives hold more data but we are forgetting to back up our working environment—entire networks found only in the minds and bonds of elders.

THE TRANSITION INTO AN ELDER

Many fathers experience their first push toward being an elder when their first child gets married. In addition to becoming involved with a whole new family, fathers must adopt a son-in-law or daughter-in-law. Weddings celebrate this adoption through the custom of changing last names. In-laws become supplemental parents to their new children and clearly feel the demands of elder status.

Fathers who all along have taken an interest in their children's friends, dates, and loves develop an eager anticipation for their new in-law children. In his song "Somewhere In The World,"[53] Wayne Watson tells of his prayers for the little girl that will some day grow up to be the wife of his little boy. In giving away his son, he gains a daughter as well. Watson has been preparing for years for that moment. When Gary and I sit in his SUV and pray, he too frequently blesses and prays for the right wives for his sons. Fathers and elders know that their love has more children as its reward. Gary is getting ready.

Being welcomed into an accepting and loving family is wonderful for brides and grooms. Since the young couple are supposed to be adults themselves, they will take pains to introduce their partners to their families in ways that create goodwill and mutual satisfaction. When parents are not inclined to be elders and exclude new children by seeing them as outsiders, you can expect the pain to last at least a couple of generations.

A second step toward elder status occurs with the arrival of grandchildren. Grandfathers delight in their children's children. The joy grandparents show can drive friends and neighbors nuts with the endless stream of pictures. Grandparenting is the most common expression of elder status. Most children love to visit their grandparents. They find a source of love there that is less prone to anger and more leisurely about time than their busy parents. Grandparents are often the saving grace for first-born grandchildren whose parents are intent on doing things right. Grandparents can take time to appreciate a child's uniqueness and special gifts.

ELDERS AS COMMUNITY FATHERS

Loving one's grandchildren is something we often take for granted and view as an extension of the biological family. We expect that a grandfather will love his grandchildren just because they are his. This raises an obvious point; Grandfather has bonded with a child he did not father. Elders extend family bonds to those they did not father thus forming a community family. Both the well-established and marginal members of his community will benefit from an elder's growing heart.

As an elder's circle of concern and care expands he will begin to care for people around him. On first examination it may appear that these people just happened across his path. He did not seek them out. He had no

---

[53] Somewhere In The World (c) 1985 by Word Music, ASCAP

previous relationship to their lives. But, it has become his nature to see God's story unfolding in the lives around him.

It is not that elders are doing something new. Giving life to others is old behavior for elders except that in earlier stages of life these men had very different understandings of "taking care of your own." Elders take whatever skills and relationships they developed in their homes and apply these skills to the life of their communities. When others will allow it, elders steady the distressed and guide whole groups into a more mature and authentic life. It has taken us eleven chapters to describe all the skills they need so let's focus on just one. Perhaps the most needed skill is remaining oneself under pressure. We can call this skill *suffering well* and it is as essential as it is unpopular.

Acting like oneself in the midst of difficulty brings stability and what Dr. Edwin Friedman called a "non-anxious presence." These obvious signs of a mature control center reveal a brain with practice returning to joy from all kinds of distress. With this capacity an elder can quiet himself and others at the same time—under all kinds of circumstances. He is the person we turn to when things go wrong, when conflicts break out and when hurt feelings swirl around. Even if he is in physical or emotional pain himself, the elder who suffers well can remember what is important. Here is a short list to remember when suffering well:

- I don't abandon when I disengage
- I share other's feelings but still know
  - Who I am
  - Who they are
- I continue to be the same person when provoked or tempted
- I bear-up well under
  - Misunderstanding
  - Accusations
  - Rage
  - Contradictions
- I see some of what God sees here
- I enjoy others

ELDERS AS SPIRITUAL FATHERS

The biological family is not the only treasure for an elder. His second treasure is his community family as we have just seen. An elder's third treasure comes in the form of his spiritual family. These three families are the rewards of many years of life-giving.

A spiritual family produces additional children for those who are not barren spiritually. A spiritual parent, or a father to others in the community if you wish, is ready to form paternal bonds with children that are not biologically his own. In addition, elders adopt men to form them as fathers, just as fathers adopt boys to form them as men. When elder men adopt women, it is to make them daughters not wives. As we will see when we study how elders build trust, any man looking for a mate cannot be fully trusted among women. This is another reason that the elder's work must wait until they are mature enough to trust.

Spiritual family is not just about adoption by elder men. Adoption by elder women helps women mature into adults, wives, mothers and grandmothers. This is how the pictures and stories in the woman's control center get expanded, supplemented and corrected. With spiritual mothers around there is hope for those who received a defective or badly trained mother core at level three of their control centers. Elder-mothers have a crucial place in our hope for future generations and their control centers.

I think back on the day that our former daughter-in-law introduced Kitty and me to her fiancé, the future father for our grandson. "I told him I come with two sets of parents," she said with a bubbly laugh. She was no longer a daughter-in-law but now a spiritual daughter. We would become grandparents to all their children not just the first one. This is how we understand this way of life.

An elder becomes a father to the mothers and fathers in the community of faith. Just as grandfathers become life-givers to their own biological grandchildren, an elder pours life into the grandchildren that God gives him through his spiritual children. So he continues to spread his tent pegs as his family grows, leading them all toward maturity.

JESUS AND SPIRITUAL FATHERS

Spiritual fatherhood, the cornerstone of eldership, makes some Protestants uncomfortable. Pastor Jack Hayford speaks to this in his book *Pastors of Promise* in which he calls pastors to become spiritual fathers and shepherds.

The grounds for protest are usually offered in Jesus' words: "Do not call anyone on earth your father; for One is your Father, He who is in Heaven" (Matt. 23:9). The spirit of the immediate context of His prohibition seems to separate a title from a truth.

…In Matthew 23, He pointedly attacks the religious pride in these leaders who paraded themselves as rulers called "fathers in Israel." Yet for all their claims of the title, they did nothing to live out the truth of fatherhood, which was to serve the interests of those they led. The New Testament not only clears the way for an appropriate mention of "spiritual fatherhood" among godly leaders, but in fact also demonstrates the meaning and desirability for such a role. It unfolds a "fathering" lifestyle that did not require the formalities of title. . .[54]

As was usual for Jesus, he cautioned people to avoid titles and claims and seek the real thing. Real fatherhood is seen in actions, not titles. Thus Paul can call himself father to the Corinthian believers. "Even though you have ten thousand guardians in Christ, you do not have many fathers, for in Christ Jesus I became your father through the gospel." (1 Corinthians 4:9. NIV) This passage occurs at a moment when Paul, like Jesus, is fighting people who claim a title but act like predators. Paul follows Jesus' example by insisting that fathers and elders be known by their "fruit."

YOU CAN CALL ME "PAPA"

We drove to Duluth to hear Walter Trobisch speak on sex. Kitty and I loved his books because they were so warm, vulnerable and personal. After the lectures, we got one of the scarce fifteen-minute appointments to talk with Walter in person. "You can call me Papa Trobisch," he said. "Many people like to." As a young married couple we were mostly impressed with how much those minutes did to help our sex life. Thirty years later the only words I can remember from that time together are, "You can call me Papa Trobisch." It was the only time we were to meet.

Encouraged by his warm reception and the fact that he wrote letters to other people, I sent Walter a letter when I was ready to graduate from college asking to come and work with him. True to form he wrote back, encouraging me to get further training and education in California before coming to Austria to train with him.

I was shooting pool in the mailroom with Sam Playfair while our little "Punkin" ran around pulling balls out of the pockets. Sam laughingly called us "the nuclear family." As Kitty checked the mail, she looked up from a magazine. "Walter Trobisch died." As suddenly as that I had no future plans.

I sent my first book to Walter's publisher about ten years later as an unsolicited manuscript. They picked it out of nearly a thousand others to publish. I dedicated *Just Between Father and Son* to Walter Trobisch.

In the long shadows of the late afternoon Missouri sunlight I spotted a small sign by the door that said **Walter's Study**. I carried in our suitcases and stopped in front of a poster with his picture. Bud and Bari had made the

---

[54] Jack. W. Hayford, *Pastors of Promise*, (Ventura, CA:Regal Books, 1997) Page 37.

arrangements for the visit to the Family Life Mission run by Ingrid Trobisch to carry on the work she and Walter had begun together many years ago. Ingrid had read some of my books and invited us to be consultants for a weekend planning session. She joined us for dinner and told the story of the day Walter died. He felt something wasn't right and lay down for a nap. He never got up.

That night my mind replayed my life and his as I listened to Kitty's rhythmic breathing. Neither Bud nor Bari had ever met Walter, they told us at a staff meeting the next day, but they kept his vision alive. Most of the rest of the staff nodded in agreement.

"Kitty and I knew Walter. We heard him speak in Duluth and even had a counseling session with him for fifteen-minutes." Some gasps were heard and every eye in the place was on us.

"You knew him?"

"We didn't know!"

"Ingrid, did you know?"

"No I didn't!" Ingrid leaned forward and smiled.

"He said, 'You can call me Papa Trobisch.'"

Ingrid nodded, "Yes," she said, her voice a bit tremulous, "That would be Walter."

Chapter Thirteen
Grandfathers and Common Types of Elders

Mr. Hansen was a tough old Norwegian. He lived in the North woods, cut his own firewood, built his own buildings, made his own roads and probably even cut his own hair. Mr. Hansen led church, taught and sang songs with a conviction that was gripping. He took young men under his care from time-to-time. They started out doing hard labor like splitting wood or grading his road with a rake. Together they drank stout coffee, ate robust foods and prayed to God as though He were right there in the woods with them.

Gruff, direct, a man of few words and hard work, Mr. Hansen thought of each boy as his responsibility. He saw to it that the boy became a man. He made sure that men around him became responsible fathers. He expected to see each father become an elder; and he thought nothing of it. To Mr. Hansen these were the responsibilities of every elder and he was not one bit unique. His temper flared if boys did not work hard and learn their lessons so he chose those who worked and discarded those who wouldn't. It was his way--the way of the North-woods elder.

I am glad I knew Mr. Hansen. His driveway was long and full of holes each spring. His woodpile needed careful stacking. I found the work itself was no worse than my previous job in the granite quarries of North Carolina, but Mr. Hansen's quietly fierce way of grasping life and his pungent view of people were well worth the discipline I learned there at seventeen.

Not too long ago, older men called all boys of their acquaintance "Sonny." This was part of the general sense of eldership in older men. In some places the term elders used for the young was, "Child" for either gender. The problem came with the term many elders used for girls, because the term for daughters was not "Daughter" but "Honey" or "Sweetheart." While this posed no problem with little boys and girls, a difference developed as children grew. Elders tended to call young men "Son" but continued using "Honey" or "Sweetheart" with young women. Either term could imply a daughter but it certainly did not have to because the terms were just as easily used for mates, dates, and general sexual harassment. In essence, the male terms allowed development and growth while the terms used for women did not. Because of these demeaning uses, society shook off these terms for women in the last quarter of the 20th century. Even though there was no organized opposition to older men calling the younger men "son," the end of paternal interest in young women spelled the end for young men as well. Neither young men nor women were treated as one's children by the end of the century. The concept passed out of culture.

While the term "son" did not guarantee in the slightest that an older man would treat a younger man like he would his own child, it did remind both the older man and the younger man of the possibility. The young man developed awareness that at some age all young men might be "sons" to him. Language created a context for the elder to develop. While the tacit knowledge was revealed in language, any actual teaching of eldership within our North American culture vanished even earlier. What we have left is Grandpa and Santa Claus.

GRANDPA

"Gee," as he was known by his little grandson, loved to take the boy everywhere. Grandpa visited amusement parks, tool stores, sandwich shops and especially ice cream stands. Gee had a grin on his face all day when the two of them were together. Grass was fun, puddles were fun, trees were fun—the world was a blast long before the boy could even talk. Gee's daughter was a single mother and it made her happy anytime she could leave her son with Grandpa. Grandma had not retired yet so Gee took over childcare while his daughter worked. She knew they would both have a great day. Three generations of joy is a good thing.

Grandfathers and babies: The love affair between grandfathers and grandbabies is heavily slanted toward a mutual enjoyment. No trip through the elder stage would be complete without discussing this naturally occurring source of joy for all elder candidates. Grandparents provide a trusted environment for young parents to leave their baby while they get away for a few hours or even overnight. After the usual parental fussing and checking to see if the grandparents have the phone numbers and special instructions they settle in to enjoy the baby. They have no other real goals; well, maybe a few pictures and videos are in the plan. Grandparents try out all the things their children particularly liked and, with a bit of luck, the baby will like at least one of them, too. About the time the grandparents have discharged their joy batteries, the parents come to take the baby back home with them. Ain't it grand!

It is a rare grandfather who will change diapers. That may change in another generation.

A good deal of the trust between young parents and grandparents hinges on the respect that the grandparents show for the young parent's parenting style. They know grandpa's sweet tooth and don't want their toddler getting a lot of candy so grandpa's self-control handing out candy will make a big difference to their overall level of joy. This is not to say that healthy discussions are out of the question because grandparents can be very helpful in easing parents out of their parenting fears if they listen carefully to their children.

Still, joy is the big deal that gives babies their strength for life. Grandparents that synchronize with babies and build joy during their first year of life are really building the baby's brain for the future. Granddads can grin with the best of them! Granddads get tired, too, so baby has an even better chance for "quiet together time" with granddad than with dad.

During the second year of life, baby must practice all that "returning to joy" from sad, angry, scared, disgusted, ashamed and hopeless. If Grandpa has learned the path back to joy they can certainly practice together. (You can review Chapter Two for more details.) But if Grandpa is not so good at returning to joy, the great news is that joy never goes out of season. Grandpa can still build both joy and quiet in baby's brain even when the control center in Grandpa's brain knows little else.

Grandfathers and children: There is a nice match between a child's capacity to care for himself and the length of excursions to see the world with grandpa. Unlike many other challenges of childhood these adventures can be planned according to both grandpa's and the child's capacities. Parents, as we know, are in the middle of a twenty-year-long season of stretching their capacities beyond their wildest ideas and limits. Vacations, weekends, trips and holidays with grandparents can usually be planned for the best results. Sure, we guess incorrectly but with a little practice most of us get it right. The results for most families are a stack of great memories.

Grandpa often learns to "bite his tongue" about the way the grandkids behave and how their parents are raising them. When a man sees a problem he wants to solve it but, for the most part, raising these kids is not his problem. Grandpa will get farther by encouraging everything his kids do right.

These are the education years and children love to learn. Anything that grandpa does or buys to help them learn is usually well received provided it is age appropriate and interesting. Trips to national parks, interesting events, and historical sites can be part of this education. Trips really begin to sparkle when grandpa takes time to hear what the children are learning from their trip. Mutual story telling about the day and its adventures helps all three generations remember what they learned about the world and each other.

Between eight and twelve years of age, Grandpa has a special opportunity to tell family stories. During this time, trips to places where the stories happened help make them vivid. Grandpas should take advantage of family reunions and holidays and tell stories. Keep them short. Ten short stories are better than one long one—unless you are a great storyteller. Grandkids like stories where they or one of their parents is the focus. Grandpa can tell a few stories on his kids to keep it interesting.

Grandfathers and young adults: Grandparents find their interest in trust building has a growth spurt about the time that the parents and adolescent grandchildren are having a rough time. During these times, grandparents can be a real shelter for teens that are locked in conflict with their parents. Sometimes grandparents can help grandchildren get away from drugs, gangs and bad friends or even get back into school. By providing a sort of second start at independence, grandparents help teens learn to return to joy after a rough time with their parents. This can prove to be particularly crucial when conflicts with stepparents in blended families leave the parents in conflict with each other.

Grandparents as parents: Fairly often, grandparents actually raise their grandchildren for part of their childhoods. We will do little other than acknowledge that reality here for it deserves its own book. What we should note is that because so many parents must have someone else care for their infants while they work, grandparents sometimes take up the slack. Grandparents can be the source of joy for infants and help them develop a much stronger brain. Even if they can only help for a while, a month's investment in joy when a baby is nine months old can change a brain for a lifetime.

Grandparents who live close by or who live far away: Grandparents who live quite close to their grandchildren need to work at promoting a sense of being special for their grandchildren. While grandchildren can come by often enough to feel comfortable and familiar, these grandparents sometimes feel a bit put-upon for free babysitting. They can lose the special joy of having grandchildren until they stop to think about it. Taking time to make special trips or take grandchildren along one-at-a-time on short trips can help. If Megan likes seeing the horses, take her to the post office when you must drive past the horse farm. If Maxwell likes Home Depot then work that stereotype to your advantage. Just don't take your trips when their favorite TV shows are on. It also helps to have each one's favorite snack on hand at the house and take time to memorize who likes what treat—you would be amazed how many parents and grandparents get that wrong every time. Write it down if you have to, then check your list.

Grandparents who live far away need to work at providing a sense of belonging for their grandchildren. This means making frequent contact by phone or e-mail so the grandchildren never go more than three months without some reminder that they are in their grandparent's lives. It also means that grandpa needs to keep something at his house that is just for each grandchild on his or her visits. This can be something like buying each one his own fishing pole, story books with their name, a picture album of their visits, a tree planted when they were born (you might want to plant two in case one dies the first winter) or even their own croquet mallet in their favorite color. Since the visits to grandpa's house are not that frequent, grandchildren easily feel special when they are treated to joy during their visits.

LATE BLOOMERS

Many men were just not ready to be fathers. They simply did not seem to grasp relationships at all. Sex, work, food and play made sense to them but that was about it. They were not just a quart low on joy when their kids were born; their crankcase was dry. Their wives and children suffered as a result. By the time they started to catch on to parenting, their kids were grown.

Sometimes the change only took one or two children. The oldest child in a family often reports in therapy that the father who raised him or her is not the same one that raised the younger brothers and sisters. They wistfully wish they had gotten the later version of a father and angrily wish the family would validate the harsh deal they did receive. The truth is, men sometimes do change and become better fathers.

The retraining of these male brains has often been costly. Some men lose two families before they realize that they can't dismiss their attachments. Getting through that *everything is work and work is everything* phase, raising children, getting divorced, wearing out a "therapeutic girlfriend," meeting a new wife who makes relational demands and watching the mistakes others made all eventually pay off. Finally he learns that people are not problems to be solved. Twenty years of trying to treat his wife (wives) and her conversations as "problems to be solved" yielded ZIPPO before he got it.

Now as a wiser and poorer man he becomes a grandfather. He no longer really wants to solve problems or control others. From almost a selfish point of view, he just wants to enjoy life—including children. Then, just when it seems like no one is left in the world to find him exciting—grandkids arrive! Suddenly, the door to joy flies open as his grandchildren run to him, smile, climb on him and drag him by the hand.

Many a man has found more joy as grandfather than he ever did as a father. The late blooming man has a chance to get in on the joy children bring and give some life with his children's children. This time, relationships are not completely strange to him. Children are not strange to him. Grandpa does not wonder what to do with their energy and excitement.

He will not get to be an elder in the full sense but tastes, for the first time, the joy of giving life.

A few men who as fathers were angry, even physically or emotionally abusive on occasion, turn out to be good grandfathers. This is not to say, by any stretch of the imagination, that all men change; but some men who were lousy fathers do become fit for society by the time they become grandfathers. These men found joy too late for their own children, some of whom still carry fear of their fathers well into adult life. Their children will wonder at the way their fathers enjoy and play with grandchildren. The children will watch carefully to see if their fathers treat their children differently than the ways that hurt them.

The time when grandchildren are being born is often a period of fence mending between generations. Even those children whose relationships with their parents (and in particular with their father) have been rough, feel a strong draw to let their children get to know their grandfather. The more honest the grandfather is about his contributions to the problems, the better these conflicts will resolve.

While we are saying that men who were somewhat controlling, authoritarian, crusty, rough and insensitive as young fathers may make good grandfathers, this is not to suggest that we should trust all abusive fathers to become good grandfathers. What we are describing are men who did a poor job of protecting others from their emotions and who lived out of fear as young men. Bonding with grandchildren is free from almost any possibility of failure so they now have little to fear. They have learned to protect others emotionally, return to joy and enjoy children. It certainly helps if they are able to articulate their change (what they have learned) but that is not always necessary for real change to have taken place.

Often the late bloomer still shows unmistakable signs of immaturity. He may even have a little "revenge" pleasure as his children "get theirs" from his grandchildren. His own resentments about his parents and parenting sometimes get transformed into aiding and abetting the grandchildren's misbehavior. But, for all his continued faults, the attraction to joy has been too much to resist. He has learned how to love his grandchildren and they will bless him for it. For the late bloomer, grandbabies are his last chance.

JUST HOPING GRANDPA CHANGED IS DANGEROUS

Has grandpa changed or has it just been a while since he had a child to target? As a general rule, if a man has not learned to suffer without blaming others he has not changed. Three patterns are particularly prone to linger: addictions, sexual abuse and narcissism.

210

When a man has not trained his nucleus accumbens that he will not die if he does not get what he craves, he loses his judgment each time his craving hits. Men who continue abusing alcohol and other drugs should not be with children. Other cravings can put children at risk as well so treat this problem seriously. Even when sober, these addiction patterns are always in the brain waiting to be activated.

The second serious problem is sexual abuse. Most serious abuse comes as a reaction to attachment pain that has gone unrecognized so the man who has not accepted responsibility for the attachment pain he has created can be considered "armed and dangerous." The most sinister form of attachment-pain-related-abuse is sexual abuse. There are many patterns of sexual abuse but all involve a failure of the intimacy and attachment functions in the mind. These child molestation patterns can be temporarily blocked but are always present in the brain and can potentially be activated at any time.

Any truly reformed child molester will insist that children be supervised 100% of the time he is around. He takes responsibility for the attachment pain he has created and takes steps to protect others from himself. This is like any recovering alcoholic will tell you that he or she cannot drink. Anyone who has sexually abused his children and still regards himself as safe around children has not reformed. He should not be trusted at all. Hoping he has changed is a very dangerous hope and becomes more dangerous the more he pleads to be trusted.

The third dangerous pattern is called narcissism. Narcissistic parents continue to insist that the children and grandchildren do not love them well enough. Narcissists react very badly to any hint that they are not trusted, any hint that they have done something wrong or any suggestion that they are hurtful to be around. They insist on being loved, while they punish, withhold love, rage and "guilt" or humiliate anyone who does not love them well enough.

Schore has pointed out the two types of narcissism.[55] I call them the peacock and the skunk. The peacock insists that he is perfect and wonderful. He has little empathy for others and what empathy he has he uses to hurt others when they bring up his faults. The peacock is self-aggrandizing and demanding. He wants to be the center of attention. Whenever he feels rejected he humiliates others until he gets his way.

The skunk has low self-esteem, avoids attention, is socially inhibited and has a high sensitivity to rejection. Whenever he feels rejected he beats up on himself until he gets his way. Narcissists of both types react to rejection but one beats up his family while the other beats up on himself.

---

[55] Schore, p. 423.

When the narcissist is told, "Sorry Dad. We won't be coming home for Christmas this year. Phil's Dad is not feeling well and we have not been there the last four Christmases" he will answer:

Peacock: "Is Phil some kind of Mommy's boy? Hasn't he got the balls to stand up to that sniveling family of his? Listen, I'm sending you tickets to fly down here and that's final."

Skunk: "Your brother is going to be really disappointed. His little girl Lisa sure does like you. We don't put on much of a spread here like the Morgans do. I can't blame you for liking them better. You probably get better gifts there too. They have all those fine discussions around the table— guess you are getting to meet important folk now. This place is really a dump anyway."

It really hurts to be told you do not love someone when you really do. Since the love of a child is about the purest form of love you can find, this attitude from the grandfather will harm the new generation just like it harmed his own children. While his children may still come around to see him, there will be little joy in the visits. What joy does grow will be shallow and die quickly as everyone learns to pretend to be what grandpa requires of them. Trust will not grow in that family.

Late bloomers don't imply subtlety or directly that there is something wrong with you if you want a change. Late bloomers are very different from unchanged liars who simply insist that: they were never the problem, it was never their fault, you owe them family devotion, you should overlook the past, you should get on with life and you should forgive and forget. Perhaps it seems harsh to call them liars since they all seem to sincerely believe what they are saying. The most convincing liars are those who believe their own lies.

SEMI-ELDERS

Besides the grandfather who bloomed late there are a variety of men whose trek through life has cost them some points. While they have holes in their development that keep them from fully seeing their communities as their own, they still can function as elders under limited conditions.

Willie is a teacher. Josie, his third wife, is a teacher. They have a daughter who works part-time in a school while attending college. Willie has the stuff to be a father. When his daughter grew up, he took in a relative from his wife's side of the family named Peter who was going to school near him. Willie could see that Peter was lost and needed a dad. Even though Peter proved to be self-centered and even a bit of a freeloader, Willie persevered. He had experienced enough losses to know the value of perseverance. There had been enough pain in his life to open his eyes. He saw that some people have to be loved just because a parent decides to love them. So it was that Willie loved Peter, talked to him, guided him, fed him, and housed him until Peter was ready to live on his own. Willie was stretching his tent pegs for his extended family.

Semi-elders are elders in a limited sort of way. Many men who have not finished their basic preparations still make helpful contributions to their communities. It is not unusual to find men who are able to treat their sons-in-law and daughters-in-law like family. They may even welcome step-grandkids without distinction but quite a few grandfathers stop stretching at that point. Many families, let alone grandfathers, end their benevolent sense of family when it comes to stepchildren. They manage their step-grandchildren rather than embrace them. Their "hearts," you might say, are slightly too small.

Many older men take an interest in community and civic groups but have trouble when a more personal touch is needed. Some befriend and help groups of their own kind—the Sons of Norway or Breast Cancer research after a family member dies from the disease. Often these semi-elders contribute to their alma mater or religious group and faithfully promote its interests.

What really describes the semi-elder is that his interests are personal to him in a naturally occurring way. He seeks the welfare of "his kind" or kin. He does not go beyond his family group but rather excludes or, in some cases, even exploits strangers. To him, the beautiful woman he does not know is still a "hubba hubba" to be ogled. People of color (or whites) get left out of his care. Arabs or Jews will always be a "them." Gays may give him the creeps.

Semi-elders, for their limitations, do care for more than their families and that is a good trend. Perhaps a few of them might be inspired to grow bigger "hearts" if they understood what it takes to be an elder. Elders need other elders; how much more semi-elders need fully developed elders to show them a better way. Meanwhile, let's encourage life where we find it.

GARDEN VARIETY ELDERS

Glen has been around for three quarters of a century. In his younger days he drove a delivery truck. Perhaps it was his wife's chronically disabled sister or his recovery from cancer that opened Glen's eyes to the needs around him, but he has never been so busy as since he retired. Besides volunteer work in the hospital, weekly visits to relatives in nursing homes, and care for his nieces, nephews, and grandchildren, Glen has adopted his mobile home park. When Sylvia had a stroke, Glen made sure that she got to the hospital. He looked after Sylvia's trailer, managed her checkbook and kept her life in order until her daughter could be persuaded to take an interest. Sylvia is just one of many that Glen has seen through a time of crisis when they could not take care of themselves. It is very hard to be so sick that one is entirely at the mercy of others. As an elder, Glen took care of each one as he would have cared for his own child. Glen is like a father to many widows and men in their old age.

Sam is an engineer and a craftsman. Sam designs and makes tiny parts for spacecraft and so, a decade or more after he should have retired, his company keeps him on as a master craftsman. Sam is not a talker; he quietly does what he does. Every Saturday he takes two women from his neighborhood grocery shopping. They don't have cars and can't get around well. Perhaps it was his wife's recurrent illness that helped Sam see the need others experience but whatever the reason he is there each Saturday. The women are very picky shoppers, partly due to fixed incomes, and greatly due to their proclivity toward pickiness. Sam patiently waits for them to finish shopping then takes them home where he helps fix the things that need care around their house without upsetting the two pack-rats who live there.

Dick had a good heart. He and his wife Nancy found tires for people's cars and furniture for their houses, helped people save their homes from foreclosure, kept businesses from closing, helped folks promote their ideas, paid for treatment expenses of orphans, helped his church reduce its debt, brought words of encouragement and guidance to many people, and taught in church each week. When one friend lost his house, Dick said quietly to me, "I could not save him even if I had the money." For Dick now knew that the life he had to give did not consist of solving people's problems but in helping people live and even suffer like themselves.

One Easter, Willard and Virginia Olwin had to sleep in their camper; they had seventeen houseguests. Among them were their granddaughters from San Francisco who invited three boys to visit them at their grandparents' house. The boys bicycled down for the weekend; it took them three days but they had a great time. The granddaughters knew where to invite friends to visit and the Olwins knew how to be hospitable.

Willard is almost eighty and a retired salesman. He and Virginia travel regularly and encourage Christian leaders who have visited their home and enjoyed their hospitality. Willard is the precinct leader at the polls each election day. He looks after the grounds at church, he is in several civic organizations, on the board of a camp, raises funds to send children to a Christian summer sports training, serves meals each week at a homeless shelter and he collects and delivers food for needy families.

214

ELDERS AND SPIRITUAL FAMILY

Some dreamy, hot summer afternoon, as clouds drift through deep blue skies over the tops of houses and trees -- stop a moment. With a cool glass of lemonade in your hand, watch the leaves rustle. Everything you see is real but there is something more. Beyond that blue sky are stars, lights without number and even though you can't see them now, they are there. Constellations and galaxies just beyond your sight wait for dark so you may know their beauty. And beyond the stars, even at night, there is even more you cannot see without help from the Hubble Telescope. Does your spiritual family hide from your eyes like the stars in the afternoon sky? Just because you can't see it doesn't mean it isn't there.

Haven't you gasped at a photograph of a concentration camp even though you did not know anyone in the picture? Have you winced when a child you never saw before was being yelled at in a grocery store? Hasn't a face on the cover of National Geographic gotten in your soul? Didn't some part of you get seared when you heard the stories of Nagasaki? Did you feel the relief when miners were pulled out alive after a cave-in or a child was dug out of a well? There is some connection we do not see between us all. It is a rare person indeed who has gotten through life without becoming attached to someone outside their family who became closer to them than many of their relatives.

An elder goes beyond this pretty sentiment by seeing people as family before a wonderful relationship has developed—often in the absence of camaraderie. As we have said, no culture develops elders without a religious values system that sees a place in the social matrix for those who have yet to be born, be included or reach their place. Elders are the guardians of this spiritual family life.

Now, you might think that in Christianity, a religion that sees all its members as one family, this type of eldership would flourish. This is not the case. Regrettably, Christians often prove the most difficult to persuade of a real dimension to a family they cannot see.

Most Christians are aware that God frequently refers to followers in family terms. Scripture mentions quite a few spiritual family relationships. One of Jesus' last acts on the cross was to perform an adoption ceremony between his elderly mother and her new adult son, John. John became a replacement son for Mary before her first son died. Thus Jesus highlighted the theme of spiritual family in a prominent way for his followers.

Spiritual adoption is frequently mentioned in the Epistles. The apostle Paul develops a theology of adoption in Romans 8:15, 23; 9:4; Galatians 4:5; and Ephesians 1:5. In these passages he highlights the believers' new relationship with God. Even if they were once sinners or even non-Jews, they are now adopted children of God. Still, it is his personal practice of adopting other men that illustrates his belief in the family of God on earth most clearly. If God adopted us, Paul was ready to adopt others as well. Adoption was an expected experience for Paul and other early church leaders.

One example of adoption can be found in the letter Paul wrote on behalf of Onesimus, whom he called "my son... who became my son while I was in chains" (Philemon 10). Paul clearly was pleased to have this son, and Onesimus was not his only son. In writing to Titus, Paul greets him as "Titus, my true son in our common faith" (Titus 1:4). In the same way he calls Timothy both "my true son in the faith" (1 Timothy 1:2) and his "dear son" (2 Timothy 1:2). Paul said of Timothy "as a son with his father he has served with me in the work of the gospel" (Philippians 2:22).

Paul is not alone in this practice. His "dear brother" the apostle Peter refers to Mark as his "son" in 1 Peter 5:13. They traveled together and Mark interpreted for the old fisherman. Mark probably wrote his gospel as a traveling companion and catechist for Peter--at least such was the traditional belief in the early church.

Adoption and mentoring are intricately combined in these biblical models. Spiritual family provides enduring relationships for growing both an individual and group identity to those who find themselves in grown bodies but immature inside. Elders are parents for those whose natural families did not help them grow up. It is in the context of a spiritual family that the stages and metamorphoses of life are best lived out. The community provides a continuity of life and the wealth of resources needed to help each individual grow, each family form and each generation build on the last.

LEVELS OF ELDER INVOLVEMENT

The need vulnerable people experience for an elder to take a family interest in them can come in many degrees of severity. These moments of need may happen to any of us at moments across our lifespan. When elders sense the call to share life with unsupported people it can require different levels of commitment. Elders can become supplemental, stand-in or replacement parents just as we saw in Chapter Eleven with spiritual fathers. These arrangements are sensed and directed spiritually but have several general characteristics: they are based on maturity not age, they create dependency on the elder and elders work to keep the dependency as limited and short-lived as possible.

Supplemental: Supplemental relatives are rarely even recognized as such. These elders fill in the holes left by everyone's parents and relatives. The semi-elders we mentioned in the last chapter supplement in

216

the holes left by family, as do beginning elders, as they are getting to know the ropes. Once in a while, teenagers will say of a friend's parents, "They are like a second family to me." These are supplemental parents.

Walter Watts was the pastor in Lake George. Now, all in all, Lake George will not put a pastor on the map. There will only be a few speaking invitations at Emmaville or maybe Kabekona Corners. I might never have known Walt except that he had a darkroom in his basement. Walt taught me how to use his equipment and then said, "Replace the chemicals you use and you are free to use the darkroom whenever it is free." After the first few visits, I never worried about being welcome in Walt's house. Sometimes, after a long project, I would lock up the house as I quietly left Walt and his sleeping family. The skills I developed in Walt's darkroom provided me with several jobs over the years. Walt was an elder who used his home, resources, and abilities to supplement my life.

Stand-in: Ceremonial or repeated long term involvement require an elder to stand-in at times like weddings and graduations when parents or other relatives would usually be present. There are, of course, stand-in brothers, sisters, aunts and even grandparents.

Christmas morning Denver Brown stopped by with Christmas lights blinking all over his jacket to say "Merry Christmas!" Denver adopted my children as grandchildren. He loves to see how they are doing and remembers them on holidays. Neither set of our children's grandparents lived near us so Christmases came and went without grandparents at our house. Denver stood in for them.

Denver is in his eighties. He works out at the gym each day, eats healthy food, filters his water and works five days a week. It was no surprise that his Christmas gift was high protein rice.

Denver knows what it means to be without family. His mother died when Denver was barely out of infancy. She had a seizure, fell into the fireplace and burned to death while little Denver and his sister tried to pull her out of the flames. Now Denver also missed his wife who died recently. Mentioning either woman brings tears to his eyes. Before he left, Denver gave a blessing prayer and talked about the God who had brought him through the years and tears.

Replacement: While the courts often step in for children whose parents die, the same is not true for moral and emotional failure. Some people come from families where everyone is on drugs, in crime or abusive. Once they clear 18 years of age no one really cares or notices that they may be at infant maturity. While elders may step into such a mess and become replacement parents, a whole family is often needed so elders must also include their community. We will examine this process in depth in Chapter Fifteen.

The interesting thing about elders is that they seem to find nothing unusual about what they do. They almost can't understand why everyone in their community doesn't join with them. Sadly, both functioning elders and healthy communities are not common. In the next chapter we will see what it takes to bring an elder and his community together.

Chapter Fourteen
An Elder Develops In His Community

Dr. Brubaker came flying up the right side of the auditorium toward the podium after one of my talks about elder maturity. His spontaneity and energy were uncommon among the psychiatrists I had met before. His trademark beard without a mustache marked him as an Anabaptist. The doctor launched into a story about the intentional Christian community he had been in for almost 20 years; a spiritual, therapeutic community where he blended his personal, professional, spiritual and family life to such an extent that all members lived from a "common purse," that is to say, they shared finances.

This Brethren group placed people with emotional disorders in homes where they could live with supportive families. After a number of years of raising their children this way, someone studied the community for a thesis. The study noted that some younger children had suffered from living in intentional families while older children had often prospered from them. In the larger community houses, a child under 13 was not able to compete successfully for the attention he or she needed.

I had just gotten through saying that one could not be an elder as long as one had children under 13. As a psychiatrist and elder, Dr. Brubaker immediately saw the link. There are jobs that only an elder can do safely. There is also a need for elders to do their jobs when the time is ripe. Dr. Brubaker was just reaching that time himself. Once he left the common purse community he became aware he needed to be an elder to a community of his own.

Elder is the longest developmental stage and the most slow-growing. Beginning by keeping an extended biological family going, an elder slowly extends his influence as the life around him becomes increasingly personal. Elders learn to synchronize biological, spiritual, social and community life into a coherent and trustworthy unity. Prayer and meditation harmonize spiritual and natural experiences as life becomes increasingly spiritual for the elder. There is much to harmonize.

For men who have lived and motivated others through fear, old age is a perilous time. Living through fear kept them from reaching elder maturity. Their rigidity is a sign of fear-based thinking. Fearful old men keep control, when they can, through money. Money controls those who fear losing their inheritance or some "benevolence." Old age makes it very clear when someone stayed rigid and shriveled in his or her thinking.

Flexibility and creativity are gone and so their lives reflect increasing restriction rather than growing synchronization.

Storytelling is the means of synchronizing these many aspects of life into one fluid whole. Transparent and deeply felt stories bring together the disparate elements of life and synchronize the mind of the storyteller. Telling the stories synchronizes the group mind of the community.

Tradition, ritual and liturgy synchronize the rhythms of life into a fluid story. Whether told to one person or to a group, the stories of the elders illustrate the meaning in customs, cultures, family histories, storms, politics, religions, the arrival of a stranger or a change in our lives. Elders synchronize the rhythms of life—when to celebrate with joy, when to mourn, when to face our shame, when to be angry, when to return to joy, when to be quiet together and when to go home (our separate ways) as a community. Neither too much synchronization nor too much isolation produces a healthy group identity.

Elders build trust through their spontaneous warmth, authenticity and transparency. Men who are reserved and play their cards close to their shirts will not create this kind of trust.

True elders are known by their ease around the vulnerable members of their communities. Both the unattractive who trigger rejection and attractive who trigger exploitation require care from elders. Vulnerable people have their trust betrayed. Elders rebuild trust when they attach to and include the Jean Valjeans and Marilyn Monroes in their lives.

In Victor Hugo's novel *Les Miserables* we find the old priest investing his greatest possessions in Jean Valjean knowing that Valjean was a thief and not because he hoped he was not. It is precisely this kind of bad investment of personal and community resources that characterize elders. Later in the story Valjean tries to be an elder by raising a town. After he has to flee the town, Valjean again takes an elder role when he raises a little orphan girl. In this fictional portrayal Victor Hugo has captured a society in turmoil for lack of elder influence. Valjean was among the most unattractive members of that society.

Marilyn Monroe is known as one of the most attractive members of society in our recent cultural history and yet if you look at her personal life it is a remarkably sad story. From a trust perspective, whom could Marilyn trust? Not her mother, father, agents, the press, Bobby or even President Kennedy. Trust issues continue clouding the cause of her death to this day because we are not even sure the government is telling the truth. Her life was one without elders.

DEVELOPMENTAL PROCESS FOR THE ELDER STAGE

Elders, like those in every other stage, must grow into their new identity. Just because their youngest child is now an adult or they have grandchildren does not complete an elder's identity. Elder is the longest of the stages of life—often approaching half a lifespan. This stage starts with a man at the height of his productivity and continues well into the decline of his energy and strength.

Increasing maturity brings increasing complexity. A developing brain continues to build complexity if its growth is not stunted, so a lifetime of learning is available to the elder. True elders are known by the complexity they can easily grasp and the simple directness of their responses.

Life becomes increasingly personal for elders. History, government, spiritual life, culture, work and what they see in the media all become personal concerns. Elders speak of their town, their houses, their churches and their schools. They no longer dismiss or ignore trends in the cultural life around them. Community life is a personal matter for elders.

Elders must deal with an environment where their control is decreasing at the same time that their investment is increasing. Elders live in constant flux. Their environment is heavily influenced by less mature people around them who have the energy to make changes. This makes it crucial for elders to stay involved and accessible in order to have influence.

More than any other stage, elders are formed by their spiritual life. Less need for sleep at night together with some financial freedom at retirement provide more elders with more reflective time. Spiritual values and viewpoints increasingly dominate active older minds. When Dirk Zweibel retired from psychology he told his younger colleagues, "I have learned that theoretical models, techniques and practice do not replace love. Love is what matters."

Merv Dirks, whose very presence brings a sense of well-being to a room, recalled how his dad walked with God. "I always wanted to emulate him. For my dad it wasn't a complicated thing. He had a really simple walk with God. It was like a little child walking with his father. That is not complicated or profound!" Then Merv laughed. He told me we should love each other. No one is around him for very long before they know that to Merv it is that simple.

This long stage of maturity has an equally long learning curve. Elders will make many mistakes. Elders are often "pushing the envelope" of what human community and compassion can attempt. When elders attempt extravagant love and it goes well, the elders are usually as amazed as anyone! Often things don't go well. Mistakes do not mean they are unfit elders. Elders make mistakes while they are learning, but these mistakes are not cause for moral concern—elders just need help restoring relationships with the people whose feelings got hurt. When things go wrong, elders need more community support but they often get the opposite response from their fearful communities. Elders must help their communities recover from each elder failure. Elders must teach their communities to understand and support their efforts.

Dr. Peters encountered this problem when his community reacted to the discovery that he had a spiritual daughter. Dr. Peters had always done his work "by the book." He was Mr. Clean and he worked his way to the top of the command chain in his denomination for his region. About the time Dr. Peters was just barely old enough to become an elder he happened to sit by a young woman in a restaurant. He knew Mrs. Valjean from the church they both attended. She was well known at church for her unstable emotions. For some reason, Dr. Peters began to develop a trust relationship with her that day. As Dr. Peters continued to take an interest in her life, her trust in him grew.

Dr. Peters began to relate to Mrs. V. like he did with his adopted daughter since they both had histories of sexual abuse. To the others around them, her growing trust in Dr. Peters was not a problem but his trust in her set off alarms in his staff and board. They did not trust Mrs. V. at all. The staff got in an uproar when they discovered that Dr. Peters let her know his cell-phone number! She might sue him or them, they insisted. Every sort of fear and immaturity came to the surface in the members of his organization and they behaved badly toward Dr. Peters. Dr. Peters was demoted and then replaced. The organization saw only a risk to their reputation and resources in Lady Valjean.

Helping his organization learn to trust and create trust proved much harder for Dr. Peters than achieving stability and growth for a sexually abused woman. Soon he began to withdraw from his peers. This was not a good time for Dr. Peters, a new elder, to be guided by fear. Like adults and parents, elders rely greatly on the encouragement and direction of their peers. Men spend a lot of time talking at this stage. Men who had little to say before can now spend most of their day talking. Comparing stories lets elders review results and correct mistakes. Dr. Peters was missing out on his review time.

Like all stages, eldership often ends with a repair and maintenance phase before the final transformation at the end of the stage. The research on dementia and Alzheimer's strongly suggests that the elderly who are active in their social networks are far less prone to the loss of their mental faculties. In fact, the life patterns needed to achieve an earned elder maturity combine many of the factors that predict longevity and a clear-minded old age.

WHY ELDER TASKS CAN'T BE DONE YOUNGER

Experience is required for all the elder tasks. We know it is hard to raise normal children. Experience raising normal children is needed before starting to raise people whose development has serious problems. Fathers have just figured out how to raise normal kids about the time they have escorted their youngest child into puberty. That is the minimal training an elder should have.

Dealing with problems outside the home provides less structure or trust to work with than men find within their families. Elders always work with fewer resources outside their homes and yet they must face larger problems. Yet, because they deal with problems through personal relationship, it is inevitable that elders will bring community problems home—the way children bring home stray cats. If it is not clear already, it should be firmly noted that elders need strong experienced marriages and secure children before attempting such outreach. The elder's group identity with his wife and children must be running well and free from fear-bonds or the strain will soon show.

When I would ask Dr. Peters how his family was accepting his spiritual adoption he would say his wife was delighted in his growth. When pressed, he would tell me that she was not really included in all that was going on—not yet. He was giving her time to get involved at her own rate. It seemed like he was trying to protect his family from the cost of elder life-giving. This does not work and is a frequent mistake for new elders.

The high emotional cost of life-giving and teaching people with damaged control centers how to return to joy is why elders need both their communities and families to synchronize with them. Like the parent stage, being an elder is a costly experience. It took many years of joyful family life—night and day, day after day—to build a really deep well of joy for the elder. Deep joy keeps us from delaminating our right hemispheric control centers under pressure. This deep joy is what elders give freely to their communities. Those who run out too quickly should not try to be elders.

Returning to joy from all of our different intense feelings takes a long time to perfect. If bringing your family back to joy and peace is hard, helping strangers get emotionally regulated is harder. Achieving a non-anxious presence when many people are upset takes years of practice. Suffering well becomes even harder when others see us as the source of their problems. Elders need all that practice feeling hopelessly out of control with their teenagers before they can face even larger emotions on a community scale.

Elders must be eager to stay involved. Elders must respond quickly to needs and problems in their communities. It is too late to be figuring out what people really need when you have a community crisis on your hands. Maturity must be smoothly integrated before the elder steps up to bat.

Elders take risks with community resources every time they attempt building trust with someone. "Betting the farm" is the risk elders take when building trust with people who do not know how to handle trust. The people they attempt to help can (and sometimes do) sue, molest, abuse, accuse, steal and damage reputations with the trust they are given. Other times it is the marginal person's friends, lovers, parents, pushers and relatives who betray trust. Because of the risks, it is only those who built the family farm who are grudgingly given the right to take chances with it. The elder never pays this price alone.

One thing an elder does not risk is his children. Since his children have had the attention they need to become adults, even the youngest is ready to form a group identity and see the value in taking care of "our people." No hostages in the form of defenseless children are involved when an elder takes chances.

Because elders take these risks in order to build trust they must first be men of known integrity whose actions and relationships are well known to their community. Most communities won't trust a man before he has raised his children. It will be very hard to trust him anyway—particularly if his actions put the community resources at risk or if he gets close to really vulnerable people.

You will find for yourself that even hearing the stories of elders and their actions may raise trust issues for you. Should they really do that? Can a man be trusted? Are you sure he is not up to something naughty? Is that wise? These questions all rest on the community's readiness to receive a man as an elder. Trust is not a cheap or quickly found commodity.

Identities take time to mature. The enormous failure rate of immature men trying to be elders and the tremendous costs of their failures for individuals, families and societies should give us reason to reflect carefully on this point. Comparing Bill Clinton and Jimmy Carter will give thoughtful observers a good contrast on this point. One man left stains on dresses while the other fought lust in his mind. One was disbarred and the other received a Nobel Peace Prize.

Years spent caring for babies, teenagers and their bodies teach an elder how much to trust himself. Raising children shows him how to teach others their safe limits. Protecting others from his limitations and helping them with theirs only happens for those who are comfortable in the presence of shame feelings. Old men feel their weaknesses. Younger men are simply too confident.

JOBS ONLY ELDERS SHOULD ATTEMPT

Fabio was a successful businessman. He and his wife Hilda brought a young woman with a history of severe abuse to live in their home—knowing there were risks involved. It was not easy living with Alba because she had few social skills—which is exactly why the young lady needed to live with people. After a few months Alba began to feel accepted. Acceptance brought out parts of her personality she kept hidden. Alba's whole experience of herself and life was being challenged and that started a crisis.

To try and gain some control of this new situation Alba tried to seduce Fabio by crudely grabbing his crotch. When he pulled away, Alba tore off all her clothes to become more powerful. Does that bring up trust issues for you like it does for most people? She alternately tried to assault him sexually and throw herself off the balcony. Fabio had to physically restrain her. Fabio yelled for Hilda to help him but the young woman proved to be too fast and strong for them to subdue together. Alba further added to the impasse by threatening to tell the police that Fabio was trying to rape her if he called them to help. When Fabio blocked her way to the balcony Alba threatened to dash out the door and run naked through the town yelling rape. Hilda then blocked the door while Alba ran about naked. It took over six hours to get Alba to put her clothes back on while Fabio and his wife restrained her suicide and escape attempts.

Should the community trust Fabio if naked women shouting rape come running out of his house? Should this couple trust Alba to stay longer in their home? Would your thinking change if she were a relative? Should Alba be placed in institutions with professionals but not with a family? If she has no money or safe relatives and there is no government institution to lock Alba in should we trust her to live on the street? These are a few of the trust issues faced by elders and their communities.

Hilda was hot after that night and not in a way likely to improve her sex life for some time. The picture she saw when first entering the room was locked in her mind. She had seen about all she wanted of her husband wrestling naked women. Who could she talk with about her feelings? People only understand one level of maturity above theirs so Hilda would only find understanding from other elders or mature parents. Everyone else just became upset or afraid so Hilda would end up having to calm them down.

"How can we keep this from happening again," was at the top of Fabio's thinking. He was not a happy camper. Fabio found himself short on fellow elders to help him with this dilemma. Many men would be ready to condemn his failure or want a chance at naked woman wrestling. Neither response would help. Fabio now had fears about his plan, his wife's capacity to handle the situation, what Alba would do tonight and what his community would do if this got out. His old tendency to cover fear with anger didn't make his stomach any happier either. Fabio was in a knot. This had not turned out at all like he had planned.

Alba continued to live with them for more than a decade after that although it was not the last outburst they had to face. We can be grateful that the couple's children were adults during this difficult time, as they needed to take care of themselves for the most part. The adult children paid part of the cost when Fabio and Hilda "bet the farm" on a stranger. Should they trust that their father could handle this mess? Could they trust that their mother would resolve her pain? Could they trust Alba to live in their house and not ruin everything? Should they trust their stomach's urgings to "get out now?" Much would rest on their parents' capacity to suffer well and remain a non-anxious presence. Showing everyone the way back to joy each day became the test of elder maturity for Fabio.

Elders do not just face hard situations in the form of problems that no one else would want, they also face situations where they must care for the things everyone else would want. Elders care for the community treasures and prepare treats for future generations but the cost to them is that the elders themselves can never possess what they cultivate for their community and future. Since we are talking about human treasures, this means building joy. Elders do what no one else would be advised to do: love everyone, kiss all the babies, give resources to bad risks, let the pretty girls sit on their knees, hug and snuggle and give back rubs. These all raise trust issues. Dirty old men have made us believe these kinds of contact are impossibilities for men. Whom do you trust?

Here we see the importance of a stable marriage to one woman over many years as the basis for the trust his community must place in an elder. No community can trust younger men and those seeking additional partners. A young man without a track record can't be trusted yet. Men with a history of taking a "better deal" when she came along and dumping their first wife or adding to their harem cannot be elders. No one in their right mind will trust them.

The deeper we look, the more emotionally charged the risks become for elders. Will we let anyone touch the vulnerable Marilyn or even the undesirable Alba? Precisely because immature people betray trust using the same activities that could build trust (such as touching, holding and sharing a home), there is a social prohibition against allowing such intimacy at all. We should not show the silver to Jean Valjean. Sometimes the prohibition is

226

even a legal one. Married couples should not lock a naked lady in a room with them for the night as Fabio and Hilda might be accused of doing. It is a sticky legal wicket.

A COMMUNITY DILEMMA

An elder and his community face an interesting dilemma. If there are activities that require elder maturity to complete safely, these same activities should harm the community when immature people try them. We have no trouble thinking that youngsters should not drive, manage money, drink alcohol or marry until they reach a certain capacity but that is our ceiling for thoughts about maturity.

With little concept of maturity beyond high school, and a culture that recently proclaimed "don't trust anyone over thirty," our westernized communities have no framework for restoring trust. Vast ignorance about maturity clouds this topic while strong feelings and fears run rampant. What I am claiming here is that the processes needed to build and restore communities to trust are unsafe except when guided by elders with earned maturity.

The reversal problem: The simplest way to see this problem is to think of any restricted activity. Until he is properly trained, George can't take a knife and cut your heart out. After he becomes Dr. George, heart surgeon at large, you will pay him to do just that if you think it will help.

How the reversal applies to trust: To build trust, an elder must do exactly the same activities he was prohibited from doing at a younger age. Since we are talking about building trust and belonging for vulnerable people, the activities we mean are the very ones that build intimacy and trust. We know that confidence artists, unscrupulous leaders and codependent relationships exploit these means of building trust.

We are in obvious need for restored trust in our society. Racial and ethnic groups distrust each other. We distrust our leaders, courts, law enforcement, accountants, brokers, business owners, employers, employees, neighbor's children (particularly teens), car salesmen, newspapers, media, doctors and increasingly our teachers. They in turn increasingly distrust us. Wherever we lack trust as a society we must move to shut down intimacy and risk taking since trust is built through intimacy and risks. Most societies have developed some cultural fears and prohibitions against building someone's trust or sense of belonging because we know the potential for abuse is very high. This is for our protection we feel—and correctly so. We compile a long list of people or situations we don't trust. Men don't take girls to the bathroom. Employers can't ask your birth date. White people can't raise Native American children. Doctors run billions of dollars in unnecessary medical tests so patients they don't trust won't sue them. Girls don't smile at strangers while children are taught not to get in their cars. My 89-year-old father has to take off his shoes in the airport to see if he has got bombs in there. We don't trust. We feel fear.

Most of what builds trust we won't allow because of previous abuses: Trust is built through intimate relationships. Those who have been burned by people they trusted are very reluctant to try again. Do you feel any of your trust issues getting stirred up by this discussion? We all do and yet we want a community we can trust. If you wanted a society based on fear and exploitation, chances are you would not be reading this book. Therefore, someone has to rebuild trust within the social fabric when it has been broken. Some members of society must develop the character maturity needed to build and restore that trust. Someone must enter the frightening and vulnerable spaces around those we do not trust ourselves around as well as those we do not trust around us. To build trust someone must teach the girls to smile at him, take children on trips in his car, cancel unnecessary medical tests and let old men wear their shoes in airports. The ones we must trust to make these choices are the very same people we would not trust when they were unprepared. How can we know when to reverse the ban on their building trust with the vulnerable?

We have tried a professional solution: We have not thought through how to build trust. The closest we come is describing "roles" or professions we can trust. Teachers are safe with children we say to ourselves—but can we trust that teacher with the sexually abused friend of his niece while they are on vacation? There by the campfire, the teacher is drinking beers and not in his teacher role. As the camp smoke drifts by it will be his identity and not his role that governs how he treats the girls near him. Do you trust him?

Our cultural question is, "How do we know when someone is prepared to build trust?" For our culture the answer has been to raise the *professional qualifications*. Professional qualifications usually mean education, supervised experience and a government issued approval. We will see in a moment that this solution has not worked for trust issues—it may have made them worse.

Professionals abuse trust too when they were not of elder maturity: When lawyers speak of "fiduciary duty" in malpractice lawsuits against professionals, they are speaking about trust. The essence of the charge is "we trusted you and got hurt." Professionals are supposed to be trustworthy but a look at the court record will show pastors, psychiatrists, doctors, counselors and all kinds of professionals getting into their patients' pants and pocketbooks. Laws have been passed in many states banning sexual activity between professionals and clients (with a noticeable

228

loosening of restrictions for lawyers—who write the laws for us. In other words, it is harder to sue your lawyer for breach of fiduciary duty than it is your minister.) The result of many professionals attempting to build trust is a violation of trust by a good number of professionals—some would estimate about 25%. There is something wrong with this picture.

Professionals are now effectively banned from building trust: Because of the fear produced by malpractice suits and state licensing board charges, most professionals will not trust their clients very far at all. Professionals know that it is very expensive and draining to fight a false charge. One psychologist of my acquaintance fought off a false charge only to have her insurance rates raised to nearly half of her yearly income. Nearly every continuing education course for counselors has the same message, "do not trust your clients." You cannot build trust while taking every precaution to not trust someone. Doctors don't want to say what they are thinking about your diagnosis—they don't trust you. They run extra tests—they don't trust you. Pastors stay aloof from their congregations—they don't trust you. Police officers only make friends with other officers—they don't trust you. Professionals are now effectively banned from building trust in communities and with vulnerable people. The few professionals who still would like to trust are warned that they, their centers and churches could get sued so they receive little community support toward building trust with those who need it.

We need elders to build trust—not professionals: There is nothing about education, training and government certification that lifts us above fear. We have all been to school. Did anything happen there that would help you control your fears and desires? Does school help you stay out of an attractive person's pants? Did you ever pass a test that made you calmer when in trouble? Did any grade you finished make you a noticeably better parent? Did you ever get a license that made you more generous?

If school did change your disposition it was likely through a relationship with a teacher or peer. Relationships produce a well-trained control center through long years of experience. Professional training does little for the control center. Professionals are needed for technical work. To build trust we need elders.

In fact, when professional counselors do become elders one of their most common mistakes is failing to build trust with anyone but the "wounded" person. They work hard to help their spiritual child learn to trust but fail to work equally hard to help their spouse, community and church develop trust. This error can be fatal if, when mistrust arises, the elder reverts to child maturity under pressure and starts to take sides. Mistrust will surely arise! The very presence of elders, their transparency and the risks they take bring mistrust out of hiding. Elders must deal with accusations and distrust everywhere—and without fear.

Professionals should not be banned from building trust when they become elders: While being a professional is no substitute for maturity, every once in a while a professional does reach maturity. Human relations professionals even have some skills that can be helpful when building trust with hurt people. They should not be banned from becoming elders just because they are also trained professionals.

Sarkis Balian, a man of elder maturity and grown children, began to see a spiritual connection with the people he prayed for as a minister. Some of the abused women he helped eventually began to see him as the father they had never had and he saw them as spiritual daughters. His colleagues and board, fearing lawsuits, questioned whether he could minister to anyone he felt this spiritual connection with as a father. They also perceived correctly that spiritual adoption of a counselee was far too difficult, complex and risky to teach as a method for their prayer counselors' use. They could not have been more correct for their training had nothing to do with maturity and elders take 30 to 50 years to grow. Even when ready, elders only form good bonds under spiritual direction not just because there is a need and certainly not because it is their work.

In the end, the board "grandfathered" Sarkis but barred any future ministers in their organization from following Sarkis' example. His moral character was not in question but the level of trust required was higher than normal and it made people feel it might not be professional enough. The problem was not that the women should trust him but that he should also trust them opening his heart and attaching to the women as well.

It might be well to note that this ministry board did not take maturity into account in their decision. They wisely noted that developing spiritual family ties was desirable and necessary. They also noted that being a minister or prayer counselor was no assurance that someone could handle a spiritual family bond. In addition, spiritual families grow in communities and their counseling center was not a community—it was not designed that way. Their fourth observation was that something about Sarkis' trust relationships were very good and healing so the board left them intact. With no standard for maturity, however, the board's concerns that someone would get hurt, brought the inevitable rules—no more personal trust bonds for ministers in their organization.

Building trust is hard for a community—even when elders are in charge: Suppose you grant my point that at some point in maturity men and women can do what they previously could not do—handle intimacy in a trustworthy way with people who are not their biological family. Just thinking about this brings our trust issues right to the surface. People below parent maturity will not be able to understand at a felt level how this works. Elders are a mystery to infants, children and adults. Infants must *do what they feel* so elders are "just attracted to these people" for infant minds. Children must *take care of themselves* and assume elders are "in this for themselves" too. Adults are *achieving mutuality* through their bonds and feel compelled to believe elders are "getting something out of this." Only parents and other elders understand they are "giving something out of this."

Trust issues: Trust involves touch. Nowhere does the trust issue get hotter and harder to handle than when people touch. Touch is a big part of bonding and human relationships. Touch builds and betrays trust more than any other activity. Once I have their confidence, older men who are elders will confide in me that girls and women seem to need touch—even sexually abused girls. My observation is that sexually abused children and adults need more touch than average. "Good touch to fill in where there was only bad," as Dr. Brubaker would say. The first reaction to touch by sexually abused women is to have sexual thoughts and feelings in reaction to almost any contact. They often fear their own feelings more than they fear another assault.

Pretty girls can also be starved for nurturing touch. The power of their looks can be a double-edged sword. Many pretty women have confided in me that they can "get a man to do whatever I want" but at the same time these women do not trust any man's interest in them. Attractive women often experience the distrust and rejection by other women as well. Since elders carry the major burden of establishing and re-establishing trust, it should not surprise us that some elders touch and give attention to girls. That is a troubling thought for those who feel the power of attraction.

Trust involves attraction. Walter Trobich almost always had young people living with his family. Many of the young women "fell in love" with Walter at some point and wished they could marry him—a normal reaction known by all kind and loving men who raise daughters. Ingrid and Walter helped them use this normal desire to make this happiness last forever to help the young women learn to say what they wanted in their husband and future. They were building trust in the young ladies. The only regret his family has seems to stem from Walter's beginning his elder work too young and it took a toll on the family time for a family with younger children.

Trust involves friendship. Dr. Lee Travis was a pioneer psychologist who helped discover brain waves. He was warm, transparent and generous. Dr. Travis and his wife took Kitty and me out to dinner at the top of the Hilton while I was in school. He was an elder. Dr. Travis told me once that all his long-term clients became his friends. It was not hard to see why. He could not build their trust without ultimately coming to trust them, too. They came to his house and his parties not just his office. Even his relatives came to Dr. Travis for therapy and help because they trusted him.

Trust involves sharing life. The early therapists in the field of dissociative disorders, or Multiple Personality Disorder (MPD) as it was then known, often reached similar thresholds making their patients members of their households, taking them on vacations, helping them buy homes and often writing the story of their pilgrimage together. Evidence suggests that sharing life together took years off recovery time. Dr. Frances Howland comments about one young woman's recovery, "Joan's integration occurred after four years; this is impressive in view of the fact that successful integrations of multiples may take between eight and twelve years. Lynn Wilson was able to devote part of her life to and share her family with Joan; the work was effective and quite rapid."[56]

Trust involves spiritual family bonds. These older, experienced and wise therapists moved out of the office and into the life of elders. In this case, Lynn Wilson and her husband Gordon took Joan Casey into their lives and family. "I love you like a daughter," Lynn said to her as she hugged her close.[57] As the three built a trusting relationship, parts of Joan called Gordon "Dad" in their sort of Zen-style spiritual family.

While Lynn was a social worker by trade, Gordon was not. What they had together was maturity. Thinking of this as a "therapeutic family" rather than a spiritual one has led some younger therapists to speed recovery through taking someone into their family. These immature therapists did not achieve such good results. Young therapists ended with disasters, emergency hospitalizations, severed relationships and a great loss of trust. Maturity, not education or professional training, makes one an elder.

Society's fears are causing problems for elders: Organizations, communities, churches and society have a problem with elders because to achieve trust, elders must do what our courts and laws and immaturity prohibit in less developed men and women.

Dr. Daniel Amen faced these societal limits when he began using brain scans to diagnose and treat psychiatric problems. When he began to tell others of his results and teach his methods he was reported to the state authorities for malpractice. The result was a painful and expensive battle to retain his license that eventually exonerated his work and led to his becoming a member of the state board.

Society patrols the people we trust. Dr. Amen fought for his method and won—probably because it was high-tech—but would Dr. Travis have made it with his low-tech love and trust? Dr. Travis, along with doctors like

---

[56] Joan Casey, *The Flock*, (New York: Alfred A. Knopf, 1991), p. 303.
[57] Casey, *The Flock*, p.164.

Cornelia Wilbur, M.D., Trula LaCalle Ph.D.[58], and Lynn Wilson[59] who built trust with their patients, would potentially face the loss of their licenses today. We would not trust them because they trusted their clients enough to share life together. We know that has a high potential for abuse—or for healing. Great good or great evil can come from how we handle personal power.

Society has a problem with whom to trust. If these elders were taken before a jury whose members were of child and infant maturity, the very immaturity of the jury members would make it impossible for the elders' motives to be understood. The law takes a very different view of what a "jury of one's peers" requires because laws rarely take maturity into account. Rules and laws are made to protect us from the worst elements of society but do you want to be protected from becoming Dr. Travis' friend?

Dr. Brubaker took a woman under his wing whose life had fallen apart. In time Lonnie became a daughter to him. Lonnie has four children that he hopes to reach in time. None of them have trusted men before and their trust is slow to grow. All four have major psychiatric disorders. Dr. Brubaker treats the youngest for her disorder and she is now back in school and doing very well. Dr. Brubaker is pleased and proud.

Lonnie's boy is on-and-off drugs but Dr. Brubaker trusts him around the Brubaker house. The young man is a good worker and Dr. Brubaker loves to have him around. When the young man goes back to drugs it brings tears to the doctor's eyes because he misses their times together.

What people have trouble understanding is how Dr. Brubaker trusts them with his life and resources. Dr. Brubaker, his wife, his parents, his brother, children and grandchildren are all sharing life together. There were 25 people around their Thanksgiving table this year and his children and grandchildren won't be home until Christmas!

ELDER'S NEEDS

An elder needs *a community to call his own*. Taking the kinds of risks we have been talking about in order to build trust in strangers can only happen among people who have known you for a long time. Since communities are wise to stop anyone with less than elder maturity from taking personal interest in the vulnerable members of society, *elders need to be recognized as such by their communities*. Once recognized, elders need the freedom to "bet" some part of the farm on the "long-shot" strangers that

---

[58] Trula LaCalle, Ph.D., *Voices,* (New York: Dodd, Mead & Co., 1987).
[59] This is a pseudonym.

grow a place in their hearts. This permission to use community resources comes from *a recognized place in the community structure* where the unique contribution of *an elder is trusted, valued and protected.*

One of the earliest descriptions in literature of an elder and his community can be found in the three or four-thousand-year-old poem of Jôb (rhymes with robe). Job describes his community, his recognition, place in the community structure and the way he was trusted and valued.

> If I went through the gate out of the town to take my seat in the public square, young men saw me and kept out of sight; old men rose to their feet, men in authority broke off their talk and put their hands to their lips; the voices of the nobles died away and every man held his tongue. They listened to me expectantly and waited in silence for my opinion. When I had spoken, no one spoke again; my words fell gently on them; they waited for them as for rain and drank them in like showers in spring. When I smiled on them, they took heart; when my face lit up, they lost their gloomy looks. I presided over them, planning their course, like a king encamped with his troops. Whoever heard of me spoke in my favor, and those who saw me bore witness to my merit
>
> Job 29:7-10, 21-25, 11 TNEB

Elders require their communities' contributions in order to thrive. In the poem, Job has a series of calamities that result in his becoming an outcast. Job describes the loss of his community's support and concludes with this lament.

> So now my soul is in turmoil within me, and misery has me daily in its grasp.
>
> Job 30:16 TNEB

Elders build and maintain a growing group identity for their clan and people. No longer do they limit themselves to a strictly genetic definition for family, clan or people. They have lived long enough to find that some who are "kin" tear down life while some who were total strangers build life up. Elders nourish life, protect life and enjoy life. A friend of life must be a friend of theirs.

Extending life to the vulnerable and marginal is not always safe. Sometimes the stray "bites." That alone is not enough to stop an elder from working with the stranger. However, people who do not know how to build trust around themselves will often use threats, blame and accusations to get

234

their way. More than a few people lie to get what they want. Elders need the trust of their communities to deal with these problems.

Elders are vulnerable to false accusations and misunderstandings by both those they are teaching how to trust and the perceptions of immature bystanders. Innocent touch can bring back sexual feelings for those whose sexual abuse has caused them to distrust their own bodies. People can misjudge an older man's interest in a pretty girl rather easily—it sure brings up trust issues for those who do not know the man! Consequently, elders need a community that will examine the evidence carefully and recognize when they are dealing with an elder. This is not the case with lawsuits or state licensing boards so most professionals stay away from getting involved. True elders need to be defended and have community advocates. Charges against an elder should require two credible witnesses. (1 Ti 5:19) It will make society a much more affectionate and trusting place to live for those who have been hurt or neglected by their families.

ELDER'S TASKS

Elders *build and rebuild trust relationships* around themselves by *living transparently and honestly* with people who have lost trust. *Elders are parents at large*, showing *hospitality* to the vulnerable and *becoming family to the disenfranchised*. Because they give life to the "bad risks" in their towns, they must also continue to *act like themselves in the midst of difficulties*. As the *keepers of their community's identity* they *raise their people to maturity* and *enjoy the beauty in everyone*. Elders protect, serve and enjoy their communities and people.

Hospitality: Hospitality was the hallmark of the Quail house. Together they were parents to more college students than they could count. When the need arose to borrow a car, Dad Quail would turn over the keys so someone could get back to see his girlfriend. The Quails understood matters of the heart. In their home many nervous, insecure college students found a place to take a boy or a girl home and meet "mom and dad." Rare as it might seem to those who like to choose their dates and mates in bars, poetry readings, cappuccino houses, and video arcades, the Quails let their "adopted" children invite someone "home for dinner." Kids and their dates could come over for an evening that included the comforts of home rather than the clutter of dorm rooms and the elegance of Denny's Restaurant.

More than one woman who didn't know where or who her dad was found comfort in seeing Dad Quail talk to her date even if she never talked directly to him about boys. To hear Dad Quail say, "You know that Bert is a fine young man," seemed to make a difference and reassured young women's hearts. He did what a father would do. My parents met at the Quail's.

Giving life to the "familyless": Francisco was a union foreman in a sugar processing plant. He had a small farm and raised a few farm animals. Francisco hated to see anything go to waste. As a result he rarely had an empty room in his small house. Clementina moved in after her husband's death. She had no money to speak of, and at 85 couldn't get a job but she could make preserves. No fruit ever went to waste with Clementina around the neighborhood. She fed the chickens and helped Francisco's wife with the business she ran out of their house.

Nor was Clementina the only one to live in Francisco's house. His teenage niece roomed with his daughters after being abused by her father. Francisco was only 60 years old but he knew the meaning of hospitality, he knew how to be a father to the men in his union and the women of his community. Francisco brought life to the "familyless."

Raising and maturing his community: Over about 25 years, Fabio and Hilda went from one woman in their home to a large house with over twenty people inside. Other members of their community live in apartments in the neighborhood. He finds people with no skills and eventually gets them working. Some community members have become leaders. People with very little potential are growing and learning to receive and give life.

Building and maintaining a community identity: Our church is known as "the Toaster" because of the funny platform on top of the building where a steeple should go. Construction on the steeple was stopped by a threatened lawsuit from neighbors who claimed it would block their view. When the Church Board was ready to find lawyers and fight, Pastor Earl Lee stopped them by saying, "We came here to win our neighbors not to fight them in court." The building looks like a spaceship to this day but the church community learned a bit more about their identity. Pastor Lee was an elder.

Acting like himself in the midst of difficulty: When his son was held as a hostage in Iran and media attention became intense, Pastor Lee would invite the media to his home. He would make sure that they had coffee and snacks. He figured these men and women were in his life for a reason so he should look after them. Sure, it was a very hard time for the Lee family, but Pastor Lee remembered who he was. Years of suffering and returning to joy in India paid off for him. In fact, one young reporter was so moved that she eventually became a pastor at the "Toaster" herself.

Enjoying what God put in everyone: Both the *hard to enjoy* and the *too easy to enjoy*, the old and the young, the fat and thin, the capable and incompetent, the successful and the failures and even the hostile community members need their joy built up. We just can't get too much joy strength.

236

Living transparently and spontaneously: Transparency is a prerequisite to building trust. We do not trust people who are hiding something. When we hide, even our own responses, we let others know we do not trust them either.

The day before Easter, Gary Bayer and I were walking around a monastery for our usual prayer time when we were greeted by a very old man walking energetically up the hill. He smiled and stopped to talk. There was something warm, unguarded and open in his manner. His white hair, what little there was of it, was tied behind his head in a little ponytail.

"Do either you espeak Espanish?" he asked. "Vengan a comulgar" he said, opening his mouth and putting in imaginary food and then tossing back his head as he downed an imaginary cup. He gestured with such vigor and zest that Gary and I had to laugh.

"Come, come a comulgar. It is Holy Saturday. God love you! I love you! Come!" He hugged us with delight.

"Come my sons!" he said again and repeated the gestures with the bread and the cup. "I will pray for you!" and with that he hugged us again with such spontaneous joy that Gary and I giggled like two schoolgirls. This elder had no fear, no embarrassment no hesitation about what life meant.

Building and rebuilding trust: It is very interesting that the brain circuits involved with trust are the same ones used for recognizing and interpreting faces. Trust, you might say, is a familiar face. These face circuits are the ones we use for authentic right-hemisphere-to-right-hemisphere communication. Trust is built and rebuilt by familiar faces we have known a long time. Trust is built face-to-face with honest, authentic people who share our feelings.

Pastor Luke Kim is an elder of impeachable sincerity. When he heard that something was wrong between Dr. Peters and the denomination staff, Pastor Kim got involved. Pastor Kim spent days talking to the parties in conflict. He personally examined Dr. Peters in depth and then vouched for his integrity. Pastor Kim listened to all sides and took their concerns seriously. Because everyone in the community trusted Pastor Kim, he used himself to build bridges and reduce damage. Pastor Kim wanted to bring everyone involved in conflict to a resolution. Because Pastor Kim cared, a few people began to trust Dr. Peters again but there was a condition. Dr. Peters, who was not trusted, would have to stay under the care and mentoring of Pastor Kim who was trusted. Dr. Peters agreed but it was later discovered that he did not do as he said he would do. Instead of confiding in the elder, Dr. Peters pretended to Pastor Kim that he had nothing more to do with Mrs. Valjean while continuing to meet her in secret. Dr. Peters fears were winning as he isolated himself from his community and family. His identity and integrity were coming apart. Elders only survive in communities.

Nothing new: An elder's tasks have not changed in four thousand years as we read in the poem of Job. His classic description of his actions as a father to his community can still inspire developing elders who want to give life to the vulnerable and "familyless."

> I delivered the poor that cried, and the fatherless, and him that had none to help him. The blessing of him that was ready to perish came upon me: I caused the widow's heart to sing for joy. I put on righteousness, and it clothed me: my judgment was as a robe and a diadem. I was eyes to the blind, and feet was I to the lame. I was a father to the poor: the cause which I knew not I searched out. And I broke the jaws of the wicked, and plucked the prey out of his teeth.
> Job 29:12-17 RWEBSTR

We recall that elder is the longest of our life stages and requires the most growth and development of any stage. The elder must learn to synchronize with more different people and in more different circumstances than he has ever done. Having your youngest turn thirteen qualifies a man to start learning the elder tasks if he has kept his maturity up to date.

WEALTH PRESERVATION BLOCKS ELDER DEVELOPMENT IN AMERICA

Perhaps the greatest enemy of elder maturity in America is not our serious disrespect for the old, the rapid changes in society or fallout from the industrial revolution but greed. Greed is the hallmark of the dissatisfied person, proof that greedy people never reached the childhood goal of learning what satisfies. Having never completed the childhood tasks means that greedy individuals are not ready for the demands of manhood let alone elder status.

Greed in the old is seen most often in the form of "wealth preservation," that is, holding on to what they have. Nor are the elderly the only people interested in wealth preservation; it can infect any age. There is nothing wrong with investments or protecting what one has, the problem is with fear-based thinking. When the fear of loss becomes the governing force in our minds, the wrong part of the brain takes over our finances. No longer do our goals govern our choices or investments, instead fears take over stopping us from acting like ourselves—this fear thinking breeds greed and wealth preservation. Older people have bumper stickers that read, "We are spending our children's inheritance." All of these forms of greed agree that

238

money is best spent on **ME**. This thought is as beautiful in a child as it is ugly in an elder.

When we talk about investments we reach a major value conflict when we look at children. Are children a liability or an investment? American culture often equates having many children with a loss of wealth. Young adults wait to have children until they can afford them, all the while buying cars, ski lift tickets, education and home theater systems. Children and family are a liability to those who wish to reduce expenses and preserve their wealth; consequently, having children seems more like a curse than a blessing.

Parents and elders see children as a blessing and their future as an investment. Elders seek this blessing. Elders cannot have many children and seek to keep all their wealth for themselves. Elders work to see their family grow and invest accordingly. Elders have children through bringing in the "orphans" of society and treating the discarded children of others as their own. For most elders this is a deeply religious activity.

The Christian scriptures make a great deal of developing a spiritual family that ever widens our area of concern. The Bible makes over 100 references to the "stranger." The stranger is one who lacks the necessary supportive relationships and can therefore be easily ignored or used by others. Strangers are mentioned in the company of widows and orphans, who obviously suffer from the same problems. The treatment of these groups becomes the test of true religion for the Old Testament prophets and, according to Christ, the test between sheep and goats at the great judgment. (Mathew 25:31ff) God had decreed that one blessing given faithful followers is to have many descendants. They can have those who have no real support in their lives. Supporting the unsupported is the church's business—a business directed by elders.

It would seem that with so much attention given in Scripture to the care of others, greed would be almost unheard of in the Christian church. Such is not the case. Wealth preservation is a form of greed frequently found in churches among members of all ages. Some people don't want to lend things to anyone who will not return them or might wreck them, even in the face of clear instructions from Jesus that we should lend to those who can't repay. The same is true for lending money, some will only lend to those who pose no risk of loss. Others carefully include only the people who will preserve their resources with them and exclude those who will deplete their supplies. Whether it is choosing whom to invite out for dinner or who will share a vacation, considerations usually favor those who will pay their own way.

Greed, envy and jealousy are mentioned by James the brother of Jesus as the source of trouble in churches. (James 4:2) Paul therefore directs that elders oversee churches. An elder will not be greedy according to Paul. (Titus 1:7) No elder could be effective if his desires ran toward his own comfort. Investing in life wins over protecting our wealth.

Loss of wealth is the fear behind the threat from lawsuits. Nothing blocks organizations (as well as individuals) from reaching out to the victimized and marginal members of their communities like the fear of lawsuits. Neither the expense nor the poor level of results that benevolence often achieves chill the well-intentioned like the phrase, "We are leaving ourselves open to a lawsuit." That phrase has put the brakes on more good ideas than any other objection I have heard uttered. Helping people is one thing, but trusting them with the power to take our wealth away through the courts is a way different one. Lawsuits are a big fear in communities of all kinds.

Greed, wealth preservation and other fears are not overcome by moralizing but through relationships. Elders slowly build trust with all who fear whether in the church, at home or on the street. It is hard to consider building trust when we might lose our wealth in the process. Elders think of this as investing.

NOT EVERYONE CAN BECOME AN ELDER

Sometimes we just start too late: Sylvia got married at 50. She will not have a family and raise kids. Sometimes we do not have the capacity: Sam was born with cerebral palsy. Sam will not play professional sports. Bob is a 67-year-old businessman with failing health. Bob will not become a university professor. Gary is a 56-year-old leader of his community with two divorces and a grandchild. Gary will not become an elder. Richard is a 47-year-old priest who has devoted his life to the care of his parish. Richard will never become an elder either.

As unfair as it might seem, sometimes it is too late or we lack the capacity and the resources to reach a goal. Some people can never achieve elder maturity. Marvin spent his life avoiding feelings and at 72 will never get his make-up work done in time. William was a woman's man and played the field all his youth and most of his adult life. Even though William eventually married, he had several affairs and could only fight off sexual feelings for his daughters with some difficulty. William so sexualized his brain that the best he can do now is protect women from himself—he will never be an elder and care for young women. Melville drank and smoked pot for over twenty years. While he has been sober for 25 years he is still at infant maturity. Lynn never tamed his anger until after his children were grown. He controlled their lives through fear. While he has four grown kids,

240

Lynn still does not know how to raise a child. Paul never married. He devoted his latter life to missionary work and wrote many letters that became widely published—even before his death. While he was greatly loved by his many spiritual children, Paul died without ever becoming an elder.

Reaching the highest level of human maturity comes only from a life-long effort by a community as well as an individual. Crucial mistakes along the way will eliminate contestants from reaching the goal.

MATURITY IS NOT THE SOURCE OF HUMAN VALUE

As we immediately sense when we hold a baby, maturity is not the same as human value. While those who fail to mature at the same rate as their surrounding culture expects often annoy us, immature people still make valuable contributions to life. As long as we can still understand our maturity goals it is not too late to pursue greater maturity.

Maturity is not a pecking order. Maturity is capacity. While it is sad to see someone who has not fully developed his capacity, value comes from how we use the capacity that we have developed.

DO YOU WANT AN ELDER IN YOUR LIFE?

Myrtle was in her 80s and her slow mental decline no longer interested her doctors. As she became more combative and resistant, Earl had a harder and harder time taking care of her. He was too old to lift her and Myrtle was too resistant and agitated to move on her own. Nurses would not come to the house because Myrtle would not sign a consent form and she would not sign the form because she no longer could. Earl couldn't get her to the doctors very easily and when he did they were not interested in her case.

When he heard about it, Dr. Brubaker drove to Myrtle and Earl's home and prescribed a medication for her paranoia. As a result, Earl and Myrtle were able to enjoy some sweet times together before my Mom died a few months later. Dr. Brubaker stopped by regularly to encourage my dad and check on his patient. After my mother died Dr. Brubaker came to visit my dad to help him with his loss and depression. He treated Earl as he would his own father.

Last year Dr. Brubaker brought his father to stay the night with my dad while he took his mother to the emergency room. It was a rainy, stormy night. Dr. Brubaker and his family had been camping near my dad's town when Dr. Brubaker's mother developed severe heart problems. Dad was glad to help with a bit of shelter.

What makes this unusual is not that my dad trusted his psychiatrist (well that is a little unusual knowing my dad) but that this psychiatrist trusted my dad. Dr. Brubaker's concern could get him sued or cost him his license if anyone complained to the state. His crime would be trusting and building trust. Do you want to be protected from Dr. Brubaker? Do you want your mother kept away from his kind of medicine?

It is not his medical license but his elder status that qualifies Dr. Brubaker to rebuild community trust and treat strangers as though they were his family. Some of you might like him as your psychiatrist if he lived near you. The sad part is we cannot use Dr. Brubaker's real name. If we gave his real name, anyone in California could call the state board with the material in this chapter and cost him a long fight and maybe his license. We can't take a chance on losing Dr. Brubaker to social immaturity and fear. Sorry we can't help. But, should you happen to meet a fatherly man in a Brethren beard with spontaneity and energy that is uncommon among the psychiatrists—your life might have just started looking up!

Chapter Fifteen
An Elder and His Children

As she got off the bus in Visalia California, Arlis carried everything she owned in a bandana—not much for a fourteen-year-old girl. Mark Heinz was there to meet her; even though she did not know him well she recognized his smile. Mark and Gloria had sent the bus ticket that had brought her here. She tried not to think about her last time in this town. The girl had many things she did not like to remember.

Arlis' mother and her eight brothers and sisters moved a great deal. She had never stayed in one place long enough to complete even one semester in school. Visalia was one more town. A shy and retiring girl, Arlis had been glad when one of her classmates invited her home on Friday night.

"Can I spend the night?" she asked her mother.

Looking around the motel room the eight of them shared her mother answered, "All right, but be back tomorrow morning to help me clean the room."

Saturday morning Arlis rode her bicycle back to the motel but no one answered the door. Her mother had taken everything and everyone and left town. Having no other idea of what to do Arlis went back to the home she had visited over night where they let her stay another day.

Sunday morning she went to church. It was a small church, about forty people in all. Mark was the youth minister. Gloria was the director of music. Mark's dad was the pastor. With their help Arlis contacted her grandmother in Washington state who said she could come there to live. Before she left Mark took her aside. He was saddened by the loss this young girl faced and wishing to set her mind at rest told her, "If you ever need a place to stay we will help you find one."

Arlis got a ride to Washington with an associate pastor and was about to take the bus the rest of the way to her Grandmother's house when Grandma abruptly changed her mind and told Arlis she was not welcome. Arlis wrote to Mark.

"We knew it would impact our daughter Carol the most," Mark remembers, "so we asked her if she wanted an older sister. Carol had been an only child for eleven years and we left the decision up to her." Suggesting that she pray about it a while her parents waited two days for their answer. Carol now says that she could have given the answer at once, for she did want an older sister. Mark sent Arlis a bus ticket to Visalia.

Sitting in their living room that night Mark told her, "You can't be a guest here. That just won't work. You will be part of the family." And as they talked Arlis' confidence rose until she said, "Could I have a piece of bread?" The Heinzes realized suddenly that the girl had not had anything to eat and Gloria hurried to the kitchen to fix her supper.

As they sat down to pray Arlis asked if she could pray. It was a prayer that Mark never forgot. "Lord, help me to learn to obey my new mother and father," Arlis asked and with that request became a daughter to the only real father she would ever know.

"I made a commitment to Arlis then and there that she would be just like the daughter born to me," Mark remembers. "It was instantaneous. The two girls became sisters and we were a family."

Arlis got her own room painted bright yellow even though Gloria hated yellow. Arlis loved yellow. It was her room to do as she wanted and she kept her door tightly closed.

A few weeks later, Gloria, who was a bug about sleeping with fresh air, tiptoed into the girl's room to open a window. Arlis sat up screaming, clutching her blankets in terror. Mark and Gloria tried to comfort her to no avail. Hours later, the girl sobbed out, "If I tell you then you won't like me anymore."

"It won't change a thing," Mark told her and taking courage from his words the stories poured out. Mark found himself with a daughter who had not only been abandoned but also abused. Her own mother had arranged the encounters that made this girl's bed a terrifying place. Far into the night the stories poured out in torrents of tears until at last her small body lay quietly snuggled in Mark's arms. Gloria dried her tears and reassured Arlis that they would never allow another crime to rob her rest.

The door to Arlis' room was open after that as was the door to her soul. "She loves me so much it's almost scary," Mark tells almost forty years later. "It is the closest to the love I have with my Heavenly Father that I have ever felt. Over the years we have continued to grow closer. I am a very blessed man. Some people say that a thirty year old can't adopt a fifteen year old but I did," Mark states with a certain tone of finality. Elders often do what others say can't be done. Elders look at strangers and see family.

"Some people think that it must be a sacrifice. We didn't have much money, but I am the one who was enriched. I only wish the church and my relatives could have accepted what our family accepted. They continued to refer to the girls as 'Arlis and your daughter' when they were both my daughters. My brother and sister have never really accepted my girl. They still invite us over and tell me not to bring Arlis. Almost all her birth family has died and the family that should be hers won't have her." Arlis still cries about that.

Here was a family and church that could look at the sky and not see stars. To them, spiritual things were not real. Arlis was never a real daughter regardless of what Mark and Gloria said. This community let their elders down and broke their hearts. Mark's deep love and bond with his daughter was never legitimate in their eyes. Results followed from this community response.

Mark cries when he remembers how Arlis was blamed for Gloria's death because Arlis was divorced just as Gloria was dying. Some want to believe that the stress was the cause of Gloria's decline, but Mark does not believe it.

As a result of her divorce Arlis was "read out"[60] of her church. Because of the divorce the pastors at the girl's church told Carol that she should treat Arlis as though she were dead and never speak to her again. This drove a wedge between the two women that has never been removed. It brought a wall between Carol and her father who had always been extremely close. Arlis' children turned away from God and the church after seeing how their mother was treated.

"I just can't reconcile this rejection by my family and church with being a Christian," Mark told me sadly. "I can be dad for my girl but I can't be cousin, uncle, aunt, nephew, church or sister." He nearly choked on the last word. No elder can be a whole family and community. He too had been abandoned.

"If I could, I would ask them what the word forgiveness means. I would tell them of the joy and blessing they are missing. I have definitely gotten the best part of this bargain. They have really missed out." His elder's heart still reaches out to his community inviting them back to joy.

After forty years of an elder's life Mark still lights up like a Christmas tree at the mention of Arlis. Many times he has confided the same secret to me, always with the same pleasure and melody in his voice. His face breaks into a smile behind his white mustache, he leans forward ever so slightly and says, "She calls me 'dad,' and I call her 'daughter'!"

BUT IS IT REAL?

Ah! But there you have it! Is this a story of a man with his daughter or a story of a 30-year-old man holding a pajama clad 15-year-old girl he just recently met? It seems like a crude question to ask of such a heroic story but we must remember that Mark's brother, sister and church all failed to see a father and a daughter in Mark and Arlis.

Mark's story is actually a fairly conservative one as stories of elders and daughters go. Arlis was still legally a child and, regardless of our maturity, we can see how children need fathers and homes. Most elders

---

[60] Excommunicated

discover their spiritual daughters when the woman is full-grown physically—perhaps even with children of her own. Sometimes the woman must escape her family or even an abusive marriage before she is free to heal and learn to trust. If she finds a spiritual father can she really be his daughter? Everything they build hinges on the reality of this bond. How we as a community will treat them hinges on their bond being real and legitimate.

The women and men who most need spiritual parents are remarkably immature. Many are emotionally unstable. They are living at infant or child maturity in full-grown bodies. By this point in the book, you are well aware of the many ways people can fail to complete their emotional development. This failure is often due to what they did not receive. To grow up, as we will see in chapters 17-19, often requires that someone provides what we didn't receive in childhood. What makes this troublesome here is that we are talking about being a father to a girl personality state in a woman's body. Are you ready for that? Are we as a culture ready for that? Speaking of fathers and daughters quickly gets into intimate subjects full of emotions! We speak romantically of the child within us all but what if that child never developed and now lives in a woman's body? Can she still have a father? I mean, a real father's love that will hold her when she cries and teach her not to fear in the night?

Children need touch, affection, warmth and closeness. Children need to depend on someone, be vulnerable and make mistakes. Children need to learn about their bodies and how to live with others. When their own families failed them, their bodies grew up anyway and now we are talking about complete strangers, men often not much older than they are physically, becoming the fathers they never had. We are all familiar with adults whose intellect is developmentally delayed. They may be thirty years old but their minds function like a three-year-old. Their teachers do not need to be older than they physically—only mentally. In the same way elder-parents can train emotionally underdeveloped minds once they have a bond between them even when their "child" was born before they were.

Can we trust that a parent-child bond between two people is real even for people in full-grown bodies? Mark said the relationship was instantaneous and just as real as with his biological daughter. Although not everyone experiences an instantaneous change, elders repeatedly report that the bond with natural and spiritual children is the same. This makes sense since the attachment center in the first level of the brain's control center appears to have only one secure form of attachment.

There is often more fear about men as fathers to women than when men are spiritual fathers to men. Perhaps this would be a good place to remember that elders have first been boys then men and then fathers before becoming elders. We are not talking about old men here. Being old guarantees nothing but wrinkly skin and hair on your ears and other places where it does no good. True fathers and elders are very good for women just as they are for men. They worked hard for many years and arrived one stage at a time—no exceptions.

It is well known that many Christian leaders who have affairs start out feeling fatherly toward the woman. This affection later turns to arousal and disaster. In every such case I have examined the man has reached elder status prematurely having skipped stages, passages and above all, having failed to learn what really satisfies his need for closeness. He has still not come to terms with his attachment pain. (In fact, most men who get in trouble would say confidently that they do not have attachment pain—a clear giveaway.) Often simple joy or trust unlocked a need he did not know he had thus releasing a need he did not know how to satisfy. (See Becoming An Elder Too Soon in Chapter Twenty.) Instead of turning to an elder who would teach him what really satisfies he turned to the man or woman who he thinks just unlocked his soul.

Dr. Peters and his fatherly care for Mrs. Valjean turned sexual within two years after he turned away from the help (and conflicts) offered by his elder Pastor Kim. During an explosive time that resembled the Columbia Space Shuttle breaking up over Texas, we watched years of hard work and life be destroyed. Dr. Peters had feared the attachment pain that both he and Mrs. V. would feel if Pastor Kim and the community kept them apart—a sign of a strong bond and a sign of an even stronger fear. Dr. Peters had not faced his attachment pain or the cry of his nucleus accumbens, "You are going to die and so is she!" As his control center delaminated and fears began to guide his choices, he found himself alone with no community or family to get him synchronized again. The very attachment pain he feared came upon them both, and his wife, and his children, and his church and his friends—Pastor Kim and me. Fear-bonds had struck again. Dr. Peters may recover but will never fly again. Mrs. Valjean is in intensive care in critical condition.

If you are a man or woman stuck in or fleeing such a situation, find an elder now to help you. You will not find the answers alone. Unless you are quite narcissistic you already know a lot of people are going to get hurt.

THE PROBLEMS WITH TOUCHING

The problems and risks created by touching are not nearly so great as those created by leaving all touch to the sexually driven members of our society. We will never solve the problems created by poor parenting by waiting for people to grow up and have sex. It is even worse when we don't wait for them to grow up. Wounded and immature people need nurturing touch. It is a crime to deprive them of what they need to grow and heal.

We are not where we need to be yet for emotionally wounded people in our churches or society. We still treat those who received terrible parenting as untouchable for life. We overlook the most essential parts of their humanity—the need for a bonded, affectionate and trusting relationship with a parent. We hold ourselves to be moral and professional because we do not touch, bond or care for the emotionally disabled. We are ready to punish, sue and defrock any who would try—especially if the wounded person is a woman. A change is needed!

Elders are the only potential source for the touch that wounded and immature people need. If we are going to understand and protect our elders and their children we must look at what may well be the most uncomfortable and easily misunderstood topic in this book—affection between a father and his daughter. This subject triggers pain and fear for almost every woman, that alone makes it hard to think about. Expressions of affection between fathers and daughters change as women grow up but individual differences leave a wide range of expressions to choose from at any age. When we add in that elders are dealing with women they did not raise, who live in adult bodies and may, at any given moment, be at almost any emotional and developmental age, it gets even harder to know how to think about affection. We are left to trust the intuitive and spiritual sense between father and daughter of what fits for them in that moment. Can we trust the elder-father and his daughter to do the same?

An elder's affection cannot be fully understood by those still at adult, child or infant maturity even when they are receiving his love. We can really only understand the motivation of one level of maturity above our own. In spite of all this risk of misunderstanding, the only way we can protect elders and their children is to teach what it takes to build trust with those whose trust has been destroyed within the intimate family sphere. This will not be easy. It will make us all uncomfortable. Our trust issues will be exposed as we examine what happens in an elder's love for his daughter.

Once a woman feels comfortable and she trusts her elder-father, the woman will begin to wonder if she is really his daughter. She will want to be touched and held the way she imagines that good fathers treat their daughters. She starts with hugs but eventually two other needs arise: the need for physical contact during "quiet together time" and the need for skin contact. Quiet together time is often called "snuggling" and can be interspersed with small eruptions of words and feelings between them like bubbles bursting at the surface of carbonated water. Sometimes they use quiet together time for reading, watching clouds or listening to music. During extended quiet together times the nervous system not only turns off its alarms but begins to learn a new, restful state of normal. The elder-father is transferring generations of family closeness into a void. Occasionally the woman will even fall asleep but the elder usually remains slightly vigilant. Sadly, for many wounded people this is the first time they have slept in peace and security. Only elders can give such a gift to those with no safe family.

ELDER-FATHERS AND SEXUALLY ABUSED WOMEN

The women and men most likely to need elders as replacement fathers are those who were sexually abused by their parents—particularly if their mothers sexually abused them. While elders are not providing any sort of therapy for sexual abuse, they do provide an atmosphere of trust, which includes trusting attachments, limits, needs, touching, feelings and living in our bodies. Sexual abuse produces the illusion in the victim that the other person is producing sexual feelings rather than these being feelings that belong to her own body. Alarms go off for abuse victims if their sexual feelings are triggered because these have always been tied to out of control experiences.

The elder-father and daughter have had to work through the initial sexualization of touch for each of them. For most men this means working through some of their own thoughts about intimacy and sexuality. At first they must remind themselves of how they would treat their biological children if they were at the same emotional age and state. This is one reason that only true elders who have completed all their maturity tasks can safely build these kinds of bonds. Before long, thoughts about how they held their own children combine with the pain they feel hearing about the sexual abuse their spiritual child suffered. The result of blending these two thoughts is a natural revulsion to any possibility of sexual contact with their spiritually adopted child.

For most sexually abused women, touch from a father figure means facing both thoughts and occasional body reactions of a sexual nature. Safe resolution requires enough trust between them that she can talk about sexual feelings when they are triggered. For her to learn how to calm her own nervous system, they must stop any touching until the sexual feelings have been put back to sleep. She will not know how to do this at first. Instead, the daughter will feel some combination of terror, shame and arousal. These are expected reactions for the woman given the terrible training her nervous system received but they leave her so vulnerable that great trust and love must be there to surround her. The crucial point is that neither she nor her spiritual father must linger to enjoy these feelings. They are beautiful feelings but not for fathers and daughters to enjoy together. Sexual feelings must be put back to sleep *as soon as they wake up*. None of these intense emotions should distract the elder from acting like himself or cause him to withdraw. This is more proof that maturity is required for elders.

Elders will encounter sexual abuse and its damage very frequently. Most women who need a new father are likely to have some degree of sexual abuse in their past. Learning to trust touch involves a process of learning to own, enjoy, set limits and quiet one's own body. It is more than abundantly clear that the man who has not had long years of experience with this himself cannot teach it to anyone.

Often women who have been sexually abused want to reenact events that led up to their abuse in order to experience a different outcome and form new memories and associations. Susie, at age 35, still wanted to go camping and stay in the same tent with her dad. She had gone camping with her stepfather when she was 12 and he had sex with her in the tent. She still wanted to have a close, warm family camping trip where she could curl up in her sleeping bag, enjoy the sounds of nature and be safe. Susie had an elder who saw her as his daughter so she asked him to take her camping. These actions all followed a secret impulse to see if she really had been molested because of something she had done or requested. Susie was 33 when she met her elder-father.

Tahisha wanted to sit on dad's knee. We know what had happened there before. She wanted to kiss dad on the lips and she wanted to tickle. Next, Tahisha wanted to serve dad coffee on the couch in the afternoon when no one else was home. Finally, she wanted to lay her head on dad's lap. Tahisha was 28 and had a young son when she met her elder-father.

Lisa left her bra and panties lying out where they could be seen. She wanted her dad to notice what she was wearing and tell her if she was pretty. Every time they were together, Lisa would throw her arms around her new father and ask to snuggle. Lisa was 36 when she met her elder-father.

All three daughters wanted to put on her pajamas and have dad tuck them into bed, say goodnight prayers and give them backrubs. Their desires to form new memories were presented to their spiritual fathers—all elders.

Most of these requests were granted but they lead to paradoxical results. While new experiences create new memories they also reveal that what happened before didn't have to be. At least half of the time a period of grief, anger and sadness followed good touch instead of the happiness the women hoped to have. Sometimes they conclude that what they asked for was a mistake. Sometimes they just don't like it. Tahisha decided that dad's knee was bony and besides she felt uncomfortable. She tried it several more times just to be sure but got the same result. She was learning about herself and making mistakes. Part of creating trust is providing an environment

250

where it is safe to make mistakes, learn and change your mind. Elders do that.

The results of father-daughter affection in these women's lives were remarkable. Susie's actual parents were her mother and older brother. Her mother, father and that same older brother, had sexually abused her. Susie had sex with almost every man or woman she ever met and had almost every one of her attempted relationships disintegrate on her. She severely distrusted all women. Several years of therapy produced no noticeable change. After her camping trip and chance to learn proper father-daughter affection, Susie only had two more impulsive sexual episodes in over ten years. She began to have and keep friends.

Tahisha would cut herself in her vagina. Every day that she could remember, she threw up in the toilet and then ate it all out of the toilet bowl again. Therapy had failed to change these behaviors. Once she began experiencing father-daughter affection this self-abuse stopped in less than two months and never returned.

Lisa spent her childhood working part-time as a child prostitute for her parents. Between her father, brother and customers she experienced over 3,000 sexual assaults before reaching puberty. She could never sleep through the night and was terrified of toilets flushing. She feared men but distrusted women even more. She kept her floor so cluttered that no one could walk in the room without tripping. She shocked her elder-father one day by saying, "I shaved myself down there because that is how you men like girls." She had to know if that was what made men attack. After learning to be tucked in bed she was able to sleep through the nights, no longer feared night sounds and was able to clean and enjoy her house for the first time.

For the first time, these women were learning how to live with others as human beings. They were learning to trust their homes, trust their bodies, trust their needs and live in community like members of society. They began to feel joy, even wake up happy some mornings. These daughters poured out their love and found peace in return. But, not one of them found a community capable or willing to accept and support the relationship with her elder-father. To a woman, they found that elder-daughter affection crossed the line that cut them off from acceptance and yet was the very thing that gave them new life.

On the other side of the coin we have seen how a lack of community support and acceptance is exactly what makes elder-daughter affection dangerous. Perhaps just having children is dangerous. More women across human history have died during childbirth that at any other moment in their lives. We have done a great deal to make it less dangerous (although not nearly enough.) Rather than say that having children is a dangerous idea and we should quit having babies we have worked to make the process safe. Let's take one more look at the postmortem for Dr. Peters and Mrs. Valjean and see what we can learn to prevent future disasters.

Like most disasters we may never fully know what went wrong. What we do know is that Dr. Peters was on his first try at becoming an elder and had no previous experience. He greatly needed the support of his family and community to survive. As far as we know, his community did not believe in or support spiritual adoption in any form and did everything possible to abort it. When Pastor Kim examined Dr. Peters several months after the spiritual adoption had taken place he could find nothing wrong with Dr. Peters spiritually—a sign that was overlooked by the community when deciding what God was doing. People already had their ideas about what was good and evil. For his part, Dr. Peters avoided pain and withdrew from community rather than trust Pastor Kim thus dismembering his individual and group identities. He needed to build trust with his community even if he took a terrible beating for staying. From that point on the incineration on re-entry was inevitable. When Dr. Peters later began to delaminate his control center under attachment pain he had no one to synchronize with but Mrs. Valjean.

Let us compare Dr. Peters' case with what happed to Harvey on his first entry into spiritual adoption. Harvey's wife became alarmed after he felt God told him to receive a teenage orphan girl as a spiritual daughter. He took steps to educate his community about spiritual adoption and stay involved with them as he tried to resolve his wife's concerns. At the advice of his community, he separated from his spiritual daughter leaving her in the arms of a caring community while he devoted himself to improving his marriage. Two years later he was reunited with his spiritual daughter. His community continues to learn from him about what God can do through spiritual adoption relationships. Harvey faced his fears and is helping his community and daughter face theirs.

Harvey's situation was not the perfect solution either because of the unnecessary separation of father and daughter for nearly two years but is shows what can happen when a new elder stays with his community and the community supports his spiritual child. What would have happened to Dr. Peters if his community had helped him learn to be an elder rather than taking away his job, doing all they could to abort the adoption, ignoring high levels of attachment pain and acting out of fear? What could have been done for the community if Dr. Peters had faced his fears and stayed involved with Pastor Kim even if it got him a beating?

As we walk around the crash site and smell the stench of burning wreckage some will say, "Scrap the program." If it is just my idea, I suggest we do exactly that. If this spiritual family is God's plan we should teach men and their communities to fly.

THE ELDER AND HIS SONS

There is no pretty way to say it—he just started too soon. Clement tried to be an elder too soon and both his family and community suffered a bit for it. But let's be fair, Clement was a pioneer. He never heard of an elder in the sense we have used in this book. Like all pioneers, he had to learn as he went. His guidebooks were wrong in several crucial ways and he had no elders to lead him through. Still, you have to give Clement credit for perseverance because he kept at it rather than giving up.

By the time he was really ready to take an elder's place, Clement had a community and a spiritual family around him. His marriage was strong and his three children were adults. They lived and participated in an extended church community where families helped each other (as well as strangers) to live fully. The Brethren, like many other groups at the time, were attempting intentional communities. With a name like "Brethren" you might expect a spiritual family but it was not the name that attracted Clement and Grace. They found a passionate love for life and others in their friendship with Jesus that was too good to keep to themselves. Their life together became a healing and living fellowship.

Clement's problem was his job for Clement was a psychotherapist. Not that there wasn't need for his help but because we put therapists in a peculiar place. As we saw in chapter 14, few jobs make it harder to be an elder than mental health jobs. As a culture we have determined that mental health is a medical matter and as such should be managed by dispassionate people who do not care at a personal level. Above all, mental heath workers do not get involved in other people's lives.[61]

Clement and Grace often had people stay in their home. People who came long distances in search of healing would find the quiet and gentle atmosphere created by Grace as healing as the therapy Clement provided. Some visitors became deeply loved and accepted by Clement's natural family. His daughter was 17 years old when she adopted one lady as her sister. Sometimes Grace would cradle someone while they cried and Clement would hold a hand. Much healing happened in the simple time

---

[61] Robert Jay Lifton, *The Nazi Doctors*, (New York: Basic Books, 1986) contains a penetrating analysis of the dangers in this medical model. Although his question is why medical training does not make one a humanitarian, he does explore the failure of Nazi doctors to act like elders.

preparing meals or working around the house. The atmosphere was saturated with trust and blessing.

Clement was a deeply spiritual man with a tendency to see the whole world as his area of concern. In his paradigm, like that of philosopher Dr. Dallas Willard, the primary requirement for the care of the soul or psyche (from which psychotherapy takes its name) is that you love that soul. Clement soon had a growing number of spiritual children—both men and women.

Tim and Tina were members of Clement's community. Tim was a young doctor who struggled to deal with his emotional reactions to his work and community. Tim first opened up to Clement about difficulties he was having with his patients. He looked to the wise older man for supervision with the emotional issues raised in his medical practice. Soon Tim began talking about his relationship with Tina. Clement realized that both Tim and Tina would not mature correctly without more help. He sensed that he was in their lives at just that time for just that purpose. Clement took the initiative to visit the young couple's home and it was there Tina recognized her own need and began a healing journey with him. Tina was resolving childhood abuse issues from a man so Clement held and nurtured her through her healing.

As his trust grew, Tim started a time of intensive therapy with Clement. Tim's traumas had started young—in utero—and led to a premature birth. His mother nearly died herself in the following hours. The nurses handed tiny Tim to his father to "hold while he can" because Timmy was not expected to live. Inhumane medical procedures, that have long since been abandoned, nearly caused his death during his three weeks in the neonatal unit. The lack of touch was bad enough but the worst thing for Timmy was the timed feeding schedule. Timmy lost almost a quarter of his already low birth weight and was sent home to die or be saved by mother love. He lived because his mother carefully synchronized to Timmy and his needs.

Clement brought in Florence to hold Tim because he needed so much mother love to face the agony of those first three weeks of his life. Florence was one of Clement's spiritual daughters. She had been brought to maturity by his care and sometimes joined him in the loving care of other souls. In this warm nest, Tim found what had been missing with the nurses in his days of newborn peril—loving affection for his needs.

In those nine years of sorting, Clement helped me make sense of this crazy stuff. I remember how enraged and angry I would feel at the nurses in the nursery for just letting the babies cry in their bassinets and not going to get them to see what was needed. I remember being just livid with rage and wanting to kill the nurses. Clement taught me to just keep looking for connections and ask the Lord where it was coming from. Clement was a support, he was a mentor and he became a friend. I not only respected and appreciated him; he showed me respect and appreciation.

Over their nine years together, Clement taught the young doctor to care for his patients, deal with unsupportive community leaders and develop the characteristics of an elder within himself. He grieved and raged and grew until in his heart Tim heard the words, "The gift of the long ordeal is life." Tim and Clement often traveled together to spiritual and professional events. They became friends attending conferences together. Twenty years later they still visit each other's homes and care deeply for one another's families even though Dr. Tim Brubaker has now moved to California and works as a psychiatrist. He is a man of spontaneity and energy that is unusual among psychiatrists.

"And now," as Paul Harvey would say, "you know the rest of the story."

GREED IN SPIRITUAL ADOPTION

Among wounded and lonely people are a number who believe their pain entitles them to care. When exposed to elders and their families they quickly begin to feel entitled to what everyone else is receiving. While they are initially attracted by the care given by elders, soon after their arrival they become competitive, often expressing contempt for others who seek help. Instead, these wounded ones insist that their problems, hurts and needs are the biggest, most pressing and deserving of anyone's. Simultaneously, their untamed nucleus accumbens screams that they will die if they don't get what they want. Often they threaten to kill themselves or, in time, others.

Narcissism, as you may recall, is an inability to return to joy from shame. Shame is the feeling that someone does not want to be with me. Rather than face and feel the shame feeling when someone really does not want to be with them at that moment, narcissists will beat themselves or the other person emotionally. They beat themselves for not being lovable enough (the skunk) or others for not loving them well enough (the peacock).

The peacocks are often in some kind of prominence or leadership position and like attracting attention or being in charge. The skunks won't participate with others and draw attention to themselves by the strangely disruptive things they do so no one will notice them—while, of course, everyone does. If they were only narcissistic and not wounded, these people would be glad to pass themselves off as elders but their wounds are too obvious.

Laura was very helpful and soon made herself seem indispensable. I say "seem indispensable" because on close examination it was not clear what Laura really did. She seemed to be in the center of activity in her community. She was always discovering some new, deep and tragic secret about her life that was worse than what anyone else had suffered. Laura seemed to always be hearing some new truth from God; at least twice she was miraculously cured of all her troubles just in time to be the highlight of a healing conference. Laura also had troubling "words from God" about people around her. She would discern that certain leaders should not be trusted, other members of her community had a "dark side." Laura "felt called" to become the "intercessor" for the man who was praying through past wounds with her. With her special spiritual discernment on his side, the leader soon found flaws in his peers and began to withdraw from them and depend more on Laura. This withdrawal from community is exactly the opposite of what an elder would do. Elders stay involved with their communities and build trust rather than withdraw when there is suspicion. In time everyone but the two of them was on the "dark side" as they saw it. Laura took up much of the minister's time with her deep sufferings and other indispensable things while he depended on her spiritual vision. They trusted no one else and no one else trusted them.

It is usually one of these narcissists who eventually accuses an elder of misconduct and succeeds in destroying trust within a community. Unlike many wounded people who do not trust others, narcissists readily seek to be trusted and use this trust to their advantage and to harm others. Communities who do not protect their elders will eventually lose trust in them through the attacks of a narcissist who is not getting his or her way. Communities must so value their elders that they are willing to face hostile narcissists and be humiliated. Communities that abandon their elders when under attack find it spells an end to trust.

Annie had three elders who served as stand-in spiritual fathers for her. She was vivacious and popular; in fact her only dark cloud was an ongoing conflict with a narcissistic colleague. One of her spiritual fathers offered to help her resolve the situation. He introduced Annie to his pastor, an elder with even more capacity for intimacy than the first three. She quickly became attracted to this church community and wanted to be closer to pastor Daniel than anyone else—including his wife. She flirted, she threatened, she physically assaulted Daniel and she made accusations both privately and publicly whenever she didn't get her way. Annie took pleasure in killing small animals as a way to threaten others about what she would do to them. When Daniel refused her demands to take her to Six Flags Over Texas for the day, Annie decided to destroy him by accusing him of sexual misconduct. So Annie sent letters to the church where he worked as well as to the national headquarters. The results of this accusation didn't cost Daniel his job but for years distrust followed him. When it came time to find a new church, he had to find other work—he was no longer trusted.

When they are forced to prove that the other does not love them well enough, narcissists will destroy trust and with it any communities, careers and relationships built on that trust. This too is greed. Narcissists happily destroy whatever they can't have—if not, they spoil it so no one else will want it either. Destroying trust accomplishes most of these objectives for them very nicely.

If narcissism and greed are the chief enemies of trust then an elder must find himself remarkably purged of them before he starts his contribution to society. A narcissist will eventually take down men who try to be elders but have not dealt with their own narcissism. No community can protect a man from the consequences of his own avoidance of shame.

Keri found her way into a small, intentional religious community where there were no real elders but did have two somewhat narcissistic leaders who called themselves elders. The community had been active for about ten years when Keri arrived. She quickly let them know that her pain was terrible and she could trust no one. Keri required all the attention from the two semi-elders because of her own special needs and special abilities. The leaders began praying with her for her healing.

With the first leader, a man, she eventually required more than twenty hours of attention each week. John frequently sat up all night with her so she would not kill herself. Meanwhile Keri worked her way into the home of the other semi-elder, a woman. Threats kept opening doors for her. Keri said she would kill herself if the family didn't help her more. Keri couldn't help it, she just hurt more than anyone had ever hurt; in fact, the little community had made her hurt more with their poor handling of her needs. She publicly berated both the elders for their mistakes and poor treatment of her.

In time, Keri convinced the woman semi-elder to get rid of her husband because he was preventing Keri from getting the care she needed. His anger was proof that he was no Christian. He moved out under protest.

Sooner or later, Keri publicly humiliated anyone in the community who trusted her—berating them for their failures to care enough. Keri herself could do no wrong. There were no full elders in Keri's community but the leaders found themselves distrusted by the community members as well as alienated from others around them as Keri's accusations spread. Many members of the intentional community left and no new members joined.

How do narcissists get into a spiritual family? Elders are very resistant to opening themselves to strangers at first. The first time they feel a spiritual bond with a stranger, an elder always questions and re-questions the legitimacy of the relationship. Over a number of years of internal struggle the elder eventually becomes convinced of two things: 1) this is a spiritual reality much bigger than himself and, 2) nothing short of a father's love and commitment would have met the need of his spiritual child. He has yet to learn the third lesson.

In time the door to his soul swings open more easily. Because of all the rejection his first spiritual child received, a journeyman elder will notice someone in need and respond more quickly. It is during this phase that narcissists usually get in. Narcissists are rarely the first people adopted by elders but they usually do their damage early in an elder's learning curve when the elder has learned to build trust but not yet learned that the wounded are not always the victims. Near the beginning of their experience many elders see the widows, orphans and strangers as victims or as harmless. The journeyman elder has received anger because he was careless and hurt someone so he sees anger as a healthy sign. Narcissists use anger as a way to avoid feeling shame because they can manipulate and coerce others that way. The journeyman elder reacts to this manipulative use of anger because to him all hurt people are innocent victims. He fails to notice the intelligent and controlling use of anger and humiliation by someone he sees as his child. He is about to learn that some of the wounded are also mean and greedy.[62] This will be his third lesson, one that without community support and the help of other elders may end his career.

Joel was a homosexual man who, like many others, craved a close relationship with a male father figure. Larry was a pastor and semi-elder with several spiritual sons, all with same-sex attractions, when he met Joel and welcomed him in without questions. In fact, Larry trusted him to stay in his house, take short trips together and live in his home like a family member.

Joel began telling stories about his neglect and abuse as a child and Larry had some prayer times with him asking God to heal these old wounds. Joel quickly expanded what he expected and wanted. He became increasingly demanding and flew into rages when he didn't get his way. Joel demanded that Larry exclude his wife, friends and children from their relationship or he would never get better. He insisted that Larry not go with his family on vacation so Joel would not be alone. All the while, Joel claimed that he was only asking for what he deserved and still getting cheated. When he still didn't get the attention he wanted he threatened to go to court and sue, tell the police he had been assaulted or destroy Larry's

---

[62] For a detailed description of malignant narcissism see *People of the Lie* by M. Scott Peck, and in particular the story of Charlene in chapter four. M. Scott Peck, *People of the Lie*, (New York: Touchstone, 1983).

reputation—he settled on the latter. Joel made sure that all the influential people he knew did not trust Larry anymore.

Soon after that, one of Larry's teenage boys attempted suicide because he felt hopeless about his family conflict over Joel. While his parents were with the boy in the emergency room after the suicide attempt, Joel arrived saying he was suicidal and succeeded in convincing Larry to leave his son and spend his time with Joel instead, supposedly because Joel's need was greater. Actually, Larry was now scared of Joel. Eventually, Joel sued Larry for not taking good enough care of his needs and planting false memories in his mind. Larry's attempts to build trust backfired on him leaving him in fear and distrust. Failure to detect a narcissist cost Larry and his community hundreds of thousands of dollars and several years of their lives.

A community must protect and defend its elders but to do so it must also recognize and qualify its elders. Right now it is not very popular to be an elder—the term means almost nothing. As soon as there is any perceived advantage to being an elder, all kinds of folk will want to have the title and have access to the trust it creates. If being an elder is equated with an office in an organization, narcissists will come running, touting their qualifications and arguing why the "details" that might disqualify them should be overlooked. If being an elder becomes socially desirable, narcissists will seek the position. Narcissists abound on church elder boards. Even for cultures without a well-defined concept of elders, the social need for the things elders provide has always kept false elders in the queue. Society is at risk anytime someone with narcissistic tendencies sits as an elder.

FALSE ELDERS

Men need elders and this has always provided an opportunity for wolves to find sheep by dressing up a bit. For thousands of years the hallmark of elders has been their willingness to suffer for others without gaining power, control, money, or another advantage in return. Imposter elders are very sensitive to the needs of others and usually very warm in their concern, unless one crosses them or causes them any suffering, embarrassment, or loss of face. They are really narcissists.

False elders use loyalty to replace trust. "If you are loyal," they say, "you will trust me." True elders expect loyalty to grow from earned trust and earned trust from their own transparent living. True elders do not use loyalty to consolidate power but to distribute it.

Women who, like men, need fathers and elders are also open to exploitation by wolves. This exploitation is usually financial but can often be sexual as well. While any kind of relationship between men and women is viewed with suspicion and even alarm these days, elders can be distinguished in due time by their desire to live openly in their community and have their fathering examined, improved and emulated by others. Wolves do not desire this review although at times they wish to brag shamelessly about themselves to their followers.

The young are also in need of elders and vulnerable to wolves in sheep's clothing. Young Americans flock to cults in great numbers seeking elders, with tragic results. People intuitively seek the secrets known by elders that will let them see themselves, the world, and God more clearly. The young are particularly vulnerable to leaders who give them important jobs and group identities and miss the leaders' narcissism. Cults have their versions of spiritual families but at the center one finds that attachments are used to serve the leader. An elder, on the other hand, is one who believes it is more blessed for him to give and you to receive than the other way around. It is hard to exaggerate the enrichment brought to a community by true elders. Elders will teach the young to be life-givers, not strangers.

WHY TRUST MEN AT ALL—A FINAL OBJECTION

We can say with some degree of certainty that much of the immaturity and most of the sexual violence in our culture is found in men rather than women. For many people this simply closes the door on any consideration of using men as elders. I would suggest three reasons why we should trust some men as elders.

Some men have trained the necessary 35 to 50 years and can do it. We should not discriminate based on gender alone. Further, if you don't like the way men currently develop and behave but we don't train them in a better way, our society will continue to get the same behavior out of men forever. Someone has to be the guide and model the goal.

Secondly, some mothers are abusive. Mothers are a sacred cow in our society and we don't often think about the children who grew up with really bad mothers. Those whose mothers sexually, physically and emotionally abused them and neglected their needs are not going to bond to a woman elder—in fact, many will be quite hostile. The elder-fathers I know who have spiritually adopted women are dealing with the infant maturity women who would not get close to a woman after what mother, and often her female relatives and friends did to her. The same abhorrence can be found in many men who were sexually abused by their mothers. They need an elder-father to build a bridge back to human contact.

The third reason we should trust men as elders is that we don't have many elders of any kind. We need to use what we have. Judging from those

I have known, they get good results. They can do what no younger and less mature person could without emotionally or sexually violating others.

Before we're finished, we should address three common ways of preventing sexual misconduct while helping one's community. The first is to have women do all the caring. The notion here is that women never have problems—perhaps because women are still viewed by some as less sexual than men. There is still some sexual misconduct by women, however. Furthermore, this approach excludes the small number of men and women who cannot trust a woman because of their emotional wounds.

The second solution, often proposed by conservatives, is to have men help men and women help women. Again, the reason for this is to prevent sexual misconduct. Same gender sexual misconduct is a growing problem that simply is not prevented by this arrangement. The problem that causes sexual misconduct is not the presence of the other gender but immaturity in the caregiver.

The third solution actually works better and that is to always give care in groups. Groups can be of great help to people stuck at child maturity because they need to become a part of a group identity as they move into adult maturity. This approach eliminates almost all the sexual misconduct but it misses the main point of this section—people stuck at infant maturity do not need to belong to groups. Infants need to belong to parents and families. In addition, having a third person or group present changes the attachment patterns. Often people at infant maturity will withdraw or hold back because they cannot be themselves and express needs in the middle of a group.

The price for eliminating the risk of sexual misconduct with any of these solutions is that it eliminates some people from receiving help. In addition it does nothing about a major root of the problem—counselor immaturity. If you send a boy or girl to do a parent's job you will simply have trouble. There is a better solution—maturity. Some parents and elders are capable of becoming family to people stuck at infant maturity. Mature parents and elders provide the needed bridge because they have learned to be the same person when alone as they are in their group identity.

While infants need one-on-one private time, elders need to be actively involved in a group. A working solution is very much like solution number three above, except that it is the elder who stays active in community. The elder builds trust by helping the community maintain strong love and joy bonds during difficult times. The elder builds a bridge from the infant to the elder's community so that when the infant is weaned the community will come to the feast. The elder prepares the way for the day when his child can learn self-care among a people and find a group identity should he or she mature that far.

We cannot afford to shut down our elders and create a society devoid of trust simply because some people pretend to be elders when they are not. We should train ourselves to know the real thing. What if we taught our boys that they could be like Mark, Clement or Tim if they trained for 30 to 50 years? What if even one-in-twenty made it? What if our communities supported elders who were spiritual parents for those who missed their chance to learn how to be human? Will you support and protect an elder and his children? Don't let your fears keep you in the back of your brain on this issue. Even now, futures hang in the balance.

Chapter Sixteen
The Death of an Elder

Darling, I am growing old,
Silver threads among the gold,
Shine upon my brow today;
Life is fading fast away.

*Silver Threads Among the
Gold* – Eben Rexford 1873

The ceiling slanted down on both sides of the front bedroom where a faintly dusty smell seemed to radiate from every treasure. I could never get over the feeling of trespassing as I searched the covered piles below the darkened knotty pine. It was play to my mind then but now it seems I was looking in his things for my grandfather. The south wall held the prize, an old cylinder style phonograph. The head was remarkably heavy and the wooden needle had to be sharpened every day. Sharpen, wind, put on a cylinder, lower the head and a foxtrot wavered out. That was a funny word *foxtrot*. It made me laugh.

The only cylinder I can remember by name was called *Silver Threads Among the Gold*. It always made me cry although I never understood why. "I don't like that one," I'd say when my brother Tim was there. We would play the foxtrots. But, when no one else was home I would pull back the dusty smelling cloth and listen to the scratchy remnants of a husky baritone voice and cry.

One day there were no more wooden needles left in the little can. The player was silent. Tim and I searched the yard for hard wood to make needles but found none. The next time I visited the player was gone. No one knew what happened to it. The room was silent. Before I got back again my grandmother was gone. The house was sold. The dark knotty pine was torn out, I'm told, but the room and the song still haunt me. I smell his voice and feel the heavy head of the player in my hand.

I can't remember my grandfather's voice. My dad says he was a rather good baritone.

AGING

Remember also your Creator in the days of your youth, before the evil days come, and the years draw nigh, when you will say, "I have no pleasure in them"; before the sun and the light and the moon and the stars are darkened and the clouds return after the rain; in the day when the keepers of the house tremble, and the strong men are bent, and the grinders cease because they are few, and those that look through the windows are dimmed, and the doors on the street are shut; when the sound of the grinding is low, and one rises up at the voice of a bird, and all the daughters of song are brought low; they are afraid also of what is high, and terrors are in the way; the almond tree blossoms, the grasshopper drags itself along and desire fails; because man goes to his eternal home, and the mourners go about the streets; before the silver cord is snapped, or the golden bowl is broken, or the pitcher is broken at the fountain, or the wheel broken at the cistern, and the dust returns to the earth as it was, and the spirit returns to God who gave it.

Ecclesiastes 12:1-7 (RSV)

Chronic loss becomes the traveling companion for the aging. It takes a robust capacity for joy to maintain a life-giving attitude while skills, senses, health, strength, independence, friends, companions and most that is familiar disappears. For the past forty years it has gotten harder for dad to see and hear. The last ten years saw his sense of balance go downhill. Now he has trouble with shaky hands.

Marvin Monk lived the last years of his life tethered to a plastic tube and an oxygen tank. He once captured 1000 enemy soldiers. He told stories until his lungs failed him at 85. Like him, Larry Bone can no longer get out to see the squirrels on the squirrel feeder because of his need for oxygen. Larry was a newlywed at 88 but is always short on breath. In spite of constant pain Larry has a ready sense of humor—a great funny bone his friends say.

Keeping warm and regulating body temperature generally becomes more difficult with age. Dad always seems cold and plans his walks for the warm times of day. Weather is a genuinely interesting topic. My brother and I both sweltered and looked for chances to open a window when we visited the folks' house. Dad quickly came out and reported a cold draft. Tim raised an eyebrow, "At 82 degrees?"

Health and health care costs are big issues for the elderly. The last few years of life are often the most expensive and elders hate to see the money they have saved spent on medicine and special care facilities. Elders with earned maturity are more able to receive the care they need from their children and grandchildren. They have mastered the infant task of receiving.

Health and strength decline for all men as they age so less information gets in through their senses. This lack of stimulation produces a sense of isolation and sensitivity to stimulation. It also leads to a loss of connection with the world around them. Men who always did things for others lose that connection. They feel left out of conversations. Many things simply go past too fast for them to grasp with their diminished senses. Old men begin to separate from the stream of life—not so much because they want to but because they can't keep up.

THE EMOTIONS OF AGING

Because their decline is slow, aging men routinely overestimate what they can do. This produces conflicts with their helpers. We like their fighting spirit but those who have never learned to synchronize well with others will wear heavily on their helpers. Old people should have the chance to do everything they can; they just guess incorrectly sometimes about what they can do for themselves. Aging is a continual process of decline that produces sad and hopeless feelings. Who wants a wheelchair in the airport!

"Dad! We only have 20 minutes between flights to get from one gate to the other."

"I can walk fine."

Immaturity does not age well. Men who did not learn joy or how to return to joy from every kind of distress make life miserable for themselves and others as they age. Issues that could be suppressed with an effort during mid-life will no longer submerge as a man's energy runs out. Unresolved emotional and relational issues will come back to bite in their last years. Those who have kept their fears covered up by willpower find the loss of control caused by aging and disease to be frightening. If a man feared loss but kept a tough exterior as an adult, this fear will find its way back. No longer is he strong enough to cover over the fear. Perhaps it will make him quiver and beg, lock up rigidly or rage and threaten as he gets old.

Old curmudgeons who have lived unbothered because their family didn't dare to cross them find that age and disease will not be intimidated. No longer can they go back to face the childhood losses that began this fear process. Now it is too late to resolve them. Regulating the old grump's control center becomes a full time job for his care team. As often as possible, they will simply leave him alone.

Many men feel that their bodies betrayed them when they suffer heart attacks and similar system failures. Depressions follow heart surgeries and other life threatening experiences. Men who cannot get back to joy from sad, frightened, powerless and out of control feelings are in trouble. Their strength of will no longer manages to prop them up.

Elders with earned maturity rarely become grumpy old men even when a stroke takes much of their brain.[63] They have learned the ways back to joy, have followed that trail so often and with so many people that their control centers are well trained. Elders are used to loss and having things go wrong. Elders have been taken through the very things they feared often enough to learn how to be themselves with loss.

Mature or not, everyone's body wears out. A long rift slowly separates an elder from his body. Although he treasures life, signs that he will not live forever begin to gather like clouds from a distant storm. Some of his friends saw the storm that killed them. Their clouds gathered and the tempest wore them down. Others just were gone before anyone knew what happened. Not knowing when death will visit creates uncertainly for the elder and his people.

UNCERTAINTY YEARS

> The leader of the band is tired and his eyes are growing old
> But his blood runs through my instrument and his song is in my soul
> My life has been a poor attempt to imitate the man
> I'm just a living legacy to the leader of -- the band
> I thank you for the music and your stories of the road
> I thank you for the freedom when it came my time to go
> I thank you for the kindness and the times when you got tough
> And papa I don't think I said, "I love you" near enough.
> *Leader of the Band* -- Dan
> Fogelberg (1982)

Whether the elderly have declining health or not, the continuous deaths of their friends and neighbors makes each visit a potential last visit. Both old and young are uncertain when death is involved. Is this the last visit with Grandpa? Is this the last year we will make the trip up here for holidays? Will I be at the table next Christmas? "Someone should go through the picture album with great-grandpa and tape the stories." "Let's take the baby up so he can see her." Uncertainty about death gives added meaning to each reunion. Not knowing when life will end brings poignancy and urgency to each day.

The special events we share with others shift across our lives. Youngsters see birthday parties at Chuck E. Cheese as big social events. Children talk about who got what gift. In junior high, sports and teams take

---

[63] Only the loss of their right prefrontal cortex or cingulate cortex to a stroke or accident will end their joy.

266

the lead socially for boys. Conversations feature performance reviews. Senior high attention goes toward events you pay to attend. Teenagers ask who is getting paired with whom. Soon, life is full of weddings to attend. Young couples attend baby showers next. It seems like no time at all after that and those babies are graduating. A second round of weddings blows through and then grandbabies and their pictures take center stage. Conversations turn more and more to health. Reunions are times to compare diagnoses.

Finally the social gatherings are for funerals. The first wave of funerals is for parents, aunts and uncles. The second wave is for friends. While young people get uncomfortable with the topics, old people discuss funerals like they did weddings. Was the service good? Did the dearly departed look like himself or herself?

Brave souls will discuss the passing or actual moment of death itself. Some will say what they hope for themselves. Much of the emotional conversation attends the character of life the deceased lived along with the quality of life he or she enjoyed before death. "He lived a good life." "I'm glad she went peacefully." "He was ready to go." Some hope their passing will be soon, some have a goal to reach first but all hope death will be fast and gentle—a quiet passing into a deeper sleep. Perhaps, they see a brighter awakening.

SHIFTING ATTACHMENTS

A city so silent and lone, Maggie
Where the young and the gay and the best
In polished white mansion of stone, Maggie
Have each found a place of rest
Is built where the birds used to play, Maggie
And join in the songs that were sung
For we sang just as gay as they, Maggie
When you and I were young.

When You and I Were Young,
Maggie--George Johnson 1866

"They don't write songs about growing old anymore," Dad said as he untangled Pecan's leash from his cane. "When I was a boy we sang songs about being old like *When You and I Were Young Maggie*. We sang about home and family. You don't hear songs like that now."

The sun that made Southern California famous was in rare form. We only take walks on sunny days because it is increasingly hard for Dad to keep warm. Dad calls the dog "Tim" frequently (my brother's name) but "poochie" doesn't mind. Dad takes two walks a day. I walk the dog because Dad's balance has been off ever since the doctors changed his blood pressure medicine. About the only place Dad spends money now that Mom is gone is at the pharmacy. He can lose all restraint there if several prescriptions run out at once. Dad is growing old. We each feel the uncertainty.

Because we all know the depth of attachment pain far too well, elderly couples each dread the death of the other. Because we know that loneliness of grief and the vulnerability of being alone, loving partners do not want to leave their darling behind and alone, should they go first. This problem has no good solution. The human brain simply has no way to deal with the loss of our life-long partner. No wonder so many older pairs die within a short time of each other.

With each funeral, the elderly elder becomes more and more alone. No loss is as hard as that of a long time spouse or a child. With each death his social network shifts until he is more attached to the dead than to the living. Just as declining health loosens an elder's hold on his personal and physical identity, the protracted series of deaths loosen his hold on his group identity. In time, the preponderance of his attachments are with those who have gone before. The songs of death become the love songs of reunion.

SPIRITUAL FAMILY

Both biological and spiritual families must make adjustments to advancing age. Spiritual family grows throughout the elder years so elders usually have more spiritual family than biological family around them as they age. Spiritual children, like we read about in the last chapter, must increasingly trust and attach to other members of the spiritual family and community. This is one place where it is essential that elders be part of community and work to help their spiritual children from a group-identity. The grief at the death of an elder will generally be worse for spiritual children than for natural ones and without a growing a spiritual group-identity spiritual children will be inconsolable. Except in quite rare cases, the spiritual children will feel excluded by the natural family once the elder dies or no longer can take care of himself.

DOWNSIZING

Normal aging is a long slow downsizing. Muscles get smaller, appetites get smaller and stuff has to go. The property that once could be managed productively now takes more energy or strength than a man has. Productivity is for younger men. For most Americans, the hardest step is

268

selling the family home. Selling the family home to move into a smaller place is the American way since family does not move in with parents. In other cultures, the elder's space gets smaller as grandchildren and great grandchildren fill the home. Elderly people in America must often give up their house for a condominium or residential care facility. During their last years they often extract the investment they made in their home to pay for residential care. Few stay with their children.

With the reduction in property size comes a reduction in possessions as well. Even if they are not sold, possessions slowly disappear from daily activities or get passed on to others. Elders usually prefer to give their possessions along to someone who will appreciate their memories and stories. "This is the bench I made in shop class back in McKinley High." Selling and giving away furniture can bring very intense feelings. So much can happen in a chair over 80 years. Memories and stories flood in as an old desk or coffee table goes out the door.

Once Mom died, Dad's attachment to things all but disappeared. Money and the house were for his "Sweetheart." Without her these possessions were only props in an old play. That didn't mean that they had lost their meaning. As each bit of their home went out the door, the stories came back. It took Dad a year to take his leave of them all.

With his eyesight failing, passing his license renewal eye test came down to which Department of Motor Vehicles clerk Mr. Magoo would get. He knew both clerks. One was lenient with seniors. Mr. Magoo drew the hard-line clerk and lost his license. As with many older people, his car was clean, old, low mileage and not worth much on the market. Still, it represented his independence, security and capacity to take care of his own business. Two weeks later he was at the mercy of his friends and the notoriously unreliable and expensive public transportation.

Losing the ability to drive and selling the car is hard for the men who must pass that way. Owning his first car was his rite of passage into manhood. My father kept track of his life by two things: where he lived and what car he drove. Family pictures were taken in front of the house. Travel pictures usually included his car in the scene.

GIVING STUFF AWAY

In downsizing, elderly elders still kept their treasures with them. A thief might be interested in some of these treasures but most only have value for those who know the story. For the mind with the memory, the keeper of the story, the bearer of the bond, these treasures contain life. Giving away life-filled memory treasures is a sign that an elder is getting ready to leave. Even the stuff memories are made of becomes heavier and less shiny as eyes dim and hands weaken. What treasures they still guard begin to find new homes. This is a very sentimental and meaningful time. Their recipients, who guess correctly that the gift is also a "goodbye," almost always accept these gifts with discomfort. Receiving suddenly feels like a loss.

Clothing and jewelry are usually last gifts given. With them comes the message, "I will not be in this body much longer." Our clothes are very personal to us. All that is left are our bodies.

DEATH AND METAMORPHOSIS

It was his work that finally killed him. "I never knew dying was such hard work," Walter told a friend just days before his death. Like many men, Walter worked hard. He loved teaching chemistry but, in the end, his prolonged exposure to chemicals produced the emphysema that led to his death. In the course of a conversation with an old friend Walter noted with surprise how hard it was to die. A few days later he died surrounded by friends and loved ones. His work was over.

Death is the last metamorphosis we are able to observe, and then only from one side. Like all transformations, death leads to a new identity; one we can't really understand ahead of time. Yet, for those who passed through weaning, from being boys to being men, from men to fathers, from fathers to elders, there develops a certainty that such passages are not only possible but also highly desirable. Elders know that we can survive the unknown and unknowable. They have made at least four transformations already and have learned expectancy. Those who have watched elders die have noticed this expectancy.

For our own good, and in order to know this expectancy we should never let an elder die alone. Their last great gift to us is the expectancy of a safe transformation. This hope is a blessing to people of all ages and stages.

We do not need to fear the death experience of an elder. Children, when accompanied by good parents, can draw courage from an elder's expectancy for their transformations. Boys can face the unknown changes in their bodies and the weighty implications of their histories through this expectancy. Men can give their lives away to their children knowing that in the end all will be purified by death, and elders can give freely to others with the certainty that soon they too will take with them only the life they have given away and leave behind all that they have kept.

While it is good for all ages to be close when an elder dies, the same is not true of the deaths of the unprepared. Those who cannot face death are a great trauma to be near in their final moments and it remains for parents and elders to stay close while children should clearly be kept away. Like all transformations, success is not automatic and the process is not inevitably good.

At times some youngsters with a terminal disease will be given a readiness for metamorphosis that is beyond their years. Perhaps it is the experience of surviving the negative transformations of disease that allows these young travelers their peaceful expectancy, but it is also the certainty expressed by their elders that such change is possible which quiets their souls.

Like all passages, death is experienced by each person alone and yet to succeed requires the help of others. Each elder must uniquely experience his own transformation but without help this transformation will end in disaster for none can give birth to themselves or see themselves through death.

Death itself represents the final decontamination of men from all that is not life giving. Precisely for this reason it is dangerous, for should the man prove to be non-life giving he will find this last visible transformation leading to permanent death rather than permanent life. Like all parts of his history he will be unable to remove the consequences of his actions on those who follow him.

Death builds on the stages that have gone before. Those who have received and given life go on to permanent life, while those who have refused to receive or give life go on to permanent death. Precisely because of the seriousness of this passage there is a tendency toward deathbed conversions. For those who care to leave a legacy of hope and life to their loved ones this last act is life-giving and will serve to see them through decontamination for they have received and given life. Others, seeking to beat God's judgment on their lives make such last minute conversions to try and cancel their bad record. In doing so they make a mockery of Jesus' death as if to say, "Better him than me" and in so doing their last act is death giving. Having neither received nor given life they will die dead. This attempt to cheat God of his justice is what the Church has called the mortal sin of presumption.

Although we all must die, we do not consider all deaths alike. We sense an inner revulsion to anyone who tries to take the passage to death out of turn. We bear a special grief when babies and children die. Mourners keep saying, "It is such a pity," and similar expressions of exceptional grief. When teenagers die we have almost the same response, yet because we know more of their history we have more to remember with the loss of young life. How many of us can remember being teens and saying, at least to ourselves, "I don't want to die before I fall in love, or get married, or have sex or have children." Such are the dreams of youth.

The death of a father is a tragedy to his family. "What will his wife and children do now?" we wonder. Yet already the sense of loss for the man himself is far less than it would be for a teenager or child. We mourn the loss of the life he would yet have given. There is less of a sense that he died before he had a chance to live. And yet fathers have their dreams as well. I can clearly remember my father telling me that because he married late and had his first son at thirty-eight that he feared he would not live to see his grandchildren. I remember my satisfaction at presenting his first grandchild to him and my deep secret joy that he was wrong. In fact, he lived to see all his great-grandchildren.

Considering how little we like seeing death taken out of turn, or a pregnancy in a child, one would think that the entire community would devote itself to helping every member achieve each stage of growth and successfully make each metamorphosis into the next stage. It is elders who direct and best understand such concerns. This is one reason why many family members fear the loss of their influence. As elders approach death their families wait for blessing and direction from them. It is impossible for younger people to completely imagine themselves filling the elder's shoes. They do not know what elders know. Often it is clear that the next generation has less character and resolve than their elders. They need blessing and instruction before the elder leaves. All our transformations prepare us for death and the death of an elder, when properly observed, prepares us for the lesser metamorphoses we face.

THE LAST DISTILLATION OF LIFE

Every new person triggers an old elder to pour out the distilled lessons and values of his life. It does not seem to matter if the new person is just cleaning their room or is their granddaughter's new boyfriend—the old elder will talk to them. "You should eat less sugar and you will be healthier." "Don't buy on credit because the economy is getting worse." "Read to your children and teach them at home." "Find a good husband and then don't cheat on each other." "Expensive cars should have more chrome."

Elderly elders give away stories. The old appreciate nothing so much as a good listener. Harold Smith would tell how on the night of March 7, 1945, he found himself with a glowing disk on his back guiding US Army vehicles across the Bridge at Ramagen. He saw his first jet airplane on that bridge. He wondered what happened to people he befriended on his long march across Germany. For Harold, however, the old, old story was the one he liked the best.

Dick Birkey came down with three different kinds of cancer at once. He was one who saw the gathering storm. Over his last months of life we discussed several times the unique power his words now carried—those of a dying man. The aim of an elder, to build trust in relationships that matter, has a unique opportunity in those who are dying. We inherently give more weight to deathbed confessions because we realize the person has less to fear and less self-interest. There is little we distrust more than self-interest. At no time in his life did Dick's words carry the weight they did those last months. Although the disease made him feel totally weak, Dick was never so powerful in his life. Dick used those days wisely then he died.

Elders are giving away their stories. The older the story the better they remember.

BLESSINGS

These are the blessings from the elders: the lack of fear with which they face life and death, the freedom with which they love, and their simple certainty of how they want to live, the way they see others, their understanding of death and resurrection, the expectancy they bring to death itself.

The time around the death of an elder has always been connected with great blessing. Thousands of years ago Isaac blessed his children on his deathbed, just as Jacob blessed his. The prophet Elijah blessed Elisha with a double portion of his spirit and power, but to achieve this blessing, Elisha had to stay with his teacher during his metamorphosis.

Blessings are both affirmation and inheritance. Naming the kind and quality of life in each of those who has received life through you is a large part of the blessing. Blessings capture the essence of someone's true self in a short story or image. "Sara, you have the deep kind heart that keeps this family together."

Regrettably, some blessings are not so positive. Elders sometimes must say, "I see you have a problem. Your life is at a crossroads and your choices are. . ." Sometimes the message is, "You have a long way back home but great value will come if you face the pain." Blessings are not magic. They are firmly founded in the daily reality of life but with a spiritual view to what might yet be.

Blessings also transfer authority and position. "Bill, you are the head of this clan now." Blessings are not magic; they do not transform a cur into a prince. Rather, blessings confirm and establish what has already been found in each heart. Blessings are the sign that an elder has carefully observed and tended the life in his care. They are his way to say, "I see who you were meant to be and I like it."

LAST GOODBYES

Often those who have been sick or even in dementia have a surge of clarity in the hours or days before their death. This is their goodbye. Sometimes they linger until a special date or event has passed. Others do not feel free to die until their family gives them leave to go. People who are dying often hold on to life until their family members arrive at their side. Perhaps they know we need to watch them go.

The sky opens in the last few hours and as life fades they become more aware of the spirit world than the physical world. We observe them looking up, reaching out, calling out names of loved ones who have died who seem to be right there. Already the dying seem beyond our reach and reality. For just a moment we see them suspended between earth and sky.

METAMORPHOSIS

The next breath is never drawn. Warmth quietly slips away.

Now, suddenly, we are the people. We are the founders of the feast, leaders of the clan, the tellers of the tales—if they are told at all.

Lives turn into memory—memories to feed the souls of another generation. Memories become stories. Some stories linger near the heart, some fade like morning mist. Lives well lived. Lives wasted. Foolish moments. Glory times. Deep paths worn through fields covered long ago by asphalt. Councils among forest trees shorn for parking lots.

Voices whisper in the night. We hear songs of far away places. Smoke rises from campfires at the edge of Iceberg Lake.

RESTORATION
&
TRANSFORMATION

UNFINISHED
TASKS

Chapter Seventeen
When A Man Is Still An Infant

You Can Tell A Man Is Still An Infant When...

- Everything is about him—at his pace, when he wants it, how he wants it.
- If others have a problem with him it gets turned around to be his problem with them.
- When you go to him for comfort you end up comforting him.
- He grunts instead of asking.
- You have to read his mind to know what he wants.
- He can't say what he feels.
- If he is upset you can't reason with him.
- He can't/won't take care of himself or his home.
- He doesn't know what he really needs.
- He consumes (food, drinks, toys, TV, sports, sex, buys stuff) to feel good.
- Communicating with him does not solve problems.
- Whenever there is a problem he lets you know you don't love him well enough.
- He can't control his emotions or impulses.

The classic example: An elderly woman fell and broke her hip. Her husband was in such a state about her fall that when the ambulance got there they took him to the hospital leaving the woman with her broken hip to drive herself to emergency.

THE ADULT "MAN" WITH INFANT MATURITY

Okay, so the bottom line here is that you, your mother, sister or daughter married him. The bad news is that although trying to make husbands and fathers grow up is a cottage industry in America—it won't work. The good news is that if anyone can motivate a man to grow up it usually is his children.

In some ways we could describe the dysfunctional family as one in which the members are trying to get the rest of the family (or a particular person) to act like an infant's mother to them. A father, for instance, might expect his wife, or even his children, to guess what he wants without his having to ask. A little grunt, a turn of the head, or a tug at his coffee cup means he wants more coffee; and "Mother" whoever she is, must jump to meet her baby's needs. How very much those actions resemble the infant's cries, turning his head toward his mother's breast, or tugging on her blouse for his supper. If the immature father's needs are not met, then like a baby, he believes he has a grievance--proof that he was not loved in the way that every nursing baby requires.

Wives of men with infant maturity are at a special disadvantage. The more wives attempt to make their husbands grow up the harder the infants resist. For decades we have been told that the solution to marital problems is better communication but bad communication is not the source of all marital problems. Immaturity causes relational problems all on its own. Infants do not keep their word. Infants do what their feelings dictate at the moment. This is true even when the infant can't express or even denies the feelings. Life with infants is a constant manipulation of feelings to get results. If you make him feel good you get what you want more often. If you avoid upsetting him you get less of what you don't want. Words mean very little with infants.

Because weak or fear-based bonds lead to weak identities, men with infant maturity have trouble with anything that upsets them, or anyone near them. Sometimes they don't care who they upset and other times it is the opposite extreme--they are afraid to upset anyone. It can be extremely debilitating to be afraid of upsetting people.

Bud was the nicest guy you ever met. One would think all his relationships would prosper, but Bud was always worried. He was late, most of the time, because he was afraid of upsetting friends by leaving. He always arrived apologizing, "I'm sorry I'm late but . . ." Bud worried about people's opinion of him. He was pointedly indecisive.

Bud married an infant woman who became upset very easily. He actually married her because she got mad that he had not proposed to her. He wasted his days trying to keep her happy. Trying to keep her from getting upset cost him jobs, friends, sleep, health, and time with his children. After awhile many people became upset with him, but the harder he tried the worse it got. He was controlled by the most upset person he knew. Bud was beside himself with agony--a nice guy going nowhere.

Before we get full of contempt for the immature man we must realize that not everyone makes it out of the infant stage. Some babies never develop an adequate foundation. They spend the rest of their unhappy lives looking for someone who will read their minds, know what they need, and do it for them without their having to ask. Often these unhappy souls mistake this kind of care for love. Worse yet, they feel unloved if others do not guess what they want without having to ask. "If I have to tell them or ask for something it doesn't count," they say. These sad people never made it to child maturity. They still want love the way a baby does.

278

ADDICTIONS – PARTICULARLY SEX ADDICTIONS

All addicts have a failure completing their infant task of returning to joy. Addicts, particularly sex addicts, also have some unresolved attachment pain. This early failure is combined with a catastrophic failure to reach adult maturity. All addicts are stuck at infant/child maturity. For this reason, we often consider infant and child needs together when talking about addictions.[64]

An infant-man with weak bonds will continue a desperate search for connection. It is this lack of a secure connection with his mother that produces frantic men. Without his crucial baby-mother bond, the baby-boy-man will continue a sporadic, frantic search for connection with someone or something. He will fear being abandoned and rejected by women. He may attach to his bottle and drugs instead. He will fear his own needs. He may act tough. This is the man who will do anything for the love of a woman, yet never find her love to be enough. He needs someone to be interested in who he is. Someone *has* to be interested in defining who he is. That special someone must find him interesting and approve of him.

A woman once told me, "You know, it is the easiest thing in the world to get a man, all you have to do is act interested in him. You can have your pick."

An actor candidly told me, "I just can't resist it when a woman is attracted to me. I have to have that love. I can't turn it down." As a result of his failure to turn down any woman's attention, he had lost several important women in his life and gotten herpes. He looks frantically for a strong love-bond to tell him he is good, valuable, and interesting. He is still trying to find a connection with a woman that will let him nurse contentedly and take in the loving gaze he has always needed. Without a healing touch deep in his soul, he will never give up his frantic search.

This helps us understand why the typical sexual fantasy of men can be reduced to this: he finds a woman or man who goes crazy over him and can't get enough of him. While there are many variations, this fantasy remains the prototype. By their teenage years, infant-men have usually sexualized their need for connection. They use orgasm to turn off the message from their nucleus accumbens that says they are going to die. Men who are attracted to pornography, for example, should consider that they may lack a connection with someone who will tell them who they really are—someone who is eager to be with them. Such a man might think that his highest glory would come from having a woman go nuts over him. He

---

[64] For an in-depth answer to addictions see my book with Raymond Jones called, *Out Of Control: Life With a Sex Addict.* (In progress.)

has a deep wound that needs to be healed before he regains control of his life. Sex will not heal that wound, for as nice as it might seem to have a woman who is crazy about you, it does not replace your mother.

Men who grew up without learning how to meet their own needs through asking and receiving will often react to breasts as though they were some extraordinary good thing. This has nothing to do with whether the baby was breast-fed or bottle-fed. Not uncommonly, such men have a fascination with breasts, particularly big ones.

Now, indeed, breasts are an extraordinary good thing if we consider the wonder of how a woman's body becomes a fountain of life, flowing with enough milk to sustain life and promote tremendous growth. That is amazing, but such is not the fascination of the man with infant needs. To him breasts are a good object beyond his reach--a treasure cruelly kept from him by the powerful creatures that have them. Breasts are objects to be desired, looked for, stared at in a ceaseless fantasy to have them all.

How to get access to breasts can be an obsession with some men. There is no shortage of lingerie and clothing manufacturers willing to exploit the man who does not know what he really needs. He will pay through the nose for the things that do not satisfy and wonder what is wrong with him.

Girl-women who do not make it out of infant maturity are also unprepared to meet their own needs by asking and receiving. These immature women also develop their own fascination for breasts. However, since they own a set, the girl-woman's preoccupation is different from the infant-man's. Girl-women wonder about the adequacy of their own good-stuff. Their sufficiency is usually measured by attractiveness and the current fashions. For the woman with infant needs, displaying and simultaneous hiding her breasts becomes an obsession. Endless shaping, padding, covering with lace, changing necklines, finding the right tightness of blouses, buying seductive bathing suits and sleepwear, all become part of this quest for the perfect display. Surgeons can add their modifications if clothing and padding do not suffice.

If, by some chance, an infant man and woman should meet, the resulting interaction gets physical rather quickly. Even if no touching happens between the two, the woman displays her attractions to a man who works to possess them in some way, either by seeing more, or getting closer--much as an unhappy weaned child would try to get to his mother's breasts. Meanwhile, the woman tries to keep the man's attentions while staying just out of reach, acting out her interpretation of her mother's distance after infancy.

This frantic search for connection can lie behind family dysfunctions and even religious addictions. People tied to "toxic faith" often try desperately to do anything they can for God's love and attention, as though we needed to do anything in order to receive God's love. They have shaped their religion to fit the thinking of an abandoned infant.

The prophet Isaiah once wrote, "Can a mother forget the baby at her breast and have no compassion on the child she has borne? Though she may forget, I will not forget you!" (Isaiah 49:15). To replace the delight of a God who loves us like a mother nursing her child with unconnected sexual passion or religious fervor, is like eating charcoal briquettes instead of grilled steak. It is close, it is hot, but it does not satisfy.

SOME SOLUTIONS

Not being a "how to fix your life at home with twine and chewing gum" book, we won't attempt here to spell out the cure for infant maturity. We can give a few suggestions to help you get started. Usually a man at infant maturity has a hard time realizing that he needs to work on his immaturity so we will start our suggestions with ideas for family members.

If you want to help a man you love with his infant maturity, work on your own maturity until you can let his upset be his problem. The upset that infant men feel when they don't get their way is necessary for them to change. Even their brains do not register the need to change how they think until the men are stuck in an upset feeling. Infant men have mastered the technique of getting others to relieve them of their pain. If his wife stops responding, his children step in. If his children stop taking care of him his mother steps in. If his mother dies his nieces or other women he knows step in. Can you spell codependence? Let me help you. Counselors will tell you that the hardest part of getting infant men to grow is getting their enablers to stop enabling long enough to let some real discomfort have its motivating ways. Of course, this has real risks for marriages, for many an infant man has simply moved on to find another wife to enable him when his first wife grew up.[65]

Communicating is not the solution to relationship problems when one is dealing with infant maturity. Wives of infants are very much advised to read the book *How One of You Can Bring the Two of You Together* by Susan Page.[66] Forget talking it out, being understood, each taking responsibility for half the problem or coming to an agreement with infants. Page shows how anyone can put his or her maturity to work and improve a situation. She calls it "being the bigger person."

---

[65] If you are dating or married to someone on his third marriage, he is likely an infant or an enabler of infant wives.

[66] Susan Page, *How One of You Can Bring the Two of You Together,* (Broadway Books: New York, 1997)

If infant-men are in a safe environment, many men will acknowledge their immaturity and want to change. Men are much more likely to admit this need to a stranger than they are to their family. After all, strangers are not going to ask anything of them. Even most infant-men are aware at some level that they have failed to bring to their relationships what their partners needed. Here is the paradox—adult-infants need to be in pain in order to change but infants avoid pain and seek safety so they slip away from pain before they learn anything that would help them change. Infants will only look at their pain if they have someone with them to guide them through to new growth. Infant-men have to feel safe with their guide and since their wife is usually seen as the source of their pain she is not safe. Worse yet, she may ask something of him he can't give and make things worse so she cannot be his guide. His children pose similar dilemmas. The guide must come from outside the family.

Once they find a guide, infant-men begin to discover their needs. One obvious need for most infant-men is joy. Men who lack joy are easy to recognize as soon as one asks the question, "Does he live in joy?" Because joy is the one emotion that infants will seek on their own, building joy is central to helping infants mature. Joy is one of the few areas of maturity where wives and children can genuinely help. Joy smiles, pleasant voice tone and lots of eye contact build bonds between couples as well as with children. For men with low joy levels I suggest lots of practice with smiles. Children and grandchildren are good places to practice smiles.

It is particularly necessary to end each day with joy otherwise stress hormones like cortisol erase the joy developed that day during the night. For more help developing joy I suggest *The Life Model*[67] book. A group of us wrote the book to help people solve their problems in living.

As soon as we talk about building joy with infant-men we discover that the people around them are often upset with them and in no mood to build joy. What they need is help returning to joy. Adult infants will have great trouble returning to joy from at least one of the major emotions. We are talking about anger, fear, sad, disgust, shame, or hopelessness. Returning to joy is an acquired skill as we saw in Chapter Two. Staying relational and regulated in the presence of a distressing feeling is what we mean by returning to joy. In other words, "Even though I am mad/scared/sad/hopeless/ashamed/disgusted I'm still glad to be with you.

To learn how to stay relational requires synchronizing mental states with someone who already knows how to be relationally stable in that emotion. This means finding a more developed brain that is able to feel misery and still act the same as if it were feeling joy. We know how people

---

[67] Friesen, Wilder, Bierling, Koepcke and Poole, *The Life Model,* Shepherd's House, 2000 available from CARE Packaging www.care1.org or (231) 745-4950.

treat us and what they value when they feel joy. The well-trained control center in a well-synchronized brain will keep the same values and intentions no matter the feeling. This is hard to believe if you have only seen ignorant, immature and untrained brains at work.

I suggest that you make a list of the six emotions and mark the ones you avoid. Also mark the emotions in which you treat others differently. If you are dealing with a man with infant maturity make a list for him. Finally, write next to each emotion anyone you know who is good at staying relationally the same during that feeling. i.e. Uncle Virgil is just as kind when he is mad as when he is happy. Vicar Rainwater is just as warm when he feels hopeless as when things are going well.

A person with infant maturity learns by sharing a mutual state of consciousness with someone who knows what they are doing in that emotion. This training can be done by face-to-face story telling about times you each felt the feeling. If you want people to train you and "download" their control center into your brain you may want them to read this book first so they know what you are talking about. For more information on how to do these exercises read *Thriving*68 by Coursey and Wilder. Help is also available from my *Quiet Place Teachings* video series.[69]

To calculate the amount of work it will take to help a man reach child maturity, go through the list of infant tasks and needs at the beginning of Chapter One. Check off the needs and tasks yet to be done. Do the same for the child stage using the list at the beginning of Chapter Three. Now make a list of who you know that could provide the kind of care and training needed to meet those needs and guide those tasks. If you are not a person who prays, this would be a good time to start because you need someone who will give life to this man when they have no real reason to do so except, perhaps, that they are full of life to give.

Finding a spiritual family for an infant man is essential for him to develop maturity. Look, there is no way a wife or children can raise a man to maturity. His family of origin obviously screwed up so that leaves the community to provide some mature parents. Sometimes a sponsor and a twelve-step program will serve as a spiritual family. This spiritual family has saved many people's lives but twelve-step programs are limited in developing maturity by the fact that most members are at child or infant maturity. People with earned parent or elder maturity do not get addicted. For that matter, not even people with adult maturity will be addicts so the pool of people involved in twelve-step programs fairly well eliminates the

---

[68] Chris Coursey and E. James Wilder, *Thriving,* (In progress.)
[69] Quiet Place Teachings videos (In progress) are available from CARE Packaging www.care1.org or (231) 745-4950.

possibility of having parents and elders available. Hearing this really upsets people at infant maturity in twelve-step programs because they know their group saved their lives. I am not criticizing twelve-step groups, but recovery groups were designed to build sobriety not maturity.

Here is an example of a spiritual family and how it might work. A small church, comprised largely of cowboys and rodeo riders, asked me to do a men's weekend. During that weekend we talked about the levels of maturity enough that all the men identified their own level. There were two elders, about 3 fathers, 5 adults and 20 boys and infants. By the end of the weekend the elders, fathers and adults decided (on their own) to help the boys and infants mature. Remember that when I say infants we are talking about men in their 20s, 30s and even 60s. Each of the children/infants checked off a list of the needs and tasks they had yet to complete to become adults. The group, under the direction of the elders, assigned men who were strong in those areas to guide the immature men through to adult maturity. One of the least mature men was Bob, the town drunk. The elders assigned three men to him. When I returned to that town a number of years later Bob was a sober father of two with a happy wife. There were three men glowing with pride in how Bob had grown. The entire group of men was heavily involved in summer and after- school programs for the community children—a sign of life to give.

Chapter Eighteen
The Man Who Was Never a Boy

Larry had the nicest house on the street. It wasn't the most expensive house, but everything about it was as close to perfect as Larry could get it. He worked on it at least four hours a night and twelve to sixteen hours a day on weekends. He had been working this way for almost six years and, as he said, it was "coming along." The carpet, paint, moldings, garden, grass, wiring, windows, water heater, shelves, garage, retaining wall, fruit trees, sinks, counter top, and dog run were among the improvements Larry had made.

Larry felt self-conscious about his results, the neighbors teased him a bit and his wife still seemed unhappy with his results, so he could not decide whether to work more or work less. Larry had a bad case of a common fear--disapproval. If you asked him why he worked so hard, he would tell you that he only wanted to be a good husband, father and Christian. He tried to do what was expected of him and what he expected of himself. Having never enjoyed his father's attention he had become a man who had never been a boy.

Larry entered childhood flying upside down. Instead of learning how to take care of himself he learned how to take care of others. Maturity inversions occur whenever someone of lesser maturity is made responsible for the needs of a more mature person. This pseudo-maturity occurs when parents want their children to take care of the parent's needs and feelings. By flying upside down Larry always acted older than his age.

The dysfunctional family is one in which the adults try to be children, while the children try to be adults. This inversion of the roles is the best way of describing the effects of trying to be an adult without first learning the lessons of being a child. As we have also pointed out, these lessons are cumulative. Man "stuff" builds on boy "stuff" rather than replacing boy "stuff."

Probably everyone from his wife and children to his church will take advantage of Larry for the rest of his life. Like the bad joke about the woman who goes to the psychiatrist, "My husband thinks he's a dog," she says. "I can fix that," says the doctor. "Who will bring in the paper," she asks.

Flying Upside Down: Pseudo-maturity
- Very hard-working but has little enjoyment or satisfaction for his efforts
- Takes care of other's needs but discounts or denies his own

- Often afraid of upsetting others and failing their expectations
- Can't think in terms of personal satisfaction because he is focused on others
- In his view of reality he has no place for his feelings
- No mistakes are allowed for him
- Does not learn from experience except to try harder to avoid mistakes
- Perpetually gives and looks out for others
- Feels guilty receiving

A pseudo-mature man or woman could have anywhere from one to all of these characteristics. Trying to be a man without first being a boy is very discouraging. In the end, the imposter who is flying upside down will be exposed because he will consume too much or too little, work too much or too little and never be satisfied. He will run out of strength just when he needs it.

Women rarely identify their husband as an enabler (pseudo-mature) unless he is enabling his mother, father or siblings instead of her. Enablers sometimes get confronted by their wives for enabling their children, particularly if they are her stepchildren. A fight then develops over the man who was never a boy to see who has dibs on him. Who should Larry take care of next, his parents, wife, children, boss, lenders, church or civic group? Obviously this can turn out many ways depending on who has the strongest fear bond with Larry. If Larry came into marriage with the biggest fear bond to his mother then he will likely get dragged onto Dr. Phil's show for a good browbeating as a "momma's boy." If his biggest fear bond is to his wife then Larry will likely serve his whole life sentence flying upside down. Larry's child or infant maturity wife will feel entitled to sponge off Larry while never being satisfied with what he supplies. Usually it is just the opposite that happens; let's look at that.

Very often the woman enters marriage in a state of pseudo-maturity. She is flying upside down and likely to serve a life sentence as an enabler while her husband stays forever a boy. His plane is right side up so looks just as immature as he really is—he just isn't flying very high.

THE MAN WHO IS ALWAYS A BOY

The man who is obviously a child looks for a mate who will please him. If confronted with his immaturity he usually looks for a woman who will please him better—one who doesn't "bitch" at him, looks sexier, gives better sex, supports him, agrees to "swing," buys him drugs, lets him buy or hunt and fish or golf or travel or gamble—all according to what he wants to consume. He wants to get the best for himself. Rather than change his

286

immaturity, the boy-man just looks for a better "babe." He is just looking out for "number one." That is a boy's job.

Bill was meticulous about his clothes. Bill shopped at the right stores and drove a BMW with a great stereo system. Never one to make a splash, Bill was understated but always had the right wine for the occasion, the house in the right neighborhood and just the right friends. Although he was only "worth" $750,000 many of his friends were millionaires. Bill had winning ways when he wanted to.

Bill left his wife for a younger woman. Bill left his new job for one with prestige and financial security that let him spend his days with the very wealthy. He moved into a new house with his new wife in a better neighborhood and had new kids. Some of his old friends were offended by this and began saying that Bill kept his brain behind his zipper. He left his old friends for better ones who didn't bring up his ex-wife or kids. Bill now throws bigger parties for more people, has replaced his old BMW with a new one, has a faster computer, manages a larger staff, and eats in finer restaurants. Bill still has no clue what would satisfy him—he doesn't ask the question.

Bill also traded in his doctor on a new one. It seems that some of the nurses in the doctor's office were becoming amused by Bill's endless stream of worries about his body and his health. His doctor could find nothing wrong that merited treatment even though Bill's tennis game was declining a bit. He fastidiously moved to healthier and healthier foods.

Bill eventually went to see a therapist. The doctor was a prominent professor and owned several counseling centers. As Bill commented, the doctor charged top fee. Bill didn't see the need to stay long. Bill was consumed with consuming. What he could not consume he stored for later consumption. Bill had reached the American dream, but few people I know respected him as a man. The boy was flying low.

Flying Low: Obvious Immaturity
- Won't do hard things
- Expects everyone to take his side
- Consumed with his personal needs but does not find satisfaction
- Does not trust or relate to others if his feelings are upset
- Does not learn anything from his experience except to distrust more people
- No mistakes allowed for others (unless he doesn't care)
- Consumes when he wants
- Untamed passions (untrained nucleus accumbens)
- Only does what he feels like doing
- Only looks out for himself

A child-man could have one or all of the characteristics on this list and more as well. If he is at infant maturity we will note the signs listed in the last chapter. The same would go for the woman with immaturity or pseudo-maturity. Many marriages have one of each—one pseudo-mature and one immature.

These child-to-pseudo-adult maturity marriages are the status quo so there is very little motivation for most child-adults to change. Since their parents, friends, neighbors and even counselors may be just as immature as they are, men who were never children (along with those who are always children) don't ever think to change. The pseudo-adult tries harder to please or to find someone he can please. The man flying upside down looks for a woman who will appreciate him but usually only after being berated and dumped by the last immature woman he tried to please. His friends say about the women he finds, "I don't know what he sees in her. She doesn't know what she's got." The pseudo-mature man just works harder. He does not know he is flying upside down.

NO SATISFACTION

Neither the man who was never a boy or the man who is still a boy have learned satisfaction. If either one checked to see if they were satisfied the answer would be a big fat NO. What is missing for both is the satisfaction test.

Satisfaction: Learning satisfaction is a child task as you may recall. The boy who begins childhood consuming and receiving must end childhood knowing when it is more satisfying to give. The man who was never a boy must go back and learn to ask and receive with satisfaction if he is to reach true maturity.

Paul was as dutiful a pastor as any church board would ever hope to find. He was a man of experience, principle, commitment, and virtue. He did not lack compassion for his parish and visited both weak and strong. Paul was a man of vision and with his help churches grew. An excellent pastor, he taught and studied carefully but not so carefully that he left no room for change or uncertainty.

If this wasn't enough, Paul was a family man. He loved his wife and three children. Paul even loved the family dog, although he might not admit that to everyone. One day Paul came to see me because he was just not sure whether to continue as a pastor. Something was wrong and he couldn't quite put his finger on what it was. Being a man of high principle, he needed to find out what was wrong, why his work seemed to be unfulfilling. Try as he might Paul could simply not figure out what was the right thing to do.

Paul's father was a pastor. He had good parents. They cared for him and never abused him. To this day, they call and see each other often. His family had taught Paul all the right things. Paul knew how to evaluate, solve problems, and do what was right. In seminary Paul even improved on the things his family had taught him but there was one thing Paul did not know. Paul had no idea what satisfied him. He did not even realize that he should know what satisfied him. Somehow, asking what satisfied him seemed "fleshly" and wrong, a bit too selfish.

Living without knowing what really satisfied had almost burned out his flame. Paul had too many right choices every morning and no way to know which of them brought him life. A good pastor would return a phone call, drop in on a sick man, take his wife to lunch, meet with the board members over lunch, have lunch with a homeless man, stop in at his daughter's school to see her during lunch, take the dog for a run, take time away for quiet prayer, prepare carefully for Sunday's sermon, read up on the topic for the men's retreat, and then there were all the good things a pastor would do in the afternoon and evening.

Without knowing which of these things brought satisfaction, Paul could only continue to review his principles and set priorities. It troubled him that so many good things *never* got done. In time he ran out of gas, began to dread his work, and the phone calls, even meeting with his board. Perhaps, he reasoned, I am not meant to be a pastor, or I would have joy in my life.

This pastor knew that his value did not come from his work or from what he possessed. He ran out of gas, though, because as a human being he needed to be satisfied by his labor and food, but he had no hint how to choose wisely. His father before him had not known what satisfied and never thought to teach his son. As a result, they would both go until they collapsed from exhaustion and wonder where the time had flown. Satisfaction is the emotional fuel that keeps us running to meet the next challenge we face.

The three sources of satisfaction must be renewed every day. The healthy boy discovers that his joy and satisfaction in these three areas only have a 24-hour shelf life and must be actively pursued each day: 1) His food brings joy and satisfaction. 2) His affection brings joy and satisfaction. 3) His efforts bring joy and satisfaction.

The ancient wisdom literature concludes that everything consumed beyond receiving what we need is emptiness (Ecclesiastes 8:15) while there is satisfaction in the food we need. The poet points to enjoying our work as a second source of satisfaction. He is careful to point out that accomplishments do not satisfy. Accomplishments are also emptiness. It is simply the work of our hands, that which comes out of us, that satisfies. We will look at the need to receive and give (work) for satisfaction next. The third source of satisfaction is enjoying our love relationships. So, to the poet, the tasks of the boy are the center of life: enjoy our food, our love, and our efforts.

SATISFACTION REQUIRES RECEIVING AND GIVING

Maturity is a developing pattern of receiving and giving life. The man who was never a boy does not receive well while the one who stayed a boy does not give well. As a result neither is satisfied. Unlike the man who was never a boy, the perpetual boy feels entitled to everything without having to work for it or give back. By looking at entitlement we will discover why some people come out of infancy flying upside down and why other are always flying low. After that we can turn our attention to what we can do about it.

Receptive entitlement: Perhaps the best way to describe the man who has completed his infant training is to consider entitlement. The man who has finished his infant tasks knows how to ask for what he needs. He considers himself to be entitled to have those needs met just because he exists and simply by asking. The sign of a complete infant is that he can ask for and receive what he needs with joy and without guilt or shame. While this will appear selfish to some, it is absolutely essential as a foundation for giving as an adult. The one who cannot receive freely cannot give freely. Receptive entitlement precedes giving.

All-consuming entitlement: The child-man who learned to receive without learning what he can produce is in very bad shape. Eventually he goes beyond *receiving* with entitlement to *taking* with entitlement. This low flying man becomes an endless vacuum. Without guilt or shame, he consumes the world for himself. Not surprisingly, he appears to others like a giant tapeworm. He feeds freely on all he can possess, and yet he is still not satisfied.

Consuming is not a satisfying definition of a man. We must both take in and give out. A boy's work is adding satisfaction to entitlement. Anyone stuck on either receiving or giving life has only half of what he needs for satisfaction. Consuming alone will never satisfy. The person who tries to reach satisfaction by consuming is doomed to consume more and more and more in the vain hope that more will satisfy. Dissatisfaction takes root deeply in a consumer society. We believe that satisfaction will come from the resources we consume. We are what we eat, or wear, or drive. More is better. More expensive is better. Are you dissatisfied? — Then buy more!

Fear of entitlement: Entitlement without production will not satisfy and is deadly as well. For this reason many people run away from entitlement. Some people fear that teaching children that they are entitled to

290

their needs and feelings will breed selfish children. Because such parents operate out of fear, they build guilt and shame in their children rather than entitlement. These children never complete the task of childhood and so can never become adults that will give and receive freely and joyfully. These children are quite prone to flying upside down.

Christian objections to receptive entitlement: Christians have had a tendency to teach sacrificial giving at the expense of entitlement. Many Christians begin teaching preschoolers in Sunday school that it is better to give than to receive, not because giving is a step of maturity and so giving will be more gratifying in time, but because it is more "righteous" to give than to receive. Guilt then falls on any child who prefers to receive or even feels entitled to receive. This is the road to disaster.

Entitlement is approved of in the Bible—even for adults. In the trial of Ananias and Sapphira (the first Christians to die for trying to look good), a pivotal point by the prosecution was entitlement. "While it (the money and property) was in your hand were you not free to do with it what you wanted?" asked the apostle Peter. (Acts 5:4) Peter made it clear that giving was to be done freely. Gifts count as gifts only when the giver was entitled to keep the gift. God, in fact, does not want gifts given by compulsion, but he loves a cheerful giver.

A friend of mine tells a story which could be repeated by many a Christian child. Joe's father gave him a new bicycle for his tenth birthday. A few weeks later a neighbor lost his car and needed transportation to get to work. Acting on the principle that it was more blessed to give than to receive, his father gave Joe's bicycle to the neighbor. My friend was expected to be happier about this arrangement than he had been to receive the bicycle to begin with. Although Joe was old enough to understand the neighbor's plight and wanted to help he could not get past the loss of his bicycle. Try as he might, my friend was not happy, nor has he ever become happy, about his loss of a bicycle. Joe continues to give and give, he even lives out of his car at times to give his children a private school education, but he is not satisfied. Always haunting him is the feeling that Joe has lost what is precious to him.

Now, don't get me wrong, it was not losing the bicycle that made Joe live in a car. These are only symptoms of a man who never learned entitlement. The result of no entitlement is low satisfaction. Some days my friend can be one of the most dissatisfied "good Christians" you might ever meet. His joy is not always there. Joe became a man without ever having been a boy.

No Entitlement—flying upside down: The problem, for those who try to become men without first completing infant tasks, is that they can only give if they are compelled to do so by shame or guilt or fear. Entitlement is a good test for any man who wonders whether he has completed the task of being an infant. If you keep your time, money, energy, or other resources for yourself, do you feel guilt and shame? If so, you have not learned receptive entitlement. Do you experience guilt, shame or embarrassment if someone gives something to you? If so then you have not learned entitlement. You are flying upside down. The result is a loss of joy, giving from fear and a trying to please others. This is not satisfying.

What the pseudo-mature man learned during infancy was *giving*. Because he had to take care of others too soon his giving became more about *them* than about *him*. The man who was never a boy gives from fear. Because the flashlight of his attention was always on others rather than himself he did not learn satisfaction, self-expression (giving life), and developing his personal resources. He does hard things from fear. Fearing that others will be upset with him takes the place of finding satisfaction. Fear keeps his perspective upside down.

Perhaps we have some part in keeping men and women flying upside down. We often exploit the pseudo-mature man. We prefer his lack of entitlement to the unquenchable entitlement of the perpetual child who will exploit us if he can.

COMPLETING THE BOY TASKS AND BECOMING A MAN

A few men have been trying to heal the wounded boy within them for some time. Gordon Dalbey tells many stories of such men in his book *Father and Son: The Wound, The Healing, The Call To Manhood*. He provides many excellent suggestions for recovery in *Healing The Masculine Soul* as well. I recommend these resources to any man who wants to heal and grow.

Most of the current trends in psychotherapy and popular psychology address the problem of the child within. They are correct in so far as they go. We must all be children first. Men who have not been boys have no roots with which to nourish their tree. They have far less support for the growth of their fruit.

Most therapists are very good with the two-year-old to eight-year-old tasks. Therapists do poorly on either side of this development band. A very few therapists are good with deficits from the first two years of life but, because these issues require long-term help and dependency on the therapist in the presence of intense and distressing emotions, few therapists have the experience needed. Those who do are usually well worth knowing.

What is missing from most therapies is any element of growing maturity that takes men beyond the infant and child tasks. Take, for instance, the "liberated man" who, in response to the women's movement and perhaps some therapy, has learned to feel, have needs, express himself and receive. He has learned the infant tasks. If he thought this would please the women around him, he was wrong. For in learning to be sensitive, he has become an infant. Women want a man, not a baby.

After learning his feelings, the man in therapy must learn to work—do things he doesn't feel like doing at the moment. Next he learns to do hard things in his relationships. Now he has something to give. Expressing this creative life energy within him helps him fully become a boy. A boy is still less than a woman wants. He will complete his final childhood step when he learns what truly satisfies him. The boy who has learned all these things is ready to become a man.

Learning the adult tasks is quite a job as we will see in the next chapter. These adult tasks are almost never included in any therapy program.[70] Most therapy models never even reach this level of development. One reason adult tasks are not included is that they require a mature community for their development. What therapist has a community at her or his disposal? The result is that most therapy leaves men as perpetual children. You may contest this next statement but men are not all stupid. They have seen the results of therapy and, overall, are not impressed. They want to be men. They would rather fly upside down than be boys for life.

The man who is helped through his infant and child needs by his counselors and mentors then engages his adult needs. With the help of an involved community his results will be satisfying to the man himself and to any adults in his life. Although he will not live to satisfy women, he can become the man who adult men and women seek.

Satisfaction is learned: It should be obvious by now that learning satisfaction is at the heart of correcting development for the man who was never a boy just as it is for the man who is always a boy. Of course, neither of them knows that he needs to learn satisfaction so the first step is to engage the issue. Make satisfaction a matter of life and daily conversation. Simply tell stories of what satisfied you today and ask questions about how satisfied he is with all things good or bad. This is not a job for one person alone—although one person may be enough to make the difference. Everyone in the family who is over four years of age should discuss satisfaction. Often children will get farther in discussions with Dad than Mommy does.

If you do not know what satisfies you then you can't teach satisfaction and need to learn satisfaction first. However, the gap is not a long one between learning satisfaction and teaching satisfaction. Even the

---

[70] The most notable exceptions are marital therapy programs like *Imago Therapy* that use the marital diads as mini communities. They also create therapy groups and support groups for the couples to serve community functions for limited periods of time.

293

first lessons are worth discussing because we learn as much about satisfaction from our failures as from our successes.

It is usually unproductive and even counterproductive to tell an immature man he needs to learn satisfaction unless he is already upset and looking for answers. If the immature man you know needs answers then "seek satisfaction" should be near the top of the list. The man who is not looking for answers will be less resistant to learning if you "just do it" and tell your daily satisfaction stories instead of confronting him with his need to learn satisfaction.

One essential place to learn satisfaction is in dealing with attachment pain and returning to joy from the big six feelings. (The big six feelings are: sadness, anger, fear, disgust, shame and hopeless despair.) Having satisfying responses to attachment pain and upsetting feelings makes a world of difference to the quality of life and relationships. These skills are passed on from well-trained brains to untrained brains so we are talking about close mentoring relationships at this point. Remember that both the man who is flying upside down in his pseudo-maturity and the man who is always a boy are having trouble returning to joy from at least one of the big six. For the man who was never a boy we know that fear is a definite problem.

Stopping the enabler: Teaching a man about satisfaction always starts with stopping the enabler. For the man who was never a boy the man himself is the enabler. With the man who is always a boy it will be some relative—usually his wife, girlfriend or mother.

It takes a whole community, a spiritual family, to support the enabler while he (or she) stops because the enabler is actually the less mature and more easily frightened of the two. While the low flying member of the relationship seems obviously immature, he or she is usually receiving with no difficulty. The upside down enabler, however, is full of fears of what will happen if his partner is left in charge. These fears are usually quite reasonable given past experience and serve to keep the flashlight of attention off the enabler's own satisfaction. His fear driven pseudo-maturity makes him think he is the more mature and responsible party.

Seize moments of inability to help the enabler to face the fear of hopeless despair. Every so often the enabler gets out on thin ice and gets stuck in a situation he/she can't enable a way out of no matter how he tries. These wonderfully teachable moments are times when anyone who comfortably knows the way back to joy from hopeless despair can lead the way. The mature brain has a chance to synchronize with the disorganized brain and teach a return to joy. Enablers are most teachable when their worst fears come true. Up until then, enablers are usually too hopeful and trying too hard to change the outcome. If you don't know how to return to joy from hopeless despair find someone who does.

294

Once an enabler wants help changing, 12-step recovery programs are good places to locate people who do well in hopeless despair and know how to help enablers stop flapping. CODA and AL-ANON groups have led the way in supporting frightened enablers through tough times. These groups do a good job of keeping the flashlight on the enabler instead of the threat. Like all groups, some 12-step groups are terrible and you will need to find a different one. In addition, a few groups do not think they can help enablers who are not dealing with an addict to some familiar substance. Most enablers have at least one alcoholic in their extended family and with that to talk about they can get in and find help for their fears.

Low flying men (men who are always boys) need to go through pain lab. Since their lives have been about avoiding pain, however unsuccessful they have been, change starts for them during those moments when they cannot escape their pain and someone joins them in it instead. The simplest form of pain is doing hard things. Doing hard things is just an uncomfortable, boy sized challenge. Learning satisfaction from doing hard things leads in time to learning how to suffer well. Suffering well leads in time to learning how to protect others from one's self—an adult task. It takes a spiritual community to help a low flying immature man suffer well by wisely giving him just enough help and no enabling. The community must not be afraid or indifferent to his pain or discomfort the process causes if they are to help. Meanwhile, the community must protect others from the immature man until he can learn (many years later) to protect others from himself.

There has been much written over the years on suffering well. We need not re-invent the wheel. What we can add now with the help of people like Dr. Schore and Dr. Siegel is a scientific approach to retraining the brain to suffer well. It is helpful to know, for instance, that we are dealing with just a few feelings (six) and that the training involves right hemisphere to right hemisphere nonverbal communication between a brain that knows how and one that doesn't. You may want to consult some of my training materials for additional help.71

Satisfaction starts small: Learning satisfaction starts with noticing the small things. Children learn satisfaction from food, clothes, games and play. Children do not do huge projects for satisfaction. One classic error adults make is attempting to find satisfaction by doing something really big.

---

71 Look for my book *Suffering Well* (In progress.)
Chris Coursey and E. James Wilder, *Thriving,* (In progress.)
Quiet Place Teachings videos (In progress) are available from CARE Packaging www.care1.org or (231) 745-4950.
Raymond Jones and E. James Wilder, *Out of Control* (In progress).

Big projects usually blow up because they take too long to do, have too many things go wrong and the resulting satisfaction doesn't last very long.

Learn satisfaction on things like which salad dressing is most satisfying? What shirt is most satisfying at a special event? What time is it most satisfying to get up or go to bed? Which friends are most satisfying? Of all the things in the day/evening/time with friends/bowl game what was the most satisfying and what was the least.

Satisfaction only lasts a day: Satisfaction only lasts a day so every day must have its own. At first it helps to sort through each day and divide your experiences into satisfying and not satisfying. After a few weeks of sorting you can begin to rank experiences by which were more satisfying and which were less satisfying. The same can be done for the dissatisfying experiences. Finally you can begin to plan your day (or next day) to have some satisfying experiences and then check at the end of the day to see if you guessed correctly. Each day needs its own satisfaction. Once you see the difference between how you feel on satisfaction days and ones without satisfaction you will need no one to persuade you what to do next.

Anyone who is building satisfaction will soon begin to mature. If you ask your friends and children to ask you about your satisfaction when you seem to have forgotten about it you will grow even faster. "Daddy, were you satisfied with how you treated us in the car?" "Mommy, are you satisfied with what you are doing right now?" Just imagine the possible questions!

PROBLEMS FOR WHICH THERE IS NO HOME REMEDY

I am what I do: Men who are stuck at four years of age have identities created by their work; they are what they do. Some men take all their value from what they do. Sam said he would never retire. He loved construction. At six every morning, seven days a week he found himself at the pancake house with the other contractors swapping stories and sub-contracts. His truck and his tools went everywhere he did. Sam worked until late afternoon most days and took pride in his work. He was known to get in fights with homeowners who wanted inferior materials just to save money. He lost a few friends that way.

Sam's wife had a life of her own and, truth be known, had told a few of her friends that Sam just watched TV and was unpleasant at home. So she didn't care that he was still working at age 69.

Sam took a vacation one time with a friend and set off to see the country, but they got in a fight before too many miles. His friend nearly left him in a café and let him find his own way home. Sam was not much for conversation unless he was reminiscing about what quality redwood used to be like.

When Sam had a heart attack and found he could not work he became miserable. All he wanted to do was die and it took him very little time to let anyone know that. Soon his visitors began to feel that it wouldn't be such a bad idea, although perhaps they didn't really mean it in their hearts.

Sam was a contractor. It wasn't that he did construction, he was a contractor. What he built was who he was. To see his finished work was to see him. No wonder he did not like inferior materials and would rather lose a friend. Aside from what he did Sam was not able to recognize himself. Sam thought his value came from what he could put out. Those who trusted his work will miss him, especially if their next contractor does bad work.

The best inroad into a man "who is what he does" is to ask satisfaction questions. As long as there is no dissatisfaction he will not change or grow. Many of these men crack about midlife when they discover they are not satisfied. A mentor, usually at work, is the best hope for a child-man who is what he does. Sometimes a good Steven Covey style coach will help those who want to improve their work identity. Since many are what others call "workaholics" they get their wake-up-call when their wives find someone else. Sometimes it takes two or three of these wake-up-calls. Retirement is another major crisis time for men who are what they do. Many simply die because they have been flying upside down all their lives and suddenly they have no one to please. With some creativity we as a culture might be able to catch a few more of them when they are about to crash. Our mistake has been assuming men are mature because they are productive.

I am what I imagine: Fantasy-prone men got stuck about five years of age. They avoid pain through fantasy, movies, Internet, computer games, sports and gambling. Their sense of reality is very closely controlled by their subjective feelings rather than by their interactions with important people in their lives. Because fantasy can have powerful effects on the brain's pleasure center, these child-men have a hard time recognizing that they are not satisfied. This group is perhaps the hardest of all to reach at home. In order to change they must trust someone else more than they trust their own minds. To solve their dilemma requires two ingredients to be present: 1) they must be in some difficulty they can't get out of without trusting someone, and 2) there must be a trustworthy person available. The first is hard to engineer and the second requires a diligent search. For these reasons, most men who recover do so because either they are stuck in an inescapably painful situation or they have a religious experience that changes their identities.

I don't learn from my mistakes – fear of failure: Starting about six years of age, children need to learn from their mistakes. When they have trusted family members who tell them what their mistakes are and what they mean, boys will develop an interest in experimenting and learning. Boys who are left to their own when it comes to comparing results they achieve with what they expected would happen will generally compensate one of two ways: they develop ways to ignore results they don't like or they don't take risks and develop a fear of failure.

In adult aged men this problem can be addressed by a mentor or by a peer group—if a man is motivated. The hardest problem is finding motivation for the man who ignores results he does not like. Family and friends have to make the results impossible to ignore but at that point the man will be so angry at his family that someone outside the family will have to help him learn from his mistakes. This change is usually slow. Men may require months to show any progress.

I can't do hard things: While many boys are cured of this by sports, scouts, basic training, or their first job, there are some who escape all the above. Even these ways of learning to do things one doesn't feel like doing do not usually train a boy to do hard things in relationships. If the "hard thing" involves uncomfortable feelings even a few Marines have been known to run.

One expects to find lazy slobs when we talk about those who do not do hard things and there certainly are those! Generally, nothing short of cutting off their rations makes lazy men change. The women who enable them support most lazy men. In these situations, the first change must be helping the enabler straighten up and fly right. This is the harder job because, as we have seen, enablers are very afraid to stop their enabling.

Many men who would never be called lazy still fear doing hard things if it involves feelings. Some men avoid all conflict but often the way this problem shows up is with anger. When men use anger to control their families they are avoiding the feeling they find hard to deal with. Controlling others through anger always involves verbal violence. If the feelings men are avoiding include attachment pain (the granddaddy of all painful feelings) their anger will often escalate to physical violence. Because attachment pain activates the nucleus accumbens it signals the brain "I'm going to die" and the results can be deadly to anyone nearby who has an attachment to the man. This condition is very dangerous and should never be treated at home. Aggressive anger should never be ignored. All community resources should be used to address this control/anger problem before someone gets seriously hurt or killed. Men can change their angry aggression but their entire brain must be retrained and that is not easy. No wife or girlfriend can do that retraining because it is not love that makes the difference—in fact love makes it worse. Aggressive rage is most often triggered by attachment pain and those he loves trigger his attachment pain. If you face aggressive anger with someone you love, go somewhere safe and get all the help your community can give.

298

Untamed nucleus accumbens: Dealing with cravings is as difficult a job as an American can face. I mention it here because it is another child-man problem that is not given to home remedies. Frankly, cravings only give way to spiritual disciplines such as those promoted by twelve-step groups, Zen Buddhism and the Christian disciplines.[72] These are rarely successful when practiced by one man alone.

THERE IS ONE THING YOU CAN DO AT HOME

No big picture: Now here is one problem for which there is a home cure of sorts. A number of men have never grown up because they simply didn't know how to get from where they are to where they want to be. I blew it with my sons, for instance, on several points. I gave them only half the big picture and totally missed teaching them to do hard things. By the time I found out about the need to teach boys to do hard things they were in college. I explained to them how I had screwed them up and what they still needed to learn.

A year later my younger son called me to say that he was going to school part time and taking on a third part-time job. When I asked him if that was going to be more than he could handle he told me, "Maybe, but I have to learn to do hard things and this is a good way to do it." Knowing the big picture lets men be intelligent about their growth. The big picture helps men be strategic about their repairs as well.

With this book a man can figure out what is missing in his life and what to do about it. If you like him you can encourage him and enjoy his growth. If you are the man, you can find or create a group of motivated men and make the trek together.

---

[72] Dallas Willard, *The Spirit of the Disciplines*, (Harper San Francisco: San Francisco, 1991)

Chapter Nineteen
It Is Not Too Late To Be A Man

"I want to become a man. I feel like a boy inside around men who are years my junior. That is why I came." Joel's words were clear, and he looked the other men in the eye. The men gathered in the retreat center were waiting to hear the words that had never been said about them.

Joel was a strong man with a firm handshake. He had a look about him that gave one the impression Joel usually got his way. He sort of took over the couch as he sat down. Before long he informed us that he was a retired fighter pilot and father of three grown children.

Larry sat back in his chair with his legs sticking out like the ends of a wishbone. He was a federal marshal and the father of three children. "I'm always afraid," he said, "that I'll do something wrong and get yelled at. If anyone gets mad at me I feel like a little boy. I can't ever remember feeling like a man under pressure. I worry constantly."

Like many other men there, Larry and Joel were waiting for the time to come when they will feel like men inside. As they approached retirement, they experienced a sense of loss and shame because they still did not feel like men.

"I thought that when I could walk out of the bathroom smelling of aftershave I'd feel like such a man!" Steve said, remembering his childhood hopes. Although we could still smell the AquaVelva on him, he assured us it hadn't worked its magic.

"You should have used Old Spice," Joel smirked.

Other men told how they had hoped that getting a wife, a career or a promotion might make them feel like men, but it never panned out. When we were through, men gathered in small circles of 8 to 12 guys and the oldest man in the circle stood up. Joel went first. He was the oldest in his group. He went from man to man in the circle, placing his hands on their shoulders and proclaiming this simple blessing: "You are a man. God loves you and I declare in his name this day that you are a man. God is very pleased." The men shook as tears welled up in their eyes. They let the words sink in and spoke haltingly in hushed tones if they spoke at all.

It is the same way at every retreat. Inevitably, this simple ceremony is the high point of the retreats I lead. Men of all ages hear for the first time that they are men and God believes that is a good thing. It is the burden of our generation to pass on what we did not receive.

After he had blessed the others, the whole group placed their hands on Joel and repeated the same blessing on him. It was a sacred moment. Joel heard what every 13-year-old boy needs to hear from his dad and the men of his community. For Joel it had taken an extra forty years.

Before their blessing, each man had gone through a maturity checklist. Becoming an adult man means doing a reasonable job of completing the infant and child tasks. Here, for your review, is a checklist of the development tasks needed to prepare for manhood. Go through them and look for any "no" answers. You will need to address the no answers before you can develop a stable adult identity. With "yes" answers you can then ask yourself is it "yes sometimes," "yes usually," or "yes always." That will give you a good idea of how well your personality will take the heat of adult life and stress.

Infant Stage

- ❏ I have experienced strong, loving, caring bonds with mother/a woman
- ❏ I have experienced strong, loving, caring bonds with father/a man
- ❏ Important needs were met until I learned to ask
- ❏ Others took the lead and synchronized with me and my feelings first
- ❏ Quiet together times helped me calm myself with people around
- ❏ Important people have seen me through the "eyes of heaven"
- ❏ I can both receive and give life
- ❏ I receive with joy and without guilt or shame
- ❏ I can now synchronize with others and their feelings
- ❏ I found people to imitate so that I now have a personality I like
- ❏ I learned to regulate and quiet the "big six" emotions
  - o Anger
  - o Fear
  - o Sadness
  - o Disgust
  - o Shame
  - o Hopeless/despair
- ❏ I can return to joy from every emotion and restore broken relationships
- ❏ I stay the same person over time
- ❏ I know how to rest

302

Child Stage

- ❑ I can do things I don't feel like doing
- ❑ I can do hard things (even if they cause me some pain)
- ❑ I can separate my feelings, my imagination and reality in my relationships
- ❑ I am comfortable with reasonable risks, attempts and failures
- ❑ I have received love I did not have to earn
- ❑ I know how my family came to be the way it is—family history
- ❑ I know how God's family came to be the way it is
- ❑ I know the "big picture" of life with the stages of maturity
- ❑ I can take care of myself
- ❑ I ask for what I need
- ❑ I enjoy self-expression
- ❑ I am growing in the things I am good at doing (personal resources and talents)
- ❑ I help other people to understand me better if they don't respond well to me
- ❑ I have learned to control my cravings
- ❑ I know what satisfies me
- ❑ I see myself through the "eyes of heaven"

When you score "yes" answers down the list you are ready to become an adult. Men with their childhood and infant needs well in hand will find the transition to adult maturity quite doable. Men can read a book and apply some creativity to solve these problems for themselves. It will take some practice with the adult tasks before marriage will come easily or the demands of parenting become a welcome challenge. The adult stage is easy to coach when the trainees are qualified so why is it that many men still can't make the leap to manhood?

DO MEN NEED HEALING OR COACHING?

There are two major reasons why men have not progressed to adult maturity. First, they may lack the preparation and training needed. We have addressed what men need to mature rather extensively in this book so you know about that part. The second reason men do not mature is that they need healing. In addition to the lack of the necessary good things in life, men must also attend to the damage caused by the genuinely bad things that happened to them as they grew up. Some of this damage was self-inflicted through ignorance or perversity, some was accidental and some was just evil. Men must have healing from these injuries before they can go on with normal growth and maturity.

Much of the time Dr. Tim Brubaker spent with Clement[73] was devoted to healing. Tim spent hours of anguish dealing with the wounds he received from the medical world before he could become a powerful doctor. To use his power wisely as a physician meant confronting the pain and the rage caused by medical rigidity. Whenever life seemed like a collision of *Ignorant Forces* and *Immovable Walls* Tim would get in a rage. Rage made all his power seem too little and his pain made the problem too large to engage at all. Tim became tiny and no longer used his manly power wisely when his pain was intense. Nor was his birth the only pain that Tim had to face. Like all men, Tim had to engage the pain from his "father wound" before he could be a good father, let alone a spiritual father. Without healing, Tiny Tim would not have become the wise Dr. Brubaker.

Many men's groups and movements have ignored the problem of injured men and tried to use coaching, cheering, pushing and even a little brow beating to get the wounded to walk. The wounded don't walk far. The Promise Keepers movement, met with such enthusiasm by many men and considerable distrust by many women, suffered from this skewed emphasis. Talk show counselors and therapists also prefer a, "Just do it, Stupid!" approach.

Getting men to change through therapy and counseling has been remarkably ineffective. Most men just won't go to therapy except at gunpoint. Still, women persist in trying to get men into counseling. The results are generally poor because most men do not think they are wounded and because healing does not correct immaturity. Therapy is usually of great help to the pseudo-mature and turns them right side up but it does little for low flying immaturity.

Since healing alone does not bring maturity, men are not impressed with the usual outcomes for men in therapy. They have seen men who have had years of therapy and still are not powerful men. Since most therapists are ignorant about maturity this should come as no surprise. Therapists are trained to deal with healing not maturity. Therapists usually leave maturity to the family and community, which usually means maturing is left to ignorance and chance.

In the end, neither school of thought gets very promising results with men. In one they heal, heal, heal but never mature and in the other they buck up, buck up, buck up but never leave the pain behind. There is no reason for this fight between the "men need healing" and the "men need to try harder" groups when men need both. Let's just be smart about it and get a plan that includes both healing and maturity.

---

[73] See Chapters 14-15.

Healing for wounded men, coaching for struggling men: There is no reason to be carrying around old pain forever. Ways to heal are well explored and easily available in most localities. Maturity coaching is a little harder to come by but not that hard to find when you have something like this book to guide your search. Go to therapy for healing but go to your community for maturity. Go to your pastor for healing but go to your spiritual family for maturity. Get prayer,[74] EMDR®[75] or TheoPhostic®[76] ministry for healing but find coaching, men's groups, Promise Keepers, elder board,[77] your tribal counsel or wise old men for maturity.

Resources for stranded men: Even after addressing wounds and getting coaches we must remember that developing adult maturity requires community resources. Adult maturity must be worked at and earned like any other stage. An initiation only serves to start the work and rally the community support that each group of men needs. One of the main resources needed in order to become a powerful adult man is a group identity. One man in isolation cannot create a group identity. Men will need to look for all the resources mentioned in chapters 5-7.

Now that we have seen how healing and coaching are both needed let us go back and study how wounds stop men from maturing. Wounds have a peculiar relationship to power and pain.

WOUNDED MEN

Becoming a man (adult) means learning to be powerful in the company of other powerful men and women. Coaching and a good group identity are needed to develop a powerful adult identity when men are making up for lost time. However, if powerful men or the absence of well-used power injured them, men react with fear or greed to offers of adult power. Injured men avoid power or use it to hurt others and protect themselves. Neither of these patterns leads to adult maturity. Unless men receive healing for their wounds their fears and pain will keep them from becoming men.

In describing what wounds men, it is impossible to avoid mentioning their fathers. Indeed, to avoid mention of the father would be to conclude that the father had no effect on his children, hardly a reasonable conclusion. Highlighting the important role of the father and giving him

---

[74] Prayer is generally and widely available but for additional help contact Rev. Gordon Dalbey at (805) 967-3872 or www.abbafather.com.

[75] Dr. Francine Shapiro, Eye Movement Desensitization and Reprocessing (EMDR)

[76] Dr. Edward M. Smith, *Healing Life's Deepest Hurts,* (Ann Arbor: Vine Books, 2002) www.servantpub.com or www.theophostic.com.

[77] Yes I know!

honor also points out his effects, whether to his credit or shame. Fathers do not intentionally and knowingly produce a "father wound." Fathers have no idea what value they have to their sons and are uncertain how to pass on what they do understand and value. Instead, men pass on the father wound from one generation to the next because they see neither their wound nor their pain.

Men who fear adult male power because it injured them do not want to grow up to be monsters. These frightened men have sworn to themselves that they would never become like their fathers and their tormentors. In their marriages these fearful child-men often want women to be powerful but don't step up to the plate themselves. They leave all the important choices to women and eventually adult women resent this strongly. Women want a man who will pull his weight and make his half of the contribution to leading their lives, raising their children and facing their conflicts.

Child-men who see having the most power as the way to kick ass and get their way greedily grasp power and become tyrants. They make life miserable for powerful women. Often these power-hungry men reduce women to sexual conquests—real or imagined. What really generates problems is when these "little boys" inside men's bodies take control and start running homes, churches, and businesses for the purposes of avoiding any pain themselves.

MEN IN PAIN

Let's step back a moment and discover how the current attitudes about men and pain have been created. Somewhere in the mid-nineteen-seventies writers began to take notice of men. I'm not sure that they thought all that highly of men, but at least they had some compassion. They began to write about the "fragile male ego." That was wonderful for men and women because, for the first time in quite a while, men were allowed to have needs and feel pain. The fragile-male-ego school said men have needs and feelings too. They are not the rocks they appear to be, living just to do heartless things. Inside they have needs and feelings just like women. This view of men was really different than popular culture--liberating, some might say. Men were like women and not nearly as "macho" as the strong, silent type might suggest.

The fragile male ego finally made room for a man to have needs and feelings, even if he didn't acknowledge what they were. Women were taught to understand and take care of these men who did not know how to say, "I need to go to sleep." They were to understand that when men growled and harrumphed, they really meant, "I'm tired." (Actually we are describing infant maturity.) A wife needed to understand that if she said to hubby, "You mean you need to go to sleep?" she might hurt his feelings of masculinity so it was better to let him wander off to bed with the understanding that tomorrow he would be alright.

As women began to talk about orgasms, men began to feel that these, too, were somehow a reflection of his performance. Faking a climax seemed better than the truth as women believed a man might be devastated and emasculated to discover that his most intimate relationship was less than ideal.

So it was that among compassionate, enlightened circles, men were seen as having become hard and silent because they lacked the strength women received from talking. "Men can feel pain," was the basic message, "so don't beat them endlessly or they may break." It was apparent how quickly men retreated into silent or angry pain from the onslaught of women's feelings and words, so the myth of the fragile male ego was born. It was a myth or story to explain why men ran from feelings--especially women's feelings.

Men did flee in droves from women and their feelings. We can now say that this inability by men to know who they are in the presence of emotions is the sign of a badly trained control center in his brain. For some men it also represents an inability to do hard things. For all men, fleeing women's emotions represents a failure to have adult power in relationships. Fleeing is a sign of infant or child level maturity. Because women understood this flight as a fragile male ego instead of immaturity, nearly a generation of men remained immature. The myth had grown to mean more than just, "men have a breaking point," it came to mean, "men can't take the truth." When men can't take the truth, men can't be a part of real life. They can't know their part in history. They can't even begin to measure their impact. As a result, a generation of men was very much confused about how much power they really had. They didn't know how much they could handle. They particularly didn't know if they could handle pain or not.

WHY MEN LIE ABOUT PAIN

There is a fairly good chance that the strong, silent type of man, the ones who inspired the fragile male ego myth, believed that men shouldn't show pain. I think that long ago this grew out of the knowledge that men could handle pain. Men had the strength to experience pain, act like themselves and keep going. After last century men had a lot to grieve. World War I and World War II, Korea, Vietnam and genocide left men who lost fathers, sons, brothers and friends. However, most men did not grieve. Instead, showing no pain became a way to be a man and even to show off. Hiding signs of pain became a way to test other men, to become more of a man than others and even to become a man. Gangs, tribal initiations, boot camp, high school football, "cold war spies," and tough guys of all stripes relied on the "show no pain" test of manhood. To be a man meant to hide one's pain. The absolutely screwy things men have done to hide their pain would fill many books. Often the cover-up was so obvious to everyone else that the very effort seems pathetic.

Instead of learning that men can survive pain and need not fear it, men began to think that feeling no pain was manly, so they decided to not avoid pain. "I can take it!" they would brag. Their sons avoided pain in order to avoid the stupidity of their fathers. Their sons avoided talking about pain so they would not be ridiculed by their fathers.

Other men made the assumption that men who did not show pain must not feel pain. When they felt pain it caused them shame because it seemed "unmanly" so they denied the pain. Their sons avoided pain because it felt painful to them and they feared it made them less than men. It did not seem manly to hurt. They were all searching for real, adult, masculine power but found their resolve melted in the face of an upset woman. To not feel pain around women, men had to avoid engagement and conflict. Men who denied pain and would not engage drove women wild.

Men who do not speak honestly about pain will never know how much pain they can take. What started as strength ended as deception. A man might know that he can handle physical pain, especially if it is inflicted on a football field. But can he handle the pain of feeling sad, sad, sad--so sad that it would make him cry? Can he handle that? He doesn't know.

AVOIDING EMOTIONAL PAIN

A strategy some men adopt is to avoid feeling pain entirely if possible. Being in control is perhaps the main method used by people to avoid having to feel pain of any kind. The person in control can ostensibly make events turn out in ways that avoid discomfort to himself. To do so requires that all pain be borne by someone else. This is perhaps a good definition of evil; for evil is the result of letting others bear our share of pain. These men will threaten or try to take control because if they are the ones in control they don't have to feel pain.

Four-year-old Leon acted up so his father hit him and then hit him again, saying, "Shut up, or I'm going to give you something to cry about!" The boy had embarrassed his dad by making a scene, and this dad knew he was going to get control of that situation. No one was going to see that he didn't know how to control his kid. It was a power struggle right to the end over who would be in control. The dad was not going to be embarrassed and feel any personal pain. If anybody was going to be feeling some pain, he knew exactly who that was going to be. It didn't matter how much power it took, he would use all he needed to be in control and avoid the pain. Even though the only pain for the father was embarrassment, he was not going to take it. Is that what it means to be a powerful man? What did Leon learn?

Threats: A threat is a powerful way to get control of a situation but is that what it means to be a powerful man? Do you know that Jesus never threatened anyone? That caught Peter's attention. (1 Peter 2:22) What would life be like if men didn't threaten? Many people tell me that they can't raise kids without threatening them. Others say they can't run a business without threats. We all need to intimidate people from time to time they claim. Perhaps Jesus failed to grasp that point.

Actually, it is impossible to control people. A man can't control his girlfriend, wife, children, employees or anyone. He may hope to influence them in a positive or negative manner but he can't control them. The paradox is that the man who tries controlling others will soon feel out of control himself. Trying to control the uncontrollable will drive him crazy and make him mean.

Giving up control: For many men the road to healing comes from a painful event they cannot escape. When men stop thrashing about they begin to learn new ways. The first of the 12 steps is admitting we are powerless. The men most likely to grow up are those caught in painful trouble they can't control. Healing starts when they admit they hurt. To their amazement they live through the pain and a few even begin to seek healing in active ways. Perhaps if more men knew they were men they might see the value in suffering a bit.

HEALING FOR MEN

I became a therapist and was told I would mostly help women. For the first eight years that was true—I saw mostly women. Most women came in to tell me how rotten men were. When dealing with disgruntled women, instead of being a man I was a "therapist," whatever that is. I tried to hide my masculinity because I didn't really want to let it be known I was one of "them." Fortunately counselors aren't considered human by their clients, so it took most women about a year to figure out that I was present at all. The women would talk for a long time about what creeps men were and how they hated men, then one day they would notice I was there and say, "But not you, of course."

At some level I was ashamed of what men had done to them. I didn't want to be seen as a male—a representative of hurtful and evil behavior. As the truth of what evil men have done continued to collect around me, my secret shame of being "one of them" grew. After listening to horror stories about men I began to think that maybe there wasn't much good at all about being a man. A large wound was forming in my masculine identity but I never noticed. The result was that I never exercised my power as a man.

It hasn't been popular to be a man for rather a long time. In fact, being a man, and in particular a father, has been considered such a worthless thing that I never received a single class on the subject during my four years of college or six years of graduate school. I don't mean that I didn't have a course on the subject, I mean that I never even had one class lecture devoted to masculinity! That is how worthless the topic was considered to be in academic circles.[78] I never noticed how that added to my father and masculine wounds.

Two factors changed my secret shame of being a man, and before I knew it my counseling caseload changed from almost all women to mostly men. Both factors showed me the same miraculous truth: powerful men have something good to offer. The first of these revelations came from the community of men and the second from a special group of women. Without being aware of it these two groups helped me to heal.

The first factor was seeing my name on a Who's Who list of fathering advocates in America. I guess writing a book on the subject is all that is needed to become a "who." Now the truth was, I was not that impressed with myself as a father. My father guilt about not being a good-enough father festered until I heard Dr. Ken Canfield of the National Center for Fathering say that according to his research, all good fathers carry the feeling that they are not good enough. Ken's talk helped me recognize my pain and my fathering wound. Only then did it occur to me that being a father was indeed good. In fact, I had been and was good for my sons, as well as for other men who had experienced a father deficit. I began to find healing for my father wound.

The second gift that changed my secret shame about being a man came from women. Not long after I became a "who," several women read my book and told me that they would have liked to have me as their father. These women were incest survivors, some of the very ones who had been so vitriolic about men earlier. The truth slowly sunk in. Being a powerful man was good. Men were to be the source of good and life, the protectors of what is good. There was no shame in that! Good effects in the lives of others were not something that men produced from time to time but the essence of who they were. These women helped me to heal as I recognized the pain men had caused was not necessary.

I did nothing overtly to spread this good news, yet somehow men began to seek me out, asking to be taught the secret. "I want whatever it is you have," they would say. There was little to it, and for the first time in my life I was really glad to be a man. It is important to see this does not mean I was really happy that I wasn't a woman. That had nothing to do with it. I couldn't do a thing about that, I simply happened to be male and being what

---

[78] I am getting my revenge now. Did you see how long this book is?

one *is* is good--splendid, even. Whether others knew it or not, I represented good news to them because good news is what I was created to be. Everyone has been created to be good news.

With this new appreciation for myself, I began to develop my own flair for life. Perhaps this is as good a place as any to say that as men become men, their wobbly efforts should soon begin to demonstrate a sense of style. Without this enjoyment of self-expression men become merely functionaries, doers, and conveniences for others. A powerful man does not simply perform service, but service flows from him expressed in his unique style for the enjoyment of those served as well as himself. We begin to like the effects we have on the world. I began to find "Jim-like effects" quite satisfying. Healing had led to growth. I was becoming a man.

FACING THE PAIN AND THE WOUND

What are the most common kinds of wounds?
- An attachment wound
- A father wound
- A man or woman wound
- A sexual wound
- A contempt wound
- A Christian wound

We have talked about attachment pain and father pain but what is a man or woman wound? These are wounds that we associate with a gender and lead to fear or hatred of that gender. If a man or series of men breaks your heart you may develop a fear of men—a man wound. I developed a woman wound from years of hearing how women hated men.

A sexual wound develops from sexual abuse, misuse or assault. Rape leaves a sexual wound along with a man wound.

All of us have received contempt wounds. "You are FAT!" "Asshole!" "Not you again!" Contempt is a form of soul murder that creates great pain. Once wounded, we tend to pass it back or pass it on. "You too! Prick!"

The leading reason why people around the world do not want to be Christians has nothing to do with Jesus, it traces to a Christian wound. Christians are the largest block to Christianity ever invented. Christian wounds run deeply in Christians themselves. Ask Catholics about parochial school. Catholics have uniquely Catholic wounds. Mennonites have Mennonite wounds, often related to fear, silence, hiding and staying hidden. Nazarenes have their Christian wounds, like feeling they are abject failures to stay holy and be acceptable to God or the church.

It has taken me more years to heal from my Christian wound than it has for my male wound. It is only recently that I have begun to see being a Christian as a good thing to talk about. Usually I hoped no one would notice or ask. I cringed when hearing what Christians did just like I did with the damage from men. The sense that Christians were a source of life and good things in this world came after a lot of healing.

These wounds make my point that protecting others from oneself only comes after dealing with one's pain. Wounded people always use too much or too little power thus causing wounds for others. Unhealed men leave men wounds. They pass on the wounds they received and often make them worse. Unhealed Christians leave Christian wounds. Wounded people do not protect others from themselves in adequate ways. As is often said, "Wounded people wound people."

Pain informs us of a wound. Men's problem with admitting pain is one reason men don't get healing. Yet every man knows the moment will come when he must face the truth about himself. He knows, "This is going to hurt." If he really looks at himself, there is a good chance he is going to look ugly. How painful to be ugly. To be honest, what man can say, "I've never done anything ugly?" If he looks at how he grew up there is going to be something ugly there too. And then what? What will he do with that pain? Here is where a second problem kicks in—his lack of trust. Who will he trust with his pain?

In the words of a wise teacher, "Seek and you will find. Ask and you will receive." The man who knows what he needs can begin to ask other men and women, "Who helped you to heal?" "Who do you trust?" "Who understands pain?" The answers will come. Someone who is full of life in the middle of his or her pain will share his hot chicken soup with you. Face the pain, find the healing, do the work and you too will serve chicken soup to hurting men and women because you have become a man.

Chapter Twenty
An Elder Too Soon

"We never had a day in our home that someone was not living with us," she said sadly. Her husband had been an elder too soon.

"Everyone in the school thinks dad is cool. They love to be with him. He listens to them and they want his advice but he doesn't listen to me. He never went to my games because someone always needed him more." His voice was flat and lifeless and his gaze drifted away. His dad had been an elder too soon. The life his son needed had gone to someone else.

"I can't stand the word 'ministry.' Ministry is what took my parents away. Their ministry was always more important than us kids." Anger and pain showed on her face. Her parents had been elders too soon.

"Every time I even think about sex I see Mr. Marlin. He was like a dad to all us girls at the school. When we went on camping trips and the little girls got scared he would let them sleep in his tent—sometimes even in his sleeping bag. He gave us candy when we cried and sometimes came around with Mrs. Marlin and tucked us in at night. They never had kids of their own. " Mr. Marlin had been assigned elder duty and no one even checked his maturity. After all, he had credentials so why couldn't he run a girl's school. He was an elder way too soon.

When and where do we need elders in charge? Elders with earned maturity are needed at the helm of all religious communities, schools, missions and organizations that shape or direct the destiny of others. When the activity of an organization directly affects the identity of its members or surrounding community it will need elders. Having elders with earned maturity in charge is the only way to safeguard the trust others will place in a charitable group. The damage caused by allowing lesser maturity into leadership is terrible. Because of the many leadership failures in the past and the appalling consequences they bring, organizations have looked for ways to prevent future failures.

Typically, they chose leaders because of their education, gifts, availability and experience. Mature leaders are rarely available. With maturity comes deep roots into one's community so mature people are usually already where they plan to stay. For this reason alone, most candidates for any position will be immature.

Experience sometimes equates to maturity but usually it does not. When selection committees look at experience, most are looking at job skills. Experience is only an indirect indication of maturity.

Gifted people are often mistakenly placed in leadership of churches and other organizations where charisma draws a crowd. Enormously gifted preachers, evangelists, musicians, worship leaders and media figures repeatedly crash and burn in their marriages and relationships. Christians, in particular, are prone to put gifted people in leadership only to have them fail in their character, morals, family and intimate relationships because they were not mature. Tragic examples are so plentiful that pastors and leaders of Christian organizations who fall into moral failure don't even get noticed unless they were extremely popular. After each failure a new "gifted" leader is selected for the same cruel fate. Only the faintest attention to maturity goes into these hiring decisions at all. Little wonder that sexual addiction like phone sex and Internet pornography is in the top five problems for missionaries and likely for preachers too. They are trying to be elders too soon.

Education is also no alternative to maturity. We generally use education as a guide when hiring relatively young men who have had no chance to develop the higher stages of maturity. When experienced leaders go back for more education so they can improve their job skills or please the people who pay them it does not improve their maturity. Information does not bring maturity. If it did you would be at elder maturity now that you have read this book.

When it comes to explaining the cause of leadership failures, and consequently preventing them, few if any analysts point to a lack of maturity as the cause. Consequently, maturity is not used to improve success in hiring. One big contributor to overlooking maturity is that there has been no scale on which to measure maturity. Ask the average person to define maturity and rate the maturity of the people they know well and you will see what I mean. We have relied on tacit knowledge but because tacit knowledge cannot be expressed in words we have trouble putting it to use. We have known that maturity matters but have not known how to talk clearly about it.

One of the problems with a chapter like this is that people, particularly those who like leadership and power, are not prone to be mature and even less prone to notice that they need more maturity than they have. The very type of leader where trouble and damage are most likely is the least likely to understand how his immaturity is part of the problem. What we can hope for is that concerned members of groups, boards, leadership teams and voting constituents can be helped to make wise decisions about the leaders they select.

What happens when an elder was needed but an immature leader got the job? Elders have the most developed people skills and the best capacity to stay true to themselves under duress of any level of maturity. When elders are needed but less mature people take charge some of these skills are going to be missing at crucial times. For example, in a conflict infants will look out for themselves, child maturity will take sides,

314

adults will protect their group and parents will look out for their family's interests. Each level of maturity will color their ways of resolving conflict.

Let's look at another example. Immature leaders often have great ideas but their ability to stay on track when they are angry, threatened or upset is compromised. Their brain's control centers do not return to joy from all the "big six" emotions so they avoid, demote or get angry with people in their organization (or even those their mission statement says they want to reach) who make them feel badly. The whole organization and its activities become shaped so no one will upset the leadership, supporters or constituents. Eventually this leads to a lot of image building and dishonesty.

An immature leader who has not built his own group identity (the way any adult should have done) will work his people to death. There will be a lack of cohesive purpose, trust and delegation of authority. Morale will be low and an "everyone looks out for him/herself" attitude will prevail even though the rhetoric of the organization may be very different. This may work for years but show up in stress, illness, loss of key employees to other organizations and similar costs.

Elders have extensive networks of trust relationships with which they nurture their community. Their roots run deep like prairie grass. Less mature leaders fail at crucial moments to find trusted helpers and resources for their community and must turn to cannibalism--internally robbing Peter to pay Paul. Immature leaders are also more likely to rely on untested and untrustworthy external resources. Naturally, and disastrously, immature leaders do not take maturity into account when they assign people to tasks and so the damage perimeter spreads.

To understand the damage caused by putting someone into an elder's place who is not ready we will need to look in detail at the many levels where damage can occur. Perhaps if you have seen or are seeing this kind of damage in some group you represent it will help you look for the immature leader behind the trouble. My hope is that recognizing where elders are needed will prevent easily foreseeable damage—particularly in religious organizations and institutions where the potential for damage may well be the highest.

Damage to organizations:
- Their mission
- Their members
- Their internal functions
- Their finances
- Their image

We are beginning to watch the long-term cost to the Catholic Church in the US as it deals with priests who molest children. There is ongoing damage to their organization, its mission, members, internal operation, finances and image. Tremendous resources are being diverted to mop up after immature leaders.

On the protestant side, estimates run as high as a 70% failure rate on missionaries during the first term. The cost of preparing each couple, family or team is high. It is difficult to find supporters who will donate for the cause. Because so many failures are traceable to a breakdown of the control center in the missionary's brain under high stress, the euphemism "returned for health reasons" is given to maintain the mission image and income. Often the emotional breakdown is in one or more of the missionary's children. This is clear evidence that the family was sent to do elder's work before they were elders. The mission itself receives a heavy setback with each failed attempt. The costs inside the missionary organizations are high as they try to promote a successful image and keep the focus on their mission. However, little has been done to rehabilitate "failures" themselves so those recovery costs usually fall back on the casualties or their family members.

One pastor with an anger problem took a church from 2,000 to 600 members. Giving dropped dramatically after he fired six staff members. The budget went into red ink and the church into $30,000 debt within a week. Hundreds of members stood up and walked out. Few ever returned. Half the board resigned and the pastor himself left within a month, just one step ahead of the lynch mob. He tried to be an elder too soon. The church board put him up to be an elder too soon. The congregation expected him to be an elder too soon. Even though the denomination hierarchy thought of him as a megalomaniac they let him be an elder too soon. It hurt them dearly but the truth is no one thought they needed an elder with earned maturity, they thought a credential was enough.

THE HUMAN COST OF BECOMING AN ELDER TOO SOON

Damage to his children by neglect: Elders are to raise their communities like their own families and look after those who lack families of their own. These tasks often fall to churches, missions and non-profit organizations. The children of ministers, civic leaders and missionaries are often the casualties of helping others. The leader of one well-known organization that helps children around the world used to say that he took care of God's children and God would take care of his. He traveled most of the year. This man's daughter committed suicide after years of feeling depressed and unloved. Her father was an elder too soon.

Damage to his marriage: A mission organization sent a young family to encourage and build a church in the mountains. The region was full of violence and civil war. Several groups of terrorists were vying for supremacy and killing their way into control of the town. Trying to keep the church open and care for the stream of victims and their families left the missionaries constantly exposed to threats and danger. The parents constantly worried about the safety of their children. They were trying to be elders too soon. In a few months the mother had a severe nervous breakdown, the family had to return to the US but the woman never fully recovered. The church was not helped by this tragic outcome either. Elders know how to help a whole community through suffering but parents must protect their children and need a stable and safe community. Sending parents to do an elder's job cost this woman her mental health for life and with that her marriage, children and grandchildren suffered decades of loss. They were elders too soon.

Damage to his church/community: The pastor fumed, "Either she goes or I go!" In three months he was gone and so were about 1000 members of the church. The pastor was a brilliant and gifted man with no capacity to return to joy from shame or anger. He was years away from being an elder by earned maturity but he was left to help a church of 3,000 people correct some problems in their group identity. This church had slowly stopped acting like itself and various power groups had seized control. The pastor had just run squarely into one power broker and squared off to play hardball. The pastor and the older woman both looked for people to take sides (a strong clue that they were at child maturity) and soon many people did. Amidst the anger, the church began to break apart. The pastor preached well but could not live what he preached when he was threatened or angry. The church board had little more maturity than the pastor and soon there were lots of hurt members and no pastor. He had tried to be an elder too soon. Yes, he had the title, the calling, the gifting and the education but not the earned maturity.

Damage to his family by introducing dangerous people into his home: A pastor's daughter became deeply involved with drugs and actively suicidal when she was about 18 years old. Four different men who had lived in the parsonage with the pastor's family had molested her over the years. Her father would invite troubled men to stay with the family when they lost jobs, were recovering from alcoholism or dealing with emotional problems. He was being family to those who had no family but they were molesting his cute little daughter. He was being an elder too soon. His daughter not only felt unsafe, unloved and unimportant, she thought her dad cared more about his work than about her. She wanted nothing to do with his God or religion. She used sex, drugs, men, cars and even her beauty destructively. All of this could have been avoided if her parents had waited until they were elders to do the work of elders. But no one told these parents about the need for maturity so now they wait to see if their daughter will kill herself or live. Both they and their church thought that ordaining them automatically or divinely gave them elder capacities. They are in better shape than others who have had all their children, boys and girls, molested. Such damaged lives are the result of trying to be elders before the youngest child is 13 and the leadership couple has earned their maturity.

Damage to the wounded/lonely people who need help: Besides the betrayal of being sexually abused by your pastor, priest or counselor and the heartbreak of broken hopes there is more damage in the wake of those who would be elders too soon. A colleague of mine ran a hospital unit for abuse victims. Many of the survivors were brought to his unit by people who had become a spiritual family to the survivor. Often they invited the survivor into their homes and said, "You are a member of our family now." When their family and their love brought out more of the hidden pain, instead of making everything better these spiritual parents brought the person to the hospital for care. Soon after arrival, or just before discharge, the unit would get a call. "Tell her she can't come back. It just didn't work out." They were elders too soon and she…well, it was not a pretty sight.

Damage to missions (the purpose) by sending the immature: The denomination moved the pastor to his third church after getting sexually involved with multiple women in two previous churches. His wife and children were miserable. He was rarely home because of the "church work." Often he visited homes and talked with the lonely and distressed church members who were home without their husbands during the day. The pastor would end up in bed with the women. When he was "discovered" with four women in the third church, his denomination made him a traveling evangelist. That way, they figured, he would not ruin any more churches. After that the man traveled 48 weeks out of the year away from his family and moved from town to town counseling the new converts in their troubles before he moved on. Do you suppose that he was accomplishing the true mission of his denomination? We won't even discuss the mission of a minister or an evangelist. He was doing elder's work while he was still at infant maturity. Bright, gifted, charismatic in his style but not his theology, he was a menace to society and an elder too soon.

Far more subtle examples can be found of missions whose purpose was lost by immaturity. One missionary leader could not control his temper in the least. He was sent to a violent region of the world where his rages drew such attention that not even the violent local people wanted to be around him. It doesn't take a rocket scientist to figure out that no matter what mission he was on the result was a failure. He did not raise one person to maturity let alone a group of victims of violence. He was doing elder work in diapers and the results looked like what you find in diapers.

Damage to churches when they put in immature men or women on elder boards: While some churches call their pastors "elders" many other churches call their ruling board "elders." In some churches these elders hire and fire the pastor and in others they simply assist the pastor in running the church. When the title of "elder" is given to some member of the church's governing body without concern about earned elder maturity it opens the door to trouble. One fine young man was elected "elder" at 22 because he was sincere, devoted, had a degree in Bible and came from a Christian family. This concept of elder is devoid of any maturity component. His church went through three church splits in the next ten years. There were many fear-based decisions made and while the discussions were all about who had the true faith, the underlying issues were an inability to build and restore trust within the group. These "elders" were years away from the maturity they needed. The time they spent on church board conflicts took away from their family and work time so church, home and work all suffered. Immature leadership put the whole group at risk.

Damage to the potential elder and his development: Obviously the people drawn to elder work are the ones most likely to develop into elders. When men are elders too soon they fail at the very thing they desire to become. As a result of repeated or catastrophic failures from starting too young, these men are "taken out of contention" by the time they could really have been elders. Their families no longer trust and cooperate, their communities won't let them try, they feel too hopeless and ashamed to try again or they are still cleaning up the mess from their untimely efforts. A suicidal wife, for instance, can take your attention for the rest of your life.

Damage to the "big picture" for all involved: Whenever I discuss the need for elders in communities and begin to talk about what elders do, looks of fear come on the faces of old men who have seen leadership failures. Looks of pain come on the faces of younger people who lived through the disasters caused by their trusted leaders. Looks of anger come on the faces of adult children who lost their parent's time and affection while their parents did the work of elders—usually called "God's work." People, now in their 60s and 70s, were left in "homes" while their parents did missionary work in distant and dangerous places. Some were left behind as young as three years of age and only saw their parents every 5 to 7 years (when they were 10 and then 17 in the worst cases.) All these are victims of men and women who were elders too soon. For some of these victims and their communities the elder tasks sound like an invitation to heartbreak and lifelong misery. There is no joy in their minds at the thought of maturity nor do they want to grow up. The pain left by the terrible failures of those sent to do elder work before they were ready goes on for three or four generations. Where immature people have been sent to do elder's jobs the social soil will not grow maturity for generations.

Damage to the trust-building task true elders with earned maturity face: If the first five people who tried to do surgery on you were cranks, imposters and incompetent would you allow the sixth candidate to cut? Because the work of an elder is to build trust and restore the identity of a whole community, failures by those who are elders too soon affect the identity and trust of a whole community. Jobs that need elder maturity should be clearly established and only elders with earned maturity put in charge. No shortcuts.

Does this mean that there is no place for gifted, talented and charismatic young leaders? Not at all! There is plenty of work for young energy and strength but they must have elders around them to raise the community and give the young a chance to mature, raise their family, enjoy their spiritual family and then, at the right time, become elders themselves.

Chapter Twenty-One
Redemption

All the metamorphoses of maturity include a redemptive element. Redemption takes us from a state we can't get out of on our own to a new place of belonging while the cost is paid by someone else. Others must pay a price so that we can grow, mature and transform. Redemption involves receiving or giving undeserved life. When these costs are paid by mature people both the receiving and giving lead to joy. Elders and spiritual families give to those without families of their own so that all can grow and mature. We may call such spiritual families redemptive community.

In Chapter 19 we talked about the need for men to face their pain and heal if they are going to get their maturity up to date. This process of seeking resolution and finding the meaning for pain and suffering is also redemptive. Let's look at an example.

I took an interest in manly matters like girls and wheels when I turned twelve. Margie was an energetic and cute neighbor girl I had always liked. I really wanted to impress her and now that I had a new bicycle, I thought of a way.

It was the fashion for teenage boys in our neighborhood to give the girls rides on the handlebars of their bicycles and while I had a new bicycle, I had never given a girl a ride. You might think I would practice with my friends but boys did not ride on handlebars—that was for girls. I figured I'd play it safe and let Margie sit on the back instead.

Seizing an opportune moment, I rode right in front of Margie and said, "How about taking a ride on the back of my bicycle?"

"I'm not sure my parents would let me do that," she said but she walked over to my side.

I looked as cool as I knew how. "Don't worry, I am a good driver. Come on, Margie."

We headed down the driveway and around the corner. This was a new gravel driveway and made of crushed rock. Since gravel was scarce, contractors took big rocks and broke them down into little sharp pieces. The result was a pleasingly uniform, gray, crunchy surface.

As I went around the corner, fast enough to impress Margie, the bike flew out from under me. Down we went on fresh gravel. Wishing to be manly and not let Margie hit the ground, I bravely put my knee down to catch the bicycle. Margie didn't get a scratch but I took a knee full of gravel.

My knee hurt like crazy. The rocks were deeply imbedded so the few I pulled out really stung. Thinking that there must be a better way, I limped over to the clinic next door. Being manly, I was careful not to cry.

At the clinic, some angels of mercy proceeded to grab tweezers and pull the stubborn rocks out. Then they took these wonderful little scissors that start off in one direction and then take a sudden turn (for some reason medical people never have straight scissors) and began to snip. Those scissors did a great job of cutting up my knee. I wouldn't have minded if they had given me a shot first, but they just kept cutting away saying, "This stuff has got to come out of here." As they snipped away I turned pale. You know it felt terrible. When I winced and pulled away, the nurses growled, "Hold still!" They didn't need to say, "Take it like a man," because I already knew that part of my duty. A man would not be bothered by pain.

After they bandaged me up, I went home. For some reason, even though my jeans were torn up and bloody, my parents didn't notice what had happened. For one thing, I often limped because my weak ankle was constantly getting sprained. In addition, my parents were prone to a certain dismissive disregard for bodies anyway. Perhaps they were too busy with their missionary work, because if they had noticed they would certainly have taken action. For whatever reason they never noticed I had injured my knee.

A couple of weeks later I was walking around and I smelled this awful odor. I didn't know what it was, but it seemed to be coming from me, of all places. I pulled up my blue jeans and noticed that my bandage was all yellow, sticky, and nasty. It occurred to me that the highly objectionable odor might very well be coming from there. The bandage looked like something that should smell bad so I pulled it down. Suddenly everything underneath the bandage boiled up white. Hundreds of little maggots swarmed everywhere.

I knew I had seen maggots like that before when I had kicked over the carcass of a dead cat. The white swarm was everywhere under the dead body, and they moved amazingly fast. This, however, was not a dead cat. This was my leg! My first reaction veered toward loosing my breakfast. My second was, "I'm dead!" I heard the words come right out of my mouth, "I'm dead! What am I going to do?"

Logic steadied me in a bit. Obviously I wasn't completely dead, but what was happening? The only answer was to go back to the clinic again. I was terrified. The nurse yelled at me for not changing the bandages. I didn't know I was supposed to change bandages. They didn't tell me that. How was I supposed to know? The angel of mercy found her scissors. Again there was no shot for the pain. I took it like a man and didn't scream but it still makes me shudder.

That story went into my trauma history. And to tell you the truth it caused me to feel a little resentment toward my parents. How was I supposed to know when to change bandages? It seemed to me that my parents should have helped me out and noticed my plight. I felt like a

322

neglected child. Thinking about maggots in my knee did not make me feel good about myself or about my parents.

Eventually I decided I had to work through these feelings. I had to express them to God and tell Him the truth about what had happened and ask Him to heal the experience and to redeem it. By this time I was in my early thirties. Who knows how God could redeem maggots? In time I even forgot about it.

One day a woman came in for therapy and said, "When I was a child, my parents locked me in a box with maggots. They said that if I didn't do what they wanted me to do, they were going to leave me in there and those maggots were going to eat me alive."

She began to shake and cry, "You don't know what it is like to have maggots in you!"

Suddenly a very strong picture with a very intense odor came into my mind. I empathized at a very deep level with what it was like to have maggots in you, to be a child, to be terrified and think maybe you were dead.

She kept saying, "You don't know what it is like to think maybe you are dead and they are going to eat you up."

"I do, I do understand." I said.

"How can God love a person with maggots in them!"

"God still loves you and will not reject you for having maggots," I assured her.

"Oh, but I'm not like you," she said, still shuddering.

It was a redemptive moment. She knew God could love me because I never had maggots in me--but not her. We know better. That is redemption in action. And I ask you, how could someone arrange those strange bits of history on their own? I dare say most people have not had maggots. God arranged this special moment.

My doctor friends tell me that the maggots most likely saved my leg. Maggots remove the dead tissue. Without maggots the infection would have led to having my leg amputated.

REDEMPTIVE HISTORY

To the Christian, all history is redemptive.

Being a part of history has some very important ramifications. All of a sudden what we do begins to matter. Who we are begins to matter a great deal. All of history is part of an ongoing process and we participate whether we want to or not. History goes like this:

God created the world, and he said to the two people he put in charge, "I need you to know that while this is a wonderful garden, my creation has been infected by a very, very nasty virus. I am sworn to get rid of it. As life is my nature, I will wipe out anything that brings death. Only life and good will be eternal, evil and destruction will not survive. You need to know that anything that gets contaminated by that virus will get wiped out too. I am sworn to get rid of both the virus and its influence. So here is a word of advice: don't mess with that virus, because as soon as you do, you'll be on my list of things that have been infected and will not be eternal."

Of course, we humans, being the wise creatures that we are, got the virus. Now Adam had already had a lesson on how to relate to the Lord God. Remember how he said, "Excuse me, Lord God, I noticed when I was checking out the animals that there are two kinds of them. But there is only one kind of me. I liked petting the kitten, playing with the dog, riding the horse, hugging the koala, laughing with the otter, and talking to the parrot, but could I put in a requisition: do you have a form to fill out with a request for one like me? I'd like to have this corrected."

And God said, "You know what? You have a point. I like your idea, and I will do just that for you." And he did. Adam found a problem, took it to God, God said, "No problem, I like your idea, we'll work on it together," so they did and it was better than before. They all looked at the results together and said, "What a good day this is."

We can still do that. We have an idea and take it to the Lord to say, "Here is a problem. Can you do something about it?" And God says, "What a good point you have! Yes, I do like working on history with you. What do you suggest we do about it?" And so we talk it over until we have a plan.

Back in the garden, however, someone pointed out another problem to Adam. "Say! You guys don't know the difference between good and evil. There is a tree over there with the answers to all your problems." Since that time people have hallucinated. They think they can tell good from evil and it has gotten them into all kinds of fights.

Well, Adam should have known better because he knew how to be a part of history. He should have gone to the Lord God and said, "Lord God, it has come to my attention that we have another problem here in the garden. What can you do about our lack of knowing good and evil?" And who knows what the Lord God would have done? I would have never guessed the woman solution, would you? Just take a nap, lose a rib, add a few very nice features.... I would have loved to find out what the Lord God would have done about the tree, wouldn't you?

But that wasn't the way it turned out. Adam had his influence on history. We all got infected with the virus and scheduled for elimination. That is still the truth today. God will not tolerate evil to be eternal. Don't carry destructiveness and death with you or leave it in your life even to avoid pain.

The biggest surprise was that God provided a decontamination process. It could not be done by anyone who was contaminated, and it would cost us our bodies. But not to worry, new bodies would be in order after final decontamination. Now he might have given us new bodies anyway without decontamination, we don't know. Like I said, who would have guessed the Eve thing? God said he would take us from glory unto glory, which means that he isn't just decontaminating but always making the good even better. This is the history we are a part of creating.

This is an important story every man should know because we each have our maggots. When we ask God to redeem our pain and redeem the very things that brought death to us or through us, we will witness a transformation. Redemption does not make bad things good. Bad is still bad, but God can look at the bad and say, "I will make life out of that." God stays involved with history in order to restore life.

Redemption can be painful because the truth about us is often ugly. The worst times are often those when we have given death instead of life to those we loved. We grieve when our story hurts but it is not grieving that redeems stories, redemption comes by seeing through the eyes of heaven. We cannot see the true meaning of what has happened until we have seen it from God's perspective. We can examine our maggots from our personal view of good and evil but until we have the eyes of heaven we don't know their real meaning. Our painful life experiences are not resolved until we know what they mean. When we don't understand what has happened to us we do not know who we are and we fear our world.

The first thing I have men do when they arrive for counseling is to write an autobiography starting before they were born. We focus in turn on preschool years, grade school, junior high, high school, college or career starts, marriage, and on into the present. We look for the maggots in their lives and prayerfully ask for redemption of all their stories. We examine hurts from others, hurts from them to others and hurts to them from themselves. We pray about the meaning of each maggot we find then ask for God's redemption.

What happens next is a transformation. Peace and joy return. Meanings change for life's painful moments and a story once hidden becomes a story worth telling. By sharing these redemptive stories with their friends, wives and children, men become a part of redemptive history. Those things that once brought death now bring life.

******

Now it is your turn to tell stories. I trust this long trail has brought you life and the desire to give life. Tell your stories of growing and transforming. Stay close to a pure clear stream of redemption. May you enjoy life with men for a long time to come.

APPENDICES

Appendix A

The LIFE Model of Redemption and Maturity

Overview: The LIFE Model is, as its name implies, a model for life from conception to death. It is an idealized model, that is to say, it proposes what life should be like rather than describing what life on earth generally produces. The LIFE model suggests that people need five things in order to thrive:

1. A place to belong
2. To receive and give life
3. The capacity to recover from things that go wrong (desynchronizations)
4. Maturation
5. To live from their identities (hearts)

The LIFE Model covers both growth and recovery. These five elements apply whether we consider physical growth, emotional growth, family growth, community growth or spiritual growth. Taken in order from one to five, these elements are needed for strong and healthy human growth. Taken in reverse order, starting with living from our true identities, these same elements form an excellent diagnostic grid for a failure to thrive. From our analysis of a failure to thrive we can design a restoration process. In this way the LIFE Model serves as a means to restore our identities as individuals, families and communities so that we live from a completely synchronized and authentic identity we call "the heart that Jesus gives us."[79] This authentic identity is as much communal as it is individual.

We have bodies and minds that readily respond in some ways and refuse to respond in others. Our knees bend one way but refuse to go the other way. We see a certain light spectrum but not infrared or X-rays. In that sense our identities are well fixed within certain limits. In between those limits we have our potential.

Just because the potential is present does not mean it will be activated and used. We develop our identities by responding and resonating when the same characteristics we inherently possess are expressed by another living being. Identity is propagated like cuttings from live plants and not grown from seeds. This way of growing an identity by receiving the life

---

[79] This is Dr. Dallas Willard's term. He is a theologian, scholar, and professor of philosophy at the University of Southern California.

passed on from one who went before is true for us at a physical level just as it is at an emotional and spiritual level.

Redemption and maturity: What makes this a Christian model is a division between redemption and maturity. While most people will agree that not everyone matures correctly, some would say that all human beings could reach their full maturity by purely human means. Christians would say, "not without help." Some believe that everything needed for full human maturity is already contained within each person. Christians would say, "Something is still missing." If you believe that you already have everything needed to reach full maturity there is no need to read farther. If it seems possible that there are some things we can't heal ourselves then you may join this discussion already in progress for thousands of years.

In a mutual effort between people and their God to fully live and experience life as it was meant to be lived we must have some sense for what is our part and what is God's part. For me, this began as an experiment in 1969 when I decided to take God's way of life for a test drive to see if it really made me alive or not. It was soon clear to me that many people who laid no claim to religion were doing a better job of growing up than some of the pious people who were "waiting on the Lord" for things that just didn't happen. Careful study brought me to the conclusion, shared by many, that God clearly separates divine areas of responsibility from human areas of responsibility. In religious language:

- Humans are responsible for maturity
- God is responsible for redemption

Humans have been given dominion over their individual and community maturity by the creation order. Inherent in this dominion is the capacity, as a people, to understand and accomplish maturation. That is, we can know how people "grow up" and how to bring about this growth. This is our business and is not beyond our capacity. We are capable of knowing how our families and communities mature, and of directing this growth in a coherent manner. This is our dominion and is within our grasp.

Maturity for ourselves and our world is the normal object of human activity. When these two areas of responsibility are correctly maintained, we develop into our true identities as individuals, families and communities. Without our own efforts and community guidance, we remain immature.

What is redemption?

Our true identities are found in the "hearts that Jesus gives us." Without seeing God and ourselves through our heart, we fail to fully act like ourselves and miss the mark--we sin.

God's redemptive work is one of restoration. Because of our fallen state, we are plagued by corruption that blocks and perverts our attempts to

330

produce maturity. Decontamination from this evil is beyond our capacity to achieve, direct or coordinate. Redemption is not our dominion; consequently we lack the capacity to effect or grasp the entirety of the project. Redemption is the normal object of divine activity. Specifically, we are told by Saint John that a search was made throughout heaven, earth and the underworld and only the Lion of the tribe of Judah was found worthy to make sense of all calamities, evil, war, terrorism and suffering. (Revelation 5:1-14) Redemption is "Lion" territory and dominion.

Some Aspects of God's Redemptive Work:

- Regeneration - We receive a new heart
- Sanctification - We are restored to our true identities
- Healing - We are healed of the traumas of sin
- Spiritual Adoption - We receive a spiritual family
- Deliverance - The assaults of evil on us are stopped
- Spiritual Gifts - We receive the means to participate in God's redemptive work

We are incapable of understanding the "big picture" of redemption. Our inability is not due to randomness or incoherence of the redemptive work, but rather to our finitude and the magnitude of redemption. Surprisingly, the redeemed still play a significant part in redemption. This participation in redemption is a "bonus" or "gift" from God. Consequently the means by which we accomplish these tasks are referred to as spiritual gifts. Because we are not able to direct the work of redemption, these gifts often take us in unexpected directions serving both to teach us about redemption and accomplish its purpose simultaneously. As a partial result, we are returned to our normal dominion--producing maturity.

Our dominion is restored by at least four means: deliverance, healing, salvation and adoption. Our participation in these four aspects of restoration is guided by our hearts, souls, minds and community through prayer by the indwelling of the Holy Spirit from whom we receive all we need.

Deliverance refers to God's acts of strength by which the assault upon us is terminated. While the police may deliver us from an abusive spouse or burglar and an army may deliver a nation, full deliverance includes stopping spiritual assaults as well as the lesser onslaughts. God spiritually directs our intelligent and prayerful participation in this battle.

Healing is the restoration of our capacity to receive and give life. The privations and assaults of evil create real losses. Damaged through acts of violence against us, our capacity to live is greatly diminished unless we are healed as individuals and communities.

Salvation is a request for God, through Jesus, to restore us fully to life. We admit that we are producing damage instead of pure life (and even bringing destruction in some cases) and need God's help to restore us and make our efforts life-giving. This intentional change in our lives is accomplished by entering fully into the life Jesus offers and synchronizing with him in all areas of our lives.

Adoption reconnects us to others with whom we receive and give life. Once able to receive and give life we need the sources and receivers of life around us who are connected to us through loving bonds. By this adoption we become part of the family of God. Adoption is also described as being grafted into the vine. It connects us to life so that we might bear fruit. These fruits are our spiritual offspring obtained through the workings of the Holy Spirit in adoption.

Adoption is the aspect of redemption tied most closely to the normal human task of maturity. Often referred to as "after-care" or "discipleship" or "follow-up" in ministries of evangelism, healing and deliverance, adoption attaches us into the spiritual family in which we mature.

Choosing the term *spiritual adoption* rather than *community building* is necessary because we refer to more than neighborly relationships in the spiritual family. Spiritual family is God's provision to heal type A traumas caused by the absence of loving bonds in our lives. Spiritually bonded relationships challenge and change the natural family bonds by exposing their failings. This accounts for much of the resistance spiritual adoption receives in the church as well as many of its abuses in cults.

Once more in familiar religious language: There would be no need for recovery except for the damage caused to all people by sin and the fall. Since the fall all creation has groaned and no human being has grown straight and true, according to God's design, except for God's only begotten son Jesus. Through Jesus we have the salvation that will finally correct all the damage of sin. This salvation works among us directly through God's activities and indirectly through His people—the people of God—His church. Because God does not intend His salvation to simply be a ticket into Heaven, His followers must participate with him in overcoming the results of sin in our day-to-day existence here on earth. This change of our hearts and lives is the work of sanctification and redemption. Once saved through repentance and the forgiveness of our sins, we must return to living life as though God's Kingdom has come and His will is being done on earth as it is in Heaven. Far too often we have seen our salvation as something that takes effect after this life not a way of life that extends into eternity. Here on earth there is work to be done and God expects us to do it. Our work will not save us but it will express that we are new creations. It is our work to grow and reach maturity together with all the saints. To achieve this we must live from our new hearts, being sanctified, healed, delivered from evil and guided by God alone. We are both saved and being saved.

Traumas are the wounds (or injuries) left in our identities that render us less than what God had in mind when He created us. Traumas block growth. Traumas block or slow proper maturity. Traumatic wounds can be caused by adding something to us we should not have--just as a bullet adds its effect to a body it encounters. Traumatic injuries can be caused by the absence of what the soul needs--just as malnutrition can cripple the body. Traumas not only cause injury and pain, traumas block or slow the process of maturity. When the traumatized person is very young this blocked or slowed maturity can cripple, disfigure or prevent the growth of proper maturity or normal faculties of identity. When maturity is slow or blocked always look for these two types of trauma.

Sin adds to our lives what should not be there and subtracts what should be. Sin (malfunction) comes from three sources: the world, the flesh and evil spirit beings. Sin always blocks maturity. Removing the effects of sin is the work of God's redemption and He alone is worthy to direct and achieve His divine purpose in our salvation. This work can only be accomplished by life in the Spirit through hearts that are alive to God. Too often, pastors, counselors and churches attempt to plan, direct, control and make programs of God's salvation. The results are what we would expect of the flesh at work.

Not only must we follow God's leading to remove that which blocks or hinders growth and holiness and add that which is lacking for complete and full life in the Spirit but we must correct misdirected growth. I have three small trees planted together, whose trunks were braided together while they were young and supple. In the same way people may mature in crooked ways because those who guide their growth chose a twisted path for them to follow. Perhaps they were given a bad example of what a man, woman, father, mother or Christian should be. Perhaps they were taught to laugh at those who weep, curse those who curse them, to get revenge on those who betray them, drink for joy, lust after many women or other men, control others with threats or anger when they don't get their way and these habits have grown so long and so deep that they have become their character. Surely this is not how God meant us to grow.

To this misguided growth the Christian must apply instruction in the word of God. What God teaches reveals our errors and God's true desire for our growth. Repentance, confession, and forgiveness lead to healing, deliverance and spiritual relationships with God and his people. Prayer, praise, worship and the fruit of the Spirit begin to form Godly character. Now true maturity can begin its growth—but maturity only grows in the fellowship of God's family.

Having removed the two blocks to maturity and addressed the misguided maturity through the leading of God's Spirit at work in his or her heart, the Christian is now ready to begin the human part of recovery—the growth of true maturity. For true maturity to grow, every aspect of the Christian life, every provision of God for our redemption, every teaching of Scripture, every nudge of the Holy Spirit must be given free and full expression. To this we add our full commitment and effort--our whole heart, soul and strength.

Where can I find more material on the LIFE Model?

Copies of the basic version of *The Life Model* and its study guide *Bringing the Life Model to Life* can be obtained from:

C.A.R.E. Packaging
9731 South M-37
Baldwin, MI 49304
(231) 745-4950
www.care1.org or CAREpkg@triton.net

Check with C.A.R.E. Packaging for other LIFE Model materials, tapes, videos and training materials. Chris Coursey and I are writing an expanded application of the LIFE Model which we are calling *Thriving*. Raymond Jones and I are working on book applying the model to sex addiction that we call *Out of Control*. I am also preparing a series of lessons on video called *Quiet Place Teachings*. Check for these and any other materials as they become available.

History: The theory behind this book was developed at Shepherd's House Inc. in California. Pastors, counselors, prayer team members, lay leaders, people in recovery and an international advisory panel from many traditions and theoretical perspectives worked together to formulate this profoundly Christian view of life.

Shepherd's House Inc.
P.O. Box 40096
Pasadena, CA 91114

Appendix B

Research And Resources On Human Development

Many astute observers have given detailed descriptions of child development, particularly mental and verbal abilities. The last few years have produced a new level of observation. Several types of brain scans can now study actual brain activity and discover when and how the brain itself develops. Surgical studies have even studied individual brain cells--discovering such quaint things as brain cells that recognize and respond to facial expressions. Five theoreticians have strongly influenced my knowledge of the link between brain development and the growth of an identity.

Dr. Allan Schore from the UCLA School of Medicine has carefully described the many studies on development of the infant brain as it relates to the development of identity. In particular, he has studied the development of the orbital prefrontal cortex. It is called "orbital" because it sits right behind the socket (orbit) of the eyes. This is the part of the brain that is at the top of the command hierarchy and is connected to every major system in the body--even the immune system. It is the first part of the cortex to receive information from inside the body or outside as well. Dr. Schore's work is notable in describing how this part of the brain (which I have called the "joyful identity control center" in Chapter One) develops and works.

Summary of Bonding Development and the Senses
0 - 1.5 months	Taste, smell and temperature
1.5 - 3 months	Touch
2 - 12 months	Visual (facial expressions of emotion)
12 - 24 months	Auditory (voice tone)

Dr. Schore has written some of the best technical descriptions of current research on brain changes during the development of maturity. Some of the material in the first chapter of this book is based on a presentation by Schore of his soon to be published book *Affect Regulation and the Repair of Self.* He read portions of the manuscript at a conference on March 15, 1997 at the Newport Beach Psychoanalytic Institute. Dr. Schore has combined the theories and discoveries of three different disciplines in order to make sense of very complex and separate fields.

Dr. Schore's brain model is hierarchical which is a very important distinction from others I will mention. His diagram entitled *Schore's Right*

Brain Dual Corticolimbic-Autonomic Circuits outlines the ascending levels of the brain's emotional control center. I find this hierarchy particularly significant because it explains why trouble at a lower lever will affect all the levels above it. Schore's hierarchical three-level structure is the basis for the four level control structure in the right hemisphere described in chapters 2, 4 and 9. The top three levels of my model, the prefrontal cortex (4), cingulate cortex (3), and the amygdala (2) are directly from Dr. Schore's theory. The bottom layer (related to attachment) is suggested by the work of Dr. Siegel and the brain scans by Dr. Amen, who we will examine in a moment.

There are three distinctive elements to Dr. Schore's theories that, when combined, make his theories stand out above the others. First, is his understanding that brain structures function in a hierarchical way rather than a modular one. Second, his model is based on synchronization of brain activation in time "windows" not just brain area functions or biological states. Third, Dr. Schore's brain model is both individual and mutual-- subjective and intersubjective. What we can make of this is a brain where small critical areas make great differences to the rest of the brain. The overall performance of the brain is not simply a matter of what its parts can do but what they do together at a given moment in time. And our brains are not so private and locked in our skulls as we might suspect, but rather share powerful, mutual states of mind at given moments in time with other brains. These states are so closely linked that we can conceive of both an individual and a mutual mind, which must both be running well across the entire lifespan. We will return to this discussion in a moment after we examine other contributors.

Dr. Erik Erikson of Harvard was unusual in that he developed a model of human growth that did not stop with childhood but continued across the lifespan. Erikson's eight crises provide us with a useful description of development. Although he was not involved in brain growth studies, later research has found that some of Erikson's crises represent a switch in development from one side of the brain to the other. The first crisis represents right hemisphere growth, the second is left hemisphere, the third is right hemisphere. The connections between what he observed and brain development in infancy have greatly expanded as new methods and technology have been developed. The massive amounts of current knowledge have been collected and summarized by three researchers in particular—Dr. Schore, Dr. van der Kolk and Dr. Siegel.

Dr. Bessel van der Kolk from Boston University School of Medicine and Harvard University has done in-depth study in the area of trauma and deprivation. Dr. van der Kolk has written summaries of early bonding research and added his own studies on the effects of early traumas at

336

different ages. From this work we can see the tremendous deficits caused by early psychological injuries and deprivations. He details the neurotransmitter, immune system, biochemical, developmental, and social impacts of early deprivation, loss and trauma. He points out that there are critical periods for attachment and brain growth. Early trauma results in a life-long inability to regulate affect (emotion). He describes the major neurochemical imbalances and deficits resulting from early deprivation. Both he and Dr. Schore have synthesized the results of many neurobiological and biochemical studies that relate to attachment and describe what can go wrong.

Dr. Daniel Siegel from the UCLA School of Medicine has written the best synthesized treatment of attachment and brain development. As someone "down stream" from Dr. Schore, Dr. Siegel has been able to expand on Dr. Schore's theories. Dr. Siegel has done a particularly outstanding job of examining the relationship between the left hemisphere's functions and the control center in the right hemisphere. While his approach to the brain is more modular and less hierarchical, Dr. Siegel has done a marvelous job with explaining the synchronization of the brain based on: development, memory, attachment style and mutual story telling.

ADDITIONAL SOURCES

Dr. Daniel Amen has scanned over 12,000 human brains. As a psychiatrist interested in the brain's impact on emotion and personality and a practitioner of nuclear medicine, Dr. Amen has found brain patterns behind many common problems. His prolific writings, speaking, teaching and website www.brainplace.com are excellent sources of information on the brain. Dr. Amen proposes a wide variety of specific solutions from diet to brain training for each brain region he has studied. Dr. Amen has a fairly modular approach to the brain that provides clear and simple identification of activity levels associated with personality problems. His modules quite closely parallel the areas mentioned by Dr. Schore in his theories. Dr. Amen's work is excellent.

The advantage of Dr. Schore's hierarchical model over a modular one is that a hierarchy in the brain establishes both an order of brain development as well as the order in which brain functions break down if there are problems. For example, in a modular approach like Dr. Amen uses he will simply find out which modules are working and which are not and prescribe solutions for each. Dr. Schore's hierarchical model predicts that if the middle level (the cingulate cortex) is not working, the top level (orbitofrontal cortex) will also be impaired as will the synchronization between hemispheres. You get more for your nickel with a hierarchical model.

Dr. Siegel, Dr. Antonio Damasio and Dr.Vilaynur Ramachandran all create brain models based on interactive modules. These non-linear models depend strongly on the activity of the reentry circuits described by Dr. Gerald Edelman. These are faintly hierarchical concepts. Dr. Guilio Tononi, however, dismisses the modular approach entirely and depends instead on temporal synchronization and the brain's five chemical value systems for his explanations. These five chemical value systems are: dopamine, serotonin, epinephrine, norepinephrine and acetylcholine. These value systems are powerful in that they affect the responses of the brain in a global way when they are activated. These value systems feature prominently in Dr. Schore's hierarchical model that, like Dr. Tononi's, depends strongly on temporal synchronization for its explanations.

The work by Dr. Ronald A. Ruden and Marcia Byalick in *The Craving Brain* and that of Dr. Harvey Milkman and Dr. Stanley Sunderwirth in *Craving for Ecstasy* point to the importance of the nucleus accumbens in addictive behaviors. This part of the mesocortical pleasure system in the basal ganglia attaches to both the orbitofrontal cortex and subcortical structures in Dr. Schore's model. Dr. Ruden discusses the interaction of the serotonin and dopamine value systems in the nucleus accumbens while Dr. Milkman stays primarily with the dopamine system with slight attention to the norepinephrine arousal needed for cravings. While neither of the books on cravings takes into account the central role of attachment in stimulation of pleasure and pain, Dr. Schore's theory makes both the pleasure and quieting functions of the pleasure/satiation system a direct product of attachment. Together with Dr. Siegel's explanation of how the brain manages not to know about its own pain, these writers provide a powerful model of how attachment failures produce the destructive cravings of badly bonded men.

Evidence would suggest that the emotional brain is synchronized internally at five levels with primacy given to the right hemisphere at all levels except the fifth and highest where the balance shifts based on our level of distress. The first level is the attachment system in the deep limbic area. This level determines what and who is personal to me. This level determines my personal reality. Level one is strongly tied to the dopamine value system. The second level controls approach and avoidance, giving and receiving. This system, at the level of the amygdala is tied to the epinephrine and norepinephrine value systems. With these two systems we control our alertness and action. The third level of synchronization involves the emotional energy levels and interpersonal reality in the cingulate cortex. This level synchronizes the brain internally and synchronizes with other minds externally. The cingulate cortex synchronizes the activity present in the different lobes of the brain as information is received and sorted. Level three can synchronize the activity of two minds into one point of view. This third level seems to synchronize serotonin and norepinephrine value systems associated with quieting and arousal. The fourth level of synchronization involves the direction of attention. Attention is the only resource humans have to offer. The orbitofrontal cortex at level four controls the serotonin system and with it the capacity to soothe and quiet the dopamine, epinephrine and norepinephrine arousal. Level four can synchronize the activity of three minds and three points of view. The fifth level of synchronization is between experience in the right hemisphere and explanations in the left. It is this synchronization that is tested by such methods as The Adult Attachment Inventory (AAI) and the TheoPhostic® process for addressing unresolved distress from the past that intrudes into current life.

The four level control center in the right hemisphere presented in this book is a result of combining the work of these doctors. Not one of them can be said to agree with my four-level model although Dr. Schore clearly established the top three levels in his hierarchy of the brain. In addition, my vision of hierarchically synchronized modules shaped and conditioned by five value systems would exceed what any one of them would propose. Dr. Schore and Dr. Siegel would certainly agree however that we have both individual and group minds and that synchronization is not just a matter of internal brain levels but of interpersonal states of mind as well.

The material from Schore, Seigel, van der Kolk and Amen forms the basis for what I have written on the brain development. I have tried to teach these ideas in common English and in word pictures. The result is clearer but less precise. Any errors or misrepresentation of their work are purely mine.

THE LIFE MODEL

The LIFE Model is, as its name implies, a model for life from conception to death. It is an idealized model, that is to say, it proposes what life should be like as opposed to merely describing what life on earth generally produces. In short, the LIFE model proposes that in order to thrive people need five things:

1. A place to belong
2. To both receive and give life
3. The capacity to recover from malfunctions
4. Maturation
5. To stay true to their identities

Expansions on many of these themes can be found in my books including this one, which is an expansion of the maturity component of the LIFE model. The staff at Shepherd's House recorded the most concise expression of these elements during the latter part of the 1990s in a small book called *The Life Model.* This book is now in Spanish and Russian with translation underway into Korean with other languages being considered for the future. *Bringing the Life Model to Life: The LIFE Model Study Guide for Individuals and Small Groups* further expands and applies these themes.

ERIK ERIKSON'S DEVELOPMENTAL STAGES

Erik Erikson developed a model of human growth that he divided into eight stages, each one with its own crisis. In the years since his observations were made, brain development studies have shown that the brain goes through profound growth changes during many of these stages. It is currently theorized that, during important transitions the brain goes through a time of reorganization and then functions differently after that point. Without help from older brains, these transitions leave the newly transformed brain in a state of disorganization. Stages of development are physical as well as mental and social.

Erikson's Eight Crises:

1. BASIC TRUST VERSUS BASIC MISTRUST: ages 0-1, I am what I am given. The infant's identity develops out of what he is given and how he is treated.

2. AUTONOMY VERSUS SHAME AND DOUBT: ages 1-3, I am what I will. The infant thinks of himself in terms of what he can do often, pulling his hand away and insisting on doing things himself.

3. INITIATIVE VERSUS GUILT: ages 3-6, I am what I imagine I will be. The child becomes the things and people he dreams he is. He loves to pretend and try new things.

4. INDUSTRY VERSUS INFERIORITY, ages 6-13, I am what I learn. The child begins to see that he must learn things he does not yet know. He sets out on quests, adventures, and conquests. Dreams become real.

5.   IDENTITY VERSUS IDENTITY DIFFUSION: ages 13-19, I am all of the above. Each aspect of identity must be combined with the others to become an adult who contains all these attributes.

6.   INTIMACY VERSUS ISOLATION: Young adult. He must now learn how to maintain himself in close harmony with others.

7.   PRODUCTIVITY VERSUS SELF-ABSORPTION: Adulthood. He is now challenged to be the source of good things.

8.   INTEGRITY VERSUS DESPAIR: Maturity. Now his soul must be capable of maintaining itself and his influence even if he loses some abilities and strength.

As can be observed, my *LIFE* Model stages generally combine two of Erikson's into one. There are several reasons for this. First, the categories I use, infant, child, adult, parent and elder are generally recognized across cultures and languages. Second, these are the categories mentioned in scripture. Third, my categories are usually used with the qualifier *young* by language, culture and scripture to indicate that those in the early part of the stage are different from those in the later part of the stage. So a *young man* is known to be different from a *man*.

Example:

LIFE **Model**	**Erikson's Crisis**	**Neurobiological**
INFANT STAGE		
Infant 0-1	Trust versus Mistrust	Right Hemisphere Growth
Toddler 2-3	Autonomy versus Shame	Left Hemisphere Growth

WEANING - Reorganization of brain structure and identity

CHILD STAGE		
Young child 4-6	Initiative versus Guilt	Rt. peak at 4, Lf. peak at 6
Child 7-12	Industry v. Inferiority	Rt. peak at 8, Lf. peak at 12

RITE OF PASSAGE - Reorganization of identity

ADULT STAGE		
Young A 13-17	Identity vs. I.D. Diffusion	Right Hemisphere Growth
Adult 18-24	Intimacy versus Isolation	Left Hemisphere Growth

BIRTH OF FIRST CHILD - Reorganization of identity and brain growth

The periods of right hemisphere growth are important as they constitute the best times for bonding as well as for forming new identities. This observation is based on the right hemisphere's dominance for emotions, relationships and bonding. This is also where the most remediation can be done for existing bonding deficits. The best time to improve bonding, self-control, emotional expression and correct relational problems is during right hemisphere growth. During these times the right hemisphere may be more open to new experiences. These are the emotional intelligence development times. Conversely, verbal and logical development is best corrected or improved during left hemisphere growth. The times of left hemisphere growth are best for introspection and learning to speak about one's internal world to others.

PERIODS OF RIGHT HEMISPHERE GROWTH

AGE	STAGE	MAIN OBJECT
0-2 years	Early infant	Mother
4 years	Early child	Father
8 years	Late child	Friends
15 years	Early adult	Mate
First child	Early parent	Baby

It is important to note that the metamorphosis for the mind, body, and social development that occurs between stages, will be attempted by the developing individual's brain based on an internal schedule. He or she is run by a biological clock as inexorable as the one that begins childbirth at about nine months. This means that each metamorphosis is attempted whether the child is being guided or has been abandoned. His attempts to grow continue even after an identity transformation fails. The child's capacity to live and mature will simply be diminished greatly from that point onward.

Writers, such as Harville Hendricks have developed descriptions of what adults are like if they get stuck at one of these developmental crises. Hendricks particularly focuses on the effects which getting stuck produces in love relationships and mate selection. Notice the importance of this connection between the failure to grow up properly and adult life. Omitting or distorting any stage of development will produce a deficit in all the stages that come afterwards. Once again we see the power of a hierarchical model, this time of maturation. Further examples and tables can be found in *The Life Model*.

As can be seen, these stages can be broken down into many smaller steps, accomplishments and developments such as Jean Piaget has done with cognitive development or Lawrence Kolhberg has done with moral

342

development. I believe that the five stages of the *LIFE* Model are sufficiently clear and useful for community use, while admitting that there is a sixth stage--prenatal. This sixth stage is actually the first in line. Counting this stage, man has a perfect six stages. As with the other five stages, the forty or so weeks of prenatal life also can be divided into substages or steps. That would be another book. The way we are made is awesome!

REFERENCES

Allan N. Schore, *Affect Regulation and the Origin of the Self: Neurobiology of Emotional Development*, (Hillsdale, NJ: Lawrence Erlbaum Associates Publishers, 1994)

Allan N. Schore, *Affect Regulation and the Repair of the Self,* (New York, NY: W.W. Norton, 2003)

Allan N. Schore, *Affect Dysregulation and the Disorders of the Self,* (New York, NY: W. W. Norton, 2003)

Erik H. Erikson, GROWTH AND CRISIS in, *Theories of Psychopathology and Personality* Edited by Theodore Millon (Philadelphia: W. B. Saunders Co., 1973) Pages 136-156.

Bessel van der Kolk, *Psychological Trauma*, (Washington: American Psychiatric Press, 1987.)

Daniel J. Siegel, *The Developing Mind: Toward a Neurobiology of Interpersonal Experience,* (New York: Guilford Press, 1999.)

Daniel G. Amen, *Healing The Hardware of the Soul,* (New York: The Free Press, 2002.)

James G. Friesen, E. James Wilder, Anne M. Bierling, Rick Koepcke, Maribeth Poole, *The Life Model: Living From The Heart Jesus Gave You— The Essentials of Christian Living Revised 2000,* (Pasadena, CA: Shepherd's House Inc., 2000) Distributed by C.A.R.E. Packaging Baldwin, MI. www.CARE1.org.

Rick Koepcke, Ruth Ann Koepcke, Maribeth Poole, E. James Wilder, *Bringing the Life Model to Life: The LIFE Model Study Guide for Individuals and Small Groups,* (Pasadena: Shepherd's House Inc., 2002.) Distributed by C.A.R.E. Packaging Baldwin, MI. www.CARE1.org.

Gerald M. Edelman, Guilio Tononi, *A Universe of Consciousness,* (New York: Basic Books, 2000)

Harvey Milkman and Stanley Sunderwirth, *Craving for Ecstasy,* (San Francisco: Josey-Bass Publishers, 1997.)

Ronald A. Ruden and Marcia Byalick, *The Craving Brain*, (New York: Perennial, 2000.)

Appendix C
Men and Their Needs

You can't just waltz up to a man and talk to him about his needs. Men have had an uncomfortable relationship with their needs for quite some time. Not only is it not manly to be needy, it is also not cool. In addition, men like to take action and if they can't do anything about their needs they would rather not talk about them.

In the middle of a culture that denies that men have emotional needs, men aren't even allowed to need sleep. They have created euphemisms to talk about sleep. "I've got to hit the sack," or "catch a little shut-eye," anything but say, "I need sleep. I'm tired." Real men don't admit needing sleep, let alone anything else. Other needs just don't fit in. Little wonder that many men do not operate well.

The sexual revolution gave men room for one need found in the phrase, "Men have certain needs." To this day many men think sex is all they really need. Well, there is one exception to that; men might need a drink. Manly men can say that. (Of course, the drink must be alcoholic. No man would need water.) Oh, there is a third need—food. "I need some food here!" is manly enough. So, men need sex, drinks and food and the luckiest dog is the man who finds a woman-mama who will give him all three.

It is not desirable for either men or women to be needy in our culture so revealing needs is something that most people, and particularly men are hesitant to try. Because of the marked discomfort most men feel about their needs, talk about needs can be used to measure trust levels in a group or a relationship. This makes sharing needs a good indicator of trust and intimacy.

There are four levels of sharing needs.
1. I once had a need
2. I just had a need
3. I have a specific need
4. I need something but I don't know what

I once had a need showed up in old time testimony meetings where someone would reveal that as a youngster they did bad things and needed help but that was years ago and now, thank God (or their higher power), they are free of such problems. This type of sharing is the first step into intimacy for it reveals to us history we might not otherwise have known. *I once had a need* requires a small amount of trust because it reveals that long ago one had problems and deficiencies. A small vulnerability like that sometimes is the beginning of liking someone because we appreciate those who will tell us their stories—provided that is not all they do.

I just had a need is a common level of sharing in groups. Last week I felt really depressed, or I had no money but God answered my prayers and today I am much better. In such groups I have often wondered where the people were who would be bouncing up next week to say that they just had a need. But it takes trust to be able to say *I just had a need* and trust must be earned. There are often good reasons to preclude any deeper intimacy.

I have a need is the third level of intimacy and gives most people a sense of being exposed and vulnerable. This is hard to do. At this level people can say, "I am lonely," or "I need new tires and I can't afford them," directly to others. This is the deepest level of trust that many people ever reach as adults. Saying *I have a need right now* occurs in only our most intimate relationships. This is one reason people feel so defenseless when panhandlers approach them on the street and say "Could you help me with some bus fare?" (I have a need right now.)

I don't know what I need is the deepest level of trust and intimacy. At this level people know that something is wrong but for the life of them they can't figure out what it is. At this level people can easily be exploited by others. This is the level that advertising tries to reach by showing us intimate things that we don't talk about and then telling us that what we need is their product.

I don't know what I need is at this level where each baby boy begins his struggle to learn what it means to be a person. Little boys start out completely helpless in this way. They do not know who they are or what they need. Take for example a little boy who won't go to sleep. He wanders out into the living room fussing.

"You stupid, spoiled little brat!" some big person in the room says when they see him. (Now he knows who he is according to the spokesperson from heaven.)

"You need a good swat!" (Now he knows what he needs.)

Now the little boy knows who he is and what he needs and it becomes a part of his identity. Whenever he feels upset in later life he can remember this lesson. So the next time he feels upset he knows how to act and what to look for. He will fuss, look for someone to yell at him and tell him something like, "you stupid, spoiled little brat" and then hit him. He might have to provoke his wife or girlfriend for quite some time before she meets his needs but then he will settle down. At the same time they might ask each other, "Why do we have to go through this each time?" or "Why does it always end this way?"

The question we need to ask is who God would have said the infant boy was and what he needed? All of us start as infants with the need to be

346

told what we need. The people that raise us have the first and greatest chance to determine our identity. But God has the last say because if our parents build an unstable identity it won't withstand the heat of life and soon will begin to crumble. As these early errors and accidents come to light we again experience *I don't know what I need.*

I don't know what I need continues throughout life. We all need people who can tell us who we are when we can't figure it out, people with better synchronization in their brain's control center and people who see us through the eyes of Heaven.